Lecture Notes in Artificial Intelligence   2049

Subseries of Lecture Notes in Computer Science
Edited by J. G. Carbonell and J. Siekmann

Lecture Notes in Computer Science
Edited by G. Goos, J. Hartmanis, and J. van Leeuwen

W0042928

Springer
Berlin
Heidelberg
New York
Barcelona
Hong Kong
London
Milan
Paris
Tokyo

Georgios Paliouras   Vangelis Karkaletsis
Constantine D. Spyropoulos (Eds.)

Machine Learning and Its Applications

Advanced Lectures

 Springer

Series Editors

Jaime G. Carbonell, Carnegie Mellon University, Pittsburgh, PA, USA
Jörg Siekmann, University of Saarland, Saabrücken, Germany

Volume Editors

Georgios Paliouras
Vangelis Karkaletsis
Constantine D. Spyropoulos
National Centre for Scientific Research "Demokritos"
Institute of Informatics and Telecommunications
P.O. Box 60228, Ag. Paraskevi, 15310 Athens, Greece
E-mail: {paliourg,vangelis,costass}@iit.demokritos.gr

Cataloging-in-Publication Data applied for

Die Deutsche Bibliothek - CIP-Einheitsaufnahme

Machine learning and its applications : advanced lectures / Georgios
Paliouras ... (ed.). - Berlin ; Heidelberg ; New York ; Barcelona ; Hong
Kong ; London ; Milan ; Paris ; Singapore ; Tokyo : Springer, 2001
    (Lecture notes in computer science ; 2049 : Lecture notes in artificial
    intelligence)
    ISBN 3-540-42490-3

CR Subject Classification (1998): I.2, 4.3.3, H.2.8, H.5.2, J.1, F.4.1

ISBN 3-540-42490-3 Springer-Verlag Berlin Heidelberg New York

This work is subject to copyright. All rights are reserved, whether the whole or part of the material is
concerned, specifically the rights of translation, reprinting, re-use of illustrations, recitation, broadcasting,
reproduction on microfilms or in any other way, and storage in data banks. Duplication of this publication
or parts thereof is permitted only under the provisions of the German Copyright Law of September 9, 1965,
in its current version, and permission for use must always be obtained from Springer-Verlag. Violations are
liable for prosecution under the German Copyright Law.

Springer-Verlag Berlin Heidelberg New York
a member of BertelsmannSpringer Science+Business Media GmbH

http://www.springer.de

© Springer-Verlag Berlin Heidelberg 2001

Typesetting: Camera-ready by author, data conversion by PTP-Berlin, Stefan Sossna
SPIN: 10781488   06/3142   5 4 3 2 1 0

Preface

In the last few years machine learning has made its way into the areas of administration, commerce, and industry, in an impressive way. Data mining is perhaps the most widely known demonstration of this phenomenon, complemented by less publicized applications of machine learning, such as adaptive systems in various industrial settings, financial prediction, medical diagnosis, and the construction of user profiles for WWW-browsers. This transfer of machine learning from the research labs to the "real world" has caused increased interest in learning techniques, dictating further effort in informing people from other disciplines about the state of the art in machine learning and its uses.

The objective of this book is to provide the reader with sufficient information about the current capabilities of machine learning methods, as well as ideas about how one could make use of these methods to solve real-world problems. The book is based primarily on the material that was presented in the Advanced Course in Artificial Intelligence (ACAI '99), which took place in Chania, Greece and was attended by research students, professionals, and researchers. However, the book goes beyond the material covered in the course, in that it contains several position papers on open research issues of machine learning.

The book is structured in a way that reflects its objective of educating the reader on how machine learning works, what the open issues are, and how it can be used. It is divided into two parts: methods and applications.

The first part consists of 10 chapters covering to a large extent the field of machine learning, from symbolic concept learning and conceptual clustering to case-based reasoning, neural networks, and genetic algorithms. The research issues addressed include the relationship of machine learning to knowledge discovery in databases, the handling of noisy data, and the modification of the learning problem through function decomposition. This part of the book concludes with two chapters examining the basic principles of learning methods. The first of the two chapters examines the approaches to selecting the appropriate method for a particular problem or modifying the problem representation to suit a learning method. In contrast, the last chapter of the section reviews the approaches to integrating different machine learning methods, in order to handle difficult learning tasks.

The second part of the book exposes the reader to innovative applications of machine learning. This part consists of 11 chapters, presenting a range of applications, from data mining in finance, marketing, and economics to learning in human language technology and user modeling. Most of these chapters are based on the work that was presented during the workshops of ACAI '99. Each such chapter describes the types of problem that have been approached with the use of machine learning in a particular domain and gives an overview of the work in this area, as presented at the relevant workshop.

We hope that the combination of theoretical and empirical knowledge in this book will be of use to the reader who is interested in entering this exciting research field and using mature machine learning techniques to solve real-world problems. The editors of the book would like to thank the distinguished authors for their willingness and cooperation in making this special volume a reality.

May 2001

Georgios Paliouras
Vangelis Karkaletsis
Constantine D. Spyropoulos

Table of Contents

Methods

Applications

Comparing Machine Learning and Knowledge Discovery in DataBases: An Application to Knowledge Discovery in Texts

Yves Kodratoff

CNRS, LRI Bât. 490 Univ. Paris-Sud, F - 91405 Orsay Cedex
yk@lri.fr

1 Introduction

This chapter has two goals. The first goal is to compare Machine Learning (ML) and Knowledge Discovery in Data (KDD, also often called Data Mining, DM) insisting on how much they actually differ. In order to make my ideas somewhat easier to understand, and as an illustration, I will include a description of several research topics that I find relevant to KDD and to KDD only. The second goal is to show that the definition I give of KDD can be almost directly applied to text analysis, and that will lead us to a very restrictive definition of Knowledge Discovery in Texts (KDT). I will provide a compelling example of a real-life set of rules obtained by what I call KDT techniques.

Knowledge Discovery in Data (KDD) is better known by the oversimplified name of Data Mining (DM). Actually, most academics are rather interested in DM, which develops methods for extracting knowledge from a given set of data. Industrialists and experts should be more interested in KDD which comprises the whole process of data selection, data cleaning, transfer to a DM technique, applying the DM technique, validating the results of the DM technique, and finally interpreting them for the user. In general, this process is a cycle that improves under the criticism of the expert.

Machine Learning (ML) and KDD have a very strong link: they both acknowledge the importance of induction as a normal way of thinking, while other scientific fields are reluctant to accept it, to say the least. We shall first explore this common point. We believe that the reluctance of other fields to accept induction relies on a misuse of apparent contradictions inside the theory of confirmation. This leads us to revisit Hempel paradox in order to explain why it does apply and that it is also possible to avoid most of its bad effects, when analyzing more precisely its restrictions.

We shall then develop the acknowledged definition of KDD, as given by [3], and we shall show that, under an apparently innocent wording, it asks for an approach different from the one of ML, and of Exploratory Statistics (not to speak of the more classical Confirmatory Statistics that do not even consider the possibility of performing inductive reasoning).

In general, it can be said that ML, with the exception of dealing with induction, is still a classical Science in the sense that it still uses the criteria upon which knowledge is valued in Science. These criteria are mainly four: Knowledge is acceptable if proven; if it is not proven, it can be experimentally validated, using precision as the validation criterion. If both are not possible, at least knowledge must be as universal

G. Paliouras, V. Karkaletsis, and C.D. Spyropoulos (Eds.): ACAI '99, LNAI 2049, pp. 1-21, 2001.
© Springer-Verlag Berlin Heidelberg 2001

as possible that is it must be accepted by as many as possible individuals. Finally, some elegance can also be asked from knowledge, and elegance equates concision, as illustrated by the famous Minimum Description Length (MDL) principle which favors descriptions the representation of which will ask for the least number of bits to be encoded. It can be claimed that KDD, if it does not oppose frontally these evaluation criteria, at least proposes models in which knowledge must primarily be more understandable than proven, more useful than precise, more particular than universal. Finally, the principle of "adequacy of the representation" is more significant in KDD than the MDL one. For instance, a drawing may need an enormous amount of bits to be coded, but it will nevertheless be preferable if it is the casual representation given by the user.

2 Reasoning by Induction

Both ML and KDD rely heavily on the induction process. Most scientists still show a kind of blind faith in favor of deduction. An argument has been, however, recently presented [9] against the blind use of deduction, in the name of efficiency: deductive processes can become so complex that there is no hope of achieving them until their end, and an approximation of them is necessary. If this approximation happens to be less precise (and I'd like to add: less useful or less comprehensible - the latter being very often the case) than the model obtained by induction, then there are no objective grounds to stick to deduction.

2.1 Hempel's Paradox and the Theory of Confirmation

Hempel underlines the existence of the contraposition associated to each theorem as shown below:

$$A \Rightarrow B \sim \neg A \vee B \sim \neg A \vee \neg \neg B \sim \neg \neg B \vee \neg A \sim \neg B \Rightarrow \neg A$$

The existence of a contraposition proves that any theorem is confirmed by the simultaneous observation of both premise and conclusion, as well as by the simultaneous observation of both negation of premise and negation of conclusion. For example:

$$\forall x (\text{crow}(x) \Rightarrow \text{black}(x)) \quad \sim \quad \forall x (\neg \text{black}(x) \Rightarrow \neg \text{crow}(x))$$
confirmed by the observation   confirmed by the observation of
of crow(A), black(A) $\neg$crow(B), $\neg$black(B)
                                                             example: white(B), shoe(B)

Induction generates hypotheses that have to be confirmed by observation of the reality, but Hempel's paradox tells us that, so many things confirm any crazy hypothesis that confirmation by counting of instances is simply impossible, thus automatization of induction (which has to rely on some sort of counting) is absurd.

In order to show how automatic induction has been nevertheless possible, it is necessary to consider that induction contains complex chains of reasoning steps [6],

[7], and an analysis of this complexity leads to a better understanding of the conditions into which safe confirmation can be performed. Let me now summarize this argument. The first remark is that a specific semantic (or meaning) is associated to an implication, and Hempel's paradox holds in a different way depending on the semantics. If the implication is relative to the description of the properties of an object, such as the black crow above, then there is little to discuss: the "*descriptive theorem*" $\forall$ x (crow (x) $\Rightarrow$ black(x)) is indeed a theorem from the deductive point of view (the contraposition of such a theorem is valid: for instance, if anything is not black, obviously it is not a crow) but it is not a real theorem from the inductive point of view since it is not confirmed by instances of its contraposition. This is why, when dealing with induction, we have to make the difference between the descriptive theorems, and what we call *causal theorems*, where the implication carries a causal meaning. Due to the fact that Science has been concerned until now with deduction only, the difference between descriptive and causal theorems is not acknowledged. We hope this chapter makes clear how useful - and actually how simple - this difference is.

2.2   Implications that Carry the Meaning of Causality

Consider the implications that represent a causal relationship, such as:

$\forall$x (smokes(x) $\Rightarrow$ cancer(x)) with probability p. There is no point in calling on Hempel's paradox here, since indeed, observing ($\neg$smokes(A)) & ($\neg$cancer(A)) confirms also this theorem, as it should. It must be however noticed that spurious causes can introduce again a paradox. For instance the theorem:

$\forall$x (smokes(x) & French(x) $\Rightarrow$ cancer(x)) is absurdly confirmed by observing ($\neg$smokes(A) $\vee$ $\neg$French(A)) & ($\neg$cancer (A)) meaning that, say, a German who has no cancer confirms this theorem. A simple analysis of the correlations (see the definition of a spurious dependency, in definition 14, below) will show easily that nationality has nothing to do with the link between smoking and cancer. A striking example of this problem has been given recently by the so-called "French paradox" stating that Frenchmen had a higher cholesterol count than Americans and they would nevertheless die less of heart attack. It was called very aptly a "paradox" because the fact of being French has obviously no causal role, and the real cause has been found in some typical French habits.

Another disputable argument is that the conjunction of causes is dangerous, for instance:

$\forall$x (smokes(x) & drinks-alcohol(x) $\Rightarrow$ cancer(x)) is confirmed by (($\neg$smokes (A) $\vee$ $\neg$drinks-alcohol (A)) & $\neg$cancer (A)) which is confirmed by any person who does not drink and has no cancer. The counter-argument here is that the "medical *and*" is not really a logical conjunct. Actually, here, drinking increases the unhealthy effect of smoking and we have to confirm two independent theorems, one stating that:

$\forall$x (smokes(x) $\Rightarrow$ cancer(x)), and the other one that

$\forall$x (drinks-alcohol(x) $\Rightarrow$ aggravates (cancer, cause_is_smoking, x)).

More generally, the paradox originates here from a false knowledge representation, and it will indeed lead to absurdities[1], but this is not especially linked to the theory of confirmation. In other words, the theorem using a logical *and* is false, and it is confirmed by almost anything, as it should be. Inversely, when two conditions are simultaneously necessary to cause a third one, say, as in stress & age>45 ⇒ heart condition (where we suppose that both stress and aging are causal), then the disjunction in the contraposition is no longer paradoxical.

In short, in the case of causal implications, absurd confirmations are avoided by a careful examination of the meaning of the implication. Simple counting might be dangerous, but there are enough statistical methods to avoid easily the trap of Hempel's paradox.

2.3   Practical Consequences

All that shows how Science has been able to build theories using confirmation, in spite of Hempel's paradox.   Unfortunately it also shows how unreliable some confirmation measurements that are automatically performed might be.

Suppose you are looking for implications A ⇒ B (i.e., associations) coming from a taxonomy of generality, i.e., with inherited property semantics, such as, for example, dog ⇒ canine. Then only the couples (A,B) confirm this hypothesis, and the couples (A,¬B) disconfirm it. Thus, the probability of confirmation for A ⇒ B should be estimated by counting the number of corresponding items (let # be the counting function, and N be the total number of items) and approximated by the value: (# (A,B) - # (A,¬B)) / N.

Inversely, suppose you are looking for implications A ⇒ B with a causal semantics. They are confirmed by all couples (A,B) and (¬A,¬B), and they are disconfirmed by all couples (A,¬B). The probability of the confirmation of A ⇒ B should then be approximated by (# (A,B) + # (¬A,¬B) – 2*(# (A,¬B)) / N.

These remarks will explain the changes I propose to the classical definitions of coverage and confidence in section 3.2.

3   What Makes Knowledge Discovery in Data (KDD) Different

I will recall Fayyad's acknowledged definition of KDD [3], as being the most canonical one among KDD and DM scientists. This definition introduces two very new concepts that are not used in ML: the discovered knowledge is requested to be (potentially) interesting and novel. I'll insist on the consequences of asking for "useful knowledge", and I'll also refine somewhat this definition by adding three more

---

[1] There is another famous argument against induction, namely that observing that 1. drinking vodka with water makes you drunk, 2. drinking gin with water makes you drunk, leads to the generalization that drinking water makes you drunk. Some claim: "This generalization is obviously absurd, hence generalization is absurd." I leave to the reader to show that, again, this argument is due to a bad knowledge representation where the word *with* is represented by a logical *and-* which is indeed absurd!

concepts: the first one is issued from history, and it defines KDD as a melting pot of many other previous approaches, including ML; the second one opposes most of ML and other scientific fields: they all have based their validity measures on accuracy while KDD asks for other measures (including interestingness); the third one is relatively simple but practically very important: KDD is a cycle that comprises many steps and no step is "good science" while other steps are "mere engineering".

The best acknowledged definition of KDD says that:

" KDD extracts potentially useful and previously unknown knowledge from large amounts of data ".

I'll not insist on the large amount of data to be treated since it simply implies that the algorithms must be as fast as possible, which is a trend of Computer Science and is so well accepted that it requires no detailed comment. On the other hand, I'll develop the consequences of asking for "unknown knowledge" (section 3.1 below) and the measures of interest (section 3.2 below). The next four sections will develop more personal points of view about KDD.

3.1   "Previously Unknown Knowledge"

Asking for **previously unknown knowledge** contains implicitly the statement that there is nothing wrong in finding knowledge that might contradict the existing one. Until now, all efforts in Machine Learning (ML) and Statistics have been aimed at finding knowledge that does not contradict the already existing one: This is even the principle underlying the development and success of Inductive Logic Programming (ILP), where the new created clauses must not contradict the existing ones. In a sense, the very success of ILP is due to the automatical integration of the invented model into the body of the existing knowledge. This is due to the fact that ILP's so-called "inversion of the resolution", works as follows: The resolution procedure, let us call it R, allows us to deduce, from two given clauses C_1 and C_2, a third one such that $R(C_1, C_2) = C_3$. The process of inversion of the resolution is the one that (very similarly to abduction) "inverses" this process by asking for the invention of a clause 'x', such that for given C_1 and C_3, the relation $R(C_1, 'x') = C_3$ holds. From this definition, it is clear that 'x' will never contradict the body of existing knowledge.

In conclusion, it can be argued that avoiding contradictory knowledge is a common characteristic of all existing inductive reasoning approaches. On the contrary, in KDD, an interesting nugget of knowledge contradicting a large body of knowledge will be considered all the more interesting!

Discovering a large number of well-known rules is considered to be the typical trap that KDD systems should be able to avoid.

3.2   "Useful Knowledge"

This statement stresses the **importance of the user's goal in biasing the acquisition of knowledge**. Induction is always an intellectually dangerous process if not tightly controlled. It should be obvious that the user's goals are the best of the biases necessary to avoid inventing trivialities. Up to now, academic research neglected this view of the problem, and still too few papers deal with it because existing research fields try to develop techniques that are, as far as possible, universal and that pretend to be useful to every user instead of being specific (if they are, they are called "mere engineering", not "Science"). Some research has been done nevertheless in the KDD community under the name of "rule validation" or "measures of interest"(see section 3.2b, below) and it tries to take into account the user's requirements. These tests are relative to patterns discovered in the data, as opposed to the incredibly large number of tests proposed to measure the results of supervised classification.

Let A and B be two assertions, and X and Y be their supports, i.e., $\{X\} = \{x \,/\, A(x) = True\}$ and $\{Y\} = \{y \,/\, B(y) = True\}$. Suppose also that we deal with a finite set of examples, in such a way that $\{X\} \cup \{\overline{X}\} = \{Y\} \cup \{\overline{Y}\} = \{Tot\}$ the cardinal of $\{Tot\}$ is the total number of examples (it can also be said that it is the total number of records in the database). When we want to infer $A \Rightarrow B$ from the data, then the following measures will provide an estimation of the validity of this implication.

Measures of Statistical Significance. These measures compute various relations between the cardinals of $\{X\}$ and $\{Y\}$. Two very classical ones are the measures of support and confidence that are used by KDD systems that discover associations. The measurements of conviction and 'interest' have been recently introduced in [2]. Several definitions that take into account the difference between causal and descriptive implication will also be introduced here.

In order to illustrate our reasoning, let us consider the following three small data sets :

D1	A	¬A
B	2	2
¬B	2	14

D2	A	¬A
B	10	0
¬B	0	10

D3	A	¬A
B	2	2
¬B	13	13

Table 1 lists the values of various measures that can be calculated on these data sets. We shall refer to these results in the discussion that follows.

D1 obviously does not confirm directly $A \Rightarrow B$ since the number of instances of (A,B) is equal to the number of instances of (A,¬B). Besides, each of them represents only 1/10 of the instances, which means that they both can be due to noise, especially if we hypothesize a 10% level of noise. Inversely, the contraposition of $A \Rightarrow B$ is well confirmed since $P(\neg A, \neg B) = 7/10$ which is much higher than the level of noise.

In this case, a descriptive $A \Rightarrow B$, being equally confirmed and disconfirmed, should be looked upon as very unlikely. For instance, if the number of women with short hair (P(A,B)) was approximately the same as that of women with long hair (P(¬A,B)), it would become very clumsy to recognize a woman by the length of her hair. As to the contraposition, if the number of men with long hair (P(A,¬B)) was very small, it would become again possible to use this feature, but in order to recognize a man (as a person with short hair), not in order to recognize a woman. Since hair length is not causally related to sex, the contraposition is not significant for the recognition of women (as persons with long hair). In other words, the fact that most men have short hair does not mean that most women should have long hair. The number of women with long hair and the number of non-women (= men) with non-long (= short) hair are not at all related, and a measure that would relate them is unreliable. We shall see that such a relation is implicitly done in some classical measures such as the confidence, P(B | A). This so-called 'confidence' is too high when descriptive implications are looked for, and too low when real causal implications are looked for.

D2 is a kind of "ideal" case where $A \Rightarrow B$ and its contraposition are equally confirmed, with absolute certainty. It will illustrate the limits of the values we introduce, and why some normative coefficients are necessary. It shows also that the classical dependency measure (see definition 12 below) under-evaluates the strength of the causal links: its value is 1/2 only because the confirmation by contraposition has been only partly taken into account.

D3 is a case where the correlation between A and B is exactly zero, using the classical dependency measure, or our "putative causal" measure. Its "confirm" measures are negative, meaning that it is more often disconfirmed than confirmed: correlation and confirmation both reject the hypothesis that $A \Rightarrow B$.

Table 1. Measures that can be calculated on datasets D1, D2 and D3.

D1	D2	D3
P(A,B) = 1/10,	P(A,B) = 1/ 2,	P(A,B) = 1/15
P(¬A,¬B) = 7/10	P(¬A,¬B) = 1/ 2	P(¬A,¬B) = 13/30
P(¬B,A) = 1/10	P(¬B,A) = 0	P(¬B,A) = 13/30
P(A) = 2/10, P(B) = 2/10	P(A) = 1/ 2, P(B) = 1/ 2	P(A) = 1/2, P(B) = 2/15
P(¬A) = 8/10, P(¬B) = 8/10	P(¬A) = 1/ 2, P(¬B) = 1/ 2	P(¬A) = 1/2, P(¬B) = 13/15
P(B | A) = 1/ 2,	P(B | A) = 1	P(B | A) = 2/15
P(¬A | ¬B) = 7/8	P(¬A | ¬B) = 1	P(¬A | ¬B) = 1/2
P(¬B | A) = 1/ 2	P(¬B | A) = 0	P(¬B | A) = 13/15
P(A | ¬B) = 1/ 8	P(A | ¬B) = 0	P(A | ¬B) = 1/2
Causal support = 8/10	Causal support = 1	Causal support = 1/2
Descriptive confirm = 0	Descriptive confirm = 1/2	Descriptive confirm = -11/30
Causal confirm = 6/10	Causal confirm = 1	Causal confirm = -11/30
Causal confidence = 11/16	Causal confidence = 1	Causal confidence = 19/60
Dependency = 3/10	Dependency = 1/2	Dependency = 0
Putative causal dependency=3/8	Putative causal dependency=1	Putative causal dependency=0

We do not illustrate the typical case where $A \Rightarrow B$ is mostly directly confirmed, since it is of little interest relative to our argumentation: it would obviously illustrate the case where our proposed measures are useless.

Note: In the following, 'the implication' will always be $A \Rightarrow B$, and 'the contraposition' will be $\neg B \Rightarrow \neg A$.

Definition 1: Support-descriptive = P(A,B)

The support of the implication expresses how often A and B are True together. It is measured by the size of the intersection between {X} and {Y}, divided by the size of {Tot}:

$$P(A,B) = | \{X\} \cap \{Y\}| / | \{Tot\}| .$$

All algorithms that detect associations perform a kind of counting based on this last formula. Generally speaking, the importance of support must be stressed before presenting any other measurement. If an implication has too little support, even with the terabytes of data now available, it might very well happen that it is then confirmed by a very small number of instances that come from noise only. This is why it is always dangerous to look for implications with small support, even though they might be very "interesting" since they show a behavior at variance with the normal one. This explains why the "intensity of implication," presented below in section 3.2b, since it might look for implication with little support, takes much care to take into account a possible effect of random noise. The above definition of support is a very classical one, and it implies that descriptive implications are looked for. In the case of causal implications, we claim that this approximation has no meaning.

Definition 2: Support-causal = $P(A,B) + P(\neg B, \neg A)$
This measure is not usually presented in the literature. It is approximated by:
$$(|\{X\} \cap \{Y\}| + |\{\overline{X}\} \cap \{\overline{Y}\}|) / |\{Tot\}|.$$
Notice that:
$$P(\neg A, \neg B) = 1 - P(A) - P(B) + P(A,B),$$
thus adding the confirmation of the contraposition, i.e., computing $P(A,B) + P(\neg A, \neg B)$ amounts to computing either
$$1 - P(A) - P(B) + 2*P(A,B)$$
or
$$P(A) + P(B) + 2* P(\neg A, \neg B) -1.$$
It follows that, in a finite world as the one of KDD, taking into account $P(A,B)$ simultaneously gives some indication on the value of $P(\neg B, \neg A)$. Nevertheless, causal support can be seen as taking into account the size of $P(A)$ and $P(B)$, a behavior not displayed by descriptive support. For instance, the causal support of D1 (4/5) is much higher than its descriptive support (1/10), as it should be since $A \Rightarrow B$ is confirmed mainly by its contraposition.

Definition 3: Confirm-descriptive = $P(A,B) - P(A,\neg B)$
Notice that $P(A,B) + P(A,\neg B) = P(A)$ thus $P(A,B) / P(A) = 1 - P(A,\neg B) / P(A)$ which means that confirmation and disconfirmation are not independent. It follows that:
$$P(A,B) - P(A,\neg B) = P(A) - 2* P(A,\neg B) = 2 * P(A,B) - P(A)$$
In the case of D1, the descriptive-confirm equals 0, as it should be.

Definition 4: Confirm-causal = $P(A,B) + P(\neg A,\neg B) - 2*P(A,\neg B)$
All the equivalencies already noticed obviously apply, and there are many ways to approximate this measure. Our causal-confirm raises from 0 to 6/10 in the case of D1 since it takes into account the confirmation of the contraposition, as it should be in the case of causality.

Definition 5: Confidence-descriptive- = $P(A,B) / P(A) = P(B | A)$
The descriptive support is divided by $P(A)$ in order to express the fact that the larger $P(A)$ is, the more it is expected that it will imply other relations. For instance, if $P(A) = 1$, then $P(A,B)=P(B)$ for any B. Thus, the implication $B \Rightarrow A$ is absolutely trivial in this data set. In general, the confidence is approximated by
$$|\{X\} \cap \{Y\}| / |\{X\}|$$
Since by definition $P(B | A) = P(A,B) / P(A)$, the confidence is nothing but the a posteriori probability of B, given A. Since $P(B | A) + P(\neg B | A) = 1$, a high confidence in $A \Rightarrow B$ entails a low confidence in $A \Rightarrow \neg B$. In other words, it can be believed that it is now less interesting to introduce explicitly the number of examples contradicting $A \Rightarrow B$, since:
$$P(B | A) - P(\neg B | A) = 1 - 2*P(\neg B | A) = - (1 - 2*P(B | A)).$$
A critique of this definition

In the definition of confidence and of dependency (defined below as $P(B \mid A) - P(B)$), the value of $P(A,B) / P(A) = P(B \mid A)$ is used in order to measure the strength of the dependency. We claim that this measurement of strength is not adequate. For instance, in D1 above, $P(B \mid A) = 0.5$. This says that the probability of B given A is relatively high, even in this case where the confirmation is doubtful for a descriptive confidence and dependency. Confidence is 0.5 and dependency is $0.5 - 2/10 = 0.3$. Both values are too high for a descriptive implication so weakly confirmed by the data. With our definition of confirmed descriptive confidence and dependency, both are equal to 0, as they should be since the dependency is as much confirmed as disconfirmed.

Definition 6: Confirmed-Confidence-descriptive = $(P(A,B) / P(A)) - (P(A,\neg B) / P(A)) = P(B \mid A) - P(\neg B \mid A)$

This measure is zero in D1 since the implication is as much confirmed as it is disconfirmed. It is 1 in D2 since no example disconfirms the implication. It is negative in D3, because the data does not support the hypothesis of the implication.

Definition 7: Confidence-causal = $1/2\ (P(A,B) / P(A)) + (P(\neg B, \neg A) / P(\neg B)) = 1/2\ (P(B \mid A) + P(\neg A \mid \neg B))$

This measure adds the confidence due to the direct instances of the implication, and the confidence due to its contraposition. The 1/2 coefficient stems from the fact that each a posteriori probability can be equal to 1, as in D2 above, and we want the measure to take values between 0 and 1. $P(B \mid A) + P(\neg A \mid \neg B)$ are linked but their link introduces again the values of $P(A)$ and $P(B)$ which can change the value of the confidence in an interesting way. Let us use again that $P(\neg A, \neg B) = 1 - P(A) - P(B) + P(A,B)$. It follows that:

$$P(\neg A \mid \neg B) \quad = P(\neg A, \neg B) / P(\neg B)$$
$$= (1 - P(A) - P(B) + P(A,B)) / 1 - P(B)$$
$$= 1 - (P(A) / 1 - P(B)) (1 - P(B \mid A))$$

A critique of this definition

The same critique as above applies, since this definition does not take into account disconfirmation. For instance, in the case of D1, the causal confidence is 11/16, which is too high for an implication that shows such an amount of disconfirmation.

Definition 8: Confirmed-confidence-causal =
$$1/2\ ((P(A,B) / P(A)) + (P(\neg B, \neg A) / + P(\neg B))) - P(\neg B, A) / P(A)) = 1/2\ (P(B \mid A) + P(\neg A \mid \neg B)) - P(\neg B \mid A)$$

The normative coefficient 1/2 is needed here because each of $P(B \mid A)$ and $P(\neg A \mid \neg B)$ can be equal to 1, as in D2 above, for instance. In the case of D1, the causal confirmed-confidence decreases from 11/16 to 3/16 since the data confirm rather weakly the implication.

Let us see now examine two other measures that have been introduced [Brin et al., 1997], with the goal of expressing better the confirmation of the hypothesis $A \Rightarrow B$. They both ignore the difference between causal and non-causal implications.

Definition 9: Conviction = $[P(A) * P(\neg B)] / P(A, \neg B)$

When A is True and B is False, then the implication $A \Rightarrow B$ is disconfirmed. This is why the larger $P(A, \neg B)$ is, the lower the conviction. Obviously, the larger $P(A)$ is, the larger the conviction. Inversely, suppose that {Y} is tiny, then its intersection with {X} can hardly be due to simple chance, and we have more conviction in favor of A ⇒ B. Thus, the larger the support of P(¬B), the larger the conviction. This measure is valid for descriptive implications only.

Definition 10: 'Interest' = P(A,B) / [P(A) * P(B)] = P(B | A) / P(B)
The more probable P(A) and P(B) are, the less interesting is their intersection since it is expected to be always large. In fact, the ratio P(A,B) / P(A) is also the conditional probability of B knowing A, and it is written as P(B | A). This measure is valid for descriptive implications only.

Definition 11: Correlation coefficient
Yet another very classical measure is the measure of correlation, valid for continuous variables. Consider variables x and y taking real values x_i and y_i for each of the N items of the data base. Let M_x be the mean value of x, and E_x be its variance. Then, the correlation of x and y is defined as:

$$1 / (N-1) \sum_{i=1}^{N} (x_i - M_x / E_x) * (y_i - M_y / E_y)$$

The intuition behind this measure is that when x and y are correlated, then x_i and y_i tend to be together "on the same side" of the mean. The correlation measure is called 'dependency' when dealing with discrete values.

Definition 12: Dependency-descriptive = Abs(P(B | A) - P(B)) if P(A) • 0
Abs is the function "absolute value." If A is not absurd, i.e., its probability of occurrence is not zero, and in practice this means that P(B | A) = P(A,B) / P(A) is computable, then the probability of meeting B given A should increase when A ⇒ B. This is why the value Abs (P(B | A) - P(B)) is used to measure the strength of the dependency. It is approximated by

Abs ((P(A,B) / P(A)) - P(B))) =Abs (| {X} ∩ {Y}| / | {X}|) - (|{Y}| / | {Tot}|))

A critique of this definition
The probability of meeting B given A should also decrease when A ⇒ ¬B is confirmed. This is why we propose now a more complex definition of dependency.

Definition 13: Putative causal dependency =
   1/2 ([P(B | A) - P(B)] + [P(¬A | ¬B) - P(¬A)] - [P(¬B | A) - P(¬B)] - [P(A | ¬B) - P(A)]).
In general, the definition of putative causal dependency contains a measure of dependency and time orientation: One says that B is causally dependent on A if : Abs(P(B | A) - P(B)) • 0 and if A occurs before B [17]. This definition is not convenient for our purposes, since we do not always know the time relationship among variables, and, worse, there are causal variables that depend on time in a twisted way, e.g., in the medical domain: sex, skin color, weight, height, sexual orientation, habits etc., in all cases of so-called "aggravation factors." As an example, it might well happen that a smoker dies of heart attack and although smoking has been causal, the heart disease started before the habit of smoking. The smoking habit acted as a reinforcement on an existing disease, and it is participating to the cause of death by this disease, if not to the cause of the disease. Besides, the approximation proposed for the computation of dependency does not fit at all the notion of causality. Since most authors do not make explicit the approximations they do when measuring P(B | A), it is impossible to check if they have done the error of approximating it by (|{X} ∩ {Y}| / | {X}|). I

find it anyhow more elegant to give a different definition of causal dependency, to which a correct approximation will be more obviously linked. The classical definition expresses the fact that when A ⇒ B then B should occur more often when A is true than when it is not. The complete accounting on this topic is then the following:

When A ⇒ B holds, for the *direct theorem*,

B should occur more often when A holds,
which asks for a highly positive P(B | A) - P(B) and
¬B should occur less often when A holds,
which asks for a zero or even a highly negative P(¬B | A) - P(¬B),

while for the *contraposed theorem*,

¬A should occur more often when ¬B holds,
which asks for a highly positive P(¬A | ¬B) - P(¬A) and
¬¬A should occur less often when ¬B holds,
which asks for a zero or even a highly negative
P(¬¬A | ¬B) - P(¬¬A) = P(A | ¬B) - P(A).

The definition of putative causal dependency can thus be computed as:

1/2 ([P(B | A) - P(B)] + [P(¬A | ¬B) - P(¬A)] - [P(¬B | A) - P(¬B)] - [P(A | ¬B) - P(A)]).

Notice the main differences between this definition and the classical one. It might happen that relationships which are highly confirmed by their contraposition but which occur in very few cases, are forgotten by the classical measure. It may also happen that relationships that are both largely confirmed and largely disconfirmed (because they are actually due to some noise) are accepted by the classical measure, while they are rejected by ours, as exemplified by D1 where the descriptive support is 1/10, while the causal one is 8/10, and where the descriptive confirm is exactly 0. The same kind of remark as the one made for confidence applies here: classical measures might over-estimate a dependency by not explicitly taking into account what disconfirms it, or they can as well under-estimate a causal dependency by not using explicitly the contraposition.

This definition does not exhaust all the cases. We shall define as really causal, any putative causal dependency that is neither indirect nor spurious.

Definition 14: Spurious causal dependencies = spurious (C ⇒ B)

Consider the case where the computations lead to accept that A ⇒ B, and A ⇒ C & C ⇒ B. Since A implies both B and C, B will be true when C is true, even if C is not causal to B, that is, even if the implication C ⇒ B does not hold in reality. If C is really causal for B, then B must be more frequent when A and C hold than when A alone holds, that is, P(B | A,C) must be higher than P(B | A). Hence the classical definition of a spurious causal dependency is P(B | A,C) = P(B | A).

Example: Suppose that we mine data relative to rain, umbrella sales, and grass growing. Obviously, one should find implications such as: rain ⇒ grass growing, rain ⇒ umbrella sales. The problem is that the data will contain also the information that umbrella sales ⇒ grass growing, since the two facts will occur together very often. The *a posteriori* probability of grass growing given umbrella sales will be a good instance of a spurious causal link. However, the probability of grass growing should be the same, given rain and umbrella sales, or given rain alone.

This definition characterizes spuriousness, i.e., the difference between by P(B | A,C) and P(B | A) can be used to measure the "degree of spuriousness." Spurious dependency is thus confirmed directly by Abs (P(B | A,C) - P(B | A)). Nevertheless, and in accordance with the measures already defined, we think it should be rather defined as the difference between everything that confirms that 'B depends on A to occur,' and everything that confirms that 'B depends on A and C to occur.' Since we claim that causal confirmed-confidence (A ⇒ B) = 1/2 (P(B | A) + P(¬A | ¬B)) - P(¬B | A) is the best measure of the existence of a causal link between B and A, we shall extend slightly this definition to get a new definition.

Definition 15: Confirmed-spurious (C ⇒ B) =
Abs(confirmed-confidence-causal (A ⇒ B) - confirmed-confidence-causal
(A,C ⇒ B))
Where confirmed-confidence-causal (A,C ⇒ B) = 1/2 (P(B | A,C) + P(¬A,¬C | ¬B)) - P(¬B | A,C).
This definition does not change the nature of the measure since conditional dependencies take also into account contraposition and disconfirmation. However, the exact amount of spuriousness could be wrongly evaluated by the classical definition. In the case of noise, some real spuriousness could be overseen, and some non-existing spuriousness could be "invented."

Definition 16: Indirect causal dependencies = indirect (A ⇒ B)
This case is symmetrical with spuriousness. Consider the case where we find again that A ⇒ B, A ⇒ C, and C ⇒ B but, now, the causality flows only through C, that is the implication A ⇒ B is not really valid.This should show in the a posteriori probabilities, and here it should be observed that P(B | A,C) = P(B | C) since C carries all the causality.
   Example: Consider a hypothetical database relative to insecurity feelings, sugar consumption, and tooth decay. The data should convey the theorems that insecurity-feelings ⇒ sugar-consumption and that sugar-consumption ⇒ tooth-decay. Unfortunately, the data will also lead to insecurity-feelings ⇒ tooth-decay. We should however observe that the probability of tooth-decay given insecurity-feelings and sugar-consumption is the same as the probability of tooth-decay given sugar-consumption. This definition characterizes indirectness, i.e., the difference between P(B | A,C) and P(B | C) can be used to measure the "degree of indirectness." Indirect dependency is thus confirmed by the difference Abs (P(B | A,C) - P(B | C)). For the same reasons as above, we shall propose a new definition.

Definition 17: Confirmed-indirect (A ⇒ B) =
Abs(Confirmed-confidence-causal (C ⇒ B) - Confirmed-confidence-causal
(A,C ⇒ B))
The definition of causality is a very tricky problem where significant progress has been achieved with the recent introduction of Bayesian networks that rely on a causal structure. Most researchers use a definition of causal dependency due to Pearl and Verma [10]. When the time dependency between variables is not known, then causality can be defined only for a set of more than two variables, as the above

definitions of spuriousness and indirectness show, since they need three variables at least for their definition.

Definition 18: Causality-global (A ⇒ B)
This definition relies on two different computations. One is the measure of correlation of A and B, when their values are continuous, and the measure of dependency, when they are discrete. The variables that show very little correlation or dependency are called independent. The second computation builds all possible geometries, i.e., all causal schemes, globally compatible with these independencies. The simplest of all is called 'the' causal scheme.

Let us present a new definition of a causal implication, that we shall call Causality-naive because it relies on a naive, albeit convincing, reasoning.

Definition 19: Causality-naive (A ⇒ B), in a network of variables, AND ¬Causality-naive (B ⇒ A)
   IF   Putative-causal-dependency (A ⇒ B) = high
   AND Putative-causal-dependency (B ⇒ A) = high
   AND Confirmed-indirect (A ⇒ B) = low
   AND Confirmed-spurious (A ⇒ B) = low
   AND Putative-causal-dependency (B ⇒ A) >
        Putative-causal-dependency (A ⇒ B)

Note that the computation of Confirmed-indirect (A ⇒ B) and Confirmed-spurious (A ⇒ B) imply that there is a network of variables. Imagine the data generated at a particular instance by a causal relationship, such as $\forall$ x (smokes (x) ⇒ cancer(x)). Since smoking is causal it takes place before cancer is observed. More generally, if A ⇒ B is suspected, and A is really causal to B, then A takes place before B. An important issue that arises then is whether A and B will be observed simultaneously in a dataset capturing a particular point in time. There are two cases.

Case 1: A causes B and thus takes place before B, but A is still True when B also starts being True. Then all individuals for which B is True A is also True. Inversely, for some individuals, A might be True, but its effect on B might not be apparent yet (in our current example, this is the case of all the smokers that did not get a cancer … yet!). Thus, there will be fewer individuals for which A True entails B True. In other words, the confirmation of A ⇒ B will be less than the confirmation of B ⇒ A.

Case 2: Suppose that A causes B, but A does not exist anymore when B takes place. Smoking, for instance, can cause cancer long after the sick person has stopped smoking. Then A and B can even look uncorrelated in a slice of the population taken at time t. Thus, the only way to observe the causality is to introduce implicitly time in the data, by counting A as True if it is or has been true. This leads to case 1.

It follows that in both cases, if the time effect is correctly taken into account - and this for implications of high putative causal dependence that are neither spurious nor indirect - one should compare the putative causal dependency of both A ⇒ B and B ⇒ A. The one with the *smallest* value is the one orientating the causal link between A and B. This definition, even though opposing others, strictly follows the intuition we have of what should happen when A causes B.

Measures of Interest. It is quite usual that the number of associations detected by using some of the above measures is still enormous. In the case of text mining, our experience is even that megas of texts generate gigas of associations with very high support and confidence. At any rate, experience shows it is always necessary to sort among the associations those that are of "interest" for the user. We shall see now four extensions to the classical measures of statistical significance, that are devoted to the measurement of some kind of interest for a user, or at least proposed to the user in order to help him or her to choose these associations that might be more interesting.

- **The first extension** is Bhandari's **Attribute Focusing** [1], linked to the selection of features that can possibly surprise the user. It relies on the application of correlation measures to discrete valued features. Suppose we know that feature q_1 is always interesting for the user (e.g. the amount of sales). It is possible that the values of the other features that are very strongly (or very weakly) correlated to q_1 are also of interest. The correlation between the value u of q_1 and the value v of q_2 is measured by:

$$I_{Bhandari} (q_1 = u, q_2 = v) = Abs (P(q_1 = u, q_2 = v) - P(q_1 = u) * P(q_2 = v)).$$

I want to insist here on three facts:

1. The impossibility of using the classical definition of correlation. Imagine that, following Bhandari, we replace each feature by its probability in the data. It is then easy to define a mean probability $P(\overline{q_1})$ for feature q_1, its variance σ_1, and normalized values: $N_u (q_1) = [P(\overline{q_1}) - P(q_1 = u)] / \sigma_1$. However, the sum of the products of $N_u (q_1) * N_v (q_2)$ cannot even be computed in the usual case where q_1 and q_2 do not have the same number of values.

2. It would perhaps be better to measure the correlation between two discrete variables by the formula for dependency: Abs (P(B | A) - P(B)) if P(A) • 0, which we introduced in section 3.2 above. In this representation, Bhandari's formula becomes:

$$I_{Bhandari} = Abs (P(B,A) - [P(B)* P(A)]) \text{ and since } P(B,A) = P(B | A) * P(A)$$
$$I_{Bhandari} = P(A) * Abs (P(B | A) - P(B)) = P(A) * \text{dependency}.$$

   In other words, $I_{Bhandari}$ measures the product of the dependency between A and B by P(A): the "interesting" variable is all the most interesting if its probability of occurrence is relatively high.

3. Bhandari's formula is thus restricted to the case where the data are purely symbolic. Consider now the case where they are mixed. It will be easy to measure independently the correlation between continuous variables and the correlation between symbolic variables separately. It is an open problem to propose a convincing measure of dependency among continuous and discrete variables. Suppose that we would like to prove or disprove a causal dependency between a typical symbolic feature, such as hair color and a typical continuous one, such as height. There is nothing we could do.

The second extension, named "**intensity of implication**," [5], instead of being based on the implicit postulate that associations with high support are interesting, it is based on the postulate that associations with low disconfirmation are interesting. In other words, instead of looking for association with high values of P(A,B), the intensity of implication detects associations with low values of P(¬A,B), whatever their P(A,B) is. In order to take into account the possibility of noise in the data, the value of P(¬A,B) in the actual data is compared to the value of P(¬A',B') where A' and B' are random sets with the same cardinality as A and B.

Let {Tot} be the set of all available observations. Let {X} be the subset of {Tot} such that the assertion A is true (we already have called it the support of A). Let {Y} be the subset of {Tot} such that the assertion B is true. Then {X} ∩{Y} supports the assertion A ⇒ B, and {X}∩{ $\overline{Y}$ } contradicts this assertion. Consider now two sets of the same cardinality as {X} and {Y}, {X'} and {Y'}, that are randomly chosen from {Tot}. Then the relation A ⇒ B can be said to be much more confirmed than by random choice if $|${X}∩{ $\overline{Y}$ }$|$ is much smaller than $|${X'}∩{ $\overline{Y'}$ }$|$. The intensity of implication measures the difference between these two quantities. The bigger the difference, the bigger the intensity of implication. The measure asks for complex calculations that are simplified by choosing an approximation to the expected random distribution. Present measures tend to use a Poisson approximation [5], which leads to the following actual measure of the intensity of the implication:

$$I = 1/\sqrt{2p} \int_{ii}^{\infty} e^{-t^2/2} \, dt$$

where the value ii is given by a computation on the observed values. Let

$$n_{ab'} = |\{X\}\cap\{\overline{Y}\}|, \ n_a = |\{X\}|, \ n_{b'} = |\{\overline{Y}\}|, \text{ and } n = \{Tot\}, \text{ then}$$

$$ii = (n_{ab'} - n_a \, n_{b'}/n) / \sqrt{n_a \, n_{b'}/n}.$$

This shows that, although it is a bit more complicated to compute than the other measures, the intensity of implication is not prohibitively expensive.

The third extension looks for **exceptions.** Rules seemingly contradictory issued from the data are deemed to be more interesting. This method looks for couples of assertions of the form:

A ⇒ B, A & A' ⇒ ¬B.

An example of such contradiction in real life can be:

Airbag ⇒ increase in security; Airbag & (age = baby) ⇒ decrease in security.

It is assumed that some combination of statistical significance of the two assertions is "interesting". For instance, when A ⇒ B is statistically very significant, and A & A' ⇒ ¬B has a small cover but large confidence. Iit is then very similar to what we think of as being a "nugget" of knowledge. Suzuki [15] has studied the detection of contradiction. The problem of exception is similar to that encountered in other rules: too many statistically significant exceptions are found, and the problem is to reduce them to the "most interesting" ones. In [16] we explore the possibility of using the intensity of implication to characterize interesting exceptions.

The fourth extension does not measure the interest of an individual rule, but it tries to evaluate the interest of a whole set of rules. Global heterogeneity can be related to interest [4]. Heterogeneity is realized by adding at each step the most distant rule to the existing set, until the set reaches a pre-determined size. An obvious extension to this method would be to ask for the most heterogeneous set of rules that maintains the precision at a fixed proportion of the precision reached by the complete set of rules.

3.3   Merging Approaches

KDD integrates several knowledge acquisition approaches, without being just a concatenation of these approaches. Integrating these methods will generate new solutions, and new scientific problems, imperfectly dealt with until now. The scientific fields to integrate are various, dealing with Machine Learning, including Symbolic, Statistical, Neural and Bayesian types of learning, Knowledge Acquisition, querying Databases, Man-Machine Interaction (MMI) and Cognitive Sciences. Until very recently, these fields have developed methodologies that consider a very specific aspect of reality. Putting it in a somewhat crude way, ML has concentrated its efforts on small data sets of noise-free symbolic values; Statistical and Neural approaches worked on rather large data sets of purely numeric variables; Bayesian learning has assumed that the causal model of the problem is known, and asked for the determination of such a large number of conditional probabilities that it was often unrealistic in real life; Knowledge Acquisition has dealt with the representation of the skills of an expert (not taking data very much into account); DBMS work concentrated on purely deductive queries; MMI has been seen as a discovery process, not as fitting into a larger discovery process using other techniques (in short, they tend to show things, but provide no way of using what has been seen); and the Cognitive Sciences have no concern for computational efficiency. Each domain is improving rapidly, but, rather than integrating approaches from other fields, it tends to concentrate its efforts on solving the problems it has already met.

The first, still incomplete, instances of such an integrated approach are the large KDD systems now found on the market, the most famous of them being: *Intelligent Miner* of IBM, *MineSet* of Silicon Graphics, *Clementine* of ISL (now, of SPSS), and SAS *Enterprise Miner*.

3.4   Accurate vs. Understandable (and Useful) Knowledge

Another concept that I believe to be KDD-specific is a kind of intellectual scandal for most scientists: it is the recognition that **validation by measures of accuracy is far from sufficient**. Up to now, all researchers, including those working on the symbolic aspects of learning, have been measuring their degree of success only by comparing accuracy, and most of them do not imagine that a different approach might even exist. A method is assumed to be better if it is more accurate. KDD, or at least some of the people working in this field - and still timidly, but with an increasing strength - pushes forward the idea that there are at least two other criteria of more importance than accuracy, and calls them "comprehensibility" and usability (described in section 3.2 above). I believe it is absolutely infuriating that while all users and real-world application people say that accuracy is less important than comprehensibility and usefulness, almost all academic people are still only concerned with the accuracy of their approaches. I am convinced that clear measures of comprehensibility and usefulness are the keys to future progress in the field. A positive example of this attitude is the commercial software, *MineSet*, which devoted most of its effort to providing the user with visual tools which help the user to understand the exact meaning of the induced decision trees.

As for usefulness, the above described measures of interest begin to give some objective definition to the notion of "interesting knowledge". A unifying theory has yet to be presented and we can guess that it will bring forth more ways to qualify interestingness than those explained in section 3.2.

About comprehensibility, much less work has been done except the classical "minimum description length principle" stating that when two models are equally efficient, then the less cumbersome to describe should be chosen. In practice, this leads to choosing decision trees that are as small as possible, or rules with the fewest possible premises. I would like to suggest that a complete definition of "comprehensible knowledge" will contain, among others, the following four features:

1. Comprehensibility is obviously user dependent. Comprehensible knowledge is expressed in the user's language, and with the user's semantics. Here, two options are possible. One is that the whole system works directly with the user's language. The second one, astutely proposed in [13], [14] is that the system works with its own internal representation, but provides explanations of its results in the user's language.
2. What is not comprehensible cannot be used. It follows that comprehensible knowledge cannot be separated from the meta-knowledge necessary for the use of knowledge.
3. A longer explanation might well be much more comprehensible than a shorter one. The minimum description length principle is still on the side of efficiency rather than on the side of clarity. Thus, the length of the explanations is not the only relevant factor.
4. In order to find a reliable definition of comprehensibility, it will be necessary to introduce a model of the user in the comprehensibility measurements. The results that best fit the user's model can be judged as being the most comprehensible. Building a user's model is not an easy task as shown by the difficulties met by the field of AI that attempts to build intelligent tutoring systems. This field that is obviously very much concerned with the problem of comprehensibility and therefore the need for building users' models was recognized very early.

3.5   An Epistemological Difference

The **knowledge extracted in KDD will modify the behavior of a human or mechanical agent. It thus has to be grounded in the real world**. Until now, the solutions looked for by computer scientists have been based on providing more universality, more precision, and more mathematical proofs to the "knowledge" they provide to the users. On the contrary, the results of KDD have to be directly usable, even if they are particular, imprecise, and unproved.

A typical example is the one of the overly stereotyped information provided by an OLAP query, say: "what are the three shops that sell the best?" A KDD system should deliver the differences of these three shops from the other ones, so as to allow the manager to react in improving the worse shops. This example also illustrates that one person's information can well be the knowledge of someone else. In other words, the definition of "knowledge" in KDD is user-dependent, and even goal-dependent. This is obviously linked to the point made above: the user's goals are doubly important in KDD.

Even though the KDD community is very silent about it, this requirement is linked to the famous Turing problem. Recent discussions about this problem show that ungrounded knowledge is the key to make the difference between a human and a computer (see [18], [11], [12] for a very thorough discussion of this problem). Usable, grounded knowledge is exactly what is needed to solve the Turing problem.

3.6   Engineering Is Not Dirty

The sixth important property of KDD stems more from a practical point of view: specialists in ML and Statistics tend to expect clean data to work upon. They consider that data cleaning and selection is pure engineering that does not deserve their scientific attention. KDD holds that data preparation is an integral part of the KDD process, and holds as much scientific respect as any other step. I must add that most specialists in KDD still hate dirtying their hands, but I claim this to be a *passé*-ist attitude that will have to change.

3.7   Conclusion

The last four conditions oppose current academic behavior. The argument I meet most often is the following: "Since you ask for all these requirements that make measurements almost impossible and since little can be proved of the processes you are studying, then you are defining an art and not a science." It is true that there does not yet exist an established measure of comprehensibility nor of usefulness, but we just saw that these measures are far from being out of reach. It is also true that, due to its strong industrial involvement, KDD looks forward more eagerly to new applications than to new theories, and therefore it still looks much more like engineering than science but the strong determination of the KDD community to maintain a high scientific level insures that a safe balance will be respected.

4   Knowledge Discovery in Texts (KDT) Defined as a KDD Application

The expression "text mining" is being used to cover any kind of text analysis, more due to the fashion linked to the word "mining" than for any real progress. I know of at least three different problems, already well-known in the community of Natural Language Processing (NLP), for which some industrialists claim to be doing "text mining": syntactical and semantical analysis, information retrieval (i.e., finding the texts associated to a set of key-words), and information extraction (i.e., filling up pre-defined patterns from texts). By no means, can it be said that these problems are easy ones, and they can even be part of a general KDT system, but for each of them, it would better to go on being called by its own name.

Rather than giving new names to old topics, I'd like to suggest defining KDT rather as the science that **discovers knowledge in texts,** *where " knowledge" is taken with the meaning used in KDD* (see section 2.5 above), that is: the knowledge extracted has to be grounded in the real world, and will modify the behavior of a human or mechanical agent. This definition introduces in KDT all the problems already described for KDD, and shows very well how KDT differs from NLP.

1. KDT **discovers** knowledge means that induction is used, while NLP never had the least interest in inductive processes, except in applying ML techniques to NLP.
2. Knowledge is understandable and directly usable by an agent, qualifies all the statistical tables or principal component analysis, etc. as not belonging to KDT, even though many NLP specialists present them as "knowledge". Those tables transform the text into data, and they can be used as a starting point for KDT. They can thus be very useful for KDT, and be included in the whole KDT process, but they do not constitute a complete KDT system.
3. Knowledge is discovered in a large number of **texts**, instead of one or a few text(s) shows also that KDT does not aim at improving text understanding, but at discovering unsuspected relations holding in a body of texts. I will give an example of this difference just below: the rule given describes knowledge contained in two years of miscellaneous "*Le Monde*" articles, instead of showing any kind of deep understanding of one particular article. It must be noticed that a part of the NLP community attacked this problem already (and called it very aptly " knowledge extraction "), but they used statistical tools without interpreting their results, and that did not allow them to go very far in terms of usefulness and comprehensibility of their results.

I will give here an example of a set of rules discovered by KDT, without details on the method used (see [8] for details), but with the hope that it illustrates the power of KDT, and that KDT provides knowledge of a striking nature, that has never been discovered before.

Existing NLP systems provide an analysis of the texts contents, with variations depending on the tool that is used. The problem for KDT is to transform these analyses into usable data. For example, consider the tool named "*Tropes*" (presently available for the French and English languages), sold by the company Acetic, which executes an analysis of the text. It provides, for each text, a table of syntactic and semantic results. This constitutes a table, the rows of which are the texts, and the columns of which correspond to the frequency of each feature in the text. For instance, the frequency of temporal junctors is a syntactic feature, and the frequency of appearance of a given concept in each text, is a semantic feature. An example of such a concept is "catastrophy". *Tropes* computes the probability that some of the words that are an instance of a catastrophy, such as 'accident', 'flooding', etc. are met in the text.

In an experiment we used a set of several thousands of articles found in two years of the French newspaper *Le Monde*. The only criterion for the selection was that the articles were relatively large, in order to allow *Tropes* to work at its best. A preliminary analysis, performed on the output of *Tropes*, using the KDD tool *Clementine* of the company SPSS, produced, among many others, the following rules, concluding on the fact that *Le Monde* has been largely speaking of the concept catastrophy in one of the texts analyzed. These rules are not particularly important, but they illustrate clearly the advantages and deficiencies of our approach.

catastrophy = much-talked-of
        IF
North-America = not-at-all-talked-of & Europe = much-talked-of
        OR
communication = moderately-talked-of & conflict = much-talked-of
        OR
Europe = much-talked-of & family = not-at-all-talked-of
        OR
Europe = much-talked-of & woman = not-at-all-talked-of
        OR
Economy = not-at-all-talked-of & Europe = much-talked-of

This set of rules expresses that, in the articles that refer to a catastrophic event, two concepts were also very often talked of. One is "Europe," which underlines an unexpected characteristic of this newspaper: when a catastrophy happens outside Europe, the concept of catastrophy is much less strongly evoked. The other concept is "conflict," in which case, *Le Monde* speaks also of communication. Very interesting is also the analysis of the statistically significant absence of evoked concepts: when speaking very strongly of a catastrophy, *Le Monde* does not speak at all of North America, family, women, and economy. Notice that among some 300 possible concepts *Le Monde* could avoid speaking of, those are the only ones significantly absent when speaking strongly of catastrophy. A detailed analysis would be necessary to understand why these absent concepts are significant by their absence. It nevertheless shows very clearly that we have produced knowledge that has never before been noticed in this newspaper, nor in any kind of text. The amount of potential research is enormous.

5 Conclusion

This chapter presents the most striking differences between Machine Learning and what I believe to be an entirely new field of research, and which corresponds roughly to what the existing KDD (Knowledge Discovery in Data) community recognizes as "unsolved problems." This last statement is largely unproved, but at least I can claim, in a somewhat jokingly way, that even though some will disclaim some of the properties I am putting forward, nobody will disclaim all these properties. The most striking instance of the disclaimer that KDD specialists will do is that none of the members of the existing KDD community will acknowledge that they are dealing with the Turing problem. Nevertheless, they will all acknowledge that they want to discover usable knowledge, which means grounded knowledge, which means dealing with the Turing problem, like it or not.

Moreover, the consequences of these definitions are applied to a new research field, that I name Knowledge Discovery in Texts (KDT). An example of the kind of knowledge it can yield has been provided. This kind of knowledge is absolutely new, and expresses properties that link a large number of texts together (instead of analyzing one text). It shows that, at least, the definitions proposed can lead to new results, and indeed define a new field of research.

Acknowledgments. George Paliouras did a detailed review of this chapter, and he helped me to improve it significantly.

References

1. Bhandari, I. "Attribute focusing: Machine-Assisted Knowledge Discovery Applied to Software Production Process Control", *Knowledge Acquisition* 6, 271-294, 1994.
2. Brin S., Motwani R., Ullman J. D., Tsur S., "Dynamic itemset Counting and Implication Rules for Market Basket Data," Proc. ACM SIGMOD International Conference on Management of Data, pp. 255-264, 1997.
3. Fayyad U. M., Piatetsky-Shapiro G., Smyth P., "From Data Mining to Knowledge Discovery: An Overview," in Fayyad U. M., Piatetsky-Shapiro G., Smyth P, Uthurasamy R. (Eds.), *Advances in Knowledge Discovery and Data mining*, AAAI Press, 1996.
4. Gago P., Bento C., "A Metric for Selection of the Most Promising Rules," in *Principles of Data Mining and Knowledge Discovery*, Zytkow J. & Quafafou M. (Eds.), pp. 19-27, LNAI 1510, Springer, Berlin 1998.
5. Gras R., Lahrer A., "L'implication statistique: une nouvelle méthode d'analyse des données," Mathématiques Informatique et Sciences Humaines 120:5-31, 1993.
6. Kodratoff Y, Bisson G. "The epistemology of conceptual clustering: KBG, an implementation", *Journal of Intelligent Information Systems*, 1:57-84, 1992.
7. Kodratoff Y., "Induction and the Organization of Knowledge", *Machine Learning: A Multistrategy Approach*, volume 4, Tecuci G. et Michalski R. S. (Eds.), pages 85-106. Morgan-Kaufmann, San Francisco CA, 1994.
8. Kodratoff Y., "Knowledge Discovery in Texts: A Definition, and Applications," Proc. ISMIS'99, Warsaw, June 1999.Published in *Foundation of Intelligent Systems*, Ras & Skowron (Eds.) LNAI 1609, pp. 16-29, Springer 1999
9. Partridge D., "The Case for Inductive Programming," *IEEE Computer 30*, 1, 36-41, 1997. A more complete version in: "The Case for Inductive Computing Science," in Computational Intelligence and Software Engineering, Pedrycz & Peters (Eds.) World Scientific, in press.
10. Pearl J., Verma T. S., "A Theory of Inferred Causation," Proc. 2nd International Conf. on Principles of Knowledge Representation and Reasoning, pp. 441-452, 1991.
11. Searle J. R. *Minds, brains & science,* Penguin books, London 1984.
10. Searle J. R., Scientific American n°262, 1990, pp. 26-31.
11. Sebag M., "2nd order Understandability of Disjunctive Version Spaces," Workshop on Machine Learning and Comprehensibility organized at IJCAI-95, LRI Report , Universite Paris-Sud.
12. Sebag M., "Delaying the choice of bias: A disjunctive version space approach," Proc. 13th International Conference on Machine Learning, Saitta L. (Ed.), pp. 444-452, Morgan Kaufmann, CA 1996.
13. Suzuki E. "Autonomous Discovery of Reliable Exception Rules," Proc. KDD-97, 259-262, 1997.
14. Suzuki E., Kodratoff Y., "Discovery of Surprising Exception Rules Based on Intensity of Implication", in *Principles of Data Mining and Knowledge Discovery*, Zytkow J. & Quafafou M. (Eds.), pp. 10-18, LNAI 1510, Springer, Berlin 1998.
15. Suppes P., "A Probalistic Theory of Causality," Acta Philosophica Fennica, Fasc. XXIV, 1970.
16. *Think*, June 1993, a review published by ITK, Univ. Tilburg, Warandelaan 2, PO Box 90153, 5000 Le Tilburg, The Netherlands.

Learning Patterns in Noisy Data: The AQ Approach

Ryszard S. Michalski[1,2] and Kenneth A. Kaufman[1]

[1]Machine Learning and Inference Laboratory, M.S. 4A5, George Mason University,
FAIRFAX, VA 22030, USA
[2]Institute of Computer Science, Polish Academy of Sciences, Warsaw, Poland
{michalsk,kaufman}@mli.gmu.edu

1   Introduction

In concept learning and data mining, a typical objective is to determine concept descriptions or patterns that will classify future data points as correctly as possible. If one can assume that the data contain no noise, then it is desirable that descriptions are complete and consistent with regard to all the data, i.e., they characterize all data points in a given class (positive examples) and no data points outside the class (negative examples).

In real-world applications, however, data may be noisy, that is, they may contain various kinds of errors, such as errors of measurement, classification or transmission, and/or inconsistencies. In such situations, searching for consistent and complete descriptions ceases to be desirable. In the presence of noise, an increase in completeness (an increase of generality of a description) tends to cause a decrease in consistency and vice versa; therefore, the best strategy is to seek a description that represents the trade-off between the two criteria that is most appropriate for the given application.

The problem then arises as to how to control such a trade-off and how to determine the most appropriate one for any given situation. To illustrate this problem, suppose that a dataset contains 1000 positive examples (P) and 1000 negative examples (N) of the concept to be learned (target concept). Suppose further that there are two descriptions or patterns under consideration: D1, which covers 600 positive (p) and 2 negative (n) examples, and D2, which covers 950 positive and 20 negative examples. Defining completeness as p / P, and consistency as $p / (p + n)$, we have:

$$\text{Completeness(D1)} = 60\% \quad \text{Completeness(D2)} = 95\%$$
$$\text{Consistency(D1)} = 99.7\% \quad \text{Consistency(D2)} = 98\%$$

The question then is, which description is better? Clearly, the answer depends on the problem at hand. In some situations, D1 may be preferred because it is more consistent, and in other situations, D2 may be preferred because it is more complete. Therefore, an important problem is how to learn descriptions that reflect different importance levels of these two criteria, that is, to control the trade-offs between the descriptions in a learning process. This issue is the main topic of this chapter. Specifically, the learning process is presented as a search for a description that maximizes a description quality measure, which best reflects the application domain.

Sections 2-5 introduce a general form of a description quality measure and illustrate it by rankings of descriptions produced by this measure and, for comparison, by criteria employed in various learning programs. Sections 6 and 7 discuss the

G. Paliouras, V. Karkaletsis, and C.D. Spyropoulos (Eds.): ACAI '99, LNAI 2049, pp. 22-38, 2001.
© Springer-Verlag Berlin Heidelberg 2001

implementation of the proposed method in the AQ18 rule learning system for natural induction and pattern discovery [14]. The final section summarizes the obtained results and discusses topics for further research.

2   Multicriterion Selection of the Best Description

In the progressive covering approach to concept learning (also known as separate-and-conquer), the primary conditions for admitting an inductive hypothesis (a description) have typically been consistency and completeness with regard to data. Other factors, such as computational simplicity, description comprehensibility, or the focus on preferred attributes, have usually been considered after the consistency and completeness criteria have been satisfied. As mentioned earlier, if the training examples contain errors (class errors or value errors) or are inconsistent (contain examples that occur in more than one class), some degree of inconsistency and incompleteness of the learned description is not only acceptable, but also desirable e.g. [2]. In such situations, a criterion for selecting a description is typically a function of the number of positive and negative examples covered by this description. For example, in the RIPPER rule learning program [6], the criterion is to maximize:

$$(p - n) / (P + N) \tag{1}$$

where p and n are the numbers of positive and negative examples covered by the rule, and P and N are the numbers of positive and negative examples in the entire training set, respectively.

A learning process can be generally characterized as a problem of searching for a description that optimizes a measure of description quality that best reflects the characteristics of the problem at hand. Such a measure is a heuristic for choosing among alternative descriptions. Various measures integrating completeness and consistency have been described in the literature e.g. [3]. In general, a description quality measure may integrate in addition to completeness and consistency several other criteria, such as the cost of description evaluation, and description simplicity. Existing learning systems usually assume one specific criterion for selecting descriptions (or components of a description, e.g., attributes in decision tree learning). It is unrealistic to assume, however, that any single criterion or a fixed combination of criteria will be suitable for all problems that can be encountered in the real world. For different problems, different criteria and their combinations may lead to the best results.

The learning system, AQ18, provides a simple mechanism for combining diverse criteria into one integrated measure of description quality. The constituent criteria are selected by the user from a repertoire of available criteria, and then combined together via the *lexicographical evaluation functional* (LEF) [13]:

$$<(c_1, \tau_1), (c_2, \tau_2), \ldots, (c_n, \tau_n)> \tag{2}$$

where c_i represents the ith constituent criterion, and τ_i is the *tolerance* associated with c_i. The tolerance defines the range (either absolute or relative) within which a candidate rule's c_i evaluation value can deviate from the best evaluation value of this criterion in the current set of descriptions. Given a LEF and a set of descriptions, the system evaluates the descriptions first on the c_1 criterion. Descriptions that do not score worse than τ_1 percent below the best description according to this criterion are passed to the next step. The next step evaluates the remaining descriptions on the c_2 criterion, and the process continues as above until all criteria are used, or only one description remains. If at the end of this process more than one description remains in the set, the best remaining one according to the first criterion is chosen.

To illustrate LEF, let us assume, for example, that we have a set of descriptions, S, and only two criteria, one, to maximize the completeness (or coverage), and the second to maximize consistency are employed to select the best description from S. Let us assume further that a description with coverage within 10% of the maximum coverage achievable by any single description in S is acceptable, and that if two or more descriptions satisfy this criterion, the one with the highest consistency is to be selected. The above description selection criterion can be specified by the following LEF:

$$LEF = <(\text{coverage}, 10\%), (\text{consistency}, 0\%)> \qquad (3)$$

It is possible that after applying both criteria, more than one description remains in the set of candidates. In this case the one that maximizes the coverage is selected.

The advantages of the LEF approach are that it is very simple to apply and very efficient, so that it can be effectively applied with a very large number of candidate descriptions. An alternative approach is to assign a weight to every constituent criterion and combine all the criteria into a single linear equation. One weakness of this approach is that it is usually difficult to assign specific weights to each constituent criterion (more difficult than to order criteria and set some tolerance). Another weakness is that all descriptions need to be evaluated on all criteria (unlike in LEF), which may be time consuming if the set of candidate descriptions, S, is very large.

3   Completeness, Consistency, and Consistency Gain

As mentioned above, in real-world applications, full consistency and completeness of descriptions is rarely required. Even if a data set can be assumed to be noise-free (which is usually unrealistic), the condition of full consistency and completeness may be undesirable if one seeks only strong patterns in the data and allows for exceptions. In such cases, one seeks descriptions that optimize a given description quality criterion.

As the main purpose of the learned descriptions is to use them for classifying future, unknown cases, a useful measure of description quality is the *testing accuracy*, that is, the accuracy of classifying testing examples, which are different from the training examples. By definition, the testing examples are not used during the learning process. Therefore, a criterion is needed that will approximate the real testing accuracy solely on the basis of training examples. Before proposing such a measure, let us explain the notation and terminology used in the rest of this chapter. Since in the implementation of the method that is presented here, descriptions are represented as a set of rules (a *ruleset*), we will henceforth use the term "ruleset" in place of "description," and the term "rule" as a component of a description.

Let P and N denote the total number of positive and negative examples, respectively, of some concept or decision class in a training set. Let R be a rule (or a ruleset) generated to cover the examples of that class, and p and n be the number of positive and negative examples covered by R, called *positive* and *negative* support, respectively. For the given rule, the ratio p / P, denoted compl(R), is called the *completeness* or *relative coverage* (or *relative support*) of R. The ratio $p / (p + n)$, denoted cons(R), is called the *consistency* or *training accuracy* of R, and $n / (p + n)$, denoted inc(R), is called the *inconsistency* or *training error rate*. If the completeness of a ruleset for a single class is 100%, then it is a *complete cover* of the training examples. If the inconsistency of the ruleset is 0%, then it is a *consistent cover*. In defining this terminology, we have tried to maintain agreement with both the existing literature and intuitive understanding of the terms. Complete agreement is, however, not possible, because different researchers and research communities attach slightly different meanings to some of the terms e.g. [3], [7].

Let us now return to the question posed in the introduction: is a description (a rule) with 60% completeness and 99.7% consistency preferable to a rule with 95% completeness and 98% consistency? As indicated earlier, the answer depends on the problem at hand. In some application domains, notably in science, a rule (law) must be consistent with all the data, unless some of the data are found erroneous. In other applications, in particular, data mining, one may seek strong patterns that hold frequently, but not always. Therefore, there is no single measure of rule quality that would be good for all problems. Instead, we seek a flexible measure that can be easily changed to fit any given problem at hand.

As mentioned earlier, a function of rule completeness and consistency may be used for evaluating a rule. Another criterion, rule simplicity, can also be used, especially in cases in which two rules rank similarly on completeness and consistency. The simplicity can be taken into consideration by properly defining the LEF criterion.

How then can we define a measure of rule quality? One approach to quantifying such considerations is the *information gain* measure that is used for selecting attributes in decision tree learning e.g. [17]. Such a criterion can also be used for ranking rules, because the rules can be viewed as binary attributes that take the value true if the rule covers a datapoint, and false otherwise. Suppose E is the set of all examples (an event space), and P and N denote the magnitudes of the subsets of positive and negative examples, respectively, of E. The entropy, or expected information for the class is defined as:

$$\text{Info}(E) = - ((P / (P + N)) \log_2(P / (P + N)) + (N / (P + N)) \log_2(N / (P + N))) \quad (4)$$

The expected information for the class when rule R is used to partition the space into regions covered and not covered by the rule is defined as:

$$\text{Info}_R(E) = ((p + n) / (P + N)) \text{Info}(R) + ((P + N - p - n) / (P + N)) \text{Info}(\sim R) \quad (5)$$

where Info(R) and Info(~R) are calculated by applying (4) to the areas covered by R and its complement, respectively. The information gained about the class by using rule R is:

$$\text{Gain}(R) = \text{Info}(E) - \text{Info}_R(E) \quad (6)$$

This measure represents a function of rule completeness and consistency; the higher a rule's completeness or consistency, the higher the Gain. Information gain as a measure of rule quality has, however, one major disadvantage. It relies not only on the informativeness of the rule, but also the informativeness of the complement of the rule. That is, it takes into consideration the entire partition created by the rule, rather than just the space covered by it. This concern is especially important in the case of many decision classes. In such cases, a rule may be highly valuable for classifying datapoints of one specific class, even if it does not reduce the entropy of the datapoints in other classes.

As an example, consider the problem of distinguishing the upper-case letters of the English alphabet. In this case, the rule, "If a capital letter has a tail, it is the letter Q" is simple, with a perfect or near-perfect completeness and consistency for the Q class. As it is a very specific rule, tailored toward one class, the above gain measure applied to it will, however, produce a low score. Another limitation of the information gain measure is that it does not provide the means for modifying it to fit different problems which may require a different relative importance of consistency versus completeness.

Before proposing another measure, let us observe that the overall relative frequency of positive and negative examples in the training set of a given class should also be a factor in evaluating a rule quality. Clearly, a rule with 15% completeness (p / P) and 75% consistency $(p /(p + n))$ could be quite attractive if the total number of positive examples (P) was 100, and the total number of negative examples (N) was substantially larger (e.g., 1000). The same rule would, however, be less attractive if N was much smaller (e.g., 10).

The distribution of positive and negative examples in the training set can be measured by the ratio $P / (P + N)$. The distribution of positive and negative examples in the set covered by the rule can be measured by the consistency $p / (p + n)$. Thus, the difference between these values, $(p /(p + n)) – (P /(P + N))$ reflects the gain of the rule consistency over the dataset distribution. This expression can be normalized by dividing it by $(1 - (P /(P + N)))$, or equivalently $N /(P + N)$, so that if the distribution of examples covered by the rule is identical to the distribution in the whole training set, it will return 0, and in the case of perfect training accuracy (when $p > 0$ and $n = 0$), it will return 1. This normalized consistency measure shares the *independence property* with statistical rule quality measures described in [3].

The above expression thus measures the advantage of using the rule over making random guesses. This advantage takes a negative value if using the rule produces worse results than random guessing. Reorganizing the normalization term, we define the *consistency gain* of a rule R, consig(R), as:

$$\text{consig}(R) = ((p / (p + n)) – (P /(P + N))) * (P +N) /N \qquad (7)$$

4   A Definition of Description Quality

This section defines a general measure of description quality. Since we will subsequently use this measure in connection with a rule learning system, we will henceforth use the term "rule quality measure," although the introduced measure can be used with any type of data description. In developing the measure, we assume the desirability of maximizing both the completeness, compl(R), and the consistency gain, consig(R) of a rule. Clearly, a rule with higher values of compl(R) and consig(R) is more desirable than a rule with lower values. A rule with either compl(R) or consig(R) equal to 0 is worthless. It makes sense, therefore, to define a rule quality measure that evaluates to 1 when both of these components reach maximum (value 1), and 0 when either is equal to 0.

A simple way to achieve such a behavior is to define rule quality as a product of compl(R) and consig(R). Such a formula, however, does not allow one to weigh these factors differently for different applications. To achieve this flexibility, we introduce a weight, w, defined as the percentage of the description quality measure to be borne by the completeness condition. Thus, the *w-weighted quality*, Q(R, *w*) of rule R, or just Q(*w*), if the rule R is implied, is:

$$Q(R, w) = \text{compl}(R)^w * \text{consig}(R)^{(1-w)} \qquad (8)$$

By changing parameter *w*, one can change the relative importance of the completeness and the consistency gain to fit a problem at hand. It can be seen that when *w* < 1, Q(*w*) satisfies the constraints listed by Piatetsky-Shapiro [16] regarding a desirable behavior of a rule evaluation criterion:

1. The rule quality should be 0 if the example distribution in the space covered by the rule is the same as in the entire data set. Note that Q(R, *w*) = 0 when $p/(p + n) = P/(P + N)$, assuming *w* < 1.
2. All other things being equal, an increase in the rule's coverage should increase the quality of the rule. Note that Q(R, *w*) increases monotonically with *p*.
3. All other things being equal, the quality of the rule should decrease when the ratio of covered positive examples in the data to either covered negative examples or total positive examples decreases. Note that Q(R, *w*) decreases monotonically as either *n* or (*P* - *p*) increases, while *P* + *N* and *p* remain constant.

The formula cited by Piatesky-Shapiro [16] as the simplest one that satisfies the above three criteria is just consig(R), without the normalization factor, multiplied by (*p* + *n*). The advantage of incorporating the component of compl(R) in (8) is that it allows one to promote high coverage rules when desirable. Thus, (8) is potentially applicable to a larger set of applications. The next section compares the proposed Q(*w*) rule evaluation method with other methods, and Sections 6 and 7 discuss its implementation in the AQ18 learning system.

5   Empirical Comparison of Description Quality Measures

This section experimentally compares the Q(*w*) rule evaluation measure with those used in other rule learning systems. To this end, we performed a series of experiments using different datasets. In the experiments, the Q(*w*) measure used with varying parameter *w* was compared with the information gain criterion (Section 3), the PROMISE method [1], [9], and the methods employed in the CN2 [5], IREP [8] and RIPPER [6] rule learning programs. To simplify the comparison, we use the uniform notation for all the methods.

As was mentioned above, the information gain criterion takes into consideration the entropy of the examples covered by the rule and not covered by the rule, and the event space as a whole. Like the information gain criterion, the PROMISE method [1], [9] was developed to evaluate the quality of attributes. It can also be used for rule evaluation by considering a rule to be a binary attribute that splits the space into the part covered by the rule and the part not covered by it. It can be shown that the PROMISE measure as defined in [1] is equivalently described by the algorithm:

$M_+ = \max(p, n)$
$M_- = \max(P - p, N - n)$
$T_+ = P$ if $p > n$, N if $p < n$, and $\min(P, N)$ if $p = n$
$T_- = P$ if $P - p > N - n$, N if $P - p < N - n$, and $\min(P, N)$ if $P - p = N - n$

PROMISE returns a value of $(M_+ / T_+) + (M_- / T_-) - 1$, the last term being a normalization factor to make the range 0 to 1. It should be noted that when M_+ and M_- are based on the same class PROMISE will return a value of zero. For example, M_+ and M_- are based on the positive class, when $p > n$ and $P - p > N - n$. Hence, it is not a useful measure of rule quality in domains in which the positive examples significantly outnumber the negative ones. Note also that when $P = N$ and p exceeds n (the latter presumably occurs in any rule of value in an evenly distributed domain), the PROMISE value reduces to:

$$(p - n) / P \qquad (9)$$

To see this, note that when $P = N$, $(p / P) + ((N - n) / N) - 1$ can be transformed into $(p / P) + ((P - n) / P) - 1$, which is equivalent to (9).

CN2 [5] builds rules using a beam search, as does the AQ-type learner, on which it was partially based. In selecting a rule, it attempts to minimize, in the case of two decision classes, the following expression:

$$-((p / (p + n)) \log_2(p / (p + n)) + (n / (p + n)) \log_2(n / (p + n))) \qquad (10)$$

This expression takes into consideration only the consistency, $p/(p + n)$, and does not consider rule completeness (p/P). Thus, a rule that covers 50 positive and 5 negative examples is deemed of identical value as a rule that covers 50,000 positive and 5000 negative examples. Although (10) has a somewhat different form than the rule consistency gain portion of $Q(w)$, CN2's rule evaluation can be expected to rank rules similarly as $Q(0)$, i.e., only by consistency gain. Indeed, in the examples shown below, the two methods provide identical rule rankings. If there are more than two decision classes, the entropy terms are summed. Nonetheless, the above comments regarding no consideration of rule completeness remain true.

A later version of CN2 [4] offered a new rule quality formula based on a Laplace error estimate. This formula is closely tied to a rule's consistency level, while completeness still plays a minimal role.

IREP's formula for rule evaluation [8] is simply:

$$(p + N - n) / (P + N) \qquad (11)$$

RIPPER, as was mentioned in Section 2, uses a slight modification of formula (11):

$$(p - n) / (P + N) \qquad (12)$$

Note that RIPPER's evaluation will not change when P changes, but $P + N$ stays constant. In other words, its scores are independent of the distribution of positive and negative examples in the event space as a whole. While this evaluates a rule on its own merits, the evaluation does not factor in the benefit provided by the rule based on the overall distribution of classes.

Furthermore, since P and N are constant for a given problem, a rule deemed preferable by IREP will also be preferred by RIPPER. Thus, these two measures produce exactly the same ranking; in comparing different measures, we therefore only show RIPPER's rankings below. Comparing (12) to (9), one notices that the RIPPER evaluation function returns a value equal to half of the PROMISE value when $P = N$ and p exceeds n. Thus, in such cases, the RIPPER ranking is the same as the PROMISE ranking.

The methods described above were compared on three datasets, each consisting of 1000 training examples. Dataset A has 20% positive and 80% negative examples, Dataset B has 50% positive and 50% negative examples, and Dataset C has 80% positive examples and 20% of negative examples. In each dataset, rules with different coverage and training accuracy were ranked using the following criteria: Information

Gain, PROMISE, RIPPER, CN2 [5], and Q(w) with the parameter w taking values 0, 0.25, 0.5, 0.75 and 1. Results are summarized in Table 1.

Table 1. A comparison of rule evaluation criteria. Columns labeled V indicate a raw value, while columns labeled R indicate rank assigned by the given evaluation method in the given dataset.

Data Set	Pos	Neg	Info Gain V	R	PROMISE V	R	CN2 V	R	RIPPER V	R	Q(0) V	R	Q(.25) V	R	Q(.5) V	R	Q(.75) V	R	Q(1) V	R
A	50	5	.10	7	.24	7	.44	4	.05	7	.89	4	.65	7	.47	7	.34	7	.25	6
	50	0	.12	6	.25	6	0	1	.05	6	1	1	.71	6	.5	6	.35	6	.25	6
200	200	5	.69	1	.99	1	.17	2	.20	1	.97	2	.98	1	.99	1	.99	1	1	1
Pos	150	10	.39	2	.74	2	.34	3	.14	2	.92	3	.88	2	.83	2	.79	2	.75	2
	150	30	.33	3	.71	3	.65	6	.12	3	.79	6	78	3	.77	3	.76	3	.75	2
800	100	15	.21	5	.48	5	.56	5	.09	5	.84	5	.74	4	.65	4	.57	5	.5	5
Neg	120	25	.24	4	.57	4	.66	7	.10	4	.78	7	.73	5	.69	5	.64	4	.6	4
B	50	5	.03	7	.09	7	.44	3	.05	7	.82	3	.48	7	.29	7	.17	7	.1	7
	250	25	.21	6	.45	5	.44	3	.23	5	.82	3	.72	5	.64	5	.57	5	.5	5
500	500	50	.76	1	.9	1	.44	3	.45	1	.82	3	.86	1	.91	1	.95	1	1	1
Pos	500	150	.49	2	.7	3	.78	7	.35	3	.54	7	.63	6	.73	4	.86	2	1	1
	200	5	.21	5	.39	6	.17	1	.20	6	.95	1	.77	4	.62	6	.5	6	.4	6
500	400	35	.44	3	.73	2	.40	2	37	2	.84	2	.83	2	.82	2	.81	3	.8	3
Neg	400	55	.38	4	.69	4	.53	6	.35	4	.76	6	.77	3	.78	3	.79	4	.8	3
C	50	5	.004	7	0	–	.44	3	.05	7	.55	3	.32	6	.18	6	.11	6	.06	7
	250	25	.02	5	0	–	.44	3	.23	5	.55	3	.47	4	.41	5	.36	4	.31	5
800	500	50	.07	1	0	–	.44	3	.45	1	.55	3	.56	3	.58	1	.60	1	.63	1
Pos	500	150	.01	6	0	–	.78	7	.35	3	<0	7	<0	7	<0	7	<0	7	.63	1
	200	5	.05	3	0	–	.17	1	.20	6	.88	1	.64	1	.47	3	.34	5	.25	6
200	400	35	.05	2	0	–	.40	2	.37	2	.6	2	.57	2	.55	2	.52	2	.5	3
Neg	400	55	.02	4	0	–	.53	6	.35	4	.4	6	.42	5	.44	4	.47	3	.5	3

In Table 1, the leftmost column identifies the dataset, the next two columns specify respectively the number of positive and negative examples covered by a hypothetical rule, and the remaining columns list the evaluations and rankings of the rules by the various methods on the corresponding dataset. Most of the values are normalized into a 0-1 range, although as was discussed in Section 4, a Q(w) value could fall below 0, if the rule performs worse than random guessing; Information Gain may also not fall into such a range. Since rule selection is solely based on rule ranking, the specific quality values of rules are relatively unimportant and are given only for general information.

As mentioned earlier, there cannot be one universally correct ranking of the rules, since the desirability of any given ranking depends on the application. As expected, experiments have shown that the rule ranking changes with the value of w; thus, by appropriately setting the value of w, one can tailor the evaluation method to a problem at hand. Table 1 reveals a surprising behavior of some methods. For example, for the Dataset C, RIPPER ranks higher a rule that performs worse than a random guess (case 500/150) than some rules that perform better.

An interesting result from this experiment is that by modifying the w parameter one can approximate rankings generated by different rule learning programs. For example, the CN2 rule ranking is equivalent in Table 1 to ranking by $Q(0)$; the RIPPER and PROMISE rule rankings are approximated by $Q(w)$ with w in the range 0.5 to 0.75, and the Information Gain rule ranking is approximated for datasets A and B by $Q(0.75)$.

6   Admitting Inconsistency in AQ

The AQ type learning programs e.g. [13], [15] were originally oriented toward generating descriptions that are consistent and complete with regard to the training data. With the introduction of idea of rule truncation [2], [15], AQ type learning programs could generate approximate descriptions (incomplete and/or inconsistent), but only though a post-processing method.

The implementation of the $Q(w)$ measure in the recent AQ18 rule learning program [12] enables the generation of approximate descriptions (patterns) in a pre-processing mode. This capability makes AQ18 more efficient and versatile, and is particularly important in data mining applications. It may be worth noting that the incorporation of $Q(w)$ in AQ18 does not prevent it from generating complete and consistent descriptions when desirable, unlike most existing rule learners, e.g., CN2 or RIPPER, that can generate only approximate descriptions. In addition, AQ18 generates descriptions as *attributional rules*, which are more expressive than the atomic decision rules (rules with conditions: attribute-relation-value) that are employed in the above programs, as well as than decision trees [14].

This section describes briefly how the $Q(w)$ measure is implemented in AQ18. The program allows a user to set the w parameter in $Q(w)$ between 0 (inclusive) and 1 (exclusive, because the value 1 would lead to a rule that covers all positive and negative examples). The default value is 0.5. For the default value, the code has a short-cut that avoids the exponentiation operation during intermediate calculations of $Q(w)$, since the ordering is preserved without the exponentiation.

Since AQ learning has been widely described in the literature, it is assumed for the sake of space that the reader has some familiarity with the AQ algorithm [15], [18]. Nevertheless, we will briefly review the rule generation portion of the algorithm in the context of the implementation of the $Q(w)$ description quality measure.

The introduction of $Q(w)$ to AQ18 has led to two modes of program operation. The first mode, called "pattern discovery," which assumes the existence of noise in the data, is used to determine strong patterns in the data. This mode utilizes $Q(w)$. The second mode, called "theory formation," which assumes no noise or negligible noise in the data, is used to determine theories that are complete and consistent with regard to the data [12], [14]. In pattern discovery mode, the measure is applied at two stages of rule generation:

1. *Star generation,* which creates a set of alternative consistent generalizations of a seed example (an example chosen randomly from the training set) that do not cover any of the negative examples examined so far. The negative examples are presented one at a time, and the *extend-against* operator [13] is applied such that the hypotheses from the previous iteration are made consistent. A rule selection occurs whenever alternative candidate rules are being generated.
2. *Star termination,* which selects the best rule from a star (after all negative rules have been extended against) according to a given multi-criterion preference measure (LEF).

6.1   Star Generation

In the standard procedure, star generation is the process of generating a set of maximally general consistent hypotheses (rules) that cover a selected positive example (a *seed*). AQ18 implements the $Q(W)$ measure by extending the seed sequentially against negative examples [13], and specializing partial hypotheses by intersecting them with these extensions.

In pattern discovery mode, the system determines the $Q(w)$ value of the generated rules after each extension-against operation; the rules with $Q(w)$ lower than that of the parent rule (the rule from which they were generated through specialization), are discarded. If the $Q(w)$ values of all rules stemming from a given parent rule are lower, the parent rule is retained instead. This operation is functionally equivalent to treating the negative example used in this extension-against operation as noise.

In order to speed up the star generation, the user may specify a time-out threshold on the extension-against process. If after a given number of consecutive extensions, there has been no further improvement of $Q(w)$ in the partial star, the system considers the current ruleset of sufficient quality, and terminates the star generation process.

6.2   Star Termination

In the star termination step (i.e., after the last extension-against operation), the candidate rules are generalized in different ways in search for a rule with a higher $Q(w)$. This process uses a hill-climbing method. Specifically, each rule in the star is generalized by separately generalizing each of its component conditions (see below). The rule with the highest $Q(w)$ from among all these generalizations is selected. This process is repeated; it is applied now to the rule selected. It continues until no generalization creates further improvement.

The generalization of rule components (single conditions) takes into consideration the type of the attribute in the condition, as described in [13]. Conditions with nominal (unordered) attributes are generalized by applying the *condition dropping* generalization operator. Conditions with linear attributes (rank, interval, cyclic, or continuous) are generalized by applying the condition dropping, the *interval extending* and the *interval closing* generalization operators. Conditions with structured attributes (hierarchically ordered) are generalized by applying the condition dropping and the *generalization tree climbing* operators. As a result of this optimization, the best rule in the resulting star is selected for output through the LEF process.

Table 2 illustrates the application of these generalization operators to the base rule [*color* = red v blue] & [*length* = 2..4 v 10..16] & [*animal_type* = dog v lion v bat]. In this rule, *color* is a nominal attribute, *length* is a linear attribute, and *animal_type* is a structured attribute.

Table 2. Effects of different generalization operators on the base rule:[*color* = red v blue] & [*length* = 2..4 v 10..16] & [*animal_type* = dog v lion v bat]

Generalization Operator	Resulting Rule
Removing nominal condition	[*length* = 2..4 v 10..16] & [*animal_type* = dog v lion v bat]
Removing linear condition	[*color* = red v blue] & [*animal_type* = dog v lion v bat]
Extending linear interval	[*color* = red v blue] & [*length* = 2..4 v 8..16] & [*animal_type* = dog v lion v bat]
Closing linear interval	[*color* = red v blue] & [*length* = 2..16] & [*animal_type* = dog v lion v bat]
Removing structured condition	[*color* = red v blue] & [*length* = 2..4 v 10..16]
Generalizing structured condition	[*color* = red v blue] & [*length* = 2..4 v 10..16] & [*animal_type* = mammal]

6.3   Unexpected Difficulty

Experiments with the pattern discovery mode in AQ18 exposed one unexpected difficulty. To explain it, let us outline the basic AQ algorithm as implemented in AQ18. The learning process proceeds in a "separate-and-conquer" fashion. It selects a positive example of the class under consideration, generates a star of it (a set of maximal generalizations), and selects the best rule from the star according to LEF. If this rule together with the previously selected rules does not cover all positive training examples, a new seed is selected randomly from among the uncovered examples. A new star is generated, and the best rule from it is added to the output ruleset. The process repeats until all of the positive training examples of are covered. The ruleset is tested for superfluous rules (rules that cover examples subsumed by the union of the remaining rules) and any such rules are removed from the final ruleset.

Consider the following scenario. Suppose AQ determines a consistent rule [x = 1] & [y = 2] that covers a given seed. Assuming that both attributes are nominal, in the star termination step the algorithm attempts to generalize the rule by dropping conditions, thereby generating candidate rules [x = 1] and [y = 2]. Suppose that both rules have $Q(w)$ lower than that of the starting rule, so that the starting rule is added to the list of selected rules. Let us assume also that the star of a subsequent seed includes a consistent rule $[x = 1]$ & $[y = 5]$, which is then generalized to produce various rules. It is possible that the generalization $[x = 1]$ will be found to have a higher $Q(w)$ than the starting rule, and thus be added to the list of selected rules.

After the complete ruleset has been generated, the system searches for superfluous rules. It then discovers that the rule $[x = 1]$ & $[y = 2]$ is subsumed by $[x = 1]$, and accordingly removes it from the ruleset. The latter rule is simpler and may cover more examples, but it has been previously determined as inferior to the former in terms of $Q(w)$.

How should this problem be solved? Which rule is better? The system may keep only the first rule, only the second rule, or both (as different patterns in the data). As we found experimentally, the latter solution may lead to a huge proliferation of rules. Therefore, AQ18 seeks a ruleset that strives to achieve simultaneously two goals: (1) to contain the highest $Q(w)$ rules, and (2) to cover the target training data set with the minimum number of such rules.

To this end, the $Q(w)$ expression (8) was modified by computing a new form of completeness, ncompl, defined as:

$$ncompl(R) = p_{new} / P \qquad (13)$$

where p_{new} is the number of positive events that are covered by the candidate rule and not covered by any of the previously determined rules (patterns). Thus, the ncompl of a rule is computed in the context of the rules already generated: only those examples that have not yet been covered by the previously determined rules are counted. This condition causes the algorithm to seek at each step the rules that cover the maximum number of not-yet-covered examples. This in turn leads to rulesets that avoid superfluous rules and, as a consequence, tends to reduce the size of the resulting ruleset.

6.4   The Effect of $Q(w)$ on Generated Rules

Experiments with the method presented here have confirmed the expectation that the rules generated in the pattern discovery mode are more general than those obtained in the theory formation mode. This effect is due to the fact that this mode allows rules to have higher completeness at the expense of consistency, if this increases $Q(w)$. In addition, processing time is reduced substantially.

To illustrate the influence of $Q(w)$ on the learning process, we have conducted experiments in which the learning process was repeated with different values of the parameter w. The experiments involved a medical dataset in which patients are described in terms of 32 attributes (all but 5 of which were of Boolean type). The attributes characterize patients' lifestyles and specify their disease. Experiments were run with three different values of the w parameter: 0.25, 0.5, and 0.75. For the decision class *arthritis*, the training set consisted of 7411 examples, of which approximately 16% were positive ($P = 1171$) and the rest were negative ($N = 6240$). The rules with the highest coverage learned for each of the three values of w were:

$w = 0.25$:   [education $\leq$ vocational] & [years in neighborhood > 26] & [rotundity $\geq$ low] & [tuberculosis $=$ no]: $p = 271, n = 903, Q = 0.111011$

$w = 0.5$:   [high blood pressure = yes] & [education $\leq$ college grad]
                    $p = 355$, $n = 1332$, $Q = 0.136516$
$w = 0.75$:   [education $\leq$ college grad]
                    $p = 940$, $n = 4529$, $Q = 0.303989$

As expected, increasing the w weight leads to rules with higher completeness (coverage) and lower consistency. All three rules indicate a relationship between educational level and the occurrence of arthritis; the first one specializes the acceptable range of educational levels in comparison to the other two. Furthermore, the third rule is a generalization of the second one.

7   Admitting Incompleteness in AQ

The previous sections focused on the issue of relaxing the consistency condition in AQ rule learning. This was done through the incorporation of the $Q(w)$ measure, which enables the learning program to find rules with high coverage that are not necessarily consistent. This section considers the problem of relaxing the ruleset completeness condition in AQ.

Let us start by observing that the application of AQ18 to the medical dataset described above consistently resulted in rulesets having a similar distribution of rule coverages regardless of the decision attribute, the value of w, and the training set. An illustrative example is a ruleset for characterizing the occurrence of arthritis. The training set consisted of 1171 positive examples (respondents who reported arthritis) and 6240 negative examples (those who did not report arthritis). This set was randomly selected from a larger database, and was representative of the overall distribution of positive and negative examples. AQ18 generated a complete ruleset (a cover) for the positive class (350 rules) and another cover for the negative class (314 rules). The distribution of rule coverages in these two rulesets is shown in Figures 1 and 2, respectively.

As one can see in these graphs, the distributions of rule coverages in rulesets for the two classes have a similar shape. A complete ruleset typically contains a few high coverage rules and many low coverage ones. Generating such a ruleset may take a significant amount of computation in the case of a large training dataset. This process could be significantly sped up by stopping the generation of rules at the point when the remaining rules are expected to have low coverage.

A special case of applying such a process is to generate for each decision class only the one rule/pattern that has the highest $Q(w)$. If this rule is determined from the first star generated, such a process will be very fast and simple, but the obtained rule may not be of the highest quality. It may even be a spurious one, if the seed was an erroneous example. In addition, this method would not allow the detection of multiple strong patterns in the class. A more attractive method is to learn rules from n stars, where n is a fixed parameter, and select one or more best rules from them. An even more attractive method is to allow the system to generate stars as long as it appears advantageous, rather than having a predetermined fixed stopping point (fixed n). This method has been implemented in AQ18. Specifically, the system generates rules as long as they continue to have sufficient coverage.

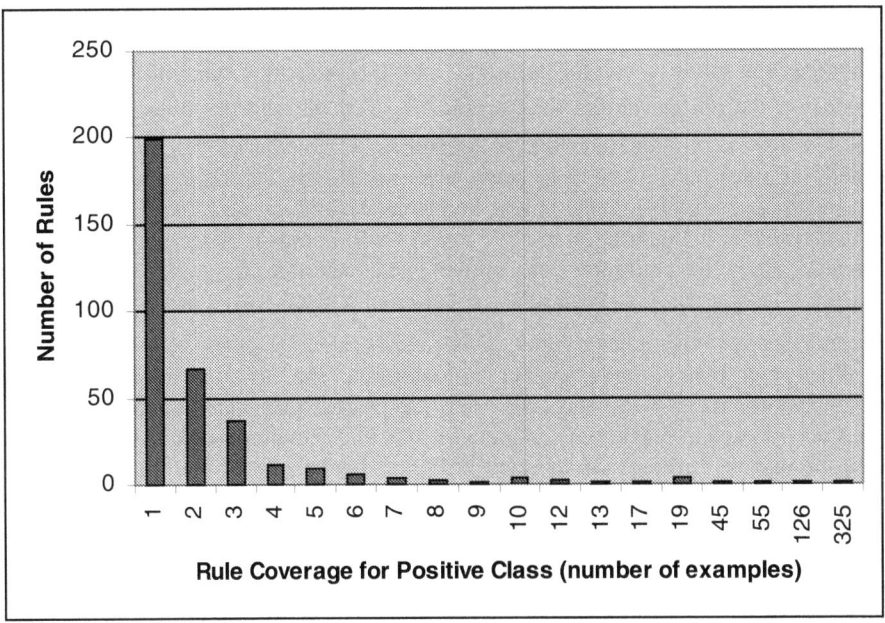

Fig. 1. Distribution of rule coverages in rulesets for the arthritis class.

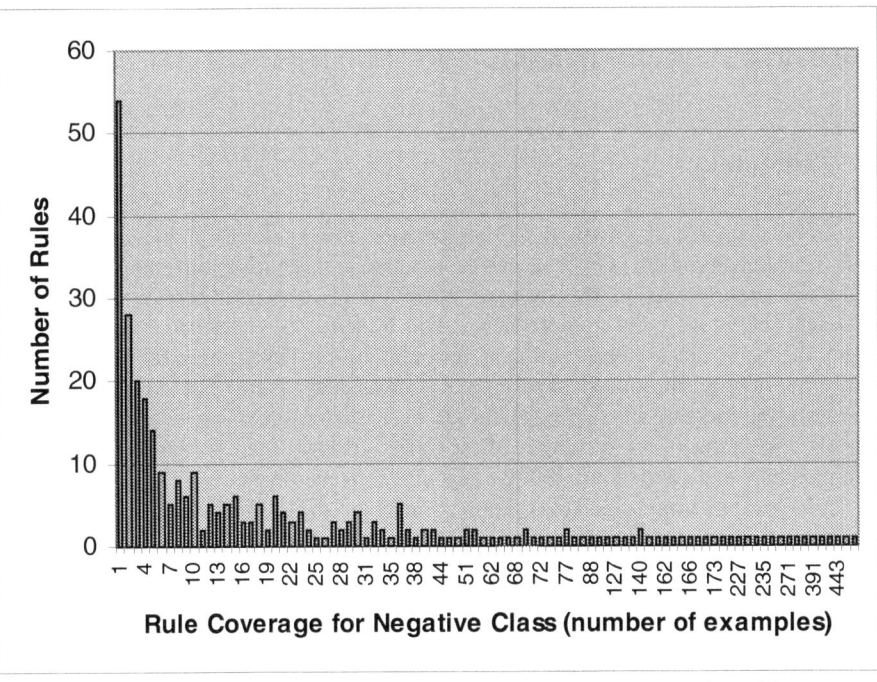

Fig. 2. Distribution of rule coverages in rulesets for the absence of arthritis

Two parameters define the termination condition for this process. The first is the *probe* that defines the length of a sequence of consecutively determined rules whose coverages fall below a certain threshold. The threshold is a function of the second parameter, the *tolerance*, and the coverage, t_{max}, of the highest-coverage rule found thus far. Specifically, the threshold is defined as $(1 - tolerance) * t_{max}$ The process of generating rules for a given class stops when the number of consecutively generated rules with coverages below the threshold has reached the *probe* value. For instance, if the *tolerance* is 0.2 and the *probe* is 3, AQ18 will continue generating rules for the given decision class until three consecutively generated rules fail to cover at least 80% of the t_{max} coverage, or the system has covered all positive examples of the class. If a new rule has coverage greater than t_{max}, its coverage then becomes the new t_{max}.

When this method was applied to determine the arthritis ruleset using the parameters *tolerance* = 0.2 and *probe* = 3, the process terminated after learning four rules (as opposed to 350 in the complete set). One of the discovered rules was the one with the highest coverage, as reported in Figure 1, and another had the third highest coverage. The other two rules had low coverage. Four was the minimum number of rules that could be generated with these parameters. The minimum was reached because every rule after the first rule generated had a lower coverage than the threshold determined by the first rule. In other words, the first rule for each case (decision class) had a dominatingly high coverage.

Such a situation does not, of course, always occur. For example, when the method was applied with the same parameters to another disease class, it generated seven rules. This was so because the dominant rule was found only after several iterations. As illustrated above, and confirmed by other experiments, the method generated a significantly smaller number of rules than would be in the complete ruleset, and the generated rules tended to have high coverage, that is, represented strong patterns.

8   Summary

This chapter presented a method for determining strong patterns in data using the AQ-type learning approach. Given a set of input examples from different classes, AQ generates descriptions in the form of attributional rules that represent a trade-off between consistency and completeness. The trade-off is controlled by a parameter, $Q(w)$, that serves as a measure of description quality by integrating rule completeness with the newly introduced measure of consistency gain. The consistency gain measures the increase in training accuracy over random guessing. The $Q(w)$ measure can be specialized to a range of specific criteria that weigh differently the completeness and consistency gain by varying the w parameter.

The $Q(w)$ measure has been implemented in the AQ18 learning and pattern discovery system during the star generation and star termination processes. By observing changes of the $Q(w)$ value in the process of rule generation, one can detect negative examples that may represent noise. This mechanism is particularly useful for data mining applications. By ignoring such negative examples (which increases inconsistency), the system often produces rules with much higher coverage than when full consistency is required. Another benefit from this mechanism is a significantly higher efficiency, which allows the algorithm to scale up to much more complex problems.

It was also shown that by varying the w parameter in $Q(w)$, the method can approximate other rule learning methods, such as CN2, IREP and RIPPER. Thus, AQ18 with the new features can be viewed not as a single pattern discovery program, but rather *as a family of programs*, each of which is defined by a specific value of the parameter w in the quality measure $Q(w)$.

The relaxation of the ruleset completeness condition is controlled by introducing two parameters, *probe* and *tolerance*. These parameters allow the system to dynamically terminate the ruleset generation process. The resulting ruleset is an approximation of the target concept.

The presented method deals solely with the issues of consistency and completeness of generated data descriptions. In practice, other criteria may also be important in discovering and evaluating patterns in data, such as description simplicity and its understandability. The method can incorporate such criteria through the lexicographical evaluation functional [10], [11]. Experiments have shown that the presented method offers a new tool for determining patterns in large datasets. Due to its flexibility obtained through $Q(w)$, *probe* and *tolerance*, it has the potential to be useful for a wide range of applications.

Acknowledgments. This research was conducted in the Machine Learning and Inference Laboratory at George Mason University. The Laboratory's research activities have been supported in part by the National Science Foundation under Grants No. IIS-9906858 and IIS-9904078, and in part by the Grant No. UMBCV/ MPO/LUCITE#32.

References

1. Baim, P.W., "The PROMISE Method for Selecting Most Relevant Attributes for Inductive Learning Systems," *Reports of the Department of Computer Science*, Report No. UIUCDCS-F-82-898, University of Illinois, Urbana, 1982.
2. Bergadano, F., Matwin, S., Michalski R.S. and Zhang, J., "Learning Two-tiered Descriptions of Flexible Concepts: The POSEIDON System," *Machine Learning* 8, pp. 5-43, 1992.
3. Bruha, I., "Quality of Decision Rules: Definitions and Classification Schemes for Multiple Rules," In Nakhaeizadeh, G. and Taylor, C.C. (eds.), *Machine Learning and Statistics, The Interface*, New York: John Wiley & Sons, Inc. , pp. 107-131, 1997.
4. Clark, P. and Boswell, R., "Rule Induction with CN2: Some Recent Improvements," in Kodratoff, Y. (ed.), *Proceedings of the Fifth European Working Session on Learning (EWSL-91)*, Berlin: Springer-Verlag, pp. 151-163, 1991.
5. Clark, P. and Niblett, T., "The CN2 Induction Algorithm," *Machine Learning* 3, pp. 261-283, 1989.
6. Cohen, W., "Fast Effective Rule Induction," *Proceedings of the Twelfth International Conference on Machine Learning*, Lake Tahoe, CA, pp. 115-123, 1995.
7. Fayyad, U.M, Piatetsky-Shapiro, G., Smyth, P. and Uthurusamy, R. (eds.), *Advances in Knowledge Discovery and Data Mining*, Menlo Park, CA: AAAI Press, 1996.

8.   Fürnkranz, J. and Widmer, G., "Incremental Reduced Error Pruning," *Proceedings of the Eleventh International Conference on Machine Learning*, New Brunswick, NJ, pp. 70-77, 1994.
9.   Kaufman, K.A., "INLEN: A Methodology and Integrated System for Knowledge Discovery in Databases," Ph.D. dissertation, *Reports of the Machine Learning and Inference Laboratory*, MLI 97-15, George Mason University, Fairfax, VA, 1997.
10.   Kaufman, K.A. and Michalski, R.S., "Learning in an Inconsistent World: Rule Selection in AQ18," *Reports of the Machine Learning and Inference Laboratory*, MLI 99-2, George Mason University, Fairfax, VA, 1999.
11.   Kaufman, K.A. and Michalski, R.S., "Learning from Inconsistent and Noisy Data: The AQ18 Approach," *Proceedings of the Eleventh International Symposium on Methodologies for Intelligent Systems*, Warsaw, pp. 411-419, 1999.
12.   Kaufman, K.A. and Michalski, R.S., "The AQ18 System for Machine Learning: User's Guide," *Reports of the Machine Learning and Inference Laboratory*, MLI 00-3, George Mason University, Fairfax, VA, 2000.
13.   Michalski, R.S., "A Theory and Methodology of Inductive Learning," In Michalski, R.S. Carbonell, J.G. and Mitchell, T.M. (eds.), *Machine Learning: An Artificial Intelligence Approach*, Palo Alto: Tioga Publishing, pp. 83-129, 1983.
14.   Michalski, R.S., "NATURAL INDUCTION: Theory, Methodology and Applications to Machine Learning and Knowledge Mining," *Reports of the Machine Learning and Inference Laboratory*, MLI 01-1, George Mason University, 2001.
15.   Michalski, R.S., Mozetic, I., Hong, J. and Lavrac, N., "The Multi-Purpose Incremental Learning System AQ15 and Its Testing Application to Three Medical Domains," *Proceedings of the National Conference on Artificial Intelligence, AAAI*, Philadelphia, pp. 1041-1045, 1986.
16.   Piatetsky-Shapiro, G., "Discovery, Analysis, and Presentation of Strong Rules," in Piatetsky-Shapiro, G. and Frawley, W. (eds.), *Knowledge Discovery in Databases*, Menlo Park, CA: AAAI Press, pp. 229-248, 1991.
17.   Quinlan, J.R., "Induction of Decision Trees," *Machine Learning* 1, pp. 81-106, 1986.
18.   Wnek, J., Kaufman, K., Bloedorn, E. and Michalski, R.S., "Inductive Learning System AQ15c: The Method and User's Guide," *Reports of the Machine Learning and Inference Laboratory*, MLI 95-4, George Mason University, Fairfax, VA, 1995.

Unsupervised Learning of Probabilistic Concept Hierarchies

Wayne Iba and Pat Langley

Institute for the Study of Learning and Expertise 2164 Staunton Court, Palo Alto, CA 94306
{iba,langley}@isle.org

1 Introduction

Since the field's inception, most research in machine learning has focused on the problem of supervised induction from labeled training cases. If anything, this trend has been strengthened by the creation of data repositories that, typically, include class information. But this emphasis is misguided if we want to understand the nature of learning in intelligent agents like humans. Clearly, children acquire many concepts about the world before they learn names for them, and scientists regularly discover patterns without any clear supervision from an outside source. Even the availability of class labels in public data sets can be misleading; many such domains are medical in nature, and medical researchers first had to discover a disease before they could diagnose it for particular patients.

Naturally, different approaches to induction from unlabeled data are possible, each stemming from different research goals. In this chapter, we report on a class of unsupervised methods designed to support learning in intelligent agents, whether human or artificial. This concern suggests some criteria that such methods should satisfy; these include:

- The aim of unsupervised learning should be to acquire *concepts* or *categories*;
- Concept descriptions should represent the *variability* that occurs in the natural world;
- These concepts should describe experience at *different levels of generality*;
- The learning process should be *incremental*, since intelligent agents interact with the environment over time.

Taken together, these criteria place strong constraints on the representation and organization of knowledge, and on the mechanisms that support performance and learning.

Our research has explored a paradigm for unsupervised learning that meets these criteria. The framework assumes that knowledge takes the form of probabilistic concept descriptions and that these concepts are organized into an 'is-a' hierarchy that describes different levels of generality. For this reason, we will often refer to the framework as one that assumes *probabilistic concept hierarchies*. However, we also assume that using this knowledge involves sorting new experiences downward through the hierarchy, and that this act of retrieval also produces changes in the concept descriptions and hierarchy structure, resulting

G. Paliouras, V. Karkaletsis, and C.D. Spyropoulos (Eds.): ACAI'99, LNAI 2049, pp. 39–70, 2001.
© Springer-Verlag Berlin Heidelberg 2001

in learning. In this chapter, we report on a large body of work that falls within this paradigm.

We begin by describing COBWEB, the system that played the founding role in this framework, and some experimental studies that reveal the importance of its various components. After this, we examine three systems that extend the basic approach; these include ARACHNE, which incorporates restructuring operators designed to handle noise and minimize order effects, TWILIX, which constructs more complex concept hierarchies that support overlapping categories, and OXBOW, which forms concepts about temporal phenomena. We also briefly review a number of other systems that incrementally construct hierarchies of probabilistic concepts. In closing, we examine the framework's relation to two more recent approaches to unsupervised induction, one based on the AUTOCLASS family and the other involving Bayesian networks.

2   Incremental Formation of Probabilistic Concept Hierarchies

As noted above, our focus in this chapter is a framework for unsupervised learning that grew out of Fisher's COBWEB [6]. We can describe the system's goals in terms of its performance and learning tasks. For the former, COBWEB aims to infer the values of attributes missing from test cases, a task that Fisher called *flexible prediction*. For learning, the system aims to carry out hierarchical clustering over unlabeled training cases that are presented in an online fashion and thus organize these instances in memory. Incidentally, this also lets it estimate the probability density function over the space of possible instances, which in recent years has become a more popular way to describe unsupervised learning. Now let us consider the manner in which COBWEB achieves these goals.

2.1   Representation and Organization of Knowledge

The central representational notion in COBWEB is the *concept* or *category*. The system generates an arbitrary name C for each such category and associates with C a descriptive summary. For each attribute A, this summary specifies a probability distribution over the values of A, conditioned on the category C. For a nominal or discrete attribute, this takes the form of a discrete probability distribution; for a numeric or continuous variable, the system uses a normal distribution, which can be characterized by its mean and variance.[1] Since it stores only marginal probability distributions, COBWEB makes the assumption that the observable attributes are independent given the category.

The key organizational theme in COBWEB is that categories are placed in a *concept hierarchy*. Each node C in this 'is-a' tree specifies a set of children and the conditional probability of C given its parent category. Moreover, the descriptive summaries between a parent and its children obeys an important

---

[1] Most implementations of COBWEB store these internally using counts for the category, counts for nominal attribute values, and the sums and sums of squares for numeric attributes.

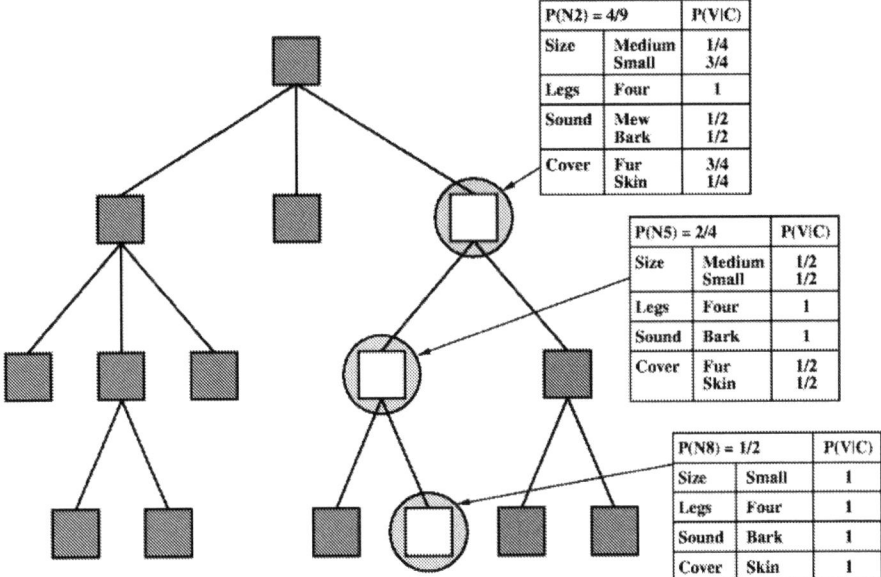

P(N2) = 4/9		P(V|C)
Size	Medium	1/4
	Small	3/4
Legs	Four	1
Sound	Mew	1/2
	Bark	1/2
Cover	Fur	3/4
	Skin	1/4

P(N5) = 2/4		P(V|C)
Size	Medium	1/2
	Small	1/2
Legs	Four	1
Sound	Bark	1
Cover	Fur	1/2
	Skin	1/2

P(N8) = 1/2		P(V|C)
Size	Small	1
Legs	Four	1
Sound	Bark	1
Cover	Skin	1

Fig. 1. A small hierarchy of probabilistic concepts for the domain of household pets, illustrating COBWEB's representation and organization of knowledge.

relation: the probability distribution for each attribute of a parent is a weighted mixture of those for its children, so that each node constitutes a probabilistic summarization of all its descendants. The terminal nodes or leaves in a COB-WEB hierarchy correspond to specific instances, typically training cases observed during learning. Thus, the root node corresponds to the most general category, which summarizes all instances the system has seen, and categories become increasingly specific as one moves down the hierarchy.

Figure 1 shows a small probabilistic concept hierarchy for the domain of household pets, with the descriptive summaries for three nodes. The leaf node $N8$ describes a single animal (a Mexican hairless dog) that is small, has four legs, barks, and has a body covered with skin. Since this category involves only one example, all attribute probabilities are either 1 or 0, and the node's conditional probability given the parent is $\frac{1}{2}$, as it has only one sibling. The parent node, $N5$, is somewhat more abstract, summarizing two instances (both dogs) that differ on some dimensions but not others. Thus, the conditional probability of having four legs and barking is still 1, given an instance of category N, but the probability distributions for size and body cover are more diffuse. The node next higher in the hierarchy, $N2$, is even more abstract, since it also covers instances (cats) that mew rather than bark, but still has little variation in the legs attribute, since all its children are quadrupeds. This node has a conditional probability of $\frac{4}{9}$ given its parent, the root, because $N2$ subsumes that fraction of the leaves in the tree.

2.2 Performance and Learning Mechanisms

Naturally, COBWEB's representation and organization of knowledge figure prominently in its use of that knowledge. Given a new test case, typically with only some attributes specified, the system sorts the experience downward through the concept hierarchy by recursively assigning the instance to the best child category at each level. This process halts when the test case reaches a terminal node or when it is not similar enough to any child to justify sorting downward further. At this point, COBWEB infers the values for attributes missing from the instance, using the modal values from the deepest (most specific) node through which it has passed.

COBWEB integrates classification and learning, so that the latter process takes place as the system sorts training cases through the hierarchy. As this occurs, the algorithm updates the conditional probability distributions for each node through which the instance passes, guaranteeing the property mentioned earlier that each category summarizes all cases below it in the hierarchy. However, COBWEB can also invoke four learning operators to alter the structure of its concept hierarchy. As illustrated in Figure 2, these include:

- *extending downward*, which occurs when a training case reaches a terminal node in memory; under these circumstances, the learner creates a new node N that is a probabilistic summary of the case and the terminal node, making both children of N;
- *creating a disjunct*, which occurs if a training case is sufficiently different from all children of a node N; in this situation, the learner creates a new child of N based on the case;
- *merging two categories*, which occurs if a case is similar enough to two children of node N that the learner judges all three should be combined into a single child;
- *splitting a concept*, which occurs when a child C of node N no longer serves as a useful category; C is removed and its children are promoted to become direct children of N.

The system considers the last three of these actions at each level of the hierarchy, as it sorts the new training instance downward through memory. Merging and splitting are designed to reduce sensitivity to training order, giving the effect of backtracking in the space of concept hierarchies without requiring the storage of previous hypotheses.

We have not yet described how COBWEB decides which category to select at each level, whether to halt at an internal node, and whether to merge or split categories. To this end, the system uses an evaluation function called *category utility* that measures the quality for a set of probabilistic categories. Given a set of K categories with discrete attributes, category utility was originally defined by Gluck and Corter [10] as the *increase* in the expected number of attribute values that can be correctly guessed over the expected number of correct guesses without such knowledge. The modification introduced by Fisher [6] and used by COBWEB is

(a)   **(b)**

(c)   **(d)**

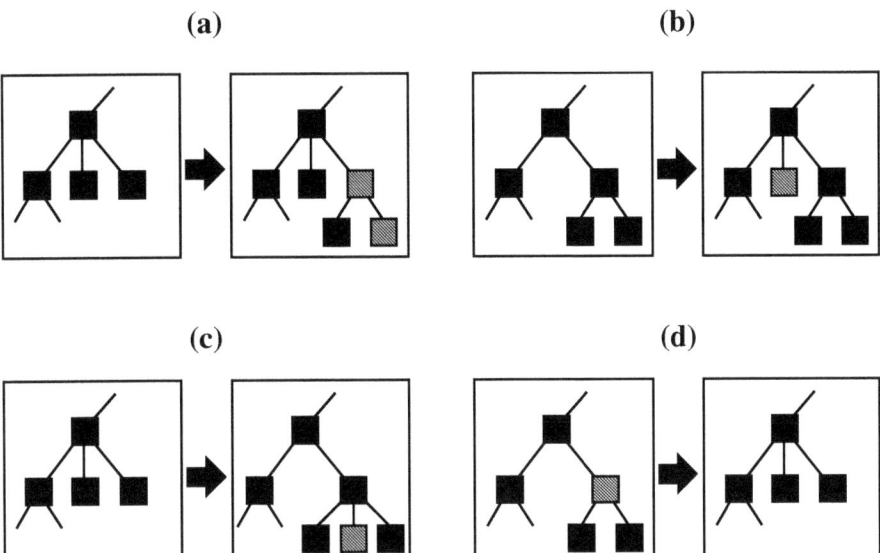

Fig. 2. Learning operators used to modify the structure of a hierarchy of probabilistic concepts: (a) extending the hierarchy downward; (b) creating a new disjunct at an existing level; (c) merging two existing classes; and (d) splitting an existing category. Newly created nodes are shown in gray.

$$\frac{1}{K}\left[\sum_{k=1}^{K} P(C_k) \sum_i \sum_j P(A_i = V_{ij}|C_k)^2 - \sum_i \sum_j P(A_i = V_{ij}|C)^2\right] \quad , \quad (1)$$

where k varies over categories, i over attributes, and j over values for each attribute. This function evaluates a *partition* — defined as a parent node C and its immediate children C_k. The probability $P(C_k)$ represents the *base rate* or the prior probability that an instance is a member of the child C_k, whereas $P(A_i = V_{ij}|C_k)^2$ is a measure of *within-class similarity* for an attribute A_i; that is, how well the instances summarized by C_k resemble one another. Subtracting the sum over the parent's within-class similarities, $P(A_i = V_{ij}|C)^2$ for each attribute, lets category utility measure the information gained by partitioning the parent class into the given set of children. Dividing by K, the number of C's children, biases the system against proliferation of singleton classes.

For numeric domains, we must modify this evaluation function because the probability that a continuous attribute will take on a particular number is zero. For such attributes, probabilities are estimated by assuming that values conform to a normal distribution with a particular mean and standard deviation. Thus, for a domain with continuous attributes, Gennari, Langley, and Fisher [9] define category utility as

$$\frac{1}{K}\left[\sum_{k=1}^{K} P(C_k) \sum_i \frac{1}{\sigma_{ik}} - \sum_i \frac{1}{\sigma_{ip}}\right] \quad , \tag{2}$$

where $P(C_k)$ is the probability of class C_k, K is the number of categories, σ_{ik} is the standard deviation for an attribute i in class C_k, and σ_{ip} is the standard deviation for attribute i in the parent node.[2] One can also combine continuous and discrete attributes in the category utility calculation simply by using the appropriate form of the equation for each attribute. That is, for nominal attributes, the inner summation over values uses Equation 1, and for numeric attributes it uses the inverse of the standard deviation.

We should close our review of COBWEB with some remarks about its assumptions and representational power. At each level of the concept hierarchy, the system assumes that attributes are conditionally independent given the category. This condition, which COBWEB shares with the naive Bayesian classifier [20], will clearly be violated in many domains. But note that the system seldom makes its predictions at the hierarchy's top level, and that categories lower in the tree describe local portions of the instance space where approximate independence may be satisfied. Indeed, recall that the leaves in a probabilistic concept hierarchy correspond to individual training cases, and that COBWEB sometimes bases its prediction on these nodes. In these situations, the system operates as a nearest neighbor classifier that uses the concept hierarchy to weight attributes and bias retrieval. In summary, COBWEB's use of a hierarchical memory gives it the ability to represent complex target concepts, at least in principle. But whether its approach works in practice is an empirical issue, to which we now turn.

3   Empirical Studies of COBWEB

COBWEB appeared on the scene during a period when machine learning researchers were first starting to carry out systematic experiments with their algorithms. As a result, the system has always been under close empirical scrutiny, though some early studies occurred before clear standards developed within the community. Here we review a number of experimental evaluations of COBWEB, concentrating on ones that have not appeared previously in the literature.

3.1   Basic Experimental Results

Initial experimental studies of COBWEB, as with all learning systems, aimed mainly to show that its performance improved with experience. Fisher [6] reported results on a number of natural domains for a task he called *flexible prediction*. This involved testing on instances with some attribute omitted and letting the system predict the missing value for each case, then repeating this

---

[2] As discussed by Gennari et al. [9], the value of $1/\sigma$ is undefined for any concept based on a single instance, so an *acuity* parameter is needed. Acuity corresponds to the notion of "just noticeable difference" in psychology.

process for each attribute and averaging the result. The technique extends naturally to continuous attributes, and Iba [15] adapted it to measure prediction errors about temporal phenomena.

Another approach, taken by Gennari [8], used labeled training data but held back the label during hierarchy construction. This scheme added the most likely class values to categories only after the hierarchy was complete, then used them to predict the classes for test cases and produce a standard measure of classification accuracy. Figure 3 shows two learning curves that McKusick and Langley [24] obtained in this manner for COBWEB and a related algorithm, ARACHNE, that we discuss later. One domain involved predicting the party of U.S. Congressmen from their voting records, whereas the other domain dealt with diagnosing disease in soybean plants. Although the latter task is clearly more difficult, COBWEB shows steady improvement in its ability to predict class labels, even though it could not use them in constructing its concept hierarchy.

Perhaps the most extensive experiments with COBWEB[3] come from Gennari [8], who wanted to understand the sources of power in the framework. His studies included varying system parameters and domain characteristics, using predictive accuracy and learning curves to measure COBWEB's sensitivity to particular settings and domain features. In the remainder of this section, we consider three of Gennari's experiments that have not appeared in the literature. These include the significance of category utility as the evaluation metric used for clustering, the importance of COBWEB's algorithm for hierarchy formation, and the effect of missing attributes on behavior.

3.2   Effect of the Evaluation Function

Let us first consider the importance of category utility, the evaluation function that COBWEB uses when sorting cases through memory and when restructuring its hierarchy. Although Fisher presents convincing arguments for using this metric, its behavior relative to other functions remains an empirical question. Gennari was interested in whether more traditional *distance* metrics, common in the clustering literature, would produce similar results. However, to embed such a measure in COBWEB required modifying them to operate over entire partitions rather than between pairs of clusters. To this end, he introduced the function

$$trace(\mathbf{W}) = \sum_{k=1}^{K} \frac{1}{N_j} \sum_{i=1}^{N_j} (x_i - \bar{x}_{jk})^2 \quad , \tag{3}$$

where $\mathbf{W}$ is the within-group covariance matrix and N_j is the number of members in class j. This expression gives an overall measure of the difference among the probabilistic summaries for sibling nodes (i.e., a distance between probability distributions). Gennari also notes that this function is similar to another metric, which he calls *category value*, that is simply category utility without information from the parent node subtracted out.

---

[3] Gennari's studies dealt with a rational reconstruction of Fisher's system, which he called CLASSIT, that also included a number of extensions. Because most of these additions were later subsumed by COBWEB/3 [25], we will also refer to it as COBWEB.

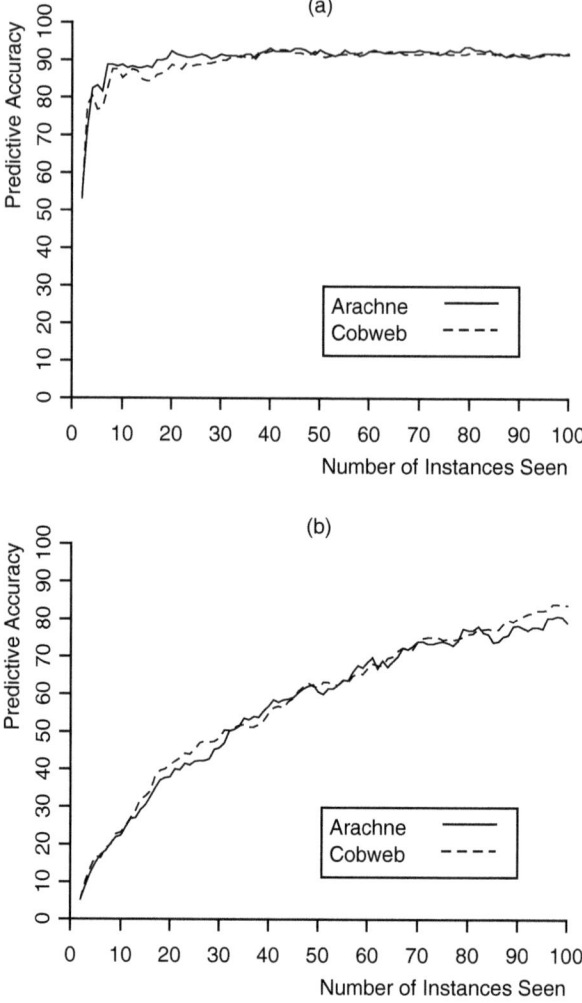

Fig. 3. Learning curves for COBWEB and a similar system, ARACHNE, on (a) congressional voting records and (b) soybean diseases, using classification accuracy as a performance measure.

Indeed, he notes that $trace(\mathbf{W})/K$ and category value are *isotonic*, in that they produce the same ordering over partitions and thus can be used interchangeably when making decisions. In fact, when the number of classes is held constant, category value is also isotonic to category utility. This means that the two functions differ primarily in that the former prefers fewer children per node than the latter. Because category value ignores the information at the parent node, Gennari expected COBWEB to perform somewhat worse using this metric than it does when relying on category utility.

An experiment with two natural data sets, one on a glass domain and another on heart disease, revealed almost identical learning curves for the two evaluation functions, violating predictions. To gain a better understanding of system behavior, Gennari designed two synthetic domains, each with nine attributes but one having three distinct classes and the other six. In this study, he measured both classification error and hierarchy depth after the system had processed 150 training cases, which were presumably enough to master the concepts in these simple domains.

Table 1. The behavior of COBWEB with category utility vs. category value on two synthetic domains.

	THREE CLASSES		SIX CLASSES	
	ERROR	DEPTH	ERROR	DEPTH
CATEGORY UTILITY	2.15	1.23	2.08	1.35
CATEGORY VALUE	2.05	2.40	1.99	3.77

Table 1 shows the predictive error and average tree depth for both evaluation functions on the three-class and six-class domains. Note that the error rates for the two metrics are very similar, replicating the result with natural domains. However, category value constructs a deeper concept hierarchy, as one would expect given its bias toward fewer children for each node, with category utility giving trees that more closely reflected the target concepts. Since COBWEB's performance element often sorts instances to terminal nodes when making predictions, tree structure often has little effect on predictive accuracy. But structural differences in the hierarchy can play a role in other contexts, as we discuss later, and category utility seems to hold advantages in such situations.

3.3   The Effect of Search Control

Another key factor in the COBWEB framework concerns the algorithm that controls search through the space of concept hierarchies. However, the literature on clustering abounds with unsupervised algorithms, suggesting that some of these approaches might give similar or even better results. Thus, Gennari carried out a second comparative study between COBWEB's incremental sorting method and two techniques that are widely used in clustering circles.

The first method also constructs hierarchies, but does this in a nonincremental, agglomerative fashion. Starting with each training case as a separate category, this algorithm finds the two categories that are nearest to each other, creates a parent node that specifies them as children, and replaces the original nodes with the new one in the set of candidates. This process continues, repeatedly combining the most similar pair of categories, until only one node (the root) remains. Because it must calculate all pairwise similarities on each iteration, this agglomerative method is considerably more expensive than COBWEB in computational terms.

The second method, known as *iterative optimization*, clusters training cases into k categories at a single level, where the user specifies the number of clusters. This process selects k instances at random as seeds to serve as initial category centroids, then assigns other cases to the cluster with the nearest seed. Next, it computes a new centroid for each cluster based on the cases it contains and reassigns each instance based on its distance to the revised centroids. This process repeats until no changes in the categories occur. This technique is sometimes known as k means clustering.

To compare the behavior of these algorithms with COBWEB, Gennari transformed the taxonomy constructed by the agglomerative scheme into a probabilistic concept hierarchy on which he could run COBWEB's performance element. In a similar manner, he transformed the clusters generated through iterative optimization into a one-level probabilistic 'hierarchy' on which COBWEB could operate. He studied the three methods' behavior on two domains. One involved a synthetic data set with nine numeric attributes and four top-level classes, two of which had two subclasses (giving six total leaf categories); the other consisted of the glass data set from the UCI repository.

Table 2. The behavior of different clustering methods on a synthetic and natural domain.

	THREE CLASSES		GLASS DOMAIN	
	ERROR	DEPTH	ERROR	DEPTH
COBWEB	2.40%	2.63	13.9%	2.93
AGGLOMERATIVE	1.71%	7.67	18.2%	11.73
ITERATIVE OPT. ($k = 6$)	5.07%	(1)	18.5%	(1)
ITERATIVE OPT. ($k = 8$)	2.82%	(1)		

Table 2 shows the results for both domains. Note that, on the synthetic data, the agglomerative method outperforms the other algorithms in terms of classification error, although it constructs a substantially deeper hierarchy than COBWEB. The latter difference comes as no surprise, since the agglomerative technique always generates binary trees. On the glass data set, COBWEB again creates a relatively shallow tree, but also gives the lowest classification error. Clearly, studies with more domains seem in order, but these preliminary results suggest that COBWEB's incremental search-control methods can hold their own with more traditional nonincremental schemes from the clustering literature.

3.4   The Effect of Missing Information

Many real-world data sets suffer from the characteristic of missing information, in that instances have no value for some attributes. Although COBWEB was designed to infer missing attributes in test cases, the omission of values during training is another matter entirely. Naturally, as the number of missing attributes increases, we would expect the learning rate to degrade somewhat, but we would also hope that COBWEB's reliance on probabilistic summaries would make this degradation a graceful one.

COBWEB's treatment of missing information is simple and straightforward. When incorporating a new instance into an existing concept description, any attributes of the instance that are marked as "missing" remain unchanged in the description. When calculating a concept's score as part of category utility, each attribute's contribution (i.e., sum over $A_i = V_{ij}$ for attributes and values) is weighted by the fraction of times it has been present in the cases that concept summarizes.[4] Equations 1 and 2, which present idealized forms with no missing information, do not show this weight factor. As an example, given a concept that summarizes four prior instances with no missing attributes and a new case with a missing attribute, the missing attribute's score would be discounted by 20% because it characterizes only four out five instances.

Gennari carried out an experimental study with a synthetic domain designed to evaluate COBWEB's tolerance to partial training data. In this domain, each instance is described by a class label and 12 attributes, six numeric and six nominal, with three attributes of each type being irrelevant with respect to the class. For this study, a filter removed attribute values from each training case with a specified probability p, replacing them with an identifier for 'missing'. Varying the parameter p produced a number of domains that were identical except for the number of omitted values. From each domain, Gennari ran the system on ten different training sets and measured classification error on a common separate test set.

Figure 4 (a) shows COBWEB's learning curves for this domain with 0%, 10%, 20%, and 30% of the attributes omitted. As expected, error increases when fewer attributes are available in the training cases, and the learning curves for higher omission levels are slower, but this degradation occurs in a graceful manner. However, the overall effect is somewhat stronger than Gennari predicted. If one removes 20% of the attribute values from training data, we would expect that 20% additional training would make up the difference. Instead, we see the curves generated with missing information needing several times the number of training cases to reach comparable levels of accuracy. Gennari attributes this effect to a higher chance that COBWEB will find local optima when enough features are absent. The fact that the learning curve for 5% (not shown) and 10% omissions are nearly identical to the curve for no omissions seems consistent with this interpretation.

In a similar study with the congressional voting data, Gennari collected a subset of the instances with missing attributes that, on average, had 12% missing values. He also took a subset of completely specified instances and randomly filtered values such that this "degraded" set also had 12% missing information. Figure 4 (b) shows the learning curves for this study. We see an interesting contrast between training on instances with missing data and training on data that

---

[4] More complex responses to missing attributes are necessary for other learning frameworks, such as decision-tree induction (e.g., [27]) and Bayesian networks, but this simple scheme is appropriate given COBWEB's assumption of conditional attribute independence given the category.

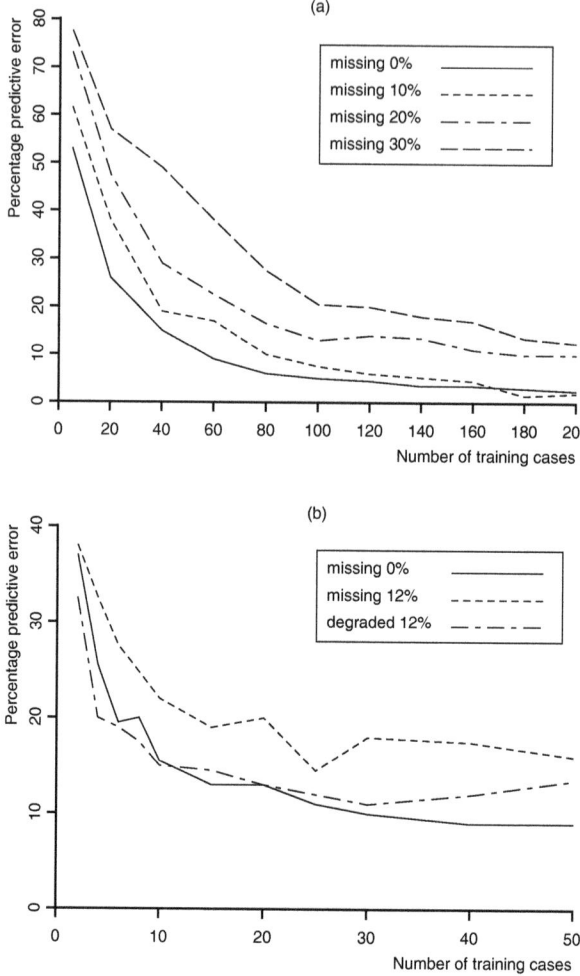

Fig. 4. Learning curves for several levels of missing information on (a) a synthetic domain and (b) Congressional voting records (from [8]).

was degraded. The former performs significantly worse than COBWEB with no missing data, while the degraded condition, with the same percentage of missing values, fares about as well as the no missing condition. Certainly, the system is robust with respect to certain forms of data loss, but missing information remains an open question that merits additional attention.

4   Extensions to COBWEB

When first developed, COBWEB appeared to offer many advantages over other approaches to learning available at the time. The system combined the hierarchical structure of decision trees with a clean probabilistic semantics, and it constructed its concept hierarchies in an incremental and unsupervised manner. However, experience with COBWEB suggested both representational and algorithmic limitations, which led to many attempts to extend the basic approach. In this section, we report on three such efforts in detail, then briefly review other research within the framework.

4.1   Minimizing Effects of Noise and Training Order

Despite its many attractions, our direct experience with COBWEB suggested that often it constructed hierarchies that did not reflect the underlying class structure of the domain. This behavior was especially apparent with noisy data and with certain training orders. In response, we developed ARACHNE, an unsupervised system that seeks to construct well-formed hierarchies of probabilistic concepts while maintaining high predictive accuracy. The algorithm bears many similarities to COBWEB, but employs different criteria for tree formation and uses alternative restructuring operators. In this section, we review ARACHNE and present some experimental results on its behavior.

The Arachne System.   ARACHNE assumes the same representation and organization of knowledge as COBWEB, but differs somewhat in its learning algorithm, classification mechanism, and evaluation function. Like its predecessor, the system includes two operators for restructuring its probabilistic concept hierarchy, one that merges children and another that promotes a child to the same level as its parent. Unlike COBWEB, the system applies these operators according to local constraints that can be tested efficiently but that should produce better structured hierarchies of probabilistic concepts. The basic learning activity involves sorting a training case downward through memory, with its values being used to update the probability distributions for the node subsuming it. However, this sorting process occurs only as the byproduct of the system's merging operator, which can lead to other restructuring along the way.

Each time such restructuring alters the children of some node N, the system checks two constraints designed to ensure a well-formed hierarchy. ARACHNE first checks each child C of N in turn to make sure the child is 'vertically well placed'; that is, it is more similar to its parent than to its grandparent. If C violates this condition, ARACHNE promotes C, removing it as a child of N and making it a child of N's parent.[5] This ensures that no children of N are more similar to their grandparent than to their parent. Thus, storing a new instance as a child of a concept can cause a sibling instance or concept to 'bubble up' to a higher location in memory.

---

[5] Actually, the system must recheck each constraint after applying the promote operator, since this changes the description of the parent node N.

The system's next step involves checking each child of N to make sure it is 'horizontally well placed', that is, it has equal or greater similarity to its parent than to any sibling. If the most similar pair of children are more like each other than either is to N, the system merges this pair by replacing these siblings with a new node that is their probabilistic average and taking the union of their children as its children. ARACHNE then recursively considers merging this new node's children. In some cases, this leads to recreation of the original siblings at a lower level in the hierarchy; in other cases, it produces further reorganizations in the subhierarchy. In particular, if the original instance is merged with an existing concept, recursive calls of the merge operator can effectively sort it down through memory.

Once it has merged two nodes at a given level, ARACHNE checks the remaining nodes for satisfaction of horizontal well-placement. If it finds another pair of nodes that violate this constraint, it merges them as well, then repeats this process until all nodes at this level satisfy the constraint. In this way, a single new instance can cause the system to merge successively many of the nodes previously stored at a given level, including pairs of nodes dissimilar from it.

For instance, suppose ARACHNE had stored four instances of cats under a common parent, and a dog instance is added (through merging from above). Here the system would first merge the two most similar cats, then merge a third into the resulting node, and finally add the fourth. The result would be two concepts, one representing the abstraction of four cat instances and the other based on a single dog. This iterative merging process differs from that used in COBWEB, which merges nodes only when they are similar to a new instance. Thus, we expect ARACHNE will create well-structured trees regardless of the order in which instances are presented.

ARACHNE's evaluation function also differs somewhat from that used in COB-WEB. The two constraints require some measure of similarity between pairs of nodes and/or instances, rather than a metric over an entire partition. To this end, the system calculates the shared area under the probability distributions for each attribute, averaged over all attributes. This usage is akin to that found in Hadzikadic and Yun's [11] INC system, which also uses a similarity function to guide the formation of probabilistic concept hierarchies. In addition, ARACHNE uses its similarity measure to determine the depth to which it should sort an instance, halting whenever the best similarity score at the next level is no better than that at the current level.

ARACHNE uses the same metric and essentially the same control structure for prediction that it uses in learning. The system sorts an instance down the hierarchy in accordance with its constraints, except that no promotion is allowed and only merges that involve the instance are executed. Thus an instance sorts to the class at which it would ordinarily become a disjunct, and a prediction is made from the last node to which it was sorted. ARACHNE also includes a simple 'recognition' criterion to foster prediction from internal nodes and thus avoid overfitting. As it sorts an instance through memory, the system makes a prediction from an internal node if its modal values perfectly match all the values of the instance.

Experimental Evaluation of Arachne. Our initial experiments were designed to show that ARACHNE is competitive with COBWEB in terms of predictive ability on natural domains. For this purpose, we followed Gennari's scheme of including the class attribute as an additional feature that the systems used for prediction but not in clustering. As shown in Figure 1, averaged results on the voting records and soybean domains revealed nearly identical learning curves, with the two systems improving at almost the same rate and reaching the same asymptotic accuracy. Although such studies show relevance to real-world problems, artificial domains provide better understanding of the reasons for an algorithm's behavior. For example, we predicted that ARACHNE's performance and learning algorithms would be more robust on noisy data, in terms of both accuracy and tree structure, since its more powerful reorganization operators should make it less subject to constructing overly deep concept hierarchies. We defined tree quality as the number of *well-placed instances*, that is, singleton nodes that are descendents of a target concept and that match 50% or more of the modal attribute values of the target concept. A high percentage of well-placed instances in a tree implies many accurate concepts.

To test this hypothesis, we designed artificial data sets with ten distinct categories, where instances were defined by four attributes, each of which could take on ten discrete values. For each concept, each attribute had a prototypical value but could take on other 'noise' values at some specified probability. In the low-noise data set, the modal value for each attribute occurred with probability 0.7, while three 'noise' values occurred with probability 0.1. In the noisier data set, the modal value for each attribute occurred with probability 0.5, while five noise values occurred with probability 0.1. Because a noise value appearing in one class was the modal value of some other class, the class descriptions overlapped to some extent. About 24% of the low-noise instances and only about 6% of the high-noise instances should conform perfectly to the modal class description, with the remainder being noisy variants.

We carried out ten runs at both noise levels, presenting COBWEB and ARACHNE with 100 training examples in each case. Figure 5 shows the learning curves for predictive accuracy at each level. As expected, increasing noise produced larger differences between the two systems. For low noise, ARACHNE asymptoted at 90% accuracy and COBWEB reaches 80%, whereas for high noise their asymptotes dropped to 76% and 56%, respectively. We observed a similar interaction regarding tree quality, with the older system being more affected by increased noise levels. Surprisingly, COBWEB's tree quality in the low-noise condition (82% well-placed nodes) was higher than for ARACHNE (74% well-placed nodes), but this order reversed for the high-noise condition, with COBWEB (37% well-placed nodes) faring worse than ARACHNE (52% well-placed nodes). Differences in accuracy were significant at the .001 level, whereas those in tree quality were significant only at the .025 level, but both measures were consistent with the predicted interaction effect.

Another one of our concerns in designing ARACHNE was stability with respect to different orders of training instances. The system's operators for merging and promotion should enable recovery from nonrepresentative training orders, leading to the prediction that COBWEB will suffer more from order effects than

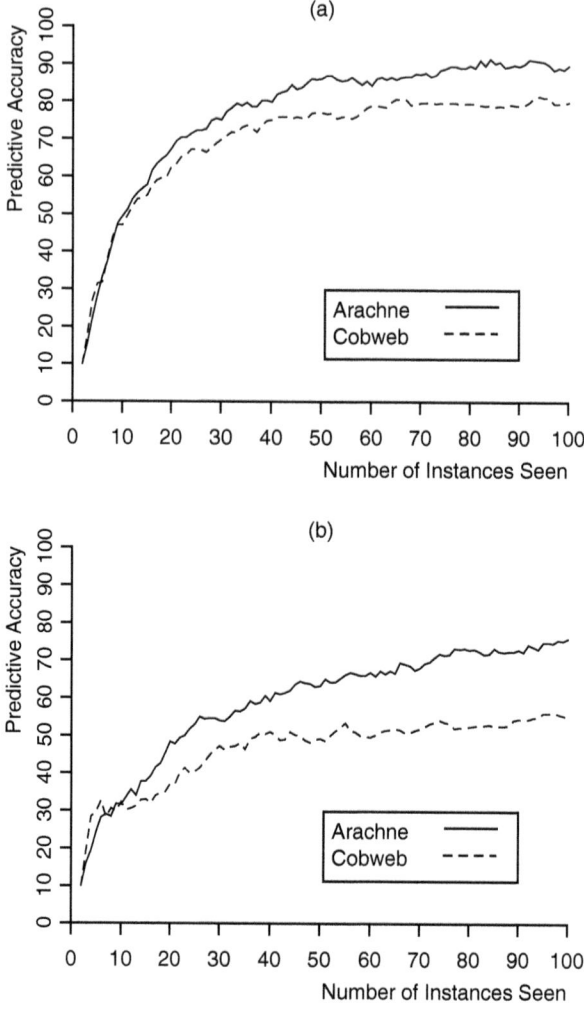

Fig. 5. Learning curves for ARACHNE and COBWEB on an artificial domain with (a) low and (b) high attribute noise, using predictive accuracy as a performance measure.

ARACHNE with respect to tree quality but not accuracy. Our experience with COBWEB suggested it has difficulty when every member of a class is presented at once, followed by every member of a new class, and so forth. Thus, we tested our hypothesis by presenting both systems with ten random orderings and ten "bad" orderings of 200 training instances from the low-noise data set described earlier. The bad orderings were strictly ordered by class, so the systems saw 20 examples of each class in turn.

The results, shown in Figure 6, indicate that instance order did not affect asymptotic accuracy for either system, although naturally learning was slower for the bad ordering, since they did not see a representative of the final class

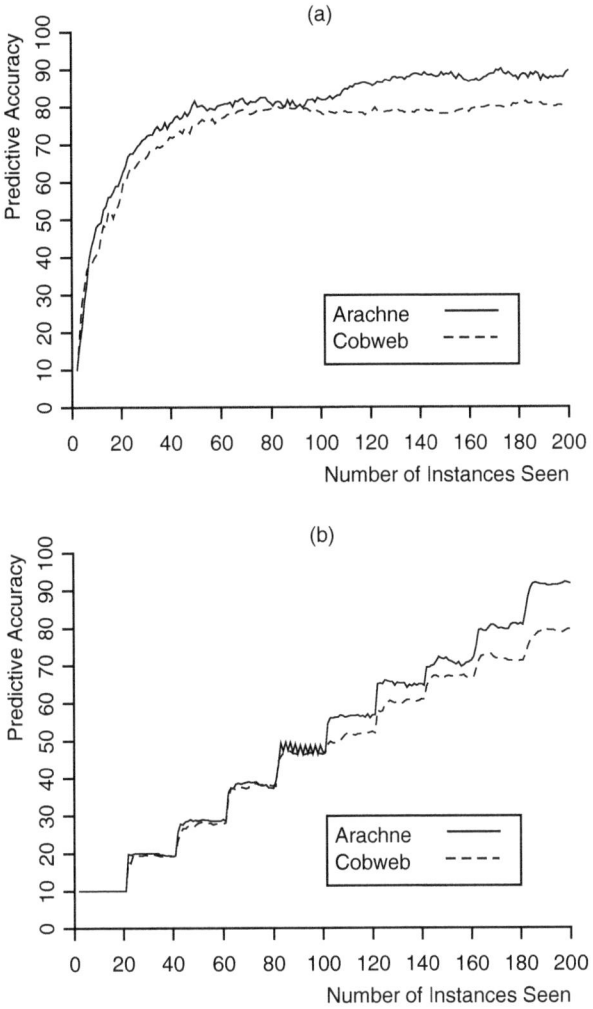

Fig. 6. Improvement in predictive accuracy for ARACHNE and COBWEB on artificial data with (a) random instance order and (b) misleading training sequences.

until the 181st instance. At this stage, random and bad orderings produce hierarchies capable of analogous predictive accuracy, approximately 90% for ARACHNE and 80% for COBWEB. However, tree quality differs significantly in the two situations. Both systems locate most or all of the concepts at some level, but COBWEB is vulnerable to misplaced instances with the pathological ordering. Whereas ARACHNE arrives at 88% well-placed nodes with the bad ordering, and a similar 86% with random ordering, COBWEB averages only 74% well-placed nodes when learning from the bad ordering, compared to 84% for the random ordering. Differences in predictive accuracy were significant for both conditions at the .001 level. Differences in tree quality between the two systems were not significant for random orderings of training cases, but were significant at the .001 level for bad instance orderings.

In summary, we found that ARACHNE's alternative control structure produced the same predictive accuracy as COBWEB on two natural domains, but we observed significant differences in both accuracy and tree quality using synthetic data. In particular, we found that COBWEB was more sensitive than ARACHNE to noisy training and test cases, and that the quality of COBWEB's trees suffers from misleading orders of training instances, while the new system's tree structure is relatively unaffected. We also saw additional evidence that predictive accuracy is poorly correlated with tree quality. These results suggest that ARACHNE embodies a promising approach to the construction of probabilistic concept hierarchies and deserves additional study.

4.2   Learning Overlapping Concepts

Another limitation of COBWEB lies in its assumption that regularities in a domain can be summarized by a single hierarchy of probabilistic concepts. One can easily imagine domains in which two or more orthogonal organizations of instances, involving different sets of attributes, are possible. If COBWEB uses one of these taxonomies to structure its experience for one attribute set, it cannot form generalizations and make useful predictions about the other attributes. Enough training cases should let the system deal with such domains, but an excessive reliance on data is a drawback of any inductive system. In response, Martin and Billman [23] developed TWILIX, a system that extends COBWEB to deal with domains that have overlapping category structure.

The TWILIX System. Like the ARACHNE system, TWILIX shares many features with its predecessor in terms of representation, organization, performance, and learning. As in COBWEB, each concept C is encoded using a conditional probability distribution for each attribute given C, along with a base rate $P(C)$ for the concept itself.[6] The system also organizes these probabilistic categories in a concept hierarchy, with higher nodes subsuming those below them. However, the immediate children of each node in the TWILIX hierarchy are not individual categories, but rather *sets* of categories. Each such 'conflict set' represents a distinct way of partitioning instances, typically emphasizing different attributes and thus supporting overlapping concepts. Each such set contains nodes for more specific probabilistic categories, which can themselves have sets of children, and so forth.

Naturally, TWILIX uses this extended memory organization to process an instance I somewhat differently than COBWEB. Within a conflict set, the system always assigns I to exactly one of the mutually exclusive categories, just as in COBWEB, updating the probability distributions that describe that concept.

---

[6] TWILIX differs slightly from COBWEB in incorporating uniform prior probabilities for each distribution, rather than estimating distributions solely from the training data.

Across conflict sets, TWILIX finds the best set by tentatively assigning I to the concepts within each set, then repeats this process to find the next best set, and so forth. The result is that the system can assign the case to more than one conflict set, but never to more than one concept within each set. Moreover, just as COBWEB sometimes decides to create a new category at the current level based on a distinctive training case, so TWILIX sometimes decides to create an entirely new conflict set. The system does not include COBWEB's split and merge operators, since it should be less sensitive to training order than its predecessor.

Like the earlier system, TWILIX relies on evaluation functions over instance partitions to direct the classification and learning process. In fact, the function for assigning cases to a category within a conflict set, which Martin and Bill-man call *set utility*, differs only in minor ways from COBWEB's category utility. However, the system also includes a function U that evaluates different sets θ of conflict sets. This can be stated as

$$U(\theta) = \left[\prod_{l=1}^{M} SU(S_l) \right]^{\frac{1}{M}} , \tag{4}$$

where SU is the set utility for cluster S_l and M is the number of conflict sets in θ. TWILIX applies this function to candidate sets of sets, selecting the one that gives the highest score. However, note that the exponent $1/M$ gives a strong bias against unnecessary conflict sets, which should lead to a single hierarchy in domains where that is appropriate.

Experimental Studies of TWILIX. Since TWILIX was specifically designed to learn overlapping concepts, Martin [21] tested the system using a data set on Pittsburgh bridges that he felt had this characteristic. This domain includes descriptions for 108 bridges that were built in the Pittsburgh area between 1818 and 1986. Each bridge is described by twelve nominal attributes, seven repre-senting design specifications or requirements, and the other five capturing the design descriptors. Martin also tested a version of COBWEB that omitted the merge and split operators to provide a closer basis for comparison.

The experiment involved running each system five separate times, training on nine successive training blocks and testing on one test block. Each block consisted of ten instances, made up from 100 instances selected randomly from the 108 total cases available. After each block of ten training instances, both systems were run without learning on the test block to obtain learning curves. The performance measure was the average accuracy on predicting each of the twelve attributes given the other eleven.

Figure 7 (a) shows the resulting learning curves (averaged over five runs) for the two systems. The graphs reveal that TWILIX has a significant advantage over COBWEB in this condition ($p < 0.001$). However, Martin conducted a tandem ex-periment in which the performance task was to predict all five design descriptors given only the specifications. As Figure 7 (b) indicates, there was no difference between the systems in this setting. Furthermore, for this performance task, COBWEB's overall performance increased (i.e., generally higher accuracy over-all), but the overall accuracy for TWILIX was actually lower. Martin speculated

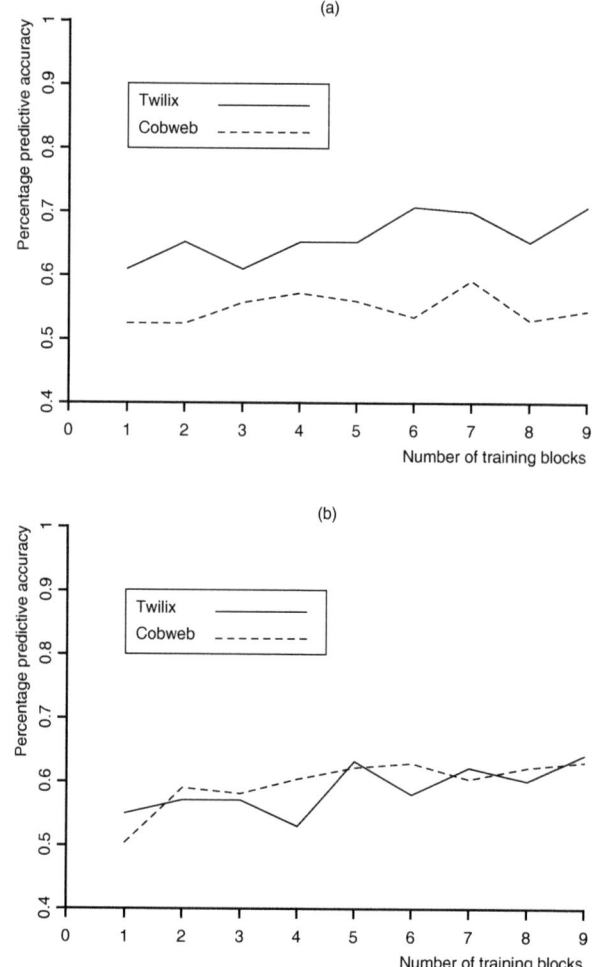

Fig. 7. Average proportion of correct predictions (a) for one attribute given the other eleven, and (b) for the five design descriptors given the seven requirement specifications (from [21]).

that the seven specification attributes in this domain might be too impoverished to make accurate predictions, yet COBWEB fared better in this condition than when only predicting a single attribute. Evidence from other empirical studies using synthetic domains generally indicates that TWILIX is more robust than its ancestor, but there seems room for additional work to identify the relative contributions of its extensions to the COBWEB framework.

4.3   Concept Formation in Temporal Domains

Many concepts in the real world describe events that occur over time with certain indicative characteristics. We can contrast such temporal concepts with those addressed to this point, which describe static objects or states of an environment. For example, motor skills correspond to a temporally structured domain in which it seems natural to use a *sequence* to characterize and discriminate among concepts. However, such domains introduce challenges for concept formation systems like COBWEB, which have no direct representation of sequence. In response, Iba [15], [16] developed OXBOW, an extension to COBWEB that forms concepts in temporal domains. Here we focus on the system's application to learning movement concepts, though the underlying approach is more general.

Design of OXBOW. OXBOW represents movements as sequences of descriptions with temporal relations among them. The system employs a movement parser, which takes a dense sequence of attribute-value descriptions as input, to create a sparse sequence based on zero crossings in velocity and acceleration. At such events, the parser creates *states* containing the positions, angles, and velocities (e.g., for the joints of a limb), as well as the time (relative to the start of the movement) associated with the zero crossing. This sparse representation is sufficient to capture and summarize the original movement with very low error.

Two issues arise for representing movements in a COBWEB-like concept hierarchy. First, the movement is a sequence of states instead of single set of attribute values. But more significantly, movements have variable numbers of states according to their complexity (number of zero crossings). In response, OXBOW represents a single movement concept using a probabilistic hierarchy of states. The top-level partition of this hierarchy is organized with respect to time only, and the nodes at this level are ordered by time to yield the state sequence of the movement.

Movement concepts are organized in a traditional probabilistic 'movement' hierarchy, each node of which points to an entire 'state' hierarchy that describes the temporal structure of the movement category. Thus, a movement hierarchy of baseball pitches might have two top-level concepts corresponding to sidearm and overhand throws, and the overhand concept might have three children: fast-ball, curve-ball, and fork-ball. Each of these concepts points to a state hierarchy in which the top level consists of an ordered AND tree that represents the sequence of states for the given movement. To continue our example, the sequence might include states for the wind-up, initial forward motion, wrist-snap, release, and follow-through.

The recognition process for a newly observed movement is similar to COBWEB's classification mechanism. The new motion is parsed into a sequence of states, which is sorted down through the movement hierarchy. At each level, OXBOW applies and evaluates the four COBWEB operators from Section 2.2. On termination, the system returns, as the retrieved category, the most recent node into which the new instance was incorporated. This category can be used to evaluate the goodness or accuracy of the classification process.

On the surface, OXBOW's learning method is quite similar to COBWEB's, but it introduces a significant variation to deal with structured objects having temporal components. Instead of simply updating attribute-value counts, the system must incorporate a new state sequence into an existing movement concept. This involves sequentially incorporating each state from the movement into the state hierarchy rooted at the movement concept. For each state, OXBOW employs the basic category utility function. However, time is the only attribute considered at the first level; in this way, the partition structure is organized by the temporal aspects of the movement. At subsequent levels, time is ignored and the state features are used in the category utility calculation.

This scheme for incorporating movements carries out a partial match between the sequence of states that comprise the newly observed movement and the sequence in the concept (as defined by the time-ordered top level). OXBOW views the top level of the state hierarchy as a 'part-of' structure. Not surprisingly, some modifications of category utility are necessary to accommodate this structured representation.

Since OXBOW works with continuous attributes, it uses the continuous version of category utility from Equation 2. However, this expression assumes that every class has the same set of attributes, so we must extend this to consider classes with different components or, in this case, state descriptions. Because the number of states is not the same for all movement instances, the information in each component is weighted by its probability. For OXBOW, the evaluation function over movements is

$$\frac{1}{K} \left[\sum_{k}^{K} P(C_k) \sum_{j}^{J} P(S_{kj}) \sum_{i}^{I} \frac{1}{\sigma_{kji}} - \sum_{m}^{M} P(S_{pm}) \sum_{i}^{I} \frac{1}{\sigma_{pmi}} \right] \quad , \qquad (5)$$

where $P(S_{kj})$ is the probability of the jth state description in class C_k, which specifies the proportion of all the state descriptions from schema instances of node C_k that have been classified at state description S_{kj}. The probability $P(S_{pm})$ is defined in a similar manner for the mth state description in the parent of the current partition.

We have extensively tested this approach to unsupervised learning over movement categories at both the movement and state levels [16] in both natural and artificial domains. We have also evaluated OXBOW on other temporal domains, including the recognition of cursive letters and events in telemetry data from the space shuttle. Here we present one study that demonstrates the temporal extension to COBWEB and highlights a variation on the performance task.

Predicting Unseen Movement. Most work in unsupervised learning has resorted to evaluating a method's utility in supervised learning contexts. We have done this with OXBOW, but we also have an opportunity to measure the error between the prototype motion, which is stored at the indexed concept, and the observed motion. We measure the error as the absolute difference in joint positions between the two movements at each corresponding point in time, which we then average over all time steps. An even more challenging performance measure requires OXBOW to predict the continuation of a movement based on its classification of a partial observation. That is, given an initial glimpse of a movement, predict its continuation over time. If we ignore issues of learning, then varying the observed percentage of a test movement provides a method for adjusting the difficulty of OXBOW's retrieval task, thereby allowing a more direct assessment of its contribution to error.

For a number of our empirical tests, we constructed an artificial movement domain that consisted of four movement types controlling a two-jointed arm. Instances of each movement type were generated by a distinct schema, the elements of which were perturbed according to a variability (noise) level. The four movement types were equally likely to occur. OXBOW learned from a series of observed movements and was then tested on a set of new movements (with learning turned off). We conducted these tests in a simulated environment with an arm that had a maximum possible error of 300 units.

To explore OXBOW's ability to predict future movement from partial observation, we ran a series of 20 sessions, each one consisting of 30 randomly generated training movements. The test set consisted of the noise-free schemas, one for each movement type. When testing, we presented an initial portion of the prototypical movement and then measured error over the remaining unobserved movement. Note that complete movements were given during training and only when evaluating system performance did we limit the extent of the observed prototype. We can compare errors among different lengths of predicted movements because the total error is averaged over the number of unobserved (i.e., predicted) time slices. Any differences in errors can be attributed to classification problems during retrieval, because the knowledge base is the same for each level of observation at a given point in training.

This formulation of the task suggests a prediction: as less of the movement is observed, classification should become more difficult and mistakes should lead to greater measured error. Simply stated, the more the system sees of a movement, the more it should know about what will happen next. Figure 8(a) shows the learning curves from an experiment in which we varied the portion of the movement to be predicted, with results averaged over ten runs of 30 training instances each.

The figure shows that the errors are consistently the highest when OXBOW must predict 80% of the movement, except very early in training, when it has not yet seen all the movement types. However, there is little difference between predicting 50% of the movement and only 20%. This result suggests that the system is not severely affected by having less information available for classification, except at a minimal level. However, from previous experiments with OXBOW, we know that increased domain variability leads to higher asymptotic errors, presumably because greater noise makes it harder to construct high-quality generalizations, which in turn hinder classification. This idea suggests a predicted interaction: as training data becomes more variable, OXBOW should require larger portions of the test movement in order to prevent increased error.

To test this prediction, we ran the system in partial prediction mode while training it on data with different levels of variability. In a single experimental run for a given level of noise, we trained OXBOW on 60 observed movements,

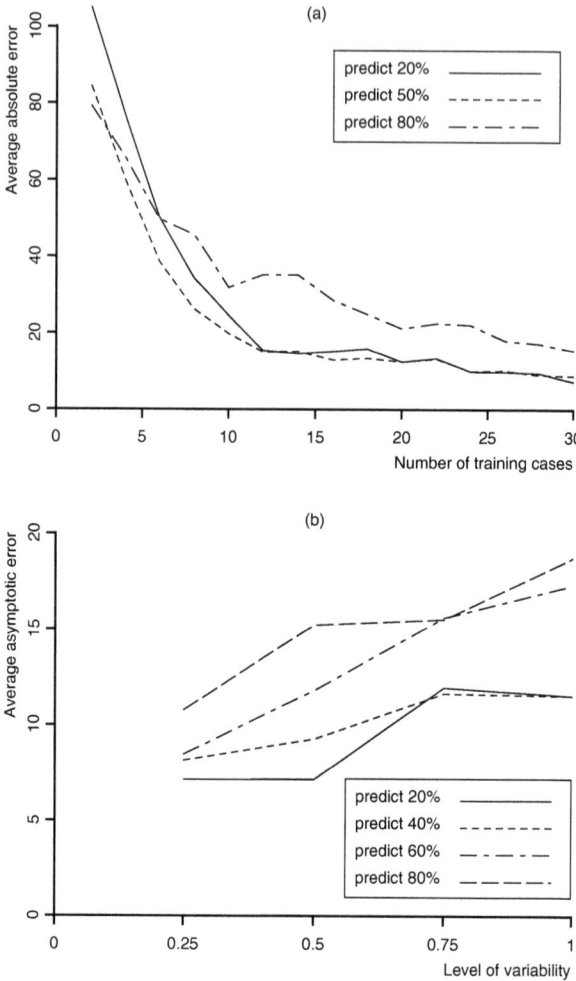

Fig. 8. (a) Learning curves showing error for three levels of partial observation, and (b) asymptotic error rates for four levels of domain variability and four levels of partial observation.

then tested on four levels (20%, 40%, 60%, and 80%) that must be predicted. As before, the system used the initial segment of the movement for classification. For each condition of noise and observation level, we averaged the results over 20 different training orders, to guard against order effects.

In this experiment, we were only interested in asymptotic error levels, having considered the effects of variability upon learning rate in an earlier study [16]. Figure 8(b) shows the asymptotic error rates for the four noise levels as a function of the portion of each test movement to be predicted. The graph indicates similar asymptote levels for the 0.25 variability condition but a wide range of asymptotes for the 1.0 level. Separate analyses of variance for these two conditions revealed a statistically significant difference for variability equal to 1.0 ($p < 0.001$) but none for the 0.25 condition ($p > 0.1$), which seems to support the predicted interaction. However, an analysis of variance over all the data shows a significant main effect of the portion to be predicted, but no significant interaction between the two factors.[7] Although the results did not strongly support our prediction, they indicate that OXBOW is somewhat robust with respect to noise; that is, the system is no more adversely affected by incomplete observations when learning from noisy data than when learning from more regular data.

Moreover, the above experiments held the learning system constant while varying the amount of information in the test movement, thus indicating the sensitivity of the classification process. The results suggest that OXBOW is not making misclassifications when given partial structures in the input. This provides supporting evidence that the increase in error associated with increased variability, is due to problems in the generalization process during incorporation of a new experience. Understanding and reducing these predictive errors remains an important topic for future research.

4.4   Other Variations on the COBWEB Framework

In addition to the extensions described above, a number of researchers have developed clustering algorithms that derive either directly from COBWEB or that bear a striking resemblance to it. Each of these systems construct hierarchies of probabilistic concepts in an incremental manner, sorting training cases through memory and updating concept descriptions in the process. Many of these methods are covered in Fisher, Pazzani, and Langley [7], but they deserve some comment here.

Pazzani (personal communication, 1990) and colleagues developed an extension to COBWEB that takes advantage of knowledge about which features one wants to predict. Their system retained the same control structure but generalized the measure of category utility so that it weights features according to the importance of predicting them. They argued that this approach should lead to better predictive accuracy than methods like COBWEB, which weights all features equally. One can view both unsupervised and supervised learning as special cases of this framework. Martin [22] has reported a similar technique that also learns the weights on features from sample queries.

Another extension to COBWEB comes from Reich and Fenves [28], who adapted the approach to problems in parametric design. Their BRIDGER system supports a variety of classification and prediction methods, including the ability to halt when all attributes that encode the design specifications have been met. The program also handles numeric attributes in a different manner than COBWEB and incorporates a mechanism for grouping nominal values into new features. Finally, BRIDGER mitigates order effects with a procedure that removes

---

[7] If we consider only the high and low variability (i.e., remove the 0.5 and 0.75 noise levels), an analysis of variance indicates a significant interaction with $p < 0.05$.

any node (and its descendents) if it contains 'characteristic' values (ones with a sufficiently high probability) that differ from those in its ancestors. Experiments using the system for synthesis of bridge designs, which involves predicting many attributes, gave encouraging results.

Anderson and Matessa [1] describe a COBWEB-like algorithm that incrementally constructs a binary tree of probabilistic concepts. One difference lies in their performance element, which follows the Bayesian philosophy of using a weighted average over all categories to make predictions about test cases. Their system also invokes Dirichelet priors to initialize the probabilistic descriptions for each category. Moreover, when deciding whether to incorporate a training case into existing children or to create a new category, it computes the probability that the case belongs to each child and that it belongs to a new category, rather than using an evaluation metric like category utility that operates over an entire partition. Their algorithm qualitatively fits numerous results on category learning from the psychological literature.

Thompson and Langley [29] report on an explicit extension to COBWEB designed to carry out concept formation over structured representations, in which the values of attributes can themselves be component objects with relations among them. Their LABYRINTH algorithm calls on COBWEB recursively, in that acquired component concepts are used to describe and influence the acquisition of composite concepts. The system also introduced a new operator for 'attribute generalization' that replaced sets of values in a composite node's description with a single value that resides above them in the component hierarchy. This required a new evaluation metric, related to category utility, that determined when to take such a restructuring step. Handa [12] has extended this approach to take context into account during the classification of component objects.

Langley and Allen [18], [19] describe DÆDALUS, another extension to COBWEB that organizes plan knowledge in an effort to improve the efficiency of problem solving. Each node in the concept hierarchy contains a probabilistic summary of problems the system has solved previously, described in terms of the relational differences involved and the operators used in their solution. DÆDALUS includes a means-ends problem solver that sorts each new subproblem through memory, using a relational variant on category utility, to retrieve an appropriate operator. After solving a problem, the system stores each subproblem and its operator in the hierarchy, updating probabilities and changing retrieval on future problems. Experimental studies of DÆDALUS's learning behavior showed reduction in search on both navigation and blocks-world tasks.

Yoo and Fisher [30] take a different approach to concept formation over problem-solving experience. Their EXOR system associates with each conceptual node the abstract solution (stated as an AND tree) for a class of problems, rather than a single operator, with nodes lower in the hierarchy specifying more detailed solutions. EXOR uses a version of category utility to sort a new problem, based on its surface features, downward through memory. The system falls back on problem-reduction search to complete the solution if this process finds only a partial solution. The learning mechanism incorporates an explanation-based component that generalizes the solution stored at each node. Experiments with

EXOR showed that its learning method improves search efficiency on algebra story problems.

Nor does this exhaust the variations and extensions on the COBWEB framework. Hadzikadic and Yun [11] report a very similar algorithm for the incremental formation of concept hierarchies that differs in details like its evaluation metric. Kilander and Jansson [17] describe a variant on COBWEB designed explicitly to deal with environments that change over time. Day [5] has adapted the basic approach to learn constraints that produce more efficient search on complex scheduling tasks. Taken together, these intellectual descendants indicate that Fisher's original approach to constructing hierarchies of probabilistic concepts lends itself naturally to a wide and interesting range of problems.

5   Relation to Other Research on Unsupervised Learning

Before closing, we should clarify the relation between the COBWEB framework and two other families of algorithms that learn probabilistic descriptions from unsupervised training data. We begin with another paradigm that also constructs probabilistic concept hierarchies, but in a quite different manner, then examine work within another representational formalism that relies on different assumptions than our own.

5.1   The AUTOCLASS Family

Soon after the initial publication on COBWEB, Cheeseman et al. [3] introduced AUTOCLASS, another clustering algorithm that has led to its own distinct family of systems. The two frameworks share some key assumptions, including the notion of describing each category in terms of probability distributions over its component attributes. Although the first system constructed only a one-level clustering, later versions like AUTOCLASS/3 [13] generated multi-level descriptions, with more general categories summarizing their more specific children. Thus, in terms of its representation and organization, the AUTOCLASS family constitutes an approach to creating and using a probabilistic concept hierarchy.

Despite this clear similarity between the two frameworks, there are also some significant differences. Unlike COBWEB and its relatives, AUTOCLASS does not store training cases as terminal nodes in its concept hierarchies or, indeed, even assign cases definitively to one category or another. Rather, the system assigns each training case to *every* category with some probability, which in turn means that its values contribute only partially to each category description. Another representational difference is that AUTOCLASS stores not only the conditional probability distribution for each attribute given the category, but also the conditional covariance matrices. For numeric attributes, this means that decision regions are not limited to ellipsoids with axes parallel to those of the instance space, as in COBWEB. More generally, the system can represent relations that violate independence at a given level of the hierarchy, albeit at the price of more parameters.

The AUTOCLASS systems also differ from COBWEB and its kin in their performance and learning mechanisms. Cheeseman et al. take a strong Bayesian position on the classification of new instances, so their algorithms assign a test case to each category at each level with a certain probability, rather than to the most probable one. Predictions about missing attributes are then based on a weighted vote that takes into account each category's prediction and its probability given the instance. In this framework, the hierarchical organization of knowledge provides no computational benefits during the prediction process, but it retains advantages in understandability.

The clustering process in AUTOCLASS also has a quite different flavor. Rather than relying on incremental sorting, as in COBWEB, it incorporates a probabilistic variant of the nonincremental k means algorithm known as *expectation maximization*. This method initializes the probabilistic descriptions for each of k clusters randomly and uses these descriptions to compute the probability of each training case belonging to each cluster. It then uses these partial assignments to update the descriptions, reassigns each instance using the new descriptions, and continues the process until no changes occur. After clustering is complete, AUTOCLASS removes those clusters that have only improbable assignments.[8] Despite their clear relationship, there exist no systematic experimental comparisons of COBWEB and AUTOCLASS or their close relatives.

5.2   Induction of Bayesian Networks

Another probabilistic approach to unsupervised learning, one that has become quite popular in the years since COBWEB first appeared, involves Bayesian networks (e.g., [14]). This framework also organizes memory using nodes and links, but their meanings are quite different from those in a probabilistic concept hierarchy. Rather than corresponding to concepts, each node represents an observable or unobservable attribute, and a link from one node to another means the values of the former influence those of the latter. Like a probabilistic concept hierarchy, a Bayesian network specifies a probability density function over the instance space, but it achieves this through very different assumptions. Information about probability distributions reside not in category descriptions but in 'conditional probability tables' stored with each attribute. These specify the probability for each value of that attribute under each possible combination of values that influence it.

Research on learning in Bayesian networks has focused on two distinct issues. The first involves estimating the conditional probability tables from training data when the structure of the network is already known. When no attribute values are missing, this simply involves counting the number of times each combination of values occurs in the training set, so effort here has focused on the issue of learning from data with omitted values (e.g., [2]). A second body of work deals with learning a network's structure from training data (e.g., [4], [26]). Most algorithms carry out a greedy search through the space of Bayes net structures, starting with no links and adding the most probable link, given the data, on each step, then halting when reaching a local optimum.

---

[8] This clustering scheme requires the user to specify the number of clusters, but the ability to remove low-probability categories mitigates this reliance.

A few researchers have also examined methods that introduce hidden attributes into learned Bayesian networks. One special form of this process introduces a single unobservable node that influences each observable attribute, which are themselves independent given this attribute. In fact, this task is equivalent to creating a set of probabilistic clusters, and the most common approach invokes the expectation maximization algorithm that is called at each level in AUTOCLASS. At first glance, this mapping suggests a close relationship between the induction of Bayesian networks and the formation of probabilistic concept hierarchies that has been our focus in this chapter.

However, closer inspection reveals deep differences between the two frameworks. Granted, both paradigms have a clear probabilistic semantics that supports unsupervised induction for the prediction of missing attribute values. But Bayesian networks assume that their graphical structure and associated probability tables hold across the entire instance space, whereas probabilistic hierarchies explicitly partition this space into regions. Bayes nets can create such a partition by using a hidden attribute, but they cannot introduce partitions at different levels of abstraction, which happens regularly in the hierarchical framework. On the other hand, each category in a probabilistic concept hierarchy assumes that attributes are conditionally independent, whereas Bayes nets can easily represent more complex situations.

Thus, the key difference between probabilistic concept hierarchies and Bayesian networks lies not in their learning algorithms. Indeed, we have seen that AUTOCLASS uses expectation maximization in a recursive manner to construct a probabilistic hierarchy, and one can imagine more gradual, incremental methods for creating Bayes nets. Rather, they differ mainly in their *representational bias*. Both frameworks can represent arbitrary target concepts, at least for discrete attributes, but each one finds it easier to describe some target functions than it does others. This means one can design synthetic domains on which either framework will learn more rapidly, achieving higher accuracy from fewer training cases, than the other. Of course, natural domains may or may not have similar characteristics, so it remains unclear which approach will fare best in practice. However, we anticipate that many real-world induction tasks will have hierarchical structure, and that methods for learning probabilistic concept hierarchies will prove useful on such problems.

6   Closing Remarks

In this chapter, we set out to address issues related to unsupervised learning in support of intelligent agents. This emphasis constrained the space of solutions in several ways and led us to focus attention on systems that represent concepts probabilistically and incorporate them incrementally into generalization hierarchies. Fisher's [6] COBWEB, which satisfies these constraints, served as our prototype system.

We reviewed the COBWEB framework as it exists after several rational reconstructions, characterizing the system's representation and organization of knowledge, as well as its processes for recognition and learning. We summarized a selected sample of empirical studies that have established the framework's robustness along several dimensions, including variations in the evaluation function, search strategy, and domain characteristics. Although these studies were generally encouraging, they also suggested some limitations and directions for improvement.

In response, we examined three extensions to the framework in some detail. One system, ARACHNE, incorporated new restructuring operators designed to improve the quality of the learned concept hierarchy, whereas another extension, TWILIX, introduced a more sophisticated memory organization to improve prediction in domains with overlapping categories. A third system, OXBOW, extended the basic framework to handle domains with temporal structure. We also briefly described a variety of other systems that build on COBWEB in some fashion. In closing, we noted links to other approaches to unsupervised learning within a probabilistic framework.

In summary, the formation of probabilistic concept hierarchies has proven a fertile paradigm for the study of unsupervised learning. Although early work on the topic made many simplifying assumptions, researchers have since extended the framework in many directions, producing methods that are both more robust and that apply to a broader class of domains. Nevertheless, each extension has raised intriguing issues that deserve attention, pointing the way for additional research in this promising paradigm.

Acknowledgements. We thank our collaborators, including John Gennari, Kathleen McKusick, Kevin Thompson, and John Allen, for their contributions to the research described in this chapter. Grant MDA 903-85-C-0324 from the Army Research Insitute supported our early work within the COBWEB framework, whereas later extensions were developed at NASA Ames Research Center.

References

1. Anderson, J. R., & Matessa, M. (1991). An iterative Bayesian algorithm for categorization. In D. H. Fisher, M. J. Pazzani, & P. Langley (Eds.), *Concept formation: Knowledge and experience in unsupervised learning.* San Mateo, CA: Morgan Kaufmann.
2. Binder, J., Koller, D., Russell, S., & Kanazawa, K. (1997). Adaptive probabilistic networks with hidden variables. *Machine Learning, 29,* 213–244.
3. Cheeseman, P., Kelly, J., Self, M., Stutz, J., Taylor, W., & Freeman, D. (1988). AUTOCLASS: A Bayesian classification system. *Proceedings of the Fifth International Conference on Machine Learning* (pp. 54–64). Ann Arbor, MI: Morgan Kaufmann.
4. Cooper, G. F., & Herskovits, E. (1992). A Bayesian method for the induction of probabilistic networks from data. *Machine Learning, 9,* 309–347.
5. Day, D. S. (1992). Acquiring search heuristics automatically for constraint-based scheduling and planning. *Proceedings of the First International Conference on AI Planning Systems* (pp. 45–51). College Park, MD: Morgan Kaufmann.
6. Fisher, D. H. (1987). Knowledge acquisition via incremental conceptual clustering. *Machine Learning, 2,* 139–172.
7. Fisher, D. H., Pazzani, M. J., & Langley, P. (Eds.) (1991). *Concept formation: Knowledge and experience in unsupervised learning.* San Mateo, CA: Morgan Kaufmann.

8. Gennari, J. H. (1990). *An experimental study of concept formation*. Doctoral dissertation, Department of Information & Computer Science, University of California, Irvine.

9. Gennari, J. H., Langley, P., & Fisher, D. H. (1989). Models of incremental concept formation. *Artificial Intelligence, 40*, 11–61.

10. Gluck, M., & Corter, J. (1985). Information, uncertainty and the utility of categories. *Proceedings of the Seventh Annual Conference of the Cognitive Science Society* (pp. 283–287). Irvine, CA: Lawrence Erlbaum.

11. Hadzikadic, M., & Yun, D. (1989). Concept formation by incremental conceptual clustering. *Proceedings of the Eleventh International Joint Conference on Artificial Intelligence* (pp. 831–836). Detroit, MI: Morgan Kaufmann.

12. Handa, K. (1990). CFIX: Concept formation by interaction of related objects. *Proceedings of the Pacific Rim International Conference on Artificial Intelligence*. Nagoya, Japan.

13. Hanson, R., Stutz, J., & Cheeseman, P. (1991). Bayesian classification with correlation and inheritance. *Proceedings of the Twelfth International Joint Conference on Artificial Intelligence* (pp. 692–698). Sydney: Morgan Kaufmann.

14. Heckerman, D. (1995). *A tutorial on learning Bayesian networks* (Technical Report MSR-TR-95-06). Redmond, WA: Microsoft Research.

15. Iba, W. (1991a). Learning to classify observed motor behavior. *Proceedings of the Twelfth International Joint Conference on Artificial Intelligence* (pp. 732–738). Sydney: Morgan Kaufmann.

16. Iba, W. (1991b). *Acquisition and improvement of human motor skills: Learning through observation and practice*. Doctoral dissertation, Department of Information & Computer Science, University of California, Irvine.

17. Kilander, F., & Jansson, C. G. (1993). COBBIT: A control procedure for COBWEB in the presence of concept drift. *Proceedings of the 1993 European Conference on Machine Learning* (pp. 244–261). Vienna: Springer-Verlag.

18. Langley, P., & Allen, J. A. (1991). Learning, memory, and search in planning. *Proceedings of the Thirteenth Conference of the Cognitive Science Society* (pp. 364–369). Chicago: Lawrence Erlbaum.

19. Langley, P., & Allen, J. A. (1993). A unified framework for planning and learning. In S. Minton (Ed.), *Machine learning methods for planning and scheduling*. San Mateo: Morgan Kaufmann.

20. Langley, P., Iba, W., & Thompson, K. (1992). An analysis of Bayesian classifiers. *Proceedings of the Tenth National Conference on Artificial Intelligence* (pp. 223–228). San Jose: AAAI Press.

21. Martin, J. D. (1992). *Direct and indirect transfer: Explorations in concept formation*. Doctoral dissertation, Department of Computer Science, Georgia Institute of Technology.

22. Martin, J. D. (1994). Goal-directed clustering. *Proceedings of the AAAI Spring Symposium on Goal-Directed Learning*. Stanford, CA.

23. Martin, J. D., & Billman, D. O. (1994). Acquiring and combining overlapping concepts. *Machine Learning, 16*, 121–155.

24. McKusick, K. B., & Langley, P. (1991). Constraints on tree structure in concept formation. *Proceedings of the Twelfth International Joint Conference on Artificial Intelligence* (pp. 810–816). Sydney: Morgan Kaufmann.

25. McKusick, K. B., & Thompson, K. (1990). COBWEB/3: A portable implementation (Tech. Rep. No. FIA-90-6-18-2). Moffett Field, CA: NASA Ames Research Center, AI Research Branch.

26. Provan, G. M., & Singh, M. (1995). Learning Bayesian networks using feature selection. *Proceedings of the Fifth International Workshop on Artificial Intelligence and Statistics* (pp. 450–456). Fort Lauderdale, FL.

27. Quinlan, J.R. (1986). Induction of decision trees. *Machine Learning, 1*, 81–106

28. Reich, Y., & Fenves, S. J. (1991). The formation and use of abstract concepts in design. In D. H. Fisher, M. J. Pazzani, & P. Langley (Eds.), *Concept formation: Knowledge and experience in unsupervised learning*. San Francisco, CA: Morgan Kaufmann.

29. Thompson, K., & Langley, P. (1991). Concept formation in structured domains. In D. H. Fisher, M. J. Pazzani, & P. Langley (Eds.), *Concept formation: Knowledge and experience in unsupervised learning*. San Mateo, CA: Morgan Kaufmann.

30. Yoo, J., & Fisher, D. H. (1991). Concept formation over problem-solving experience. In D. H. Fisher, M. J. Pazzani, & P. Langley (Eds.), *Concept formation: Knowledge and experience in unsupervised learning*. San Francisco, CA: Morgan Kaufmann.

Function Decomposition in Machine Learning

Blaž Zupan[1,2,3], Ivan Bratko[1,2], Marko Bohanec[2], and Janez Demšar[1]

[1] Faculty of Computer and Information Sciences, Univ. of Ljubljana, Slovenia
[2] Department of Intelligent Systems, J. Stefan Institute, Jamova 39, SI-1000
Ljubljana, Slovenia
[3] Baylor College of Medicine, 1 Baylor Plaza, Houston, TX 77030, USA

1 Introduction

To solve a complex problem, one of the effective general approaches is to decompose it into smaller, less complex and more manageable subproblems. In machine learning, this principle is a foundation for structured induction [44]: instead of learning a single complex classification rule from examples, define a concept hierarchy and learn rules for each of the (sub)concepts. Shapiro [44] used structured induction for the classification of a fairly complex chess endgame and demonstrated that the complexity and comprehensiveness ("brain-compatibility") of the obtained solution was superior to the unstructured one. Shapiro was helped by a chess master to structure his problem domain. Typically, applications of structured induction involve a manual development of the hierarchy and a manual selection and classification of examples to induce the subconcept classification rules; usually this is a tiresome process that requires an active availability of a domain expert over long periods of time. Therefore, it would be very desirable to automate the problem decomposition task.

In this chapter we present a method for automatically developing a concept hierarchy from examples using function decomposition. The method is implemented in the program called HINT (Hierarchy INduction Tool) [53]. As an illustration of the effectiveness of this approach, we present here some motivating experimental results in reconstruction of Boolean functions from examples. Consider the learning of Boolean function y of five Boolean attributes $x_1, ..., x_5$:

$$y = (x_1 \text{ OR } x_2) \text{ XOR } (x_3 \text{ OR } (x_4 \text{ XOR } x_5))$$

Out of the complete 5-attribute space of 32 points, 24 points (75%) were randomly selected as examples for learning. The examples were stated as attribute-value vectors, hiding from HINT any underlying conceptual structure of the domain. In nine out of ten experiments with different randomly selected subsets of 24 examples, HINT found that the most appropriate structure of subconcepts is as shown in Figure 1. HINT also found a definition of the intermediate functions corresponding to:

$$f_1 = \text{OR}$$
$$f_2 = \text{XOR}$$
$$f_3 = \text{OR}$$
$$f_4 = \text{XOR}$$

G. Paliouras, V. Karkaletsis, and C.D. Spyropoulos (Eds.): ACAI'99, LNAI 2049, pp. 71–101, 2001.
© Springer-Verlag Berlin Heidelberg 2001

This corresponds to complete reconstruction of the target concept. It should be noted that HINT does not use any predefined repertoire of intermediate functions; the definitions of the four intermediate functions above were induced solely from the learning examples.

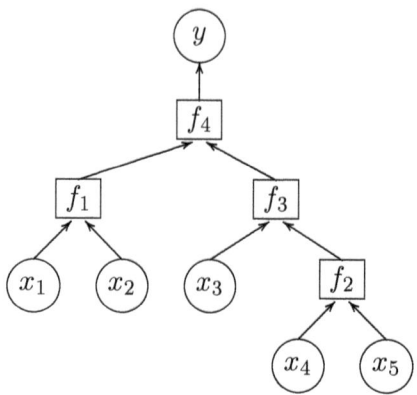

Fig. 1. Hierarchy of intermediate concepts induced by HINT for the example Boolean function.

The following results show how much the detection of a useful structure in data, like the one in Figure 1, helps in terms of classification accuracy on new data. "New data" in our case was the remaining 25% of the points (other than those 24 examples used for learning). The average accuracy on new data over the 10 experiments was 97.5% with standard deviation 7.9%. For a comparison with a "flat" learner (one that does not look for concept structure in data), the program C4.5 [35] was run on the same 10 data sets. Its accuracy was 60% with standard deviation 16.5%. This result is typical of the difference in performance between HINT and flat learners in similar domains where there exist useful concept hierarchies and illustrates dramatic effects of exploiting a possible structure in the domain. Further experiments with the HINT method are given later in the paper.

We present the HINT method in detail in Section 3. Before that, in Section 2, we review related work in function decomposition, structured induction and constructive induction. A reader not interested in this review can proceed immediately to Section 3.

2   Review of Function Decomposition Related to Machine Learning

The decomposition approach to machine learning was used early by a pioneer of artificial intelligence, A. Samuel. He proposed a method based on a *signature table system* [43] and used it as an evaluation mechanism for his checkers playing programs. A signature table system is a tree of input, intermediate, and a single output variable, and is essentially an identical representation of concept trees as used in this chapter. Signature tables define the intermediate concepts and use signatures (examples) that completely cover the attribute space. The value of an output variable is determined by a bottom-up derivation that first assigns the values to the intermediate variables, and finally derives the value of the output variable. Samuel used a manually defined concept structures with two layers of intermediate concepts. Learning was based on presenting a set of book moves to the concept hierarchy and adjusting the output values of the signatures according to the correlation coefficient computed from learning examples. Compared to his previous approach that was based on the learning of the coefficients in a linear evaluation polynomial [42], Samuel showed that the use of a signature table system significantly improves the performance. Samuel's approach was later studied and improved by Biermann et al. [2], but still required the concept structure to be given in advance.

While, within machine learning, Samuel and Biermann et al. may be the first to realize the power of using concept hierarchies, fundamentals of the approach that can discover such hierarchies were defined earlier in the area of switching circuit design. Curtis [10] reports that in the late 1940's and 1950's several switching circuit theorists considered this subject and in 1952 Ashenhurst reported on a unified theory of decomposition of switching functions [1]. The method proposed by Ashenhurst decomposes the truth table of a Boolean function to be realized with standard binary gates. Most of other related work of that time is reported and reprinted in [10], where Curtis compares the decomposition approach to other switching circuit design approaches and further formalizes and extends the decomposition theory. Besides a disjoint decomposition, where each variable can appear as input in just one of the derived tables, Curtis defines a non-disjoint decomposition where the resulting structure is an acyclic graph rather than a tree. Furthermore, Curtis defines a decomposition algorithm that aims at constructing a switching circuit of the lowest complexity, i.e., with the lowest number of gates used. Curtis' method is defined over two-valued variables and requires a set of examples that completely cover the attribute space.

Recently, the Ashenhurst-Curtis approach was substantially improved by research groups of M. A. Perkowski, T. Luba, and T. D. Ross. Perkowski and Uong [33] and Wan and Perkowski [49] propose a graph coloring approach to the decomposition of incompletely specified switching functions. A different approach is presented by Luba and Selvaraj [22]. Their decomposition algorithms are able to generalize in the same sense as examples are generalized in inductive learning. A generalization of function decomposition when applied to a set of simple Boolean functions was studied by Ross et al. [39] and Goldman [14]. The authors indicate that the decomposition approach to switching function design may be termed knowledge discovery as functions and features not previously anticipated can be discovered. A similar point, but using different terminology, was made already by Curtis [10], who observed that the same truth table representing a Boolean function might have different decompositions.

Function decomposition can be viewed as a way of constructing new features. In Figure 1, for example, a new feature was constructed as x_1 OR x_2. Feature discovery has been at large investigated by constructive induction, a recently active field within machine learning. The term was first used by Michalski [24], who defined it as an ability of the system to derive and use new attributes in the process of learning. Following this idea and perhaps closest to function decomposition are the constructive induction systems that use a set of constructive operators to derive new attributes. Examples of such systems are described in [23,34,37]. The main limitation of these approaches is that the set of constructive operators has to be defined in advance. Moreover, in constructive induction, the new features are primarily introduced for the purpose of improving the classification accuracy of the induced classifier, while the above described function decomposition approaches focused primarily on the reduction of complexity, where the impact on classification accuracy can be regarded rather as a side-effect of decomposition-based generalization. In first-order learning of relational concept descriptions, constructive induction is referred to as predicate invention. An overview of recent achievements in this area can be found in [46].

Decomposition with nominal-valued attributes and classes may be regarded as a straightforward extension of Ashenhurst-Curtis approach. Such an extension was described by Biermann et al. [2]. Alternatively, Luba [21] proposes a decomposition where multi-valued intermediate concepts are binarized. Files et al. [13] propose a decomposition approach for k-valued logic where both attributes and intermediate concepts take at most k values.

A concept structure as used in this chapter defines a declarative bias over the hypothesis space. Biermann et al. [2] showed that concept structure significantly limits the number of representable functions. This was also observed by Russel [40], who proved that tree-structured bias can reduce the size of concept language from doubly-exponential to singly exponential in the number of attributes. Tadepalli and Russel [47] show that such bias enables PAC-learning of tabulated functions within concept structure. Their approach for decomposition of Boolean functions requires the concept structure to be given in advance. Their learning algorithm differs from the function decomposition approaches in that it uses both examples and queries, i.e., asks the oracle for the class value of instances that are needed in derivation but not provided in the training examples. Similar to function decomposition, the learning algorithm of Tadepalli and Russel induces intermediate concepts that are lower in the hierarchy first. As with Ashenhurst-Curtis decomposition, the resulting classifiers are consistent with training examples. Queries are also used in PAC-learning described by Bshouty et al [8]. Their algorithm identifies both concept structures and their associated tabulated functions, but can deal only with Boolean functions with symmetric and constant fan-in gates. Within PAC-learning, Hancock et al. [15] learn non-overlapping perceptron networks from examples and membership queries. An excellent review of other related work in PAC-learning that uses structural bias and queries is given in [47].

Function decomposition is also related to construction of oblivious read-once decision graphs (OODG). OODGs are rooted, directed acyclic graphs that can be divided into levels [16]. All nodes at a level test the same attribute, and all edges that originate from one level terminate at the next level. Like with decision trees, OODG leaf nodes represent class values. OODGs can be regarded as a special case of decomposition, where decomposition structures are of the form $f_1(x_1, f_2(x_2, \ldots, f_n(x_n)))$ and where x_n is at the top of a decision graph and the number of nodes at each level equals the number of distinct output values used by corresponding function f_i. In fact, decision graphs were found as a good form of representation of examples to be used by decomposition [20,19, 13]. Within machine learning, the use of oblivious decision graphs was studied by Kohavi [16]. Graphs induced by his learning algorithm are consistent with training examples, and for incomplete data sets the core of the algorithm is a graph coloring algorithm similar to the one defined by Perkowski and Uong [33].

Of other machine learning approaches that construct concept hierarchies we here mention Muggleton's DUCE [28,29] which uses transformation operators to compress the given examples by successive generalization and feature construction. Nevill-Manning and Witten [31] describe SEQUITUR, an algorithm that infers a hierarchical structure from a sequence of discrete symbols. Although there are some similarities with function decomposition (e.g., maintaining consistency and induction of new features), DUCE and SEQUITUR are essentially different in both the algorithmic and representational aspects.

Within machine learning, there are other approaches based on problem decomposition, but where the problem is decomposed by an expert and not discovered by a machine. A well-known example is structured induction, introduced by Donald Michie and applied by Shapiro and Niblett [45] and Shapiro [44]. Their approach is based on a manual decomposition of the problem and an expert-assisted selection and classification of examples to construct rules for intermediate concepts in the hierarchy. In comparison with standard decision tree induction techniques, structured induction exhibits about the same classification accuracy with the increased transparency and lower complexity of the developed models. Michie [25] emphasized the important role of structured induction in the future and listed several real problems that had been solved in this way.

Mozetič [26,27,7] employed another scheme for structuring the learning problem. That approach was particularly aimed at automated construction of system models from input-output observations of the system's behavior. The structure of the learning problem, specified by a Prolog clause, corresponded to the physical structure of the modeled system in terms of the system's components and connections among them. In an experiment, a substantial part of a qualitative model of the heart was induced from examples of the behavior of the heart. It was shown that the structuring of the domain very significantly improved the effectiveness of learning compared to unstructured learning. Again, the structure of the system was specified by the user and not induced automatically.

Concept hierarchy has also been used in a multi-attribute decision support expert system shell DEX [6] which has its roots in DECMAK methodology [12, 3]. There, a tree-like structure of variables is defined by an expert, and several tools assist in the acquisition of decision rules. These are, like Samuel's signature tables, used to derive the values of intermediate and output variables. DEX also allows different representations of user-defined decision tables, including decision trees [44] and decision rules [38]. DEX has been applied in more than 50 real decision making problems.

The HINT method presented in detail in the next section essentially borrows from three different research areas: it shares the motivation with structured induction and structured approach to decision support, while the core of the method is based on Ashenhurst-Curtis function decomposition. Further technical details of this method can be found in [53].

3   Learning by Function Decomposition in HINT

The HINT method is based on function decomposition, an approach originally developed for the design of switching circuits [1,10]. The goal is to decompose a function $y = F(X)$ into $y = G(A, H(B))$, where X is a set of input attributes $x_1, \ldots, x_n$, and y is the class variable (Figure 2). F, G, and H are functions partially specified by examples, i.e., by sets of attribute-value vectors with assigned classes. A and B are subsets of input attributes such that $A \cup B = X$. The functions G and H are determined in the decomposition process and are not predefined in any way. Their joint complexity (determined by some complexity measure) should be lower than the complexity of F. Such a decomposition also discovers a new intermediate concept $c = H(B)$. Since decomposition can be applied recursively on H and G, the result in general is a hierarchy of concepts. For each concept in the hierarchy, there is a corresponding function (such as $H(B)$) that determines the dependency of that concept on its immediate descendants in the hierarchy.

A method for discovery of a concept hierarchy from an unstructured set of examples by function decomposition can be regarded as a process that comprises the following mechanisms:

Basic function decomposition step which, given a function $y = F(X)$ partially represented by examples E_F, and a partition of the attribute set X to sets A and B, finds the corresponding functions G and H, such that $y = G(A, c)$ and $c = H(B)$. The new functions are partially defined by examples E_G and E_H.

Attribute partition selection is a process which, given a function $y = F(X)$, examines candidate partitions of X to A and B and the corresponding functions G and H. It then selects the preferred partition of X to A and B that minimizes some complexity measure defined over G and H.

Overall function decomposition is then a recursive invocation of the above two operations on an initial example set that defines $y = F(X)$. In each step, the best attribute partition of X to A and B for $y = F(X)$ is selected. A

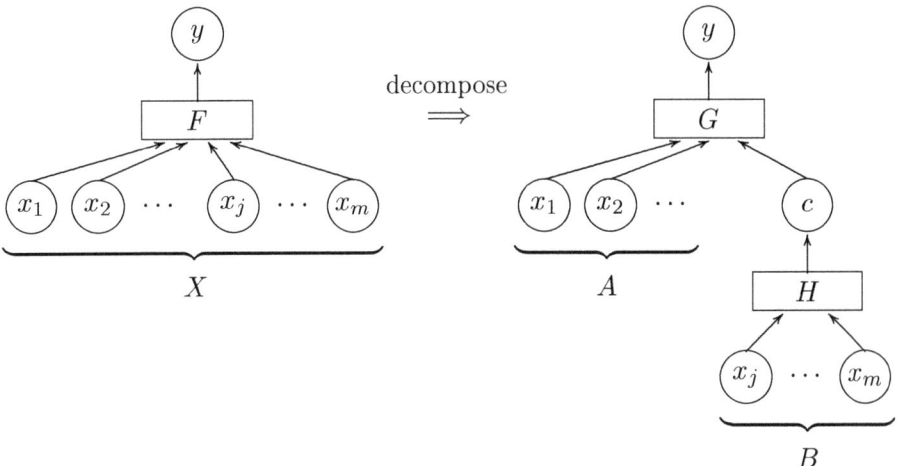

Fig. 2. Basic decomposition step.

function $y = F(X)$ is decomposed to $y = G(A, c)$ and $c = H(B)$ provided that G and H are overall less complex than F. If this is the case, this step is recursively repeated on newly constructed functions G and H.

Generalization usually occurs in the basic function decomposition step. When constructing example sets E_G and E_H, some points not included in E_F may be assigned a class value, thereby inductively generalizing the definition of F to points other than those explicitly stated in the examples E_F.

One of the most important problems with function decomposition is its time complexity. An algorithm for finding an optimal decomposition would consist of steps of exponential time complexity in the number of attributes. To cope with reasonably sized problems, these steps must be replaced by heuristic methods. The method presented here is "greedy" in the sense that it tries to optimize only a single step of the decomposition process; the whole discovered hierarchy, however, might not be optimal. The time complexity of splitting the attributes into sets A and B in a single decomposition step is reduced by bounding the size of B. For the task of determining the required number of values of a newly discovered concept c, which is equivalent to the graph coloring problem, we use a sub-optimal but efficient algorithm.

The decomposition method in HINT is limited to nominal-valued attributes and classes. It only uses disjoint partitions of attributes: $A \cap B = \emptyset$. This constrains the discovered concept hierarchies to concept trees. Furthermore, because of constraining the size of the bound set B to, say, b attributes, each internal node in the tree can have at most b descendants.

Although the function decomposition approach results in a tree, it should be noted that it is quite different from the well-known top down induction of decision trees [36]. In decision trees, nodes correspond to attributes and leaves correspond to classes. In function decomposition trees, nodes correspond to functions, and leaves correspond to attributes.

In this chapter we do not present the specific noise handling mechanism in HINT. Noise handling in HINT is described by Zupan [51] and Zupan et al. [54].

The remainder of this chapter starts with a detailed description of each of the above mentioned decomposition components (Sections 4, 5, and 6). A method that uses function decomposition to detect the redundancy of attributes and to select non-redundant and most relevant attributes is given in Section 7. Section 8 experimentally evaluates the decomposition method and in particular addresses its ability to generalize and to construct meaningful concept hierarchies. Section 9 gives conclusions and points to some directions for further research.

4   Basic Decomposition Step

Given a set of examples E_F that partially specify a function $y = F(X)$ and a partition of attributes X to subsets A and B, the *basic decomposition step* of F constructs the functions $y = G(A, c)$ and $c = H(B)$ (Figure 2). Functions G and H are partially specified by the example sets E_G and E_H, respectively, that are derived from and are consistent with the example set E_F. Example sets E_G and E_H are discovered in the decomposition process and are not predefined in any way. X is a set of attributes $x_1, \ldots, x_m$, and A and B are a nontrivial disjoint partition of attributes in X, such that $A \cup B = X$, $A \cap B = \emptyset$, $A \neq \emptyset$, and $B \neq \emptyset$.

The decomposition requires both the input attributes $x_i \in X$ and class variable y to be nominal-valued with domains D_{x_i} and D_y, respectively. The cardinality of these domains, denoted by $|D_{x_i}|$ and $|D_y|$, is required to be finite. The set E_F is required to be consistent: no two examples may have the same attribute values and different class values.

As proposed by Curtis [10], we will use the names *free set* and *bound set* for attribute sets A and B, respectively, and use the notation $A|B$ for the partition of attributes X into these two sets. Before the decomposition, the concept y is defined by an example set E_F and after the decomposition it is defined by an example set E_G. Basic decomposition step discovers a new intermediate concept c which is defined by an example set E_H. We first present an example of such a decomposition and then define the method for basic decomposition step.

Example 1 Consider a function $y = F(x_1, x_2, x_3)$ where x_1, x_2, and x_3 are attributes and y is the target concept. The domain of y, x_1, and x_2 is {lo, med, hi} and the domain for x_3 is {lo, hi}. The function F is partially specified with a set of examples shown in Table 1.

Consider the decomposition $y = G(x_1, H(x_2, x_3))$, i.e., a decomposition with attribute partition $\langle x_1 \rangle | \langle x_2, x_3 \rangle$. This is given in Figure 3. The following can be observed:

- The new concept hierarchy is consistent with the original example set. This can be verified by classifying each example in E_F. For instance, for attribute

Table 1. Set of examples that partially define the function $y = F(x_1, x_2, x_3)$.

x_1	x_2	x_3	y
lo	lo	lo	lo
lo	lo	hi	lo
lo	med	lo	lo
lo	med	hi	med
lo	hi	lo	lo
lo	hi	hi	hi
med	med	lo	med
med	hi	lo	med
med	hi	hi	hi
hi	lo	lo	hi
hi	hi	lo	hi

values $x_1 = \mathtt{med}$, $x_2 = \mathtt{med}$, and $x_3 = \mathtt{low}$, we derive $c = 1$ and $y = \mathtt{med}$, which is indeed the same as the value of $F(\mathtt{med}, \mathtt{med}, \mathtt{lo})$.

- The example sets E_G and E_H are overall smaller than the original E_F and also easier to interpret. We can see that the new concept c corresponds to $\mathrm{MIN}(x_2, x_3)$, and E_G represents the function $\mathrm{MAX}(x_1, c)$.
- The decomposition generalizes some undefined entries of F. For example, $F(\mathtt{hi}, \mathtt{lo}, \mathtt{hi})$, which does not appear in example set E_F, is generalized to $\mathtt{hi}$ ($c = H(\mathtt{lo}, \mathtt{hi}) = 1$ and $y = G(\mathtt{hi}, 1) = \mathtt{hi}$).

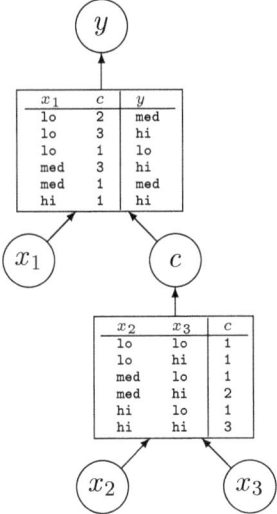

Fig. 3. Decomposition $y = G_1(x_1, H_1(x_2, x_3))$ of the example set from Table 1.

4.1   The Method

Let E_F be a set of examples that partially specify the function $y = F(X)$ and let $A|B$ be a partition of attributes X. The basic decomposition step derives new example sets E_G and E_H from E_F, such that they partially specify functions $y = G(A, c)$ and $c = H(B)$, respectively. Functions G and H are consistent with F, so that each example from E_F is classified equally by F and by its decomposition to G and H.

The decomposition starts with the derivation of a partition matrix. Given a partition of X to $A|B$, a *partition matrix* $\mathcal{P}_{A|B}$ is a tabular representation of example set E_F with each row corresponding to a distinct combination of values of attributes in A, and each column corresponding to a distinct combination of values of attributes in B. Each example $e_i \in E_F$ has its corresponding entry in $\mathcal{P}_{A|B}$ with row index $A(e_i)$ and column index $B(e_i)$. The elements of $\mathcal{P}_{A|B}$ with no corresponding examples in E_F are denoted by "-" and treated as *don't care*. A column a of $\mathcal{P}_{A|B}$ is called *non-empty* if there exists an example $e_i \in E_F$ such that $B(e_i) = a$.

An example partition matrix is given in Figure 4. Note that the columns represent all possible combinations of the values of the attributes in B. Each column thus denotes the behavior of F when the attributes in the bound set are constant. To find a function $c = H(B)$, it is necessary to find a corresponding value (label) for each non-empty column of the partition matrix.

	x_2	lo	lo	med	med	hi	hi
x_1	x_3	lo	hi	lo	hi	lo	hi
lo		lo	lo	lo	med	lo	hi
med		-	-	med	-	med	hi
hi		hi	-	-	-	hi	-

c	1	1	1	2	1	3

Fig. 4. Partition matrix for the example set from Table 1 and the attribute partition $\langle x_1 \rangle | \langle x_2, x_3 \rangle$. The bottom row shows the column labels (values of c for combinations of x_2 and x_3) obtained by the coloring of incompatibility graph.

Columns that exhibit non-contradicting behavior are called *compatible*. Columns a and b of partition matrix $\mathcal{P}_{A|B}$ are *compatible* if $F(e_i) = F(e_j)$ for every pair of examples $e_i, e_j \in E_F$ with $A(e_i) = A(e_j)$ and $B(e_i) = a$, $B(e_j) = b$. The number of such pairs is called *degree of compatibility* between columns a and b and is denoted by $d(a, b)$. The columns not being compatible are *incompatible* and their degree of compatibility is zero.

Example sets E_G and E_H are consistent with E_F only if E_H is derived from labeled partition matrix $\mathcal{P}_{A|B}$ so that no two incompatible columns are labeled with the same label. Zupan *et al.* [53] prove that this is a necessary condition for consistency.

Let us define a partition matrix to be *properly labeled* if the same label is not used for mutually incompatible columns. Below we introduce a method that constructs E_G and E_H that are consistent with E_F and derived from any properly labeled partition matrix. The labeling preferred by decomposition is the one that introduces the fewest distinct labels, i.e., the one that defines the smallest domain for intermediate concepts c. Finding such labeling corresponds to finding the lowest number of groups of mutually compatible columns. This number is called *column multiplicity* and is denoted by $\nu(A|B)$.

Column incompatibility graph $\mathcal{I}_{A|B}$ is a graph where each non-empty column of $\mathcal{P}_{A|B}$ is represented by a vertex. Two vertices are connected if and only if the corresponding columns are incompatible. The partition matrix column multiplicity $\nu(A|B)$ is then the number of colors needed to color the incompatibility graph $\mathcal{I}_{A|B}$. Namely, the proper coloring guarantees that two vertices representing incompatible columns are not assigned the same color. The same colors are only assigned to the columns that are compatible. Therefore, the optimal coloring discovers the lowest number of groups of compatible $\mathcal{P}_{A|B}$ columns, and thus induces the assignment of y to every non-empty column of $\mathcal{P}_{A|B}$ such that $|D_c|$ is minimal. An example of colored incompatibility graph is given in Figure 5.

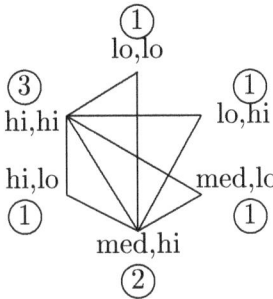

Fig. 5. Incompatibility graph for the partition $\langle x_1 \rangle | \langle x_2, x_3 \rangle$ and the partition matrix of Figure 4. Numbers in circles represent different colors (labels) of vertices.

Graph coloring is an NP-hard problem and the computation time of an exhaustive search algorithm is prohibitive even for small graphs with about 15 vertices. Instead of optimal coloring, a heuristic approach should be used. For proper labeling of partition matrix, an efficient heuristic algorithm called Color Influence Method was proposed by Perkowski and Uong [33] and Wan and Perkowski [49]. They empirically showed that the method generates solutions close to optimal. Essentially, Color Influence Method uses similar idea to a heuristic algorithm for graph coloring by Welsh and Powell [50], which sorts the vertices by their decreasing connectivity and then assigns to each vertex a color that is different from the colors of its neighbors so that the minimal number of colors is used. We use the same coloring method, with the following improvement: when a color is to be assigned to vertex v and several compatible vertices have already been colored with different colors, the color is chosen that is used for a group of colored vertices $v_1, \ldots, v_k$ that are *most compatible* to v. The degree of compatibility is estimated as $\sum_{i=1}^{k} d(v, v_i)$.

Each vertex in $\mathcal{I}_{A|B}$ denotes a distinct combination of values of attributes in B, and its label (color) denotes a value of c. It is therefore straightforward to derive an example set E_H from the colored $\mathcal{I}_{A|B}$. The attribute set for these examples is B. Each vertex in $\mathcal{I}_{A|B}$ is an example in set E_H. Color c of the vertex is the class of the example.

Example set E_G is derived as follows. For any value of c and combination of values a of attributes in A, $y = G(a, c)$ is determined by looking for an example e_i in row $a = A(e_i)$ and in any column labeled with the value of c. If such an example exists, an example with attribute values $A(e_i)$ and c and class $y = F(e_i)$ is added to E_G.

Decomposition generalizes every undefined ("-") element of $\mathcal{P}_{A|B}$ in row a and column b, if a corresponding example e_i with $a = A(e_i)$ and column $B(e_i)$ with the same label as column b is found. For example, an undefined element $\mathcal{P}_{A|B}[\texttt{<hi>},\texttt{<lo,hi>}]$ of the first partition matrix in Figure 4 was generalized to hi because the column $\texttt{<lo,hi>}$ had the same label as columns $\texttt{<lo,lo>}$ and $\texttt{<hi,lo>}$.

4.2   Some Properties of Basic Decomposition Step

Here we give some properties of the basic decomposition step. We omit the proofs which rather obviously follow from the method of constructing examples sets E_G and E_H.

Property 1. The example sets E_G and E_H obtained by basic decomposition step are consistent with E_F, i.e., every example in E_F is correctly classified using the functions H and G.

Property 2. The partition matrix column multiplicity $\nu(A|B)$ obtained by optimal coloring of $\mathcal{I}_{A|B}$ is the lowest number of values for c to guarantee the consistency of example sets E_G and E_H with respect to example set E_F.

Property 3. Let N_G, N_H, and N_F be the numbers of examples in E_G, E_H, E_F, respectively. Decomposition derives E_G and E_H from E_F using the attribute partition $A|B$. Then, E_G and E_H use fewer or equal number of attributes than E_F ($|B| < |X|$ and $|A| + 1 \leq |X|$, where X is the initial attribute set) and include fewer or equal number of examples ($N_G \leq N_F$ and $N_H \leq N_F$).

4.3   Efficient Derivation of Incompatibility Graph

Most often, machine learning algorithms deal with sparse data sets. For these, the implementation using the partition matrix is memory inefficient. Instead, the incompatibility graph $\mathcal{I}_{A|B}$ can be derived directly from the example set E_F. An edge (v_i, v_j) of incompatibility graph $\mathcal{I}_{A|B}$ connects two vertices v_i and v_j if there exist examples $e_k, e_l \in E_F$ with $F(e_k) \neq F(e_l)$ such that $A(e_k) = A(e_l)$, $i =$

$B(e_k)$, and $j = B(e_l)$. We propose an algorithm that efficiently implements the construction of $\mathcal{I}_{A|B}$ using this definition. The algorithm first sorts the examples E_F based on the values of the attributes in A and the values of y. Sorting uses a combination of *radix* and *counting sort* [9], and thus runs $|A| + 1$ intermediate sorts of time complexity $|E_F|$. After sorting, the examples with the same $A(e_i)$ constitute consecutive groups that correspond to rows in partition matrix $\mathcal{P}_{A|B}$. Within each group, examples with the same value of y constitute consecutive subgroups. Each pair of examples from the same group and different subgroups has a corresponding edge in $\mathcal{I}_{A|B}$.

Again, E_H is derived directly from the colored $\mathcal{I}_{A|B}$. The sorted examples of E_F are then used to efficiently derive E_G. With coloring, each example from E_F has obtained a label (value of c). Each subgroup can contain examples assigned to different value of c. Now, for each subgroup, and each value of c used within this subgroup, we then make an example for E_G with the values of attributes in A and a value of c, and a value of y.

Example 2 For the example set from Table 1 and for the partition $\langle x_1 \rangle | \langle x_2, x_3 \rangle$, the examples sorted on the basis of the values of attributes in A and values of y are given in Table 2. The double lines delimit the groups and the single lines the subgroups. Now consider the two instances printed in bold. Their corresponding vertices in $\mathcal{I}_{A|B}$ are (lo,lo) and (med,hi). Because these instances are in the same group but in different subgroups, there is an edge in $\mathcal{I}_{A|B}$ connecting (lo,lo) and (med,hi). □

Table 2. Examples from Table 1 sorted by x_1 and y.

x_1	x_2	x_3	y
lo	lo	lo	lo
lo	lo	hi	lo
lo	med	lo	lo
lo	hi	lo	lo
lo	**med**	**hi**	med
lo	hi	hi	hi
med	med	lo	med
med	hi	lo	med
med	hi	hi	hi
hi	lo	lo	hi
hi	hi	lo	hi

5   Partition Selection Measures

The basic decomposition step assumes that a partition of the attributes to free and bound sets is given. However, for each function F there can be many possible partitions, each one yielding a different intermediate concept c and a different pair of functions G and H. Among these partitions, we prefer those that lead to a simple concept c and functions G and H of low complexity.

Example 3 Consider again the example set from Table 1. Its decomposition that uses the attribute partition $\langle x_1 \rangle | \langle x_2, x_3 \rangle$ is shown in Figure 3. There are two other non-trivial attribute partitions $\langle x_2 \rangle | \langle x_1, x_3 \rangle$ and $\langle x_3 \rangle | \langle x_1, x_2 \rangle$ whose decompositions are given in Figure 6. Note that, compared to these two decompositions, the first decomposition yields less complex and more comprehensible data sets. While we could interpret the data sets of the first decomposition (concepts MIN and MAX), the interpretation of concepts for other two decompositions is harder. Note also that these two decompositions both discover intermediate concepts that use more values than the one in the first decomposition. Among the three attribute partitions it is therefore best to decide for $\langle x_1 \rangle | \langle x_2, x_3 \rangle$ and decompose $y = F(x_1, x_2, x_3)$ to $y = G_1(x_1, c_1)$ and $c_1 = H_1(x_2, x_3)$). □

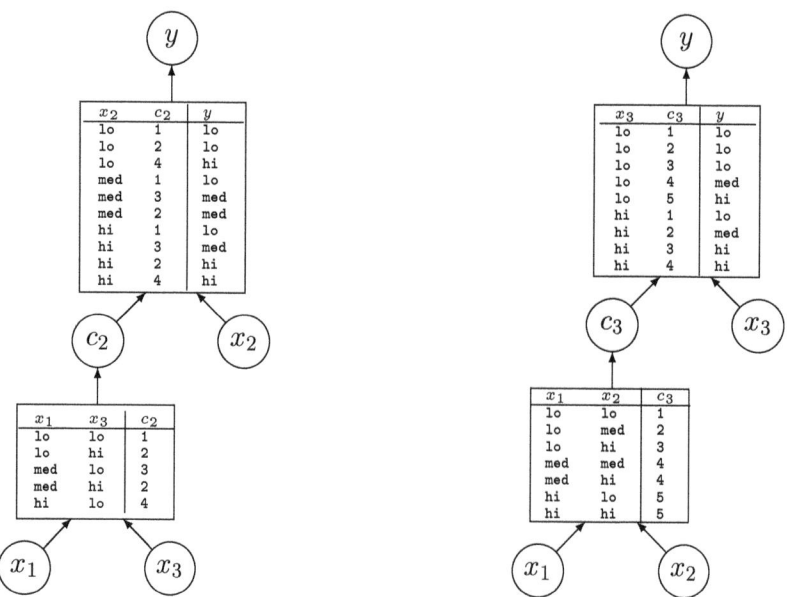

Fig. 6. The decompositions $y = G_2(x_2, H_2(x_1, x_3))$ and $y = G_3(x_3, H_3(x_1, x_2))$ of the example set from Table 1.

We introduce a *partition selection measure* $\psi(A|B)$ that estimates the complexity of decomposition of F to G and H using the attribute partition $A|B$. The best partition is the one that minimizes $\psi(A|B)$. Here we mention three partition selection measures, one based on column multiplicity of partition matrix and the remaining two based on the amount of information needed to represent the functions G and H. The three measures are experimentally compared in [53].

Our simplest partition selection measure, denoted ψ_ν, is column multiplicity. It is defined as the number of values required for the new feature c. That is, when decomposing F, a set of candidate partitions is examined and one that yields c with the smallest set of possible values is selected for decomposition. The number of required values for c is equal to column multiplicity of partition matrix $\mathcal{P}_{A|B}$, so:

$$\psi_\nu(A|B) = \nu(A|B)$$

Note that $\nu(A|B)$ also indirectly affects the size of instance space that defines G. The smaller the $\nu(A|B)$, the less complex the function G.

The idea for this measure came from practical experience with decision support system DEX [6]. There, a hierarchical system of decision tables is constructed manually. In more than 50 real-life applications it was observed that in order to alleviate the construction and interpretation, the designers consistently developed functions that define concepts with a small number of values. In most cases, they used intermediate concepts with 2 to 5 values.

Example 4 For the partitions in Figure 4, ψ_ν is 3, 4, and 5, respectively. As expected, the best partition according to ψ_ν is $\langle x_1 \rangle | \langle x_2, x_3 \rangle$.   □

Another idea is to consider the complexity of functions as a partition selection measure. The complexity of a function can be measured as the amount of information needed to encode the function. Let $I(F)$ denote the minimal number of bits needed to encode some function F. Then, the best partition is the one that minimizes the overall complexity of newly discovered functions H and G, i.e., the partition with minimal $I(H)+I(G)$. Estimating I can be done in various ways. Two of them are explored in [53]: the first one, denoted with ψ_s, takes into account only the attribute-class space size of the functions, while the second one additionally considers specific constraints imposed by the decomposition over the functions. Further, complicated refinements are possible (proposed by other authors and also mentioned in [53]). However, experimental comparison of these measures does not justify the complications involved (see [53] for details). Therefore, we recommend the simple column multiplicity as the most practical and effective partition selection measure.

6   Overall Function Decomposition

The decomposition aims to discover a hierarchy of concepts defined by example sets that are overall less complex than the initial one. Since an exhaustive search is prohibitively complex, the decomposition uses a suboptimal greedy algorithm.

6.1   Decomposition Algorithm

The overall decomposition algorithm (Algorithm 1) applies the basic decomposition step over the evolving example sets in a concept hierarchy, starting with a single non-structured example set. The algorithm keeps a list $\mathcal{E}$ of constructed example sets, which initially contains a complete training set E_{F_0}.

Input: Set of examples E_{F_0} describing a single output concept
Output: Its hierarchical decomposition
initialize $\mathcal{E} \leftarrow \{E_{F_0}\}$
initialize $j \leftarrow 1$
while $\mathcal{E} \neq \emptyset$
    arbitrarily select $E_{F_i} \in \mathcal{E}$ that partially specifies $c_i = F_i(x_1, \ldots, x_m)$, $i < j$
    $\mathcal{E} \leftarrow \mathcal{E} \setminus \{E_{F_i}\}$
    $A_{best}|B_{best} = \arg\min_{A|B} \psi(A|B)$,
        where $A|B$ runs over all possible partitions of $X = <x_1, \ldots, x_m>$
        such that $A \cup B = X$, $A \cap B = \emptyset$, and $|B| \leq b$
    if E_{F_i} is decomposable using $A_{best}|B_{best}$ **then**
        decompose E_{F_i} to E_G and E_{F_j}, such that $c_i = G(A_{best}, c_j)$ and
        $c_j = F_j(B_{best})$ and E_G and E_{F_j} partially specify G and F_j, respectively
        $E_{F_i} \leftarrow E_G$
        if $|A_{best}| > 1$ **then** $\mathcal{E} \leftarrow \mathcal{E} \cup \{E_{F_i}\}$ **end if**
        if $|B_{best}| > 2$ **then** $\mathcal{E} \leftarrow \mathcal{E} \cup \{E_{F_j}\}$ **end if**
        $j \leftarrow j + 1$
    end if
end while

Algorithm 1   Decomposition algorithm

In each step (the **while** loop) the algorithm arbitrarily selects an example set E_{F_i} from $\mathcal{E}$ which belongs to a single node in the evolving concept hierarchy. The algorithm tries to decompose E_{F_i} by evaluating all candidate partitions of its attributes. To limit the complexity, the candidate partitions are those with the cardinality of the bound set less than or equal to a user defined parameter b. For all such partitions, the partition selection measure is determined and the best partition $A_{best}|B_{best}$ is selected accordingly. Next, the decomposition determines if the best partition would result in two new example sets of lower complexity than the example set E_{F_i} being decomposed. If this is the case, E_{F_i} is called *decomposable* and is replaced by two new example sets. This decomposition step is then repeated until a concept structure is found that includes only non-decomposable example sets.

To decompose a function further or not is determined by the *decomposability criterion*. Suppose that we are decomposing a function F and its best attribute partition would yield functions G and H. Then, either one of the information-based complexity measures presented in Section 5 can be used to determine the number of bits $I(F)$, $I(G)$, and $I(H)$ to encode the three functions, where the method to compute $I(F)$ is the same as for $I(G)$. The decomposability criterion is then $I(G) + I(H) < I(F)$.

Note that because ψ_ν is not based on function complexity, it can not be similarly used as decomposability criterion. Therefore, when using ψ_ν as a partition selection measure, an information-based complexity measures is used to determine decomposability.

Example 5 Table 3 shows the application of decomposability criterion ψ_s on the example set from Table 1. This criterion only allows the decomposition with $\langle x_1 \rangle | \langle x_2, x_3 \rangle$.   □

Table 3. Complexity measures and decomposability for partitions of Figure 4 and 6.

	$\langle x_1 \rangle | \langle x_2, x_3 \rangle$		$\langle x_2 \rangle | \langle x_1, x_3 \rangle$		$\langle x_3 \rangle | \langle x_1, x_2 \rangle$	
	$I(G) + I(H)$	$I(F)$	$I(G) + I(H)$	$I(F)$	$I(G) + I(H)$	$I(F)$
ψ_s	23.7	28.5 ✔	31.0	28.5 ✗	36.7	28.5 ✗

6.2   Complexity of Decomposition Algorithm

The time complexity of a single step decomposition of E_F to E_G and E_H, which consists of sorting E_F and deriving and coloring the incompatibility graph is $O(Nn_c) + O(Nk) + O(k^2)$, where N is the number of examples in E_F, k is the number of vertices in $\mathcal{I}_{A|B}$, and n_c is the maximum cardinality of attribute domains and domains of constructed intermediate concepts. For any bound set B, the upper bound of k is

$$k_{max} = n_c^b$$

where $b = |B|$. The number of disjoint partitions considered by decomposition when decomposing E_F with n attributes is

$$\sum_{j=2}^{b} \binom{n}{j} \le \sum_{j=2}^{b} n^j \le (b-1)n^b = O(n^b)$$

The highest number of $n-2$ decompositions is required when the hierarchy is a binary tree, where n is the number of attributes in the initial example set. The time complexity of the decomposition algorithm is thus

$$O\left((Nn_c + Nk_{max} + k_{max}^2) \sum_{m=3}^{n} m^b\right) = O\left(n^{b+1}(Nn_c + Nk_{max} + k_{max}^2)\right)$$

Therefore, the algorithm's complexity is polynomial in N and n, and exponential in b (k_{max} is exponential in b). Note that the bound b is a user-defined parameter. This analysis clearly illustrates the benefits of setting b to a sufficiently low value. In our experiments, b was usually set to 3.

7 Attribute Redundancy and Decomposition-Based Attribute Subset Selection

When applying a basic decomposition step to a function $y = F(X)$ using some attribute partition $A|B$, an interesting situation occurs when the resulting function $c = H(B)$ is constant, i.e., when $|D_c| = 1$. For such a decomposition, the intermediate concept c can be removed as it does not influence the value of y. Thus, the attributes in B are *redundant*, and $y = F(X)$ can be consistently represented with $y = G(A)$, which is a decomposition-constructed function $G(A, c)$ with c removed.

Such decomposition-discovered redundancy may well indicate a true attribute redundancy. However, especially with the example sets that sparsely cover the attribute space, this redundancy may also be due to undersampling: the defined entries in partition matrix are sparse and do not provide the evidence for incompatibility of any two columns. In such cases, several bound sets yielding intermediate concepts with $|D_c| = 1$ may exist, thus misleading the partition selection measures to prefer partitions with redundant bound sets instead of those that include attributes that really define some underlying concept.

To overcome this problem, we propose an example set preprocessing by means of attribute subset selection which removes the redundant attributes. The resulting example set is then further used for decomposition. Attributes are removed one at the time, their redundancy being determined by the following definition: an attribute a_j is *redundant* for a function $y = F(X) = F(a_1, \ldots, a_n)$, if for the partition of attributes X to $A|B$ such that $B = \langle a_j \rangle$ and $A = X \setminus \langle a_j \rangle$, the column multiplicity of partition matrix $\mathcal{P}_{A|B}$ is $\nu(A|B) = 1$.

Figure 7 provides an example of the discovery and removal of a redundant attribute. The original data set (left) was examined for redundancy of attribute a_3 by constructing a corresponding partition matrix (center). Since the two columns for $a_3 = \texttt{lo}$ and $a_3 = \texttt{hi}$ are compatible, a_3 can be reduced to a constant and can thus be removed (right).

Besides attribute redundancy, we also define redundancy in attribute values: an attribute a_j has redundant values if for a function $y = F(X) = F(a_1, \ldots, a_n)$ and for a partition of X to $A|B$ such that $B = \langle a_j \rangle$ and $A = X \setminus \langle a_j \rangle$, the column multiplicity of partition matrix $\mathcal{P}_{A|B}$ is lower than $|D_j|$.

By this definition, such an attribute can be replaced by an attribute $a'_j = H(a_j)$, and a function $y = G(A, a'_j)$ may be used instead of $y = F(X)$. An example of such attribute replacement is given in Figure 8. Since an example set E_H may itself be of interest and point out some regularities in data, it is included in the representation and a'_j is treated as an intermediate concept.

It should be noted that not all redundancies according to these definitions may simply be removed. For example, after removing a redundant attribute from X, other redundant attributes may become non redundant. Therefore, redundant attributes are processed one at a time in the reverse order of their relevance. Given an initial example set, redundancy and relevance of the attributes is determined. Next, the least relevant attribute is selected, and its redundancy removed by either removing the attribute or replacing it by a corresponding attribute with

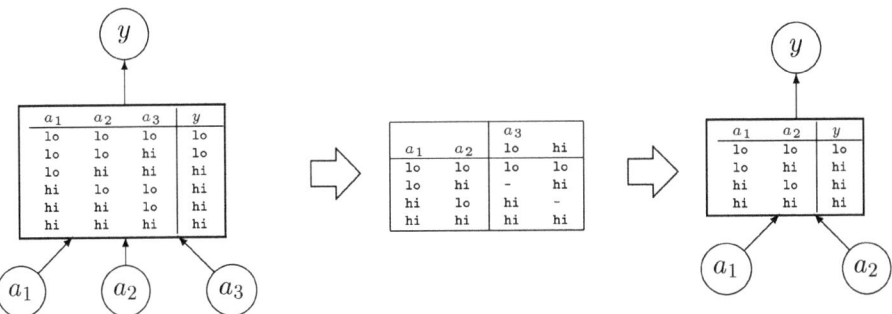

Fig. 7. Discovery of redundant attribute a_3 and its removal from the training set.

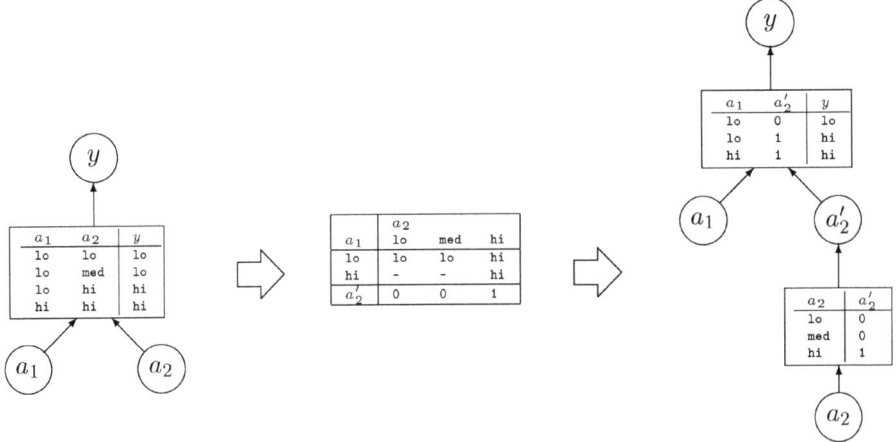

Fig. 8. Replacement of attribute a_2 with a corresponding attribute a_2'. Note that $|a_2'| < |a_2|$.

fewer values, whichever appropriate. The process is then repeated on the new example set, until no more redundancies are found. The greedy feature selection approach described here can be rightfully criticized because it tends towards local optimization only. However, due to the combinatorial complexity of global optimization, similar greedy approaches are still commonly used.

To estimate the relevance of attributes, we use the ReliefF algorithm as proposed by Kononenko [17]. This particular algorithm is used due to its advantages over other impurity functions usually used in inductive learning algorithms [18]. ReliefF estimates the attributes according to how well they distinguish among the instances that are close to each other and belong to different class. The relevance of attribute a is then

$$W(a) = P(\text{different value of } a \mid k-\text{nearest instances from different class}) -$$
$$P(\text{different value of } a \mid k-\text{nearest instances from same class})$$

We use the version of ReliefF which determines the attribute's relevance based on at most 200 randomly selected examples from the training set, and which for every example examines $k = 5$ nearest instances of the same class and k nearest instances of different class. The distance between two examples is measured as the number of attributes in which these two examples differ. Probabilities are estimated by relative frequencies. For further details of the ReliefF algorithm see [17].

8   Experimental Evaluation

This section attempts to evaluate HINT and the underlying methods from the aspects of generalization and discovery of concept hierarchies. For this purpose, several data sets are used for which either the underlying concepts hierarchy is known or anticipated, or unknown. The latter data sets are considered only for the evaluation of generalization.

First, the data sets on which experiments were performed are introduced. This is followed by an assessment of generalization and evaluation of HINT's capabilities to discover meaningful concept hierarchies.

8.1   Data Sets

Three types of data set were used: (1) artificial data sets with known underlying concepts, (2) real-life data sets taken mostly from UCI Repository of machine learning databases [30], and (3) data sets derived from hierarchical decision support models developed with the DEX methodology. To distinguish among them, we will refer to these data sets as *artificial, repository,* and *DEX data sets.* Their basic characteristics are given in Table 4.

The artificial data sets are PALINDROME, PARITY, MONK1, and MONK2. PALINDROME is a palindrome function over six 3-valued attributes. PARITY is defined as XOR over five binary attributes; the other five attributes in this domain are irrelevant. MONK1 and MONK2 are well known six-attribute binary classification problems [30,48] that use 2 to 4-valued attributes. MONK1 has an underlying concept $x_1 = x_2$ OR $x_5 = 1$, and MONK2 the concept $x = 1$ for exactly two choices of attributes $x \in \{x_1, \ldots, x_6\}$.

VOTE is a real-world database as given with Quinlan's C4.5 package [35] that includes example votes by U.S. House of Representatives Congressmen. The votes are simplified to yes, no, or unknown. PROMOTERS, SPLICE and MUSHROOM were all obtained from the UCI Repository [30]. PROMOTERS describes E. coli promoter gene sequences and classifies them according to biological promoter activity. Given a position in the middle of a window of 60 DNA sequence elements, instances in SPLICE are classified to donors, acceptors, or neither. Given an attribute-value description of a mushroom, the class of MUSHROOM instances is either edible or poisonous. Common to all four data sets is that they include only nominal attributes. Only MUSHROOM includes instances with undefined attributes, which were for the purpose of this study removed. As the

Table 4. Basic characteristics of data sets.

data set	#class	#atts.	#val/att.	#examples	maj. class (%)
PALINDROME	2	6	3.0	729	96.3
PARITY	2	10	2.0	1024	50.0
MONK1	2	6	2.8	432	50.0
MONK2	2	6	2.8	432	67.1
VOTE	2	16	3.0	435	61.4
PROMOTERS	2	57	4.0	106	50.0
SPLICE	3	60	8.0	3191	50.0
MUSHROOM	2	22	-	5644	61.8
CAR	4	6	3.5	1728	70.0
NURSERY	5	8	3.4	12960	33.3
HOUSING	9	12	2.9	5000	29.9
BREAST	4	12	2.8	5000	41.5
EIS	5	14	3.0	10000	59.0
BANKING	3	17	2.2	5000	40.8

concept hierarchies for these data sets are unknown to us and neither could we anticipate them, these data sets were only used for the study of generalization. That is, we were interested in HINT's accuracy on test data.

The remaining six data sets were obtained from multi-attribute decision models originally developed using DEX [6]. DEX models are hierarchical, so both the structure and intermediate concepts for these domains are known. The formalisms used to describe the resulting model and its interpretation are essentially the same as those derived by decomposition. This makes models developed by DEX ideal benchmarks for the evaluation of decomposition. Additional convenience of DEX examples is the availability of the decision support expert (Marko Bohanec) who was involved in the development of the models, for the evaluation of comprehensibility and appropriateness of the structures discovered by decomposition.

Six different DEX models were used. CAR is a model for evaluating cars based on their price and technical characteristics. This simple model was developed for educational purposes and is described in [5]. NURSERY is a real-world model developed to rank applications for nursery schools [32]. HOUSING is a model to determine the priority of housing loans applications [4]. This model is a part of a management decision support system for allocating housing loans that has been used since 1991 in the Housing Fund of Slovenia. BANKING, EIS and BREAST are three previously unpublished models for the evaluation of business partners in banking, evaluation of executive information systems, and breast-cancer risk assessment, respectively.

Each DEX model was used to obtain either 5000 or 10000 attribute-value instances with corresponding classes as derived from the model such that the class distribution was equal as in the data set that would completely cover the attribute space. We have decided for either 5000 or 10000 examples because within this range HINT's behavior was found to be most relevant and diverse. The only exception is CAR where 1728 instances completely cover the attribute space.

8.2 Generalization

Here we study how the size of the training set affects HINT's ability to find a correct generalization. We construct learning curves by a variant of 10-fold cross-validation. In 10-fold cross validation, the data is divided to 10 subsets, of which 9 are used for training and the remaining one for testing. The experiment is repeated 10 times, each time using a different testing subset. Stratified splits are used, i.e., the class distribution of the original data set and training and test sets are essentially the same. In our case, instead of learning from all examples from 9 subsets, only p percent of training instances from 9 subsets are randomly selected for learning, where p ranges from 10% to 100% in 10% steps. This adaptation of the standard method was necessary to keep test sets independent and compare classifiers as proposed in [41]. Note that when $p = 100\%$, this method is equivalent to the standard stratified 10-fold cross-validation.

HINT derived a concept hierarchy and corresponding classifier using the examples in the training set. The hierarchy was tested for classification accuracy on the test set. For each p, the results are the average of 10 independent experiments. The attribute subset selection was done on a training set as described in Section 7. The resulting set of examples was then used to induce a concept hierarchy. HINT used the column multiplicity as a partition selection measure and determined the decomposability based on our first information-based measure ψ_ν (Section 5). The bound set size b was limited to three.

The concept hierarchy obtained from training set was used to classify the instances in the test set. The instance's class value was obtained by bottom-up derivation of intermediate concepts. For each intermediate concept, its example set may or may not include the appropriate example to be used for classification. In the latter case, the *default rule* was used that assigns the value of most frequent class in the example set that defines the intermediate concept.

We compare HINT's learning curve to the one obtained by C4.5 inductive decision tree learner [35] run on the same data. As is the case with HINT, C4.5 was also required to induce a decision tree consistent with the training set. Hence, C4.5 used the default options except for -m1 (minimal number of instances in leaves was set to 1) and the classification accuracy was evaluated on unpruned decision trees. For several data sets, we have observed that subsetting (option -s) obtains a more accurate classifier: the learning curves for C4.5 were then developed both with and without subsetting, and the better one of the two was used for comparison with HINT. For each p, a binomial test [41] was used to test for significant differences between the methods using $\alpha = 0.01$ (99% confidence level).

The learning curves are shown in Figures 9 and 10. Drawing symbols are ∘ for HINT and ⋄ for C4.5. Where the difference is significant, the symbol for

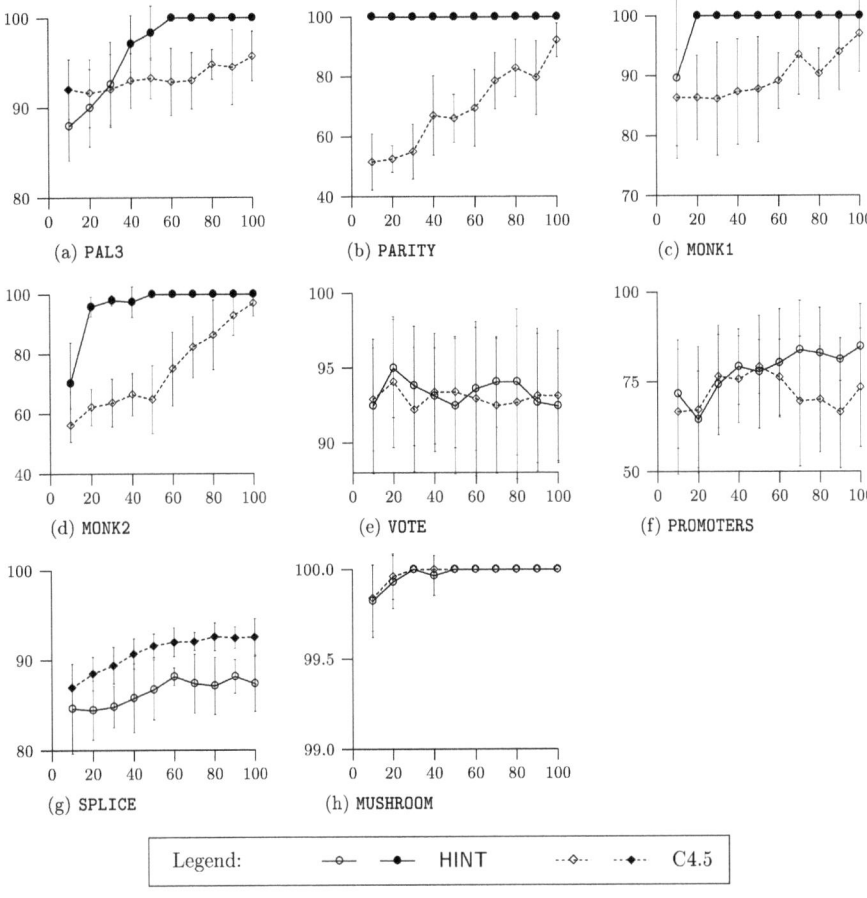

Fig. 9. Learning curves for artificial and repository datasets.

the better classifier is filled (● for HINT and ◆ for C4.5). The following can be observed:

- In general, for artificial data sets HINT performs significantly better than C4.5. For all four domains HINT's classification accuracy converges to 100% as the training set sizes increase. The percentage of instances needed to reach 100% accuracy varies between domains from 10% to 60%. Note that C4.5 never reaches the 100% classification accuracy.
- For VOTE, PROMOTERS, and MUSHROOM the differences are not significant, while for SPLICE C4.5 performs better. Only for MUSHROOM both classifiers reached the maximum accuracy.
- Common for all six DEX domains is that with small training sets HINT performs similar or worse than C4.5, while when increasing the training set size it gains the advantage and finally reaches the classification accuracy of close to or exactly 100%.

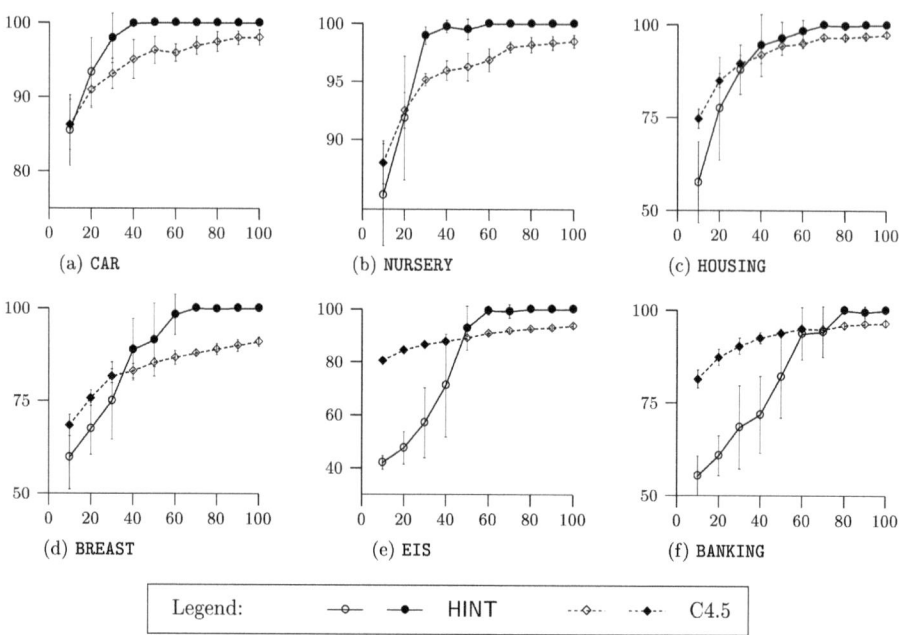

Fig. 10. Learning curves for DEX datasets.

Note that for DEX and most of the artificial data sets, there exist useful concept structures in the form of concept trees. Given sufficient training instances, it is exactly in these domains where HINT outperforms C4.5. Repository data sets do not necessarily have such characteristics, which may be the reason why for these domains HINT's performance is worse. For example, the domain theory given with the SPLICE data set [30] mentions several potentially useful intermediate concepts that share attributes. Thus these concepts form a concept *lattice* rather than a concept tree, and therefore can not be discovered by HINT. Furthermore, DEX and artificial data sets indicate that although a domain possesses a proper structure discoverable by decomposition, HINT needs a sufficient number of training examples to induce good classifiers: HINT's performance suffers from undersampling more than C4.5's.

The number of attributes used in concept hierarchies depends on attribute subset selection (training data preprocessing by removing redundant attributes). This further depends on the existence of irrelevant attributes and on the coverage of attribute space by training set. Figure 11 illustrates that with increasing coverage the number of attributes in induced structures increases and, in general, converges to a specific number of most relevant and non-redundant attributes. Interestingly, for PARITY and MONK1 domain HINT finds, as expected, that only 5 and 3 attributes are relevant, respectively. HINT converges to the use of about 10 attributes for VOTE, 12 for SPLICE, and 5 for MUSHROOM. For all DEX domains,

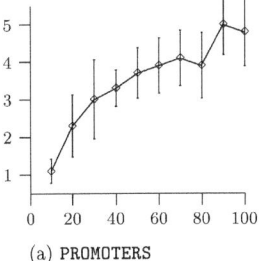
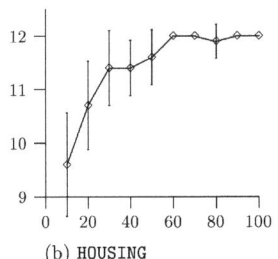
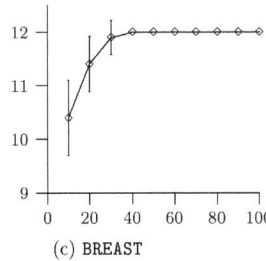

(a) PROMOTERS   (b) HOUSING   (c) BREAST

Fig. 11. Number of attributes used in concept hiearchy as a function of training set size.

with sufficiently large training sets HINT does not remove any of the attributes – this was expected since all attributes in these domains are relevant.

The use of default rule for classification had a minor impact on classification accuracy. This holds even for the smallest training sets, where 95% of instances were classified without firing the default rule. In most cases, with increasing training set size this percentage monotonically increased to 100%.

8.3 Hierarchical Concept Structures

Induced concept structures were compared to those anticipated for artificial and DEX domains. For each of these, HINT converged to a single concept structure when increasing the training set size. For PALINDROME and PARITY, HINT induced expected structures of the forms $(x_1 = x_6$ AND $x_2 = x_5)$ AND $(x_3 = x_4)$ and x_1 XOR $((x_2$ XOR $x_3)$ XOR $(x_4$ XOR $x_5))$, respectively.

More interesting are the structures for MONK1 and MONK2. For MONK1, HINT develops a concept hierarchy (Figure 12) that (1) correctly excludes irrelevant attributes x_3, x_4, and x_6, (2) transforms x_5 to x'_5 by mapping four values of x_5 to only two values of x'_5, (3) includes an intermediate concept c and its tabular representation for $x_1 = x_2$, and (4) relates c and x'_5 with a tabular representation of the OR function. In other words, the resulting hierarchy correctly represents the target concept. For MONK2, although the discovered structure (Figure 13) does not directly correspond to the original concept definition, it correctly reformulates the target concept by introducing concepts that count the number of ones in their arguments. Also note that all attributes that have more than two values are replaced by new binary ones.

For all DEX domains HINT converged to concept hierarchies that were very similar to the original DEX models. A typical example is NURSERY, for which Figure 14 shows the original DEX model and the concept hierarchy discovered by HINT. Note that the two structures are actually the same except that some original DEX intermediate concepts were additionally decomposed. Similarities of the same type were also observed for other DEX domains.

For NURSERY, no attributes were removed by preprocessing and redundancies were found only in attributes' domains: applicant's social status **none** and **medium**

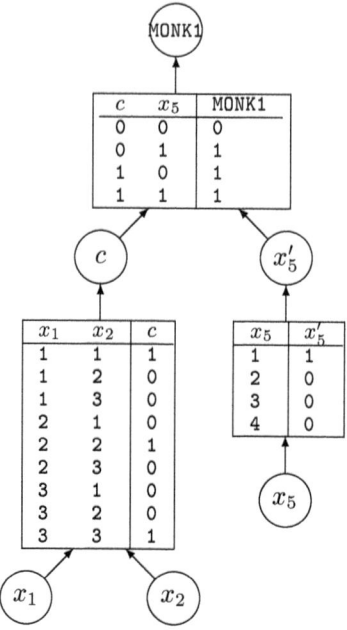

Fig. 12. MONK1 feature hierachy as discovered by HINT.

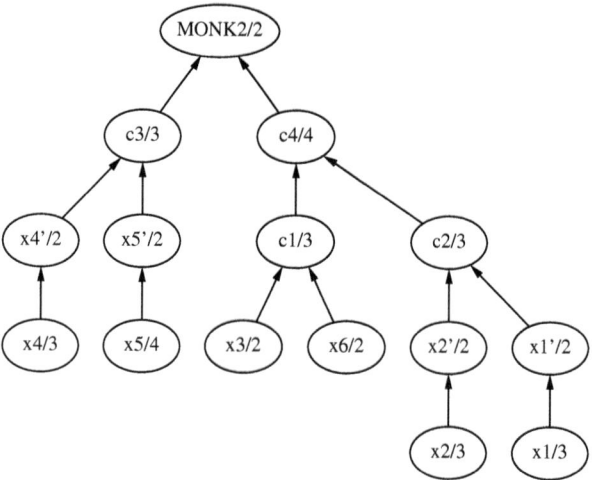

Fig. 13. The feature hierarchy discovered for MONK2. Each node gives a name of the feature and cardinality of its set of values.

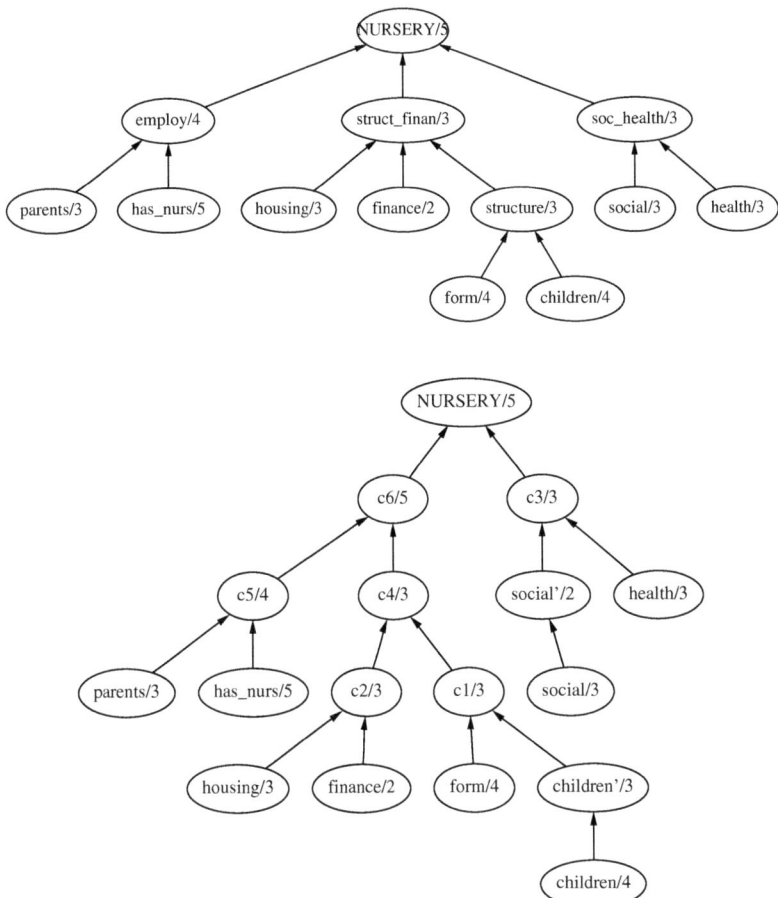

Fig. 14. Original (top) and discovered structure (bottom) for NURSERY.

were found equivalent, and there was no difference between a family having 3 or **more-than-3** children. Similar type of redundancies were also found in other DEX models. When a decision support expert that participated in the development of DEX models was asked to comment on these findings, he indeed recognized most of them as those that were intentionally used in DEX models with future extension and specialization of model functions in mind.

9   Conclusion

We presented an approach to machine learning based on function decomposition. A distinguishing feature of this approach is its capability to discover new intermediate concepts, organize them into a hierarchical structure, and induce the relationships between the attributes, newly discovered concepts, and the target concept. In their basic form, these relationships are specified by newly constructed example sets. In a way, the learning process can thus be viewed as a process of generating new, equivalent example sets, which are consistent with the original example set. The new sets are smaller, have smaller number of attributes, and introduce intermediate concepts. Generalization also occurs in this process.

We described experiments with the decomposition-based learning method on several data sets. In particular, we studied the accuracy of the induced descriptions by HINT and its capability to discover meaningful hierarchies. For all data sets where useful hierarchies existed, HINT significantly outperformed C4.5 and found relevant concept hierarchies, provided that enough examples were used for training. Experiments show that decomposition is more sensitive to undersampling and, especially in more complex data sets, C4.5 performed relatively better with small training sets. For other data sets, with no useful concept structure, C4.5 and HINT performed similarly in all but one domain.

In terms of the meaningfulness of discovered structures, the most significant experiments were those with DEX domains. For these domains HINT's task was to reconstruct the underlying concept hierarchy. We have observed that for all six domains investigated, HINT converges to concept hierarchies that are very similar or identical to those developed by human experts. It should be emphasized that we consider these similarities of concept structures as the most significant indicator of HINT's success.

The approach described in this chapter is limited to consistent data sets and nominal features. It is therefore desired to extend the approach to discover new features from noisy data, and from data that comprises continuous features. To handle noisy data, a minimal-error decomposition was recently proposed [51,54]. It is based on a representation of training examples with class distributions and uses successive column merging of partition matrix, so that the expected error of classification is minimized. For continuously-valued data sets, a function decomposition method was proposed in [11]. They both present preliminary results which strongly encourage further development in this direction and integration of their techniques into common function decomposition framework. The feature construction aspect of HINT is investigated in more detail in [52].

Acknowledgement. This research was supported by the Slovene Ministry of Science and Technology. We would like to thank Donald Michie for discussion, and George Paliouras for valuable suggestions on this chapter.

This chapter is based on the article Learning by discovering concept hierarchies (by B. Zupan, M. Bohanec, J. Demsar, and I. Bratko), *Artificial Intelligence* 109 (1999) 211-242. Material from this article was used with kind permission of the Editor of the AI Journal.

References

1. R. L. Ashenhurst. The decomposition of switching functions. Technical report, Bell Laboratories BL-1(11), pages 541–602, 1952.

2. A. W. Biermann, J. Fairfield, and T. Beres. Signature table systems and learning. *IEEE Transactions on Systems, Man and Cybernetics*, 12(5):635–648, 1982.
3. M. Bohanec, I. Bratko, and V. Rajkovič. An expert system for decision making. In H. G. Sol, editor, *Processes and Tools for Decision Support*. North-Holland, 1983.
4. M. Bohanec, B. Cestnik, and V. Rajkovič. A management decision support system for allocating housing loans. In P. Humphreys, L. Bannon, A. McCosh, and P. Migliarese, editors, *Implementing System for Supporting Management Decisions*, pages 34–43. Chapman & Hall, London, 1996.
5. M. Bohanec and V. Rajkovič. Knowledge acquisition and explanation for multi-attribute decision making. In *8th Intl Workshop on Expert Systems and their Applications*, pages 59–78, Avignon, France, 1988.
6. M. Bohanec and V. Rajkovič. DEX: An expert system shell for decision support. *Sistemica*, 1(1):145–157, 1990.
7. I. Bratko, I. Mozetič, and N. Lavrač. *KARDIO: a study in deep and qualitative knowledge for expert systems*. MIT Press, 1989.
8. N. H. Bshouty, T. R. Hancock, and L. Hellerstein. Learning boolean read-once formulas over generalized bases. *Journal of Computer and System Sciences*, 50(3):521–542, 1995.
9. T. H. Cormen, C. E. Leiserson, and R. L. Rivest. *Introduction to Algorithms*. MIT Press, 1989.
10. H. A. Curtis. *A New Approach to the Design of Switching Functions*. Van Nostrand, Princeton, N.J., 1962.
11. J. Demšar, B. Zupan, M. Bohanec, and I. Bratko. Constructing intermediate concepts by decomposition of real functions. In M. van Someren and G. Widmer, editors, *Proc. European Conference on Machine Learning, ECML-97*, pages 93–107, Prague, April 1997. Springer.
12. J. Efstathiou and V. Rajkovič. Multiattribute decisionmaking using a fuzzy heuristic approach. *IEEE Trans. on Systems, Man and Cybernetics*, 9:326–333, 1979.
13. C. Files, R. Drechsler, and M. Perkowski. Functional decomposition of MVL functions using multi-valued decision diagrams. In *International Symposium on Multi-Valued Logic*, may 1997.
14. J. A. Goldman. Pattern theoretic knowledge discovery. In *Proc. the Sixth Int'l IEEE Conference on Tools with AI*, 1994.
15. T. R. Hancock, M. Golea, and M. Marchand. Learning nonoverlaping perceptron networks from examples and membership queries. *Machine Learning*, 16(3):161–183, 1994.
16. R. Kohavi. Bottom-up induction of oblivious read-once decision graphs. In F. Bergadano and L. de Raedt, editors, *Proc. European Conference on Machine Learning*, pages 154–169. Springer–Verlag, 1994.
17. I. Kononenko. Estimating attributes: Analysis and extensions of RELIEF. In F. Bergadano and L. de Raedt, editors, *Proceedings of the European Conference on Machine Learning*, pages 171–182. Springer-Verlag, 1994.
18. I. Kononenko, E. Šimec, and M. Robnik Šikonja. Overcoming the myopia of inductive learning algorithms with ReliefF. *Applied Intelligence Journal*, 7(1):39–56, 1997.
19. Y.-T. Lai, K.-R. R. Pan, and M. Pedram. OBDD-based function decomposition: Algorithms and implementation. *IEEE Transactions on Computer Aided Design of Integrated Circuits and Systems*, 15(8):977–990, 1996.
20. Y.-T. Lai, M. Pedram, and S. Sastry. BDD-based decomposition of logic functions with application to FPGA synthesis. In *30th DAC*, pages 642–647, 1993.

21. T. Luba. Decomposition of multiple-valued functions. In *25th Intl. Symposium on Multiple-Valued Logic*, pages 256–261, Bloomigton, Indiana, May 1995.

22. T. Luba and H. Selvaraj. A general approach to boolean function decomposition and its application in FPGA-based synthesis. *VLSI Design*, 3(3–4):289–300, 1995.

23. R. S. Michalski. A theory and methodology of inductive learning. In R. Michalski, J. Carbonnel, and T. Mitchell, editors, *Machine Learning: An Artificial Intelligence Approach*, pages 83–134. Kaufmann, Paolo Alto, CA, 1983.

24. R. S. Michalski. Understanding the nature of learning: Issues and research directions. In R. Michalski, J. Carbonnel, and T. Mitchell, editors, *Machine Learning: An Artificial Intelligence Approach*, pages 3–25. Kaufmann, Los Atlos, CA, 1986.

25. D. Michie. Problem decomposition and the learning of skills. In N. Lavrač and S. Wrobel, editors, *Machine Learning: ECML-95*, Notes in Artificial Intelligence 912, pages 17–31. Springer-Verlag, 1995.

26. I. Mozetič. Learning of qualitative models. In I. Bratko and N. Lavrač, editors, *Progress in Machine Learning*. Sigma Press, 1987. Wilmslow, England.

27. I. Mozetič. The role of abstractions in learning of qualitative models. In *Proc. Fourth Int. Workshop on Machine Learning*. Morgan Kaufmann, 1987. Irvine, Ca.

28. S. Muggleton. Structuring knowledge by asking questions. In I. Bratko and N. Lavrač, editors, *Progress in Machine Learning*, pages 218–229. Sigma Press, 1987.

29. S. Muggleton. *Inductive Acquisition of Expert Knowledge*. Addison-Wesley, Workingham, England, 1990.

30. P. M. Murphy and D. W. Aha. UCI Repository of machine learning databases [http://www.ics.uci.edu/~mlearn/mlrepository.html]. Irvine, CA: University of California, Department of Information and Computer Science, 1994.

31. C. G. Nevill-Manning and I. H. Witten. Identifying hierarchical structure in sequences: A linear-time algorithm. *Journal of Artificial Intelligence Research*, 7:67–82, 1997.

32. M. Olave, V. Rajkovič, and M. Bohanec. An application for admission in public school systems. In I. Th. M. Snellen, W. B. H. J. van de Donk, and J.-P. Baquiast, editors, *Expert Systems in Public Administration*, pages 145–160. Elsevier Science Publishers (North Holland), 1989.

33. M. Perkowski and H. Uong. Automatic design of finite state machines with electronically programmable devices. In *Record of Northcon '87*, pages 16/4.1–16/4.15, Portland, OR, 1987.

34. B. Pfahringer. Controlling constructive induction in CiPF. In F. Bergadano and L. de Raedt, editors, *Machine Learning: ECML-94*, pages 242–256. Springer-Verlag, 1994.

35. J. R. Quinlan. *C4.5: Programs for Machine Learning*. Morgan Kaufmann Publishers, 1993.

36. R. Quinlan. Induction of decision trees. *Machine Learning*, 1(1):81–106, 1986.

37. H. Ragavan and L. Rendell. Lookahead feature construction for learning hard concepts. In *Proc. Tenth International Machine Learning Conference*, pages 252–259. Morgan Kaufman, 1993.

38. V. Rajkovič and M. Bohanec. Decision support by knowledge explanation. In H. G. Sol and J. Vecsenyi, editors, *Environments for supporting Decision Process*. Elsevier Science Publishers B.V., 1991.

39. T. D. Ross, M. J. Noviskey, D. A. Gadd, and J. A. Goldman. Pattern theoretic feature extraction and constructive induction. In *Proc. ML-COLT '94 Workshop on Constructive Induction and Change of Representation*, New Brunswick, New Jersey, July 1994.

40. S. J. Russell. Tree-structured bias. In M. N. Saint Paul, editor, *Proc. The Seventh National Conference on Artificial Intelligence*, pages 641–645, San Mateo, CA, 1988. Morgan Kaufmann.
41. S. L. Salzberg. On comparing classifiers: Pitfalls to avoid and a recommended approach. *Data Mining and Knowledge Discovery*, 1:317–328, 1997.
42. A. Samuel. Some studies in machine learning using the game of checkers. *IBM J. Res. Develop.*, 3:221–229, 1959.
43. A. Samuel. Some studies in machine learning using the game of checkers II: Recent progress. *IBM J. Res. Develop.*, 11:601–617, 1967.
44. A. D. Shapiro. *Structured induction in expert systems*. Turing Institute Press in association with Addison-Wesley Publishing Company, 1987.
45. A. D. Shapiro and T. Niblett. Automatic induction of classificiation rules for a chess endgame. In M. R. B. Clarke, editor, *Advances in Computer Chess 3*, pages 73–92. Pergamon, Oxford, 1982.
46. I. Stahl. An overview of predicate invention techniques in ILP. In *ESPRIT BRA 6020: Inductive Logic Programming*, 1991.
47. P. Tadepalli and S. Russell. Learning from examples and membership queries with structured determinations. *Machine Learning*, 32:245–295, 1998.
48. S. B. Thrun and et al. A performance comparison of different learning algorithms. Technical report, Carnegie Mellon University CMU-CS-91-197, 1991.
49. W. Wan and M. A. Perkowski. A new approach to the decomposition of incompletely specified functions based on graph-coloring and local transformations and its application to FPGA mapping. In *Proc. of the IEEE EURO-DAC '92*, pages 230–235, Hamburg, September 1992.
50. D. J. A. Welsh and M. B. Powell. An upper bound on the chromatic number of a graph and its application to timetabling problems. *Computer Journal*, 10:85–86, 1967.
51. B. Zupan. *Machine learning based on function decomposition*. PhD thesis, University of Ljubljana, April 1997. Available at http://www-ai.ijs.si/BlazZupan/papers.html.
52. B. Zupan, M. Bohanec, J. Demšar, and I. Bratko. Feature transformation by function decomposition. *IEEE Intelligent Systems & Their Applications*, 13(2):38–43, March/April 1998.
53. B. Zupan, M. Bohanec, J. Demšar, and I. Bratko. Learning by discovering concept hierarchies. *Artificial Intelligence*, 109(1–2):211–242, 1999.
54. B. Zupan, I. Bratko, M. Bohanec, and J. Demšar. Induction of concept hierarchies from noisy data. In P. Langley, editor, *Proceedings of the Seventeenth International Conference on Machine Learning (ICML-2000)*, pages 1199–1206, San Francisco, CA, 2000. Morgan Kaufmann.

How to Upgrade Propositional Learners to First Order Logic: A Case Study

Wim Van Laer[1] and Luc De Raedt[2]

[1] Department of Computer Science, Katholieke Universiteit Leuven Celestijnenlaan 200A, B-3001 Leuven, Belgium
Wim.VanLaer@cs.kuleuven.ac.be
[2] Institut für Informatik, Albert-Ludwigs-Universität Freiburg Am Flughafen 17, D-79110 Freiburg, Germany
deraedt@informatik.uni-freiburg.de

1 Introduction

Current machine learning systems are often distinguished on the basis of their representation, which can either be propositional or first order logic. Systems belonging to the first category are often called attribute value learners, systems of the second category are called relational learners or inductive logic programming systems.

In this paper, we describe a methodology for upgrading existing attribute value learners towards first order logic and demonstrate it at work. This method has several advantages: one can profit from existing research on propositional learners (and inherit its efficiency and effectiveness), relational learners (and inherit its expressiveness) and PAC-learning (and inherit its theoretical basis). Moreover there is a clear relationship between the new relational system and its propositional counterpart, resulting in e.g. identical results on identical (propositional) data. This makes the ILP system easy to use and understand by users familiar with the propositional counterpart.

This methodology is perhaps the most important lesson learned during the development of several inductive logic programming systems and results (including [21], TILDE [9,7], ICL [23], CLAUDIEN [20], WARMR [26]) of the machine learning group in Leuven. The methodology starts from an existing propositional learner and provides a recipe for upgrading it towards the use of first order logic. The recipe involves the use of examples which correspond to sets of ground facts (interpretations), the adaptation of the representation of hypotheses towards Prolog, the employment of θ-subsumption to structure and search the space of hypotheses, the introduction of a declarative bias, and otherwise recycles as much as possible from the original system. Following the methodology, it should be possible to turn virtually any propositional symbolic learner into an inductive logic programming system.

To show how the methodology works, we demonstrate it on upgrading the well-known CN2 [14,13] learning algorithm towards ICL [23]. In Section 6 we give an overview of other systems that follow the same methodology.

G. Paliouras, V. Karkaletsis, and C.D. Spyropoulos (Eds.): ACAI'99, LNAI 2049, pp. 102–126, 2001.
© Springer-Verlag Berlin Heidelberg 2001

The paper is structured as follows: we first elaborate on the characteristics of the propositional and the first order knowledge representation and we show how the relational representation can overcome limitations of the propositional representation. After describing the propositional learner CN2, we present our methodology for upgrading a propositional learner and illustrate each step w.r.t. CN2 resulting in the relational learner ICL. We also present some experimental results with ICL that show that the methodology is worthwhile. In the last section we discuss some related results and conclude.

2   Knowledge Representation

2.1   Attribute Value Learning

Consider Figure 1. Each example or scene can be described by a fixed number of attributes: `shape-left`, `size-left`, `color-left`, `shape-right`, `size-right`, `color-right` and `class`. The data-set can be summarized in one table as in Figure 2, where each row (or in relational database terms, each tuple) represents one example. Many well-known systems like C4.5 [56,57] and CN2 [14,13] are based on this *attribute value representation* (also called propositional representation), and are as such called attribute value learners. Also, data mining mainly focusses on learning from single tables.

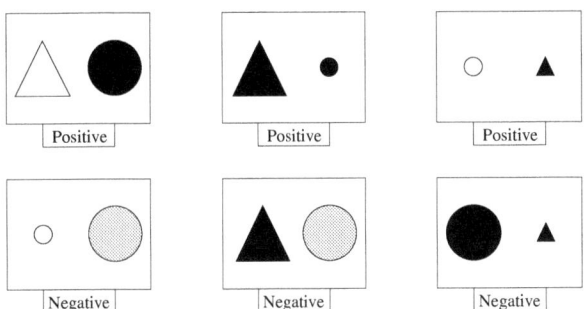

Fig. 1. A simple classification problem. One scene (example) consists of a left-side and a right-side object. Each scene is tagged with a class (positive or negative).

The examples in Figure 3 however, cannot easily be described by a fixed number of features. A scene or example consists of a variable number of geometrical objects (such as lines, points, squares, triangles, circles,...), each having a number of different properties (e.g., white, black, small, large, horizontal,...), and a variable number of relations between objects. Representing these scenes with a fixed set of attribute value pairs results in a number of problems (cf. [19]). *First*, one should fix the maximum number of objects in a scene. Given a bound b on the number of objects, one could then list attributes $A_{i,1}, ..., A_{i,j}$ characterizing each object i. Some of these attributes will yield nil values since not all

id	shape-left	size-left	color-left	shape-right	size-right	color-right	class
1	triangle	large	white	circle	large	black	positive
2	triangle	large	black	circle	small	black	positive
3	circle	small	white	triangle	small	black	positive
4	circle	small	white	circle	large	grey	negative
5	triangle	large	black	circle	large	grey	negative
6	circle	large	black	triangle	small	black	negative

Fig. 2. An attribute value representation for Figure 1 (with `id` a unique identifier for each example).

scenes may possess the same number of objects and not all attributes/properties are meaningful for each object. *Secondly*, one should also order the objects in a scene, which is more problematic. Indeed, reconsider scene 1 in Figure 1. Its representation in Figure 2 assumes that the order is from left to right. In general, the objects will be essentially unordered (as in Figure 3). Without determining the order of objects within a scene there is an exponential number of equivalent representations of a scene (in the number of objects). Scene 1 of Figure 1 corresponds to one such representation, another representation (based on a different order) would swap the left and right object. For similar reasons, the representation of rules will also require one such ordering. These two problems prohibit an efficient encoding of first order problems into the attribute value representations employed by typical machine learning systems. *Thirdly*, one should provide an attribute for each possible relation between each pair of objects (in a specific order). E.g. the first object is left of the second object, the first object is left of the third object,... Again, the number of such attributes (relations) grows exponentially in the number of objects available.

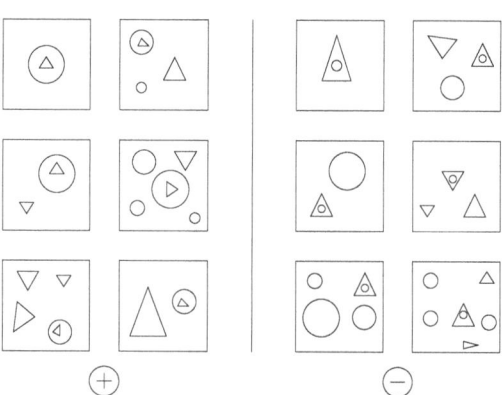

Fig. 3. A more complex classification problem: Bongard problem 47, developed by the Russian scientist M. Bongard in [10]. It consists of 12 scenes (or examples), six of class ⊕ and six of class ⊖. The goal is to discriminate between the two classes.

Though the above problem is a toy-problem, it is very similar to real-life problems in e.g. the field of biochemistry (see [43,11]) where essentially the same representational problems arise. Data consists of a set of molecules, each of which is composed of several atoms with specific properties (like charge). Similar to a scene, there exists a number of relations between atoms (like bonds, structures,...).

2.2   First Order Representations

The above sketched problems can be overcome using a *relational/first order representation*. We propose the following representation for examples:

an example is a set of ground facts

Ground facts are tuples in a relational database.

From a logical point of view this is called a (Herbrand) *interpretation* because the facts represent all atoms which are true for the example, thus all facts not in the example are assumed to be false. From a computational view this can be seen as a a small relational database or a Prolog knowledge base, so we can make use of a Prolog interpreter for querying an example.

To illustrate this representation, let's reexamine the Bongard problem in Figure 3. The upper left scene consists of a small triangle, pointing upwards and being inside a large circle. This scene can be specified as follows:

{class(*positive*), object(*o1*), object(*o2*), shape(*o1*, *circle*), size(*o1*, *large*), shape(*o2*, *triangle*), size(*o2*, *small*), pointing(*o2*, *up*), in(*o2*, *o1*)}.

The other scenes can be encoded in the same way. The number of objects in one scene is not limited, and objects are not ordered (they could be called *a* and *b* instead of *o1* and *o2*). Different objects can have different properties, e.g. a triangle can be pointing up or down, but this property makes no sense for a circle. And finally, the number of relations between objects is not fixed.

This first order representation is more general and more expressive than the attribute value representation which is a special case of it. Indeed, an attribute value table with k attributes can be mapped to a set of interpretations/examples as follows:

> For each example (a tuple/row in the attribute value table), construct the fact {example(val_1, ..., val_k).}, where val_i is the value of the ith attribute of the example in the table. Then each of these facts is the *interpretation* of the corresponding example.
>
> Instead of mapping to one fact, an alternative is to map each row or example to a set of k facts {att$_1$(val_1), ..., att$_k$(val_k)} where val_i is the value for the ith attribute.

For instance, the first example in Figure 1 can be represented by {example(*triangle, large, white, circle, large, black, positive*)}

or

{shape-left(*triangle*), size-left(*large*), color-left(*white*),
shape-right(*circle*), size-right(*large*), color-right(*black*), class(*positive*)}

At this point, it is worth noting that in the attribute value representation each example must have a single value for a given attribute. Therefore, if we know that the value of e.g. size-left=*large*, we also know that size-left≠*small*. This corresponds to making a kind of closed world assumption at the level of each example (cf. [38]). Due to the use of Prolog (and the implicit negation as failure), the meaning of each example in the above representation is correctly captured! (i.e. if color-left(*black*) then ?-color-left(X) will only succeed for X=*black*.)

This framework and use of Prolog is quite similar to what happens in the older work on structural matching (e.g. [39,40,71,72,73]).

2.3   Background Knowledge

It is useful to use not only factual knowledge in the examples, but also Prolog rules (or definite clauses). If these rules are common to all the examples, they are referred to as background knowledge. Such knowledge can take various forms: e.g. abstraction of specific values into a taxonomy or interval, deriving new properties from a combination of existing ones, summarizing or aggregating values of several facts/tuples into a single value, etc.

For our Bongard problem in Figure 3, we could add the following definitions:

polygon(X) :- triangle(X).
polygon(X) :- rectangle(X).
number_objects(NO) :- setof(O, object(O), LO), length(LO, NO).

The first two clauses state that a polygon can be either a triangle or a rectangle. This encodes a kind of taxonomy. The last clause calculates the number of objects in an example by creating a set of all objects and counting the number of elements in this set.

As background knowledge is visible for each example, all the facts that can be derived from the background knowledge and an example are part of the extended example[1]. When querying an example, it suffices to assert the background knowledge and the example; the Prolog interpreter will do the necessary derivations.

2.4   Note

The above representation of examples is known in the literature as *learning from interpretations* [21,18]. It is only one of the possible representations used within inductive logic programming. More details on the relation among various inductive logic programming settings can be found in [18].

---

[1] Formally, an extended example is the minimal Herbrand model of the example and the background theory.

3   The Propositional Learner CN2

CN2 is a well-known attribute value learning system which is described in [14, 13]. Originally, it induced an ordered list of rules using entropy as its search heuristic [14]. Two improvements to the algorithm are described in [13]: the use of the Laplace error estimate as evaluation function and the generation of unordered rules instead of ordered rules. In the rest of the paper we will only consider the algorithm for learning unordered rules.

Informally, CN2's problem specification is: given a set of examples E (represented in attribute value as described in Section 2.1) and a set of classes C (each example belongs to one class), find an unordered set of rules of the form class=*class* if *condition* (with *condition* a conjunction of attribute-value tests) such that each example is classified correctly. To classify an example, one collects all rules which fire (i.e. all rules that cover the example[2]) and predict the class by a simple probabilistic method to resolve clashes. For the moment, we will concentrate on the task to induce a set of rules for one class c: the set of positive examples P are all the examples belonging to the class c, the set of negative examples N are all the others (so $E = P \cup N$).

Reconsider the classification problem in Figure 1. CN2 might learn the following hypothesis for class *positive* (as an unordered set of rules):

class=*positive* if color-left=*white* and color-right=*black*
class=*positive* if size-right=*small* and shape-right=*circle*

Learn-For-One-Class(*Examples, Class*) **return** *Hypothesis*;

1. **let** $P := \{e \in Examples \mid$ example e is of class $Class\}$;
2. **let** $N := \{e \in Examples \mid$ example e is not of class $Class\}$;
3. **let** $H := \emptyset$;
4. **repeat**
   a) *BestRule* = **Find-Best-Rule**(P, N);
   b) **if** *BestRule* found **then**
      i. add *BestRule* to H;
      ii. remove from P all examples e covered by *BestRule*;
   until *BestRule* not found **or** P is empty;
5. **return** H;

Fig. 4. Learn a theory for one class.

To learn a theory for one class, CN2 performs a covering approach on the positive examples: it repeatedly finds a single rule that is considered *best* (that is maximizes the positive examples covered and minimizes the negative examples

---
[2] A rule covers an example if the condition of the rule is true for the example.

covered). The *best* rule is then added to the hypothesis H and all examples of P that are covered by the rule are removed from P. This process terminates when no *best* rule can be found or when no more positives have to be covered. The algorithm can be found in Figure 4.

Find-Best-Rule(P,N);

1. **let** mgr := most general rule in the search-space;
2. **let** $Beam$:= $\{mgr\}$;
3. **let** $BestRule$:= $\emptyset$;
4. **while** $Beam$ is not empty **do**
   a) **let** $NewBeam$:= $\emptyset$;
   b) **for** each rule R in $Beam$ **do**
      for each refinement Ref of R **do**
      i. **if** Ref is better than $BestRule$ **and** Ref is statistically significant
         then let $BestRule$:= Ref;
      ii. **if** Ref is not to be pruned
          then
          − **add** Ref to $NewBeam$;
          − **if** size of $NewBeam$ > $MaxBeamSize$
             then remove worst rule from $NewBeam$;
   c) **let** $Beam$:= $NewBeam$;
5. **return** $BestRule$;

Fig. 5. Beam search algorithm to find the *best* rule.

To find a *best* rule, CN2 has to search through the space of rules. The structure of this search-space is implied by the subset test. Refining a rule is simply done by adding a new attribute test to the body of the rule (also called condition). CN2 starts with the most general rule of the search-space (usually the rule with an empty body: *class :- true*). It then performs a beam search. At each step/level, all refinements of the rules in the current *beam* are evaluated. If the rule is statistically significant and better than the current best, it becomes the current best rule. From all the refinements (except those that can be pruned[3]), the $MaxBeamSize$ best rules are kept in the new *beam*. This search repeats until no more rules are in the *beam*. The algorithm for finding a *best* rule can be found in Figure 5.

---

[3] For example, a rule can be pruned if none of its refinements can become better than the current $BestRule$.

4   Upgrading CN2

In Section 2, we have motivated the need for relational representations and we have introduced a first order representation for examples. Now, we can focus on the methodology for upgrading propositional learners.

This section will provide a detailed case study with CN2 [14,13] and ICL [23] introducing the methodology. The final section will briefly review a number of other cases with the methodology.

4.1   The Propositional Task and Algorithm

Suppose that we are asked to design a learning system for Bongard type problems. Machine learning researchers would observe that Bongard problems are classification problems (another popular task is that of descriptive learning, for example discovering association rules [2,1,66]). So, the range of possible propositional learning algorithms to consider includes AQ [47], TDIDT [57] (like C4.5 [56]), and CN2 [14,13]. Suppose we fancy the latter algorithm because it combines the advantages of AQ and TDIDT, i.e. it produces understandable rules, it is efficient and can cope with noisy data. So, we decide to base our first order learner on CN2. Then we have also accomplished the first step of the methodology:

Step 1 : *Identify the propositional learner that best matches the learning task.*

Given the goal of upgrading CN2 to first order logic, the question is how to realize this. At this point, the reader may notice that CN2 will not work on the Bongard problem because:

- the representation of the examples is propositional,
- the representation of the rules is propositional,
- the search operators are propositional.

We will now discuss these issues in detail.

4.2   Examples Are Interpretations

The propositional representation of examples should be upgraded to a first order one. We propose to use interpretations for this (see Section 2) as it is a natural representation for examples and there is a clear relation with attribute value learning [19,18]. This will alleviate the first problem. Also, if desired, background knowledge can be formulated in Prolog as in Section 2.3.

Step 2 : *Use interpretations to represent examples.*

4.3   First Order Hypotheses

As the expressiveness of the examples (inputs) has been extended, we should also extend the expressiveness of the hypotheses (outputs).

Let us have a closer look at the concept representation in CN2. Recall from Section 3 that CN2 learns an unordered set of rules of the form class=*class* if *condition*, with *condition* a conjunction of attribute-value tests (e.g. color-left =*white*). An attribute-value test can be seen as a special case of a literal. For example, color-left=*white* can be mapped to color-left(*white*) (cf. also the mapping in Section 2.2). So if we allow literals (with possibly more than one argument, and with variables or terms as arguments) instead of just attribute-value tests, the hypothesis will be a kind of first order expression. When using rule sets with literals (the variables in the literals are existentially quantified), we can learn the following rule for the Bongard problem in Figure 3:

class=⊕ if ∃T,C: shape(T, *triangle*) and shape(C, *circle*) and in(T, C).

which states that there exists a triangle and a circle (thus an instantiation for the variables T and C) such that the triangle is inside the circle. At this point, the condition of the rule corresponds to a Prolog query. Furthermore, instead of the 'if' notation in rule-based approaches it is common in logic programming and Prolog to write ':-', yielding a typical Prolog clause:

class(⊕) :- shape(T, *triangle*), shape(C, *circle*), in(T, C).

As a result, a first order upgrade of unordered rule sets for CN2 is of the form:

$$\text{class}(class) \text{ :- } l_{1,1}, ..., l_{1,n_1}$$
$$...$$
$$\text{class}(class) \text{ :- } l_{k,1}, ..., l_{k,n_k}$$

where all $l_{i,j}$ are literals and all the variables appearing in the literals are existentially quantified. Note that the variables are independent between different rules.

So far, we have only sketched a syntactic adaptation. We also need to modify the semantics of hypotheses. This boils down to specifying when an example is covered by a hypothesis. An example e will be covered by a hypothesis H (a set of rules for class(c)) if $H \wedge e \models$ class(c). Thus to test coverage, one asserts the hypothesis H (resp. a rule) and the example e in a Prolog knowledge base (one could also use a relational database system) and runs the query ?-class(c). If this query succeeds, the example is covered; otherwise it is not.

Note that this coverage test is more complex in both time and space than its propositional counterpart (which is a simple subset test).

The reader familiar with CN2 may observe that CN2 also uses a simple probabilistic method to resolve conflicts/clashes when an example is covered by rules belonging to multiple classes. These probabilities can straightforwardly be used here too. It is merely the test for coverage that needs to be changed.

The third step of the methodology can be summarized as follows:

Step 3 : *Upgrade the representation of propositional hypotheses by replacing attribute-value tests by first order literals and modify the coverage test accordingly.*

This third step alleviates the second problem concerning CN2, mentioned earlier.

Note that this step also works for a wide range of propositional hypothesis/concept representations, like ordered or unordered rule sets, decision trees, regression trees, association rules,.... Indeed, all these concept descriptions have one thing in common: they are all based on attribute-value tests. For instance, in a decision tree each branch is based on an attribute-value test, and an association rule is a set of attribute-value tests.

For example, TILDE [9,7] introduces first order logical decision trees - FOLDT (of which binary trees are a special case). A FOLDT is a binary decision tree in which the nodes of the tree contain a conjunction of literals. Moreover, different nodes may share variables, under the restriction that a variable that is introduced in a node (meaning that it does not occur in higher nodes) does not occur in the right branch of that node[4]. An example of a logical decision tree is shown in Figure 6. Note the sharing of the variable T in both literals.

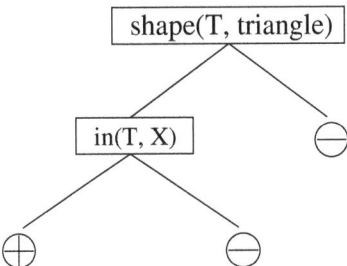

Fig. 6. An example of a first order logical decision tree that discriminates between the classes $\oplus$ and $\ominus$ for the Bongard problem in Figure 3.

4.4   Structuring the Search Space

Nearly all symbolic machine learning systems structure the search-space by means of the *is more general than* relation. When working with propositional representations this relation is often quite simple. For instance, in the CN2 algorithm one rule is more general than another rule if all literals (i.e. attribute-value tests) occurring in the first rule are a subset of those occurring in the second rule.

---

[4] The need for this restriction follows from the semantics of FOLDT. A variable X in a literal is existentially quantified within the conjunction of that node. As the the right subtree is only relevant when the conjunction fails (thus saying *there is no such X*), further references to X are meaningless in the right branch.

On the other hand, when working with first order representations the frameworks for generality become rather complex. Various frameworks have been proposed, including θ-subsumption (from Plotkin [54]), inverse implication, inverse resolution and inverse entailment (cf. [50] for an overview). However, in practice, the large majority of ILP systems (including FOIL [58], Golem [51], PROGOL[5] [49], CLAUDIEN [20], and TILDE [9,7],...) uses θ-subsumption. This is due to the excellent computational properties of θ-subsumption (as compared to inverse resolution and inverse implication, which are both computationally intractable and less understood yet). Another important property of θ-subsumption is that it works at the level of single clauses instead of sets of clauses (as inverse resolution). This is similar to propositional systems which also structure the space at the level of individual rules. On the other hand, working at the level of single clauses only may cause problems when learning recursive clauses or multiple predicates (cf. [22,4]). However, in our opinion, recursion is not essential for most real-life applications of relational machine learning and data mining. Indeed, the authors are only familiar of a few recursive rules in the mesh-design [27]. Most other current real-life applications of inductive logic programming do not involve recursive regularities (see [31,11] for overviews). So, in most applications θ-subsumption is the right framework for generality when upgrading propositional systems to first order logic.

Step 4 : *Use θ-subsumption as the framework for generality.*

Before showing in the next section how to adapt the operators, we provide a brief review of θ-subsumption and its properties.

Let us first introduce the definition:

Clause C_1 θ-subsumes clause C_2 iff $\exists \theta$: $C_1\theta \subseteq C_2$.

A clause (rule) is a set of literals and a variable substitution θ ($=\{V_1/t_1,\ldots,V_n/t_n\}$) maps each variable V_i to its corresponding term t_i. For instance:
C_1 = father(X, Y) :- parent(X, Y), male(X). is more general than clause C_2 = father(*jef, wim*) :- parent(*jef, wim*), parent(*jef, ann*), male(*jef*), female(*ann*). because $C_1\theta \subseteq C_2$ with $\theta = \{X/jef, Y/wim\}$.

Note that the propositional ordering on the search-space is a special case of θ-subsumption. This is an important property in the light of the upgrading procedure. For instance: the clause class(*positive*) :- color-right(*black*) is more general than class(*positive*) :- color-left(*white*), color-right(*black*).

At this point it is important to realize that θ-subsumption generalizes the well-known *turning constants into variables* introduced by [48]. For example, p :- q(X,Y), q(Y,X) is more general than p :- q(a,a) under θ-subsumption, but would not be regarded a generalization using the turning constants into variables. A second point where θ-subsumption generalizes Michalski's framework is that it also works for structured terms. E.g. p :- q(f(a)) is a specialization of p :- q(X).

---

[5] In Progol, the θ-subsumption lattice is searched top-down but is bounded from below by a clause computed using inverse entailment.

Some more theoretical properties of θ-subsumption include (for more details see [54,53,50,68]):

- it induces a quasi-order (reflexive and transitive) on the space of first order rules
- if c_1 θ-subsumes c_2 then $c_1 \models c_2$, i.e. c_1 logically entails c_2.
- there exist clauses $c_1 \neq c_2$ that are equivalent under θ-subsumption, e.g. p :- q(X,Y) and p :- q(X,Y),q(X,Z).
- the quasi-order can be turned into a partial order (also anti-symmetric) by defining equivalence classes in the usual way. There is then also a unique (up to variable renaming) representative of each equivalence class, which is called the *reduced* clause. The reduced clause r of a clause c is defined as the smallest subset of literals in c such that r is equivalent under θ-subsumption with c. E.g. p :- q(X,Y) is the reduced clause of p :- q(X,Y),q(X,Z).
- at the level of equivalence classes, one obtains a complete lattice, i.e. any two equivalence classes have a unique least upper bound (also called the least general generalization, the lgg) and a unique greatest lower bound.

4.5   Adapting the Search Operators

Now that we have chosen a framework for generality, we still need to define operators for searching the corresponding rule space. Given the advice of step 4, we will limit the discussion here to operators under θ-subsumption only.

Let us consider three typical operators used by concept learners. A specialization (resp. a generalization) operator that operates on a single clause, and a generalization operator that computes the least general generalization of two clauses.

The typical propositional specialization operator will basically add a condition to a rule. Using clauses, a condition can be added in two manners: either by adding a literal or by applying a substitution to the given clause. E.g. the clauses p :- q(X,Y),r(X), p :- q(X,X) and p :- q(X,a). are specializations of the clause p :- q(X,Y).

This yields the so-called refinement operators (cf. [53,68]). There are some additional complications when using refinement operators w.r.t. propositional systems:

- when simply adding literals, one might stay within the same equivalence class, and there might be infinite chains of such refinements, e.g. when refining p :- q(X,Y) to p :- q(X,Y), q(X,Z) and then to p :- q(X,Y), q(X,Z), q(X,W) ...
- it could be that even some proper refinements of a clause do not affect the coverage of the examples, this is known as the *determinacy problem* [59]. E.g. refining class(*pos*) :- atom(X) to class(*pos*) :- atom(X), bond(X,Y). As any atom will have bonds to other atoms, merely adding bond(X,Y) will not modify the coverage of the clause. This may misguide the heuristics of the learning engine.

Both difficulties can be alleviated by using a declarative (language) bias that will be discussed in the next section.

The typical propositional generalization operator will delete (or relax) a condition in a rule. Under θ-subsumption there are two ways of relaxing a clause: either delete a literal, or apply an inverse substitution to the clause. The first case is the easy one: e.g. generalize p :- q(X,Y), r(Y) towards p :- r(Y). The second case is more complicated and generalizes the turning constants into variables rule. If the constant (or term) to be generalized occurs only once in the clause, there is no problem: it can merely be generalized into a variable not yet occurring in the clause. E.g. p :- q(a,b) into p :- q(X,b). However, if the constant or term to be generalized occurs multiple times, generalization can be quite complex. Indeed, consider p :- q(a,a). This can be generalized into p :- q(X,X) or p :- q(a,X),q(X,a). One problem is the existence of infinite chains, i.e., the clause positive :- q(a,a) has the following generalizations: positive :- q(X,X), positive :- q(X,Y), q(Y,X), ... The most specific generalization is the infinite rule positive :- q(X_1,X_2), q(X_2,X_3),...,q(X_i,X_{i+1}),...).
This problem and the existence of a *lgg* operator (cf. below) explains why plain generalization operators are less popular in ILP than refinement operators. The problems with generalization operators can again be reduced by an appropriate declarative bias mechanism.

A third popular operator is the (generalization) operator that computes the least general generalization (*lgg*) of two clauses.

A clause g is a *least general generalization* (*lgg*) of the clauses C_1 and C_2
if and only if
g θ-subsumes C_1 and g θ-subsumes C_2, and for every clause g' such that
g' θ-subsumes C_1 and g' θ-subsumes C_2, g' also θ-subsumes g.

Plotkin has given a procedure to compute the *lgg* of two clauses: The *lgg* of two identical terms is the term itself ($lgg(t,t) = t$). The *lgg* of the terms $f(s_1, ..., s_n)$ and $f(t_1, ..., t_n)$ is $f(lgg(s_1,t_1), ..., lgg(s_n,t_n))$. The *lgg* of the terms $f(s_1, ..., s_n)$ and $g(t_1, ..., t_m)$ where $f \neq g$ is the variable v where v represents this pair of terms throughout. The *lgg* of two atoms/literals $p(s_1, ..., s_n)$ and $p(t_1, ..., t_n)$ is $p(lgg(s_1,t_1), ..., lgg(s_n,t_n))$, the *lgg* being undefined when the sign or the predicate symbols are different. Finally, the *lgg* of two clauses C_1 and C_2 is then $\bigvee_{l_1 \in set(C_1), l_2 \in set(C_2)} lgg(l_1, l_2)$.
For example, the *lgg* of father(*luc,soetkin*) :- parent(*luc,soetkin*), male(*luc*), female(*soetkin*) and father(*jef,wim*) :- parent(*jef,wim*), male(*jef*), male(*wim*) is father(X,Y) :- parent(X,Y), male(X), male(Z). Note that the variable X is the lgg of the terms *luc* and *jef*, Y is the lgg of *soetkin* and *wim*, and Z is the lgg of *luc* and *wim*.
The *lgg* is used in specific to general inductive logic programming systems like Golem [51]. The problem with the lgg operator is that the complexity of the lgg (i.e. the number of literals) may grow exponentially with the number of examples in the worst case.

Step 5 : *Use an operator under θ-subsumption. Use that one that corresponds closely to the propositional operator.*

In the ICL system, we choose a specialization operator under θ-subsumption. Due to the problems sketched above, we will embed it within a declarative bias mechanism.

4.6   The Need for Bias

In the previous section, several problems with pure θ-subsumption operators were mentioned. These problems are mainly due to the combinatorics of the search-space, the fact that the space is infinite rather than finite (as in the propositional case) and the determinacy problem. To make the search tractable and efficient, it is thus necessary to constrain the search-space in some way. In ILP, this is solved using syntactical or semantical declarative bias mechanisms. Various formalisms exist (see [52] for an overview), but the overall idea is to limit the number of clauses considered. The most straightforward methods merely employ some bounds on the number of variables, or literals in clauses and make the search-space finite. Other methods will specify syntactic limitations on the clauses considered (from which an operator can be derived). E.g. using a number of schemata to enforce that clauses satisfy certain patterns, e.g. the pattern P(X,Y) :- Q(X), R(X,Y), where P, Q and R are 'predicate' variables (see [42]). Other methods use a kind of grammar construction to explicitly declare the range of acceptable clauses [17]. A third class of techniques uses so-called mode-declarations to state how clauses can be refined, like in PROGOL [49], TILDE [9,7] and WARMR [26].

Step 6: *Use a declarative bias mechanism to limit the search-space.*

In ICL we selected the $\mathcal{D}$LAB declarative bias formalism of [20], which encodes a kind of grammar[6]. An example is given in Figure 7. Min-Max:List means that

```
dlab_template('
  1-len:[shape(Object1, 1-1:[circle,triangle]),
         size(Object1, 1-1:[small,large]),
         shape(Object2, 1-1:[circle,triangle]),
         size(Object2, 1-1:[small,large]),
         1-1:[in(Object1, Object2), left_of(Object1,Object2)]
         ]').
```

Fig. 7. A $\mathcal{D}$LAB bias for the Bongard problem

at least Min and at most Max literals of List are allowed (`len` is the length of `List`). Note that shape(Object, 1-1:[circle,triangle]) is a shorthand for 1-1:[shape(Object,circle), shape(Object,triangle)]. Recursion is allowed. There is also a notion of dlab_variable (not used in the example) that allows the user to define shortcuts for frequently occurring parts (like 1-1:[circle,triangle]).

---

[6] We could have used as well the mode-declarations as in Tilde and Warmr.

Given a $\mathcal{D}$LAB expression, a refinement operator can be used to traverse the (restricted) search-space. A complete refinement operator for $\mathcal{D}$LAB is given in [20]. For example, based on the $\mathcal{D}$LAB expression in Figure 7, the top rule of the search-space is

class($\oplus$) :- *true*.

The refinement operator will generate the following refinements for this rule:

class($\oplus$) :- shape(Object1, *circle*).
class($\oplus$) :- shape(Object1, *triangle*).
...
class($\oplus$) :- left_of(Object1, Object2).

These rules again can be refined further on. For the first rule:

class($\oplus$) :- shape(Object1, *circle*), size(Object1, *small*).
...
class($\oplus$) :- shape(Object1, *circle*), shape(Object2, *circle*).
...

Note that class($\oplus$) :- shape(Object1, *circle*), shape(Object1, *triangle*). is not a valid refinement.

The advantage of $\mathcal{D}$LAB is its expressive power. It allows the user to strongly bias the learning system ICL. On the other hand, a $\mathcal{D}$LAB expression can become very complex. Writing a $\mathcal{D}$LAB (and bias in general) is an iterative process and not always straightforward.

Note that some kind of lookahead can be performed by $\mathcal{D}$LAB to overcome the determinacy problem. Indeed, when using len-len:[List] in the template, all the literals in List must be added in one step as a refinement.

4.7   Implementing the Algorithm

By now, we are ready to implement our first order learner. All basic modifications needed have been sketched. In this step, it is important that as many features of the original algorithm as possible are preserved, like search strategy, heuristics, noise-handling, pruning, parameters,... For example, ICL uses the same heuristics (Laplace estimate) as its propositional counterpart CN2.

Some advanced and specific features of propositional learning algorithms may need further changes. For example, discretization on numerical attributes cannot be mapped directly towards our relational representation (see Section 4.9).

Step 7: *Implement*.

Currently, ICL is implemented in MasterProLog (formerly ProLog by BIM) and freely available for academic use (runtime version for Solaris 2.5 is available on request).

4.8   Evaluation of ILP System

A first evaluation is testing the implementation on a propositional problem, for example the problem in Figure 1. The results should be compatible with the results of the corresponding propositional learner. In the ideal case these should be the same, but in reality some minor differences might occur. Many reasons exist: small differences in implementation, lack of some features (like handling of unknown values), a slightly different hypothesis space for the propositional and relational system,...

The next test is learning on relational data. A good starting point is some artificial problem, like the Bongard problem in Figure 3, where one has already a solution (obtained by hand or by some other relational learner). Experiments with these data can give good insight in the system (the parameters, the output, the behaviour of learning, some problems,...).

Then one can start the *real* work and run the system on real-life problems. A well-known application area is in molecular biology.

Step 8: *Evaluate your (first order) implementation on propositional and relational data.*

In Section 5, some experimental results with ICL will be discussed.

4.9   Extensions to the Basic System

Many propositional systems have been extended with extra features or optimizations. These can often also be incorporated in their relational counterpart. Some extensions can be plugged in as they are, others will need some adaption/upgrade similar to the other steps in the sketched methodology. In this way, ILP learners can reuse results from research on propositional learners.

Note that also ideas from other ILP systems can be incorporated. These ILP results then also become available for propositional problems, so both communities can learn from each other.

Step 9: *Add interesting extra features.*

The system ICL has many extensions/optimizations w.r.t. the basic system described up to now (see [70,69] for more details). To handle numerical data, we upgraded the discretization method of Fayyad and Irani (see [37,29]) towards ICL. To handle multiple classes, we extended the CN2 method with a Bayesian approach (inspired by [55]). This result can be integrated in CN2 without any problem (illustrating that results in the context of relational learners can be mapped back to propositional learners). Other extensions/optimizations of ICL include: learning both DNF and CNF theories, using the m-estimate (as in [32]) instead of the Laplace estimate as heuristic, extra pruning of the search-space,... While CN2 has a specific handling of unknown values (* and ?), ICL just assumes the closed world assumption.

5   Some Experimental Results with ICL

To illustrate the utility of the method and the effectiveness of ICL, we will give an overview of some experiments performed with ICL.

5.1 Experimental Settings

The experiments have been performed with ICL version 4.2, implemented in MasterProLog (formerly ProLog by BIM). We used a Sun Ultra 2 with two 167 Mhz UltraSPARC processors running Solaris 2.6, and a SUN Ultra 10 with a 333 Mhz UltraSPARCII processor running Solaris 7.

Unless stated otherwise, we used the default settings of ICL. The most important ones: significance level is 90%, heuristic is m_estimate (with parameter m the number of classes), the size of the beam is 5, and classes are *pos* and *neg*.

5.2 Propositional Data

One of the nice properties of our methodology is its *backward compatibility*, meaning that the upgraded relational system behaves similar as its propositional predecessor on propositional data. However, some deflections occur due to differences in implementation.

To simulate CN2 with ICL, we can use the following simple $\mathcal{D}$LAB expression: 1-len:$[att_1 = 1\text{-}1\text{:}[v_{1,1}, ..., v_{1,i_1}],..., att_k = 1\text{-}1\text{:}[v_{k,1}, ..., v_{k,i_k}]]$, with $v_{i,j}$ the values of the attribute att_i.

We have run ICL on a few propositional data sets used in [13]: voting-records, breast-cancer, lymphography and primary-tumor. Some information on the data sets is given in Table 1. We have chosen these data sets because they have no (or few) numerical values and only few unknown values. So this allows a close comparison.

Table 1. Details of the propositional domains used in the experiments. We did the same data conversions as documented in [13].

Domain	Description
voting-records	predict democrat/republican from votes
breast-cancer	predict if recurrence is likely
lymphography	disease diagnosis
primary-tumor	predict tumour type

Number of			Unknown	Numerical
Exs	Atts	Classes	values	values
435	16	2	yes	no
286	9	2	few	few
148	18	4	no	few
330	17	15	yes	no

We performed a similar experimental procedure as in [13]. The accuracies have been estimated by averaging the results over 20 runs (for each run, 2/3 of the data is selected randomly for training and the remainder for testing). The results are shown in Table 2. We have run ICL with the same language bias and the same settings as in [13]: beam=20 and heuristic=laplace. The last column gives the result of the default ICL performance (with default parameters: beam=5, significance level=90% and heuristic=m_estimate).

Table 2. Comparison of ICL and CN2 on accuracy (with standard deviation) and rule set size (number of attribute tests/literals). Results for CN2 are taken from [13], Appendix 1.

Accuracy	ICL		CN2 (unordered)		ICL
Sign. Threshold	0%	99.5%	0%	99.5%	default settings
voting-records	94.1±1.5	92.5±2.0	94.8±1.8	93.3±2.1	94.1±1.9
breast-cancer	69.7±3.3	71.8±3.7	73.0±4.5	70.8±3.5	69.4±4.1
lymphography	80.3±4.0	76.2±6.3	81.7±4.3	76.5±5.3	81.9±5.8
primary-tumor	41.7±4.9	42.0±4.8	45.8±3.6	41.4±5.8	41.4±5.5

Rule set size	ICL		CN2 (unordered)		ICL
Sign. Threshold	0%	99.5%	0%	99.5%	default settings
voting-records	43.5	14.9	64.8	19.9	49.7
breast-cancer	158.5	17.4	100.5	18.0	136.1
lymphography	38.5	14.9	40.4	13.5	45.5
primary-tumor	267	115.35	351.0	131.4	253.6

When we look at the accuracy and rule set size, we can conclude that ICL's performance is similar to CN2's, what we expected. Differences can be accounted by the small differences between CN2 and ICL w.r.t. options and implementation details. There are however 2 boundary cases: for breast-cancer and primary-tumor with significance threshold 0% ICL performs worse than CN2 w.r.t. accuracy. In both cases, the theories sizes also differ significantly. We haven't found any explanation for this[7].

5.3   Relational Data

ICL has been used in many experiments with (real-life) relational data sets. We will give some results, and refer to the literature for more details.

One of the most popular data set in ILP is the **mutagenesis** one (see [65]). The data consists of 188 molecules, of which 125 are active (thus mutagenic) and 63 are inactive. A molecule is described by its atoms `atom(AtomID, Element, Type, Charge)` (the number of atoms differs between molecules, ranging from 15 to 35) and the bonds `bond(Atom1, Atom2, BondType)` between these atoms. Four different sets of background have been used (same as in [65]). Background 1 uses only the information on atoms and bonds, background 2 allows tests on the *charge* of an atom, background 3 adds 2 specific measures w.r.t. the molecule (e.g. $\log P$ and ϵ_{LUMO}) and background 4 consists of descriptions of higher-level structures that appear in the molecule (like aromatic rings).

Experiments with ICL on this data set can be found in [69]. Results with ICL version 4.2 are given in Table 3. We manually discretized the numerical values

---

[7] In other papers we have found similar results for CN2 as ours. For example in [28], the result for breast-cancer is 70.0±1.4 accuracy with a theory size of 114.5, and for primary-tumor the accuracy is 39.9±1.0 with a theory size of 302.8. These are similar to our results. The experiments in that paper used a beam of size 5 instead of 20. The other settings are the same.

(i.e. $\log P$, ϵ_{LUMO} and the *Charge* of the atoms). It seems that the multi-class theory is always better than the seperate (DNF) theory for each class. This is not so surprising as the multi-class theory combines the two seperate theories for each class, and resolves clashes between the two. The (multi-class) accuracy of ICL is significantly better than FOIL for background 1 and 2, and marginally better for background 3 and 4. ICL is also marginally better than PROGOL and TILDE for background 1. For Background 2, 3 and 4 however, the performance of ICL, PROGOL and TILDE is similar. Note that the accuracy increases as more background is added.

Table 3. Accuracies for the four different backgrounds of the mutagenesis data (estimated by a 10-fold cross-validation). The first three columns are results for ICL (with the *default settings*, except for maxbody=8, and without discretization). Pos and Neg are the two classes and for each of them a DNF theory is learned and evaluated. Multi merges the 2 theories into a multi-class theory. The results for PROGOL, FOIL and TILDE have been taken from [8].

Muta	Accuracies (%)						Timing (s)
	Neg	Pos	Multi	PROGOL	FOIL	TILDE	ICL
BG1	79.3±8.2	67.6±5.1	80.9±7.4	76	61	75	79
BG2	80.3±8.9	74.5±6.9	82.4±7.4	81	61	79	143
BG3	85.1±8.7	83.5±5.9	86.7±10.0	83	83	85	160
BG4	85.1±7.7	86.2±7.6	88.3±8.0	88	82	86	197

Results on the **biodegradability** domain can be found in [69] (preliminary results) and [35] (more recent results). The task is to predict the half-life in water for aerobic aqueous biodegradation of a compound from its chemical structure. The biodegradation time has been discretized into 4 classes: fast, moderate, slow and resistant. The structure of a compound is represented by facts about atoms and bonds, much like in the mutagenesis domain. In [35] experiments on the relational data (denoted $R1$) and 2 propositional versions of the data (denoted $P1$ and $P2$) has been performed with the propositional classification systems C4.5 and RIPPER [15], and the relational learners FFOIL [60], SRT [46], ICL and TILDE. A short overview of the results can be found in Table 4. Accuracy is classification accuracy and Accuracy (+/-1) is the accuracy where only misclassification by more than one class counts as an error (e.g. slow as fast, moderate as resistant,...). ICL has only been applied to the relational representation R1. Of all the relational learners using R1, ICL achieves the highest Accuracy and Accuracy(+/-1). Compared to the propositional systems, ICL is better than all systems in term of Accuracy(+/-1), except for RIPPER on P2. For more specific results and discussions we refer to the paper.

ICL also participated in the **PTE-2 challenge** of which the results have been published in [63,64]. The challenge was to make carcinogenesis predictions for 30 compounds, based on models constructed by Machine Learning programs. There were 9 (legal) submissions using ILP systems (TILDE, WARMR/MACCENT, ICL, P-PROGOL) and combinations of propositional systems (like C4.5) and ILP

Table 4. Accuracies of machine learning systems predicting Biodegradability. Results are taken from [35]. We have left out the results of the regression systems.

System	Representation	Accuracy	Accuracy (+/-1)
C4.5	P1	55.2	86.2
C4.5	P2	56.9	82.4
RIPPER	P1	52.6	89.8
RIPPER	P2	57.6	93.9
FFOIL	R1'	53.0	88.7
ICL	R1	55.7	92.6
SRT-C	P1 + R1	55.0	90.0
TILDE-C	R1	51.0	88.6
TILDE-C	P1 + R1	52.0	89.0

(like rules from WARMR). ICL and the other ILP systems perform unexpectedly well on scales of quantitative performance. ICL itself is in the top 3 of ILP systems (with 78% accuracy). ILP assisted models appear to be better than expert assisted ones (w.r.t. the PTE-2 data). Interesting results are obtained with propositional prediction methods using results from ILP systems (for example C4.5 using rules/sub-structures generated by WARMR).

Other successful experiments with ICL include: *finite element mesh design* by [69]; automated acquisition of knowledge on *traffic problem detection* by [34, 33]; and the problem of *diterpene structure elucidation* from ^{13}C NMR spectra by [30].

To conclude, ICL performs as well as other well-known ILP systems, and thus can be said to be a successful upgrade.

6   Related Work and Conclusions

There are plenty of other inductive logic programming systems whose development more or less fits in with the proposed methodology: FOIL [58], RIBL [36], SRT [46], TILDE [9,7], WARMR [26,25], MACCENT [24], jk-CT learner [21], CLAUDIEN [20], Probabilistic Relational Models [45], Cohen's Flipper [16] [61] and RDBC [44].

E.g. Quinlan's FOIL can also be considered an upgrade of either Michalski's AQ [47] or CN2 [14,13], RIBL upgrades the classical k-nearest neighbor algorithm (using a first order distance due to [6]), SRT and TILDE upgrade the well-known decision (and regression) tree paradigm incorporated in CART [12] and C4.5 [56,57], WARMR upgrades APRIORI [2,1], MACCENT upgrades the Maximum Entropy approach in [5], De Raedt and Dzeroski's PAC-learning results (as well as its incorporation in the CLAUDIEN system) for jk-CT are derived from results in [67] for k-CNF, Reddy and Tadepalli's results are based on the well-known results on learning horn-sentences by [3], Flipper upgrades Cohen's earlier Ripper [15], Koller's probabilistic relational models upgrade (propositional) bayesian networks, and Kirsten and Wrobel's cluster system upgrades bottom-up agglomerative clustering algorithms to first order logic.

Hence, it is clear that the methodology we presented is not really new. It has been applied - implicitly - several times before to obtain effective inductive logic programming systems. One might even argue that it has been applied in some of the pre-ILP work on relational learning (e.g. [71,48]). The most important contribution of our work therefore is to describe the underlying recipe *explicitly* and to show through a case study that it can be used to obtain novel inductive logic programming techniques. The authors would like to stress that this does not imply that this recipe is the *only* way to obtain inductive logic programming systems. Certainly, some systems, of which perhaps PROGOL [49] and MIS [62] are the best examples of well-known inductive logic programming sytems that have been derived from logical principles (without our recipe). Yet, we hope that our work gives new insights into the field of inductive logic programming and its relation to propositional machine learning.

Acknowledgements. Wim Van Laer and Luc De Raedt are supported by the ALADIN Esprit Project 28.623.

The authors would like to thank the machine learning group of Leuven, and more specifically Hendrik Blockeel, Luc Dehaspe and Maurice Bruynooghe, for their feedback, comments and interesting discussions on this topic.

The breast cancer, lymphography and primary-tumor domain were obtained from the University Medical Centre, Institute of Oncology, Ljubljana, Slovenia. Thanks go to M. Zwitter and M. Soklic for providing the data.

The Mutagenesis dataset is made public by King and Srinivasan [65] and is available at the ILP data repository [41].

More info on ICL can be found online:
`http://www.cs.kuleuven.ac.be/~wimv/ICL/main.html`.

References

1. R. Agrawal, H. Mannila, R. Srikant, H. Toivonen, and A.I. Verkamo. Fast discovery of association rules. In U. Fayyad, G. Piatetsky-Shapiro, P. Smyth, and R. Uthurusamy, editors, *Advances in Knowledge Discovery and Data Mining*, pages 307–328. The MIT Press, 1996.
2. Rakesh Agrawal, Tomasz Imielinski, and Arun Swami. Mining association rules between sets of items in large databases. In P. Buneman and S. Jajodia, editors, *Proceedings of ACM SIGMOD Conference on Management of Data*, pages 207–216, Washington, D.C., USA, May 1993. ACM.
3. D. Angluin, M. Frazier, and L. Pitt. Learning conjunctions of Horn clauses. *Machine Learning*, 9:147–162, 1992.
4. F. Bergadano and D. Gunetti. An interactive system to learn functional logic programs. In *Proceedings of the Thirteenth International Joint Conference on Artificial Intelligence*, pages 1044–1049. Morgan Kaufmann, 1993.
5. A.L. Berger, V.J. Della Pietra, and S.A. Della Pietra. A maximum entropy approach to natural language processing. *Computational Linguistics*, 22(1):39–71, 1996.
6. G. Bisson. Conceptual clustering in a first order logic representation. In *Proceedings of the Tenth European Conference on Artificial Intelligence*, pages 458–462. John Wiley & Sons, 1992.

7. H. Blockeel. *Top-down induction of first order logical decision trees*. PhD thesis, Department of Computer Science, Katholieke Universiteit Leuven, 1998. `http://www.cs.kuleuven.ac.be/~ml/PS/blockeel98:phd.ps.gz`.
8. H. Blockeel and L. De Raedt. Experiments with top-down induction of logical decision trees. Technical Report CW 247, Dept. of Computer Science, K.U.Leuven, January 1997. Also in Periodic Progress Report ESPRIT Project ILP2, January 1997. `http://www.cs.kuleuven.ac.be/publicaties/rapporten/CW1997.html`.
9. H. Blockeel and L. De Raedt. Top-down induction of first order logical decision trees. *Artificial Intelligence*, 101(1-2):285–297, June 1998.
10. M. Bongard. *Pattern Recognition*. Spartan Books, 1970.
11. I. Bratko and S. Muggleton. Applications of inductive logic programming. *Communications of the ACM*, 38(11):65–70, 1995.
12. L. Breiman, J.H. Friedman, R.A. Olshen, and C.J. Stone. *Classification and Regression Trees*. Wadsworth, Belmont, 1984.
13. P. Clark and R. Boswell. Rule induction with CN2: Some recent improvements. In Yves Kodratoff, editor, *Proceedings of the Fifth European Working Session on Learning*, volume 482 of *Lecture Notes in Artificial Intelligence*, pages 151–163. Springer-Verlag, 1991.
14. P. Clark and T. Niblett. The CN2 algorithm. *Machine Learning*, 3(4):261–284, 1989.
15. W. Cohen. Fast effective rule induction. In *Proceedings of the twelfth International Conference on Machine Learning*, pages 115–123. Morgan Kaufmann, 1995.
16. W. Cohen. Learning to classify English text with ILP methods. In Luc De Raedt, editor, *Advances in inductive logic programming*, pages 124–143. IOS Press, Amsterdam, NL, 1996.
17. W.W. Cohen. Grammatically biased learning: learning logic programs using an explicit antecedent description language. *Artificial Intelligence*, 68:303–366, 1994.
18. L. De Raedt. Logical settings for concept learning. *Artificial Intelligence*, 95:187–201, 1997.
19. L. De Raedt. Attribute-value learning versus inductive logic programming: the missing links (extended abstract). In D. Page, editor, *Proceedings of the Eighth International Conference on Inductive Logic Programming*, volume 1446 of *Lecture Notes in Artificial Intelligence*, pages 1–8. Springer-Verlag, 1998.
20. L. De Raedt and L. Dehaspe. Clausal discovery. *Machine Learning*, 26:99–146, 1997.
21. L. De Raedt and S. Džeroski. First order jk-clausal theories are PAC-learnable. *Artificial Intelligence*, 70:375–392, 1994.
22. L. De Raedt, N. Lavrač, and S. Džeroski. Multiple predicate learning. In *Proceedings of the Thirteenth International Joint Conference on Artificial Intelligence*, pages 1037–1042. Morgan Kaufmann, 1993.
23. L. De Raedt and W. Van Laer. Inductive constraint logic. In Klaus P. Jantke, Takeshi Shinohara, and Thomas Zeugmann, editors, *Proceedings of the Sixth International Workshop on Algorithmic Learning Theory*, volume 997 of *Lecture Notes in Artificial Intelligence*, pages 80–94. Springer-Verlag, 1995.
24. L. Dehaspe. Maximum entropy modeling with clausal constraints. In *Proceedings of the Seventh International Workshop on Inductive Logic Programming*, volume 1297 of *Lecture Notes in Artificial Intelligence*, pages 109–124. Springer-Verlag, 1997.
25. L. Dehaspe. *Frequent Pattern Discovery in First-Order Logic*. PhD thesis, Department of Computer Science, Katholieke Universiteit Leuven, 1998. `http://www.cs.kuleuven.ac.be/~ldh/`.

26. L. Dehaspe and L. De Raedt. Mining association rules in multiple relations. In *Proceedings of the Seventh International Workshop on Inductive Logic Programming*, volume 1297 of *Lecture Notes in Artificial Intelligence*, pages 125–132, Berlin, 1997. Springer-Verlag.

27. B. Dolsak, I. Bratko, and A. Jezernik. Finite element mesh design: An engineering domain for ILP application. In S. Wrobel, editor, *Proceedings of the Fourth International Workshop on Inductive Logic Programming*, volume 237 of *GMD-Studien*, Sankt Augustin, Germany, 1994. Gesellschaft für Mathematik und Datenverarbeitung MBH.

28. Pedro Domingos. A process-oriented heuristic for model selection. In *Proceedings of the Fifteenth International Conference on Machine Learning*, pages 127–135. Morgan Kaufmann, San Francisco, CA, 1998.

29. J. Dougherty, R. Kohavi, and M. Sahami. Supervised and unsupervised discretization of continuous features. In A. Prieditis and S. Russell, editors, *Proceedings of the Twelfth International Conference on Machine Learning*. Morgan Kaufmann, 1995.

30. S. Džeroski, S. Schulze-Kremer, K. R. Heidtke, K. Siems, D. Wettschereck, and H. Blockeel. Diterpene structure elucidation from ^{13}C NMR spectra with inductive logic programming. *Applied Artificial Intelligence*, 12(5):363–384, July-August 1998.

31. S. Džeroski and I. Bratko. Applications of inductive logic programming. In L. De Raedt, editor, *Advances in inductive logic programming*, volume 32 of *Frontiers in Artificial Intelligence and Applications*, pages 65–81. IOS Press, 1996.

32. S. Džeroski, B. Cestnik, and I. Petrovski. Using the m-estimate in rule induction. *Journal of Computing and Information Technology*, 1(1):37 – 46, 1993.

33. S. Džeroski, N. Jacobs, M. Molina, and C. Moure. ILP experiments in detecting traffic problems. In *Proceedings of the Tenth European Conference on Machine Learning*, Lecture Notes in Artificial Intelligence, pages 61–66. Springer-Verlag, August 1998.

34. S. Džeroski, N. Jacobs, M. Molina, C. Moure, S. Muggleton, and W. Van Laer. Detecting traffic problems with ILP. In *Proceedings of the Eighth International Conference on Inductive Logic Programming*, volume 1446 of *Lecture Notes in Artificial Intelligence*. Springer-Verlag, 1998.

35. S. Džeroski, H. Blockeel, S. Kramer, B. Kompare, B. Pfahringer, and W. Van Laer. Experiments in predicting biodegradability. In S. Džeroski and P. Flach, editors, *Proceedings of the Ninth International Workshop on Inductive Logic Programming*, volume 1634 of *Lecture Notes in Artificial Intelligence*, pages 80–91. Springer-Verlag, 1999.

36. W. Emde and D. Wettschereck. Relational instance-based learning. In L. Saitta, editor, *Proceedings of the Thirteenth International Conference on Machine Learning*, pages 122–130. Morgan Kaufmann, 1996.

37. U.M. Fayyad and K.B. Irani. Multi-interval discretization of continuous-valued attributes for classification learning. In *Proceedings of the Thirteenth International Joint Conference on Artificial Intelligence*, pages 1022–1027, San Mateo, CA, 1993. Morgan Kaufmann.

38. P.A. Flach. Strongly typed inductive concept learning. In D. Page, editor, *Proceedings of the Eighth International Conference on Inductive Logic Programming*, volume 1446, pages 185–194. Springer-Verlag, 1998.

39. J.G. Ganascia and Y. Kodratoff. Improving the generalization step in learning. In R.S Michalski, J.G. Carbonell, and T.M. Mitchell, editors, *Machine Learning: an artificial intelligence approach*, volume 2, pages 215–241. Morgan Kaufmann, 1986.

40. F. Hayes-Roth and J. McDermott. An interference matching technique for inducing abstractions. *Communications of the ACM*, 21:401–410, 1978.

41. D. Kazakov, L. Popelinsky, and O. Stepankova. ILP datasets page [http://www.gmd.de/ml-archive/datasets/ilp-res.html], 1996.

42. J-U. Kietz and S. Wrobel. Controlling the complexity of learning in logic through syntactic and task-oriented models. In S. Muggleton, editor, *Inductive logic programming*, pages 335–359. Academic Press, 1992.

43. R.D. King, M.J.E. Sternberg, A. Srinivasan, and S.H. Muggleton. Relating chemical activity to structure: an examination of ILP successes. *New Generation Computing*, 13(3-4):411–434, 1995.

44. M. Kirsten and S. Wrobel. Relational distance-based clustering. In *Proceedings of the Eighth International Conference on Inductive Logic Programming*, Lecture Notes in Artificial Intelligence, pages 261–270. Springer-Verlag, 1998.

45. D. Koller. Probabilistic relational models. In *Proceedings of the Ninth International Workshop on Inductive Logic Programming*, volume 1634 of *Lecture Notes in Artificial Intelligence*, pages 3–13. Springer-Verlag, 1999.

46. Stefan Kramer. Structural regression trees. In *Proceedings of the Thirteenth National Conference on Artificial Intelligence*, pages 812–819, Cambridge/Menlo Park, 1996. AAAI Press/MIT Press.

47. R. Michalski, I. Mozetic, J. Hong, and N. Lavrac. The AQ15 inductive learning system: an overview and experiments. In *Proceedings of IMAL 1986*, Orsay, 1986. Université de Paris-Sud.

48. R.S. Michalski. A theory and methodology of inductive learning. In R.S Michalski, J.G. Carbonell, and T.M. Mitchell, editors, *Machine Learning: an artificial intelligence approach*, volume 1. Morgan Kaufmann, 1983.

49. S. Muggleton. Inverse entailment and Progol. *New Generation Computing, Special issue on Inductive Logic Programming*, 13(3-4):245–286, 1995.

50. S. Muggleton and L. De Raedt. Inductive logic programming : Theory and methods. *Journal of Logic Programming*, 19,20:629–679, 1994.

51. S. Muggleton and C. Feng. Efficient induction of logic programs. In *Proceedings of the First Conference on Algorithmic Learning Theory*, pages 368–381. Ohmsma, Tokyo, Japan, 1990.

52. C. Nédellec, H. Adé, F. Bergadano, and B. Tausend. Declarative bias in ILP. In L. De Raedt, editor, *Advances in Inductive Logic Programming*, volume 32 of *Frontiers in Artificial Intelligence and Applications*, pages 82–103. IOS Press, 1996.

53. S.-H. Nienhuys-Cheng and R. Wolf. *Foundations of inductive logic programming*, volume 1228 of *Lecture Notes in Computer Science and Lecture Notes in Artificial Intelligence*. Springer-Verlag, New York, NY, USA, 1997.

54. G. Plotkin. A note on inductive generalization. In B. Meltzer and D. Michie, editors, *Machine Intelligence*, volume 5, pages 153–163. Edinburgh University Press, 1970.

55. U. Pompe and I. Kononenko. Probabilistic first-order classification. In *Proceedings of the Seventh International Workshop on Inductive Logic Programming*. Springer-Verlag, 1997.

56. J. Ross Quinlan. *C4.5: Programs for Machine Learning*. Morgan Kaufmann series in machine learning. Morgan Kaufmann, 1993.

57. J.R. Quinlan. Induction of decision trees. *Machine Learning*, 1:81–106, 1986.

58. J.R. Quinlan. Learning logical definitions from relations. *Machine Learning*, 5:239–266, 1990.

59. J.R. Quinlan. Determinate Literals in Inductive Logic Programming. In *Proceedings of the Eighth International Workshop on Machine Learning*, pages 442–446. Morgan Kaufmann, 1991.
60. J.R. Quinlan. Learning first-order definitions of functions. *Journal of Artificial Intelligence Research*, 5:139–161, 1996.
61. C. Reddy and P. Tadepalli. Learning first-order acyclic Horn programs from entailment. In David Page, editor, *Proceedings of the Eighth International Conference on Inductive Logic Programming*, volume 1446 of *LNAI*, pages 23–37. Springer, 1998.
62. E.Y. Shapiro. An algorithm that infers theories from facts. In *Proceedings of the Seventh International Joint Conference on Artificial Intelligence*, pages 446–452. Morgan Kaufmann, 1981.
63. A. Srinivasan, R. D. King, S. H. Muggleton, and M. Sternberg. The predictive toxicology evaluation challenge. In *Proceedings of the Fifteenth International Joint Conference on Artificial Intelligence)*, pages 1–6. Morgan Kaufmann, 1997.
64. A. Srinivasan, R.D. King, and D.W. Bristol. An assessment of ILP-assisted models for toxicology and the PTE-3 experiment. In *Proceedings of the Ninth International Workshop on Inductive Logic Programming*, volume 1634 of *Lecture Notes in Artificial Intelligence*, pages 291–302. Springer-Verlag, 1999.
65. A. Srinivasan, S.H. Muggleton, M.J.E. Sternberg, and R.D. King. Theories for mutagenicity: A study in first-order and feature-based induction. *Artificial Intelligence*, 85(1,2), 1996.
66. H. Toivonen, M. Klemettinen, et al. Pruning and grouping discovered association rules. In Y. Kodratoff, G. Nakhaeizadeh, and G. Taylor, editors, *Proceedings of the MLnet Familiarization Workshop on Statistics, Machine Learning and Knowledge Discovery in Databases*, pages 47–52, Heraklion, Crete, Greece, 1995.
67. L. Valiant. A theory of the learnable. *Communications of the ACM*, 27:1134–1142, 1984.
68. Patrick R. J. van der Laag and Shan-Hwei Nienhuys-Cheng. Completeness and properness of refinement operators in inductive logic programming. *Journal of Logic Programming*, 34(3):201–225, 1998.
69. W. Van Laer, L. De Raedt, and S. Džeroski. On multi-class problems and discretization in inductive logic programming. In Zbigniew W. Ras and Andrzej Skowron, editors, *Proceedings of the Tenth International Symposium on Methodologies for Intelligent Systems*, volume 1325 of *Lecture Notes in Artificial Intelligence*, pages 277–286. Springer-Verlag, 1997.
70. W. Van Laer, S. Džeroski, and L. De Raedt. Multi-class problems and discretization in ICL (extended abstract). In *Proceedings of the MLnet Familiarization Workshop on Data Mining with Inductive Logic Programming*, pages 53–60, 1996.
71. S.A. Vere. Induction of concepts in the predicate calculus. In *Proceedings of the Fourth International Joint Conference on Artificial Intelligence*, pages 282–287. Morgan Kaufmann, 1975.
72. C. Vrain. Ogust: A system that learns using domain properties expressed as theorems. In Y. Kodratoff and R.S. Michalski, editors, *Machine Learning: an artificial intelligence approach*, volume 3, pages 360–381. Morgan Kaufmann, 1990.
73. P.H. Winston. Learning structural descriptions from examples. In P.H. Winston, editor, *Psychology of Computer Vision*. The MIT Press, 1975.

Case-Based Reasoning

Ramon Lopez de Mantaras

IIIA-Artificial Intelligence Research Institute
CSIC-Spanish Scientific Research Council
mantaras@iiia.csic.es

1 Introduction

This chapter contains an overview of Case-Based Reasoning (CBR). The main goal is to have a balance between brevity and expressiveness and to provide helpful pointers to literature in the field. To do so, we first describe the CBR types and the CBR cycle, then we briefly review a representative set of systems, next we discuss the connections between CBR and learning. The main part of the chapter analyses the most important issues and problems of the CBR components, such as indexing/retrieval/selection, memory organization, adaptation/evaluation, forgetting, and integration with other techniques. Finally, we discuss the added value of incorporating fuzzy techniques in CBR and briefly describe some representative Fuzzy-CBR systems.

Case-based reasoning (CBR) is a major paradigm in automated reasoning and machine learning. In case-based reasoning, a reasoner solves a new problem by noticing its similarity with one or several previously solved problems and by adapting their known solutions instead of working out a solution from scratch. In many aspects, case-based reasoning is a problem solving method different from other AI approaches. In particular, instead of using only general domain dependent heuristic knowledge like in the case of expert systems, it is able to use the specific knowledge of concrete, previously experienced, problem situations. Another important characteristic is that CBR implies incremental learning since a new experience is memorized and available for future problem solving each time a problem is solved. Case-based reasoning is a powerful and frequently used way of human problem solving. Results from cognitive psychology have shown its psychological plausibility.

Case-based reasoning can provide an alternative to rule-based expert systems, and is especially appropriate when the number of rules needed to capture an expert's knowledge is unmanageable or when the domain theory is too weak or incomplete. CBR can work in problem domains where the underlying models used for solutions are not well understood. Historically, CBR has shown its greatest success in areas where individual cases or precedents govern the decision-making processes, as in case law.

1.1 CBR Types and the CBR Cycle

Case-based reasoning can mean different things depending on the intended use of the reasoning: adapt and combine old solutions to solve a new problem, explain new situations according to previously experienced similar situations, critique new

G. Paliouras, V. Karkaletsis, and C.D. Spyropoulos (Eds.): ACAI '99, LNAI 2049, pp. 127-145, 2001.
© Springer-Verlag Berlin Heidelberg 2001

solutions based on old cases, reasoning from precedents to understand a new situation, or build a consensus solution based on previous cases. However, these different aspects can be classified into two major types: interpretive (or classification) CBR, and problem solving CBR [73]. In interpretive CBR the key aspect is arguing whether or not a new situation should be treated like previous ones based on similarities and differences among them. In problem solving CBR, the goal is to build a solution to a new case based on the adaptation of solutions to past cases. This division, though it is useful to present the field, it is not always clear in practice because many problems have components of both types of CBR and certainly the most effective case-based learners will use a combination of both methods. For example, the labor mediation application [117], which deals with the resolution of labor-related disputes, needs both interpreting the situation and then deriving a solution based on precedents. Furthermore, many systems use interpretive CBR to evaluate the solutions reached since evaluation is one of the basic operations in any case-based reasoner. In general, given a case to solve, case-based reasoning involves the following steps :

1. retrieving relevant cases from the case memory (this requires to index the cases by appropriate features);
2. selecting a set of best cases;
3. deriving a solution;
4. evaluating the solution (in order to make sure that poor solutions are not repeated);
5. storing the newly solved case in the case memory.

According to these steps, Aamodt and Plaza in [3] describe a Case-Based reasoner as a cyclic process comprising "the 4 R's": Retrieve, Reuse, Revise and Retain, that is:

1. RETRIEVE the most similar previously experienced case or cases
2. REUSE the information and knowledge in the retrieved case(s) to solve the new problem
3. REVISE the solution
4. RETAIN the parts of this experience that are likely to be useful in the future by incorporating it into the case base

In this chapter we first briefly review some CBR systems from the point of view of existing representative applications. Next we focus our attention to case-based reasoning as a learning paradigm and we point to the main issues and problems associated with the different CBR components. Finally, we discuss the added value of incorporating fuzzy techniques in CBR and briefly describe some representative Fuzzy-CBR systems.

2   Some Representative CBR Systems

The case-based approach to reasoning and learning (Kolodner 83) has been growing impressively during the last few years. Today there are more than one hundred CBR systems reported in the literature. Kolodner in her very book [73] reports 82 CBR systems in the USA. Today we can find hundreds of CBR systems reported in the literature all over the world [76], [124]. Furthermore, there are specialized workshops and conferences held every year both in the US and in Europe with a quite large number of participants and in all major conferences in AI one can find several sessions devoted to this topic. The pioneering work in this field is that of Schank on Dynamic Memory [108], Carbonell on Analogy [33] and Kolodner who was really the first to build a case-based reasoning and learning system called CYRUS [69]. After these early works, the development of CBR continued with further work by Kolodner and students [70], [71], [118], as well as the work of Hammond and others on case-based planning [57], [58], [39].

Within the problem solving type of CBR, several systems have been built addressing case-based planning and design, among them let us mention JULIA [60], [61] to plan meals; KRITIK [54] that combines case-based and model-based reasoning for the design of mechanical assemblies; CLAVIER [19] to lay out pieces made of composite materials in an autoclave; a system developed by Faltings to represent architectural design knowledge [50]; SMART [121] whose goal is to increase the planning efficiency (speed-up learning) of the system PRODIGY [34]; CREATOR [56] for the elaboration of design requirements; ARCHIE [89] and CADRE [42] to help architects understand and solve conceptual design problems.

Another important application field of problem solving CBR is diagnosis. In diagnosis, just as in planning or design, it is often necessary to adapt an old case to fit a new problem. CASEY [74] is a well known case-based system for diagnosing heart problems of patients by adaptation of the known diagnoses of previous patients. Another very interesting diagnosis system is PROTOS [18]. PROTOS diagnoses hearing disorders using a learning apprentice approach. The difficulty of this diagnosis is that many difference diagnoses have similar manifestations and the relevant differences are so subtle that novices miss them. In such a situation, PROTOS starts as a novice and when it makes a mistake, a teacher explains the mistake and as a result PROTOS learns such subtle differences by putting difference pointers in its memory that allow the system to switch from an apparently trivial but incorrect diagnosis to the correct one. Another early work in diagnosis is that of Althoff [7] on complex diagnosis issues. Other more recent representative applications to diagnosis are CASELINE [82] for airplane maintenance; a system for maintenance of telecommunication networks [43]; a system for ultrasonic railway inspection [66]. General Electric has developed a CBR system to determine what colorants to use for producing a specific color of plastic [37]. In software design applications, we can mention a system for software project effort estimation [51], the system CBModeller [75] that applies CBR to information systems design, and a system applied to software knowledge reuse to improve productivity and reliability of software development [119].

In interpretive CBR, the first works are those of Rissland and Ashley with the development of a system for legal reasoning called HYPO [15]. In HYPO, the cases retrieved are of two different types, those supporting the new situation which are used to argument in favor and those against the new situation which are used as counter-arguments.The result is a set of three-ply arguments supporting the proposed solution. There are many other interpretive CBR systems in the legal domain, among them let us cite [16], [28], [125].

The latest field where CBR seems to be also useful is creativity [120], [113], [22], [81]. The main working hypothesis is that much creativity stems from using old solutions in novel ways. A particularly interesting application is the generation of expressive music based on examples of human interpretations achieved by the SAXEX system [11], [12]. SAXEX extracts information related to several expressive parameters from human recordings by means of spectral modeling techniques. This set of parameters and the scores of the interpretations constitute the set of cases. From these, the system decides a set of expressive transformations to apply to a new and inexpressive musical phrase given as input the sound file. This decision is based on the similarity between the new phrase and the cases. The similarity is based on background musical knowledge. Finally, SAXEX applies the transformations to the sound file using its synthesis capabilities and the results are actually audible.

3   Case Based Reasoning as a Learning Paradigm

Learning in AI is usually taken to mean generalizing through induction or explanation. Learning is in fact inherent to any case-based reasoner not only because it induces also generalizations based on the detected similarities between cases but mostly because it accumulates and indexes cases in a case memory for later use. The main difference of the CBR approach to inductive learning methods is that CBR emphasizes the semantics of a given domain through similarity based retrieval and case adaptation knowledge. Case-based reasoning as a learning paradigm has several technical advantages:

- Since each new solved case is stored in memory for later use, instead of deriving new solutions from scratch, a CBR system remembers and adapts old solutions. If such solutions have been adapted in a different novel way or combined in a different way then, when solving another similar case, these circumstances will be remembered rather than re-derived.
- A case-based reasoner becomes more competent over time, can avoid previously made mistakes, and can focus on the most important parts of a problem first.
- CBR enables prototype systems to operate with a small initial set of cases and to increase its coverage by storing new cases incrementally.

Since many efforts in CBR address the problem of finding techniques to analyze and select cases, perhaps some of these techniques could be used by the rest of the machine learning community to help in the selection of training instances.

Perhaps the most important advantage of the case-based approach to learning is its affinity to human learning: people take into account and use past experiences to take future decisions.

Instance-based learning (IBL) is a particular case of case-based learning. IBL algorithms [5] store previously categorized examples and use them to classify new inputs by assigning the same classification that was assigned to the most similar previous example. Although they may involve complex indexing, they use a limited representation (feature-value) and do not address case-adaptation.

Case-based learning algorithms have been applied to a large variety of tasks, among them we can point to the following ones : predicting power load levels for the Niagara Mohawk Power Co. [64]; speech recognition [27]; evaluating oil prospecting sites in the North Sea [38]; knowledge acquisition and refinement [112]; robotic control [85]; molecular biology [41]; architectural design [50], [109]; and medicine [92], [106], [5], [80], [83].

4   Components, Issues, and Problems

4.1   Indexing/Retrieval/Selection

The most basic problems in CBR are the retrieval and selection of cases since the remaining operations of adaptation and evaluation will succeed only if the past cases are the relevant ones. The retrieval of relevant cases depends on the good indexing of the cases. One way to do it is to fix the indices a priori for a given domain but the problem is the loss in generality. Among the techniques being explored to solve this problem we can mention: Inductive Learning methods to identify predictive features which will then be used as indices [78], instance-based learning to learn feature importance, introspective reasoning to learn features for indexing and Explanation-based techniques to identify relevant features. Explanation-based techniques are used to justify the actions of a case with respect to those features known when the case was originally executed. Demonstrably relevant features are generalized to form primary indices. Inconsistencies between the domain theory and the actual case are used to determine irrelevant features. The remaining features are marked as secondary indices that are subject to refinement using similarity-based inductive techniques [20]. In learning feature importance, each feature is associated with a weight that is adjusted after each prediction attempt during the training process. The adjustment is done by comparing the current case with its most similar stored case [5], [63], [126]. The introspective approach in [52] provides the CBR system with an introspective reasoning capability to detect poor retrievals, identify features which would retrieve more adaptable cases and refine the indexing criteria to avoid future failures. The work of [23] also uses an introspective learning approach to improve the retrieval in an application to air traffic control.

Some researchers take the approach of defining vocabularies for describing different types of problems in an attempt to discover the content of indices that allow reminding across individual domains [55]. Heuristic search techniques and Qualitative Models are also very promising approaches to the indexing/retrieval problem [102]. Heuristic search techniques [102] are used in a graph containing cases and domain knowledge to look for support for legal arguments. The idea is to narrow the gap between the available indexing scheme and the requirements of arguments through the use of best-first search guided by evaluation functions. A qualitative model of a physical system has been used in [99] to derive minimal sets of control parameters relevant to each of the desired inputs in a two stage sewage treatment plant. This approach reduces the number of features used for indexing the cases in a CBR system, which suggests the settings of the control parameters based on past experience in controlling the plant.

Selecting the best case requires being able to find matching cases together. Nearest Neighbor techniques that provide a measure of how similar a previous case is to a given problem. In general the match is not perfect because on the one hand, the values of the features of the new case and previous cases are not exactly the same and on the other hand there are ususally missing values for some or many of the features, therefore the usual approach is to define some similarity metric.

The matching problem is being studied by many researchers ([21], [26], [104] and others). An additional difficulty is that the similarity metrics must take into account the different importance of the features. In some situations a weighted similarity measure can be used to account for these differences, but often this is not possible because the importance of some features is context dependent. Usually, the context is represented by the cases already in memory and therefore they can be used to determine which features of the new case are the most important ones. There are several methods based on this observation: preference heuristics [72], dimensional analysis [101], the use of dynamically changing weighted evaluation functions [115] and the use of domain specific knowledge to influence similarity judgments [32], [111], [116]. A similar approach [21] uses a CBR+EBL similarity metric that is able to assign a relevance measure to each matching fact. Up to now, practically all the existing similarity measures assume that cases are represented just by collections of feature-value pairs, however we have started to see the need for more structured representations in complex domains [10], [107] and therefore for new approaches to similarity such as graph similarity measures already used in pattern recognition [31], [93], or using domain knowledge to describe declarative biases to guide the retrieval process [10]. In [88] a formal framework for the construction of similarity metrics which subsume boolean, numeric and structured measures of similarity is introduced.

Finally, let us mention a very interesting approach [122] that allows to incrementally learn better similarity metrics by interpreting the behaviour of the analogical problem solver PRODIGY replaying retrieved cases. To do so, the problem solver provides information about the utility of the candidate cases suggested as similar. This information is used to refine the case library organization and the similarity metric. This process starts with a simple metric that is refined by analysing the derivational trace produced by PRODIGY.

4.2   Memory Organization

Another basic problem is that of memory organization. Good indexing is not enough when the case memory is large Good organization of the memory is necessary because a simple linear organization, like a list, is very inefficient for retrieval purposes (see Watson and Perera [124] for an evaluation study). A much better approach is to have a hierarchical structure, where internal nodes are generalizations of individual cases, as in the system CYRUS [69] based on Schank's dynamic memory model [108]. Almost all the existing CBR systems use memory organizations inspired either by Schank's dynamic memory or by Porter's PROTOS approach [94].

The case memory in the dynamic memory model is a hierarchical structure of 'episodic memory organization packets'. The basic idea is to organize specific cases which share similar properties under a more general structure called 'generalized episode' (GE). A GE contains norms, cases and indices. Norms are features common to all cases, indexed under a GE, and indices are features which discriminate between cases of a GE. An index is composed of an index name and an index value. The entire case memory is in fact a discrimination network where a node is either a generalized episode, an index, or a case. When a new case description input is given and the search for the best matching commences, the input case structure is "pushed down" the discrimination network starting at the root node. When one or more features of the input case match one or more features of a GE, the case is further discriminated based on its remaining features. A case is retrieved by finding the GE with most norms in common with the problem description, and the indices under that GE are then traversed in order to find the case which contains most of the remaining problem features. In case storing, when a feature of the case matches a feature of an existing case, a GE is created. The two cases can be discriminated by indexing them under different indices below the GE. If two cases or two GEs end up under the same index, a new GE is automatically created. Hence, the memory structure is dynamic in the sense that similar parts of the two cases are dynamically generalized into a GE.

In PROTOS [94], an alternative hierarchical organization is used. The case memory is embedded in a network structure of categories, semantic relations, cases, and index pointers. Each case is associated with a category and indices may either point to a case or a category. The indices are of three types: Feature links pointing from problem features to cases or categories (called remindings), case links pointing from categories to their associated cases (called exemplars), which are sorted according to their degree of typicality in the category, and difference links pointing from cases to 'near cases' that only differ in a small number of features. Furthermore, the categories are interlinked within a semantic network that represents domain knowledge and enables to provide an explanatory support to some of the CBR tasks. Finding a case in memory that matches an input description is done by combining the input features of a problem case into a pointer to the case or category that shares most of its features with the problem case. If a reminding points directly to a category, the links to its most prototypical cases are traversed and these cases are retrieved. The semantic network of domain knowledge is used to enable matching of features that are semantically similar. A new case is stored by searching for a matching case and by establishing the appropriate feature indices. If an old case is found with only minor differences to the input case, the input case may not be retained or the two cases may be merged by generalizing some features according to the taxonomic links in the semantic network.

BOLERO [79] combines Schank's and Porter's approaches. It uses the generalized episodes of Schank together with the exemplar links, difference links and prototypes of Porter. The structure of the cases themselves is also an important issue. While most case-based systems store each case as a unit, others break the cases and store them into pieces along with pointers for later reconstruction [60], [79]. The advantage of this last approach is that it allows solving complex problems by combining partial solutions of several other problems. Finally, an obvious approach to the problem of dealing with large memories of cases is the use of massive parallelism for both the parallel matching of cases and indices [72].

4.3   Adaptation/Evaluation

A good adaptation of old cases to fit the new case can reduce significantly the amount of work needed to solve it. Early work by Hammond, Sycara, and others in case-based planning addressed the adaptation issue, which however afterwards received less attention. More recently, the interest in adaptation has increased again. For example, quite a few papers have addressed this problem in the recent workshops and conferences on CBR. One adaptation technique uses generalization and refinement heuristics. An example is the plausible design adaptation for design tasks [62]. This adaptation is a process that takes a source concept, a set of constraints and constraint violations, and a set of adaptation transformations and returns a new concept that satisfies the constraints. Chatterjee and Campbell [36] use an interpolation technique to adapt old cases. Zeyer and Weiss [128] use a similarity-based adaptation approach. Hanney and Keane [59] use inductive learning techniques to learn adaptation knowledge from case comparisons. Leake et al [77] use CBR and introspective reasoning to learn case adaptation. Portinale et al [95] introduce a technique called Pivoting-Based retrieval that exploits a heuristic estimate of the adaptability of a solution determining in this way which cases are worth to retrieve. Purvis and Athalye [97] address the situations in which initially retrieved cases are not easily adaptable, and propose a genetic algorithm to improve case adaptability. The relations between case adaptation and case retrieval are also being studied [114].

Evaluation gives feedback to the case-based reasoner about whether or not the new case was solved adequately. If the solution is not adequate, the retrieval of additional cases may be required, which may result in the need for an additional adaptation stage called repair. Some of the major issues involved include strategies for evaluating cases and the assignment of blame or credit to old cases [73].

4.4   Forgetting

Even assuming that we have solved the basic problems of retrieval and indexing there is still an additional, somehow unexpected, problem resulting from an uncontrolled growth of the case memory which may result in the degradation of the performance of the system, as a direct consequence of the increased cost in accessing memory. Existing approaches to this problem include: storing new cases selectively (for example only when the existing cases in memory lead to a classification error) and deleting cases occasionally [68]; and incorporating a restricted expressiveness policy into the indexing scheme, by placing an upper bound on the size of a case that can be matched [53].

4.5   Integration with Other Techniques

In some application domains there is a need to combine CBR with other reasoning techniques such as model-based or rule-based reasoning. Some examples are the following: JULIA [60], integrating CBR and constraints for design tasks; Aamodt's work on knowledge intensive case-based reasoning [1]; CARS [25] that combines case-based and fuzzy rule-based systems (see section 6.4); CREEK [2] which integrates rules and cases and a top level control strategy to decide whether to activate rules or cases to achieve a goal; CABARET [100], which integrates rule-based and case-based reasoning to facilitate the use of rules containing ill-defined terms; GREBE [29], which also integrates rules and cases; PATDEX/MOLTKE [8] integrating models, cases and compiled knowledge; MoCas [90], combining case-based and model-based reasoning for technical diagnosis applications; the work of Portinale et al [95], who also use a combination of models and cases for diagnosis; QMC [4], which uses a semi-qualitative model to reason about possible effects of differences between cases and about the possible causes of observed problems; IKBALS [127], which integrates rules and cases for intelligent information retrieval; A LA CARTE [87], which uses cases to tune rules in a KBS; BOLERO [79] integrating rule-based reasoning at the domain level with case-based reasoning at the meta-level in such a way that the cases guide the inference process at the domain level, allowing learning of control knowledge by experience (see section 6.2); and NOOS [91], [13], a reflective architecture capable of integrating different inference and learning methods. Karacapilidis et al [67] integrate CBR and argumentation-based reasoning to address group decision making processes. There is also work addressing the integration of case-based and inductive learning to enhance problem solving [40], [17], [84], [13], [9]. Finally, there work integrating CBR and Bayesian reasoning. This work includes the work by Myllymäki and Tirri [86] for case matching and adaptation in a connectionist network, Breese and Heckerman [30] to identify the most probable cases for diagnostic purposes, Chang and Harrison [35] to guide retrieval and indexing, and Aha and Chang [6] for agent cooperation in multi-agent planning tasks. In these cases, the Bayesian network is used to characterize action selection and the CBR is used to determine how to implement actions.

4.6   Uncertainty, Imprecision, and Incompleteness in CBR

Uncertainty, imprecision and incompleteness are problems that pervade the CBR reasoning process. Uncertainty and imprecision are present in the semantics of abstract features used to index the cases, in the evaluation of the similarity measures computed across these features, in the determination of relevancy and saliency of similar cases, and in the modification rules used in the solution adaptation phase. Incompleteness is also present in the partial domain theory used in indexing and retrieval, in the (usually) sparse coverage of the problem space by the existing cases, and in the description of the problem. In [49], the author uses probability theory to model the uncertainty associated with the main assumption of CBR that to similar problems correspond similar solutions. He shows that even if that assumption is not met for particular instances, it is correct on the average. In [103], the authors propose a Bayesian network modeling for CBR. Their model uses two networks, one for ranking categories, and another for identifying exemplars within categories. This view leads to the notion of modeling similarities by conditional probabilities. Therefore it computes the probability of an exemplar given the features to classify a new case. Probability theory cannot however model imprecision easily. Fuzzy logic provides better techniques to deal with imprecision. The following sections are devoted to discussing the Fuzzy Logic approach to CBR.

5   Fuzzy CBR: Value Added to Conventional CBR

Fuzzy Logic techniques have proven to be very useful in addressing some aspects of the above open problems such as the representation of imprecise information, case retrieval and case adaptation. For example, in case representation Fuzzy Logic provides a characterization for imprecise and uncertain information, in case retrieval it helps evaluating partial matches by means of fuzzy matching techniques [44]; and in case adaptation it helps modifying the selected case by means of gradual rules [45] and aggregating the solutions of different cases by means of fuzzy combination rules, according to well defined operators called triangular norms [110]. Early work on fuzzy case-based reasoning is represented by Plaza and Lopez de Mantaras [92], Bonissone and Ayub [25] and Salotti [105]. In this section we discuss this issue in more detail. More specifically, the following aspects have been, or are being, addressed using fuzzy techniques:

1. The casebase itself can be considered a fuzzy set since the cases it contains are not all simply "completely useful" or "not at all useful". Instead their usefulness is a matter of degree (depending on the problem at hand) and this can be exploited in a fuzzy case-based reasoner.

2. At the representation level, Fuzzy Logic allows to represent cases whose attributes have imprecise values and in particular linguistic values [92], [25], [80], [65].

3. In order to retrieve appropriate cases, fuzzy prototypes - that is prototypes described by means of fuzzy terms - can be used [92]. Additionally, viewing the description of a case as a tuple of attribute values, fuzzy logic provides a powerful weighted fuzzy pattern matching mechanism [44] to compute the overall similarity between cases from partial similarities between the attributes describing the cases. Weighted fuzzy pattern matching allows also to take into account the relative level of importance of each attribute in the comparison process, thus limiting the penalty on the matching of cases that differ on unimportant attributes. Fuzzy logic can also be used to represent the degree of similarity between attribute values that are not precisely known. When the cases are imprecisely or incompletely described, their similarity measures can be described by lower and upper bounds, obtained from possibility and necessity measures respectively [46].

4. Gradual rules of the general form "the more similar two cases are with respect to some attribute(s), the more similar they possibly are with respect to their solution" were developed within the framework of fuzzy logic and are the basis for many approximate reasoning applications. However they can also be used in case adaptation - that is in adapting to the unsolved case the values appearing in the known cases of the case base. Conditions can also include the assessment of difference between cases like for example in the rule "if two used cars are similar except for the mileage run, the difference between their prices will be a function of the mileage difference". In [47] and [48], a gradual rule-based formalization of the similarity-based inference process of CBR is proposed. This is the first attempt to provide a logical formalization of CBR.

6   A Brief Account of Fuzzy Case-Based Reasoning Systems

In this section we describe a representative sample of fuzzy techniques present in several important case-based systems. They all share the capability of using attributes with fuzzy values and using a fuzzy pattern matcher for case retrieval.

6.1   The ARC System

The memory organization of the ARC system [92] is a hierarchy of classes and cases. Each class is represented by a fuzzy prototype, which is a description of the features common to most of the cases belonging in the class. Furthermore, each class is linked to a set of sub-classes, a set of differentially indexed cases and also to cases that are near-misses. The memory organization is dynamic in the sense that classes can be modified or created after each reasoning step. The retrieval process selects first the most promising classes by means of a fuzzy pattern-matching algorithm based on common features. Next, cases are selected based on the similarities and differences between the classes and the cases. Finally, near-misses are used to avoid repeating past failures. The certainty values of the fuzzy prototypes and the matching degree are expressed by means of linguistic values.

6.2   The BOLERO System

BOLERO [80] is a system that integrates rule-based and case-based representations. The object level knowledge of BOLERO is represented by rules and the meta-knowledge contains the solved instances of problems, conveniently organized in the memory of cases. Since these solved instances can contain uncertain and imprecise values, linguistic values represented by fuzzy sets are used. Moreover, the pattern matching algorithm at the retrieval step is adapted to deal with such linguistic values. An added-value of such hybrid system is the capability of learning meta-knowledge by experience. BOLERO has been successfully applied to a complex medical diagnosis problem using, at the object level, rules about pneumonia diagnosis.

6.3   The CAREFUL System

CAREFUL [65] focuses on the first two steps of a case-based reasoner, that is, the case and problem representation and the case retrieval. CAREFUL uses an object-oriented representation based on a hierarchy of fuzzy classes. The use of fuzzy logic allows taking into account the flexibility (imprecision, incompleteness, preferences) associated with the target description, the user requests, the case description and the retrieval process. As with the other systems, the fuzzy sets represent imprecise values of the attributes of the cases. Furthermore, in CAREFUL, fuzzy sets are also used to represent vague constraints in the problem description. The retrieval process proceeds in two steps: first the problem specification and case filtering step guides the operator in specifying the problem and identifying potentially interesting cases, and second in the selection step the nearest cases are chosen. The first step is based on an existing hierarchical fuzzy classification algorithm. The result of the first step is a set of potentially relevant cases that in the second step are compared with the problem description in order to select the nearest cases. To do so, each value of a problem attribute represents a fuzzy constraint and the process selects those cases that better satisfy these fuzzy constraints according to a weighted fuzzy pattern matching technique based on computing a possibility and a necessity degree.

6.4   The CARS System

In CARS [25], cases and problems are also defined in an object-oriented environment. The representation of cases and problems is done by surface and abstract fuzzy attributes. The abstract attributes are computed using plausible inference rules. The most interesting aspect of CARS is the technique used in the selection of the nearest cases, which uses a fuzzy similarity measure between attributes based on a fuzzy algebra. The resulting similarity, which is a fuzzy set, is compared, by means of a measure of inclusion, to reference fuzzy sets such as NO-MATCH, PARTIAL-MATCH, COMPLETE-MATCH, etc., representing the matching degree for each attribute. Finally, the matching degrees of all attributes are aggregated, taking into account their importance weight, using different combination methods.

6.5   The FLORAN System

In FLORAN [105] the cases and problems are also represented within an object oriented environment, where cases and problems are instances of classes whose slots can have fuzzy values. The classes of FLORAN are linked to dependency contexts - that is objects that represent, for a given class, a specific goal, a list of relevant attributes, their importance and a set of fuzzy restrictions on the attributes. This is similar to the CAREFUL system, except that the contexts in CAREFUL are hierarchically organized.

As in the other systems, the retrieval step of FLORAN is divided into a filtering step and a selection step. In the filtering step, FLORAN first looks for the most compatible context and then gets its associated cases. In the selection step, the current problem is compared with each filtered case by means of a fuzzy pattern matching technique. The fuzzy pattern matcher takes into account a tolerance parameter associated with each context.

7   Conclusions

In this chapter we have described the main aspects of case-based reasoning from the point of view of representative existing systems and we have mentioned the main issues and open problems being faced. We have also briefly described several systems that use fuzzy logic techniques to address some of the existing problems such as the representation of imprecise information. CBR has produced very promising techniques in addressing some of the issues and problems mentioned in this chapter, but there are still several open problems. Among them we could choose the following: how to efficiently represent complex cases such as those with higher-order relations between their features and time dependent information, how to index complex cases in order to optimize their reuse, how to dynamically generate new indices depending on evolving situations, how to compute similarities when cases are highly structured and complex, how to determine relevant features, how to deal with forgetting mechanisms, how to integrate CBR with other paradigms, and how to acquire, validate, and maintain case bases. For example, Racine and Yang [98] present some methods for maintaining large unstructured case bases focusing on redundancy and inconsistency detection. We believe that in the near future we will see fast growing research activities in all these problems using richer representations, including fuzzy logic and case-based temporal reasoning.

References

1. Aamodt A. (1990). Knowledge-intensive case-based reasoning and sustained learning. Poceedings European Conference on Artificial Intelligence, Pitman, 1-6.
2. Aamodt A. (1991). A knowledge-intensive approach to problem solving and sustained learning. Ph.D. Thesis, University of Trondheim, Norwegian Institute of Technology.
3. Aamodt A. and Plaza E. (1994). Case-based reasoning: foundational issues, methodological variations and system approaches. AI Communications 7(1), 39-59.
4. Aarts R.J. and Rousu J. (1997). Qualitative knowledge to support reasoning about cases. In (Leake and Plaza, eds.) In Proceedings of the Second International Conference on Case-Based Reasoning (ICCBR-97). Lecture Notes in Artificial Intelligence 1266, Springer-Verlag, 489-498.
5. Aha D., Kibler D., Albert M.K. (1991). Instance-based learning algorithms. Machine Learning Journal 6, 37-66.
6. Aha D.W. and Chang L.W. (1996). Cooperative bayesian and case-based reasoning for solving multiagent planning tasks. Technical Report AIC-96-005, Navy Center for Applied Research in AI NRL, Washington D.C.
7. Althoff K.D. (1989). Knowledge acquisition in the domain of CBC machine centres: the MOLTKE approach. In Proceedings European Knowledge Acquisition Workshop (EKAW-89), 180-195.
8. Althoff K.D. and Wess S. (1991). Case-based knowledge acquisition, learning and problem solving in diagnostic real world tasks. In Proceedings European Knowledge Acquisition Workshop (EKAW-91).
9. An A., Cercone N., and Chan C. (1997). Integrating rule induction and case-based reasoning to enhance problem solving. In Proceedings of the Second International Conference on Case-Based Reasoning (ICCBR-97). Lecture Notes in Artificial Intelligence 1266, Springer-Verlag, 499-508.
10. Arcos J.L. and Lopez de Mantaras R. (1997). Perspectives: A declarative bias mechanism for case retrieval. In Proceedings of the Second International Conference on Case-Based Reasoning (ICCBR-97). Lecture Notes in Artificial Intelligence 1266, Springer-Verlag, 279-290.
11. Arcos J.L., Lopez de Mantaras R., and Serra X. (1997b). SaxEx: A case-based reasoning system for generating expressive musical performances. In Proceedings of the 1997 International Computer Music Conference, Thessaloniki, Greece, 25-30 September 1997, pp. 329-336.
12. Arcos J.L., Lopez de Mantaras R., and Serra X. (1998). Saxex: A case-based reasoning system for generating expressive musical performances. Journal of New Music Research 27 (3), 194-210.
13. Armengol E. and Plaza E. (1993). A Knowledge Level Model of Case-based reasoning. First European Workshop on Case-Based Reasoning. Springer Verlag LNAI 837, 63-64.
14. Armengol E. and Plaza E. (1994). Integrating induction in a case-based reasoner. Second European Workshop on Case-Based Reasoning. Springer Verlag LNAI 984, 3-17.
15. Ashley K.D. (1988). Arguing by analogy in Law: A case-based model. In (Helman ed.) Analogical Reasoning: Perspectives of Artificial Intelligence, Cognitive Science, and Philosophy. Reidel.
16. Bain W. (1986). Case-based reasoning: A computer model of subjective assessment. Ph.D. Thesis. Yale University.
17. Bamberger S.K. and Goos K. (1993). Integration of case-based reasoning and inductive learning methods. In (Richter, Wess, Althoff, Maurer, eds.) Preprints First European Workshop on Case-Based Reasoning, SEKI-Report SR-93-12 University of Kaiserslautern Press. Vol.2, 296-300.
18. Bareiss E.R., Porter B., Weir C.C. (1988). PROTOS: An exemplar-based learning apprentice. Int. J. of Man-Machine Studies 29, 549-561.

19. Barletta R. and Hennessy D. (1989). Case adaptation in autoclave layout design. In Hammond (ed.): Proceedings Second Workshop on Case-Based Reasoning, Pensacola Beach, Florida, Morgan-Kauffman, 203-207.

20. Barletta R., Mark W. (1988). Explanation-based indexing of cases. Proceedings AAAI-88, Cambridge, AAAI/Morgan Kaufmann, 541-546.

21. Bento C. and Costa E. (1993). A similarity metric for retrieval of cases imperfectly described and explained. In Proceedings First European Workshop on Case-Based Reasoning. Vol. 1, 8-13.

22. Bhatta S.R. and Goel A.K. (1997). An analogical theory of creativity in design. In Proceedings of the Second International Conference on Case-Based Reasoning (ICCBR-97). Lecture Notes in Artificial Intelligence 1266, Springer-Verlag, 565-574.

23. Bonzano A., Cunningham P. and Smyth B. (1997). Using introspective learning to improve retrieval in CBR: A case study in air traffic control. In Proceedings of the Second International Conference on Case-Based Reasoning (ICCBR-97). Lecture Notes in Artificial Intelligence 1266, Springer-Verlag, 291-302.

24. Bonissone P., Blau L. and Ayub S. (1990). Leveraging the integration of approximate reasoning systems. In Proceedings 1990 AAAI Spring Symposium in Case Based Reasoning, Stanford, California, 1-6.

25. Bonissone P. and Ayub S. (1992). Similarity measures for case-based reasoning systems. In Proceedings of the International Conference on Information Processing and Management of Uncertainty in Knowledge-Based Systems (IPMU-92), Universitat Illes Balears Press, 483-487.

26. Borner K. (1993). Structural similarity as guidance in case-based design. First European Workshop on Case-Based Reasoning, Springer-Verlag, LNAI 837, 197-208.

27. Bradshaw G. (1987). Learning about speech sounds: The NEXUS project. Proceedings Fourth Int. Workshop on Machine Learning, Irvine, Morgan Kauffmann, 1-11.

28. Branting L.K. (1988). The role of explanation in reasoning from legal precedent. In Kolodner (ed.): Proceedings Case-Based Reasoning Workshop, Clearwater Beach, Florida, Morgan-Kaufmann, 94-103.

29. Branting L.K. and Porter B.W. (1991). Rules and precedents as complementary warrants. Proceedings AAAI-91. AAAI/Morgan Kaufmann, 3-9.

30. Breese J.S. and Heckerman D. (1995). Decision-theoretic case-based reasoning. In Proceedings of the Fifth International Workshop on Artificial Intelligence and Statistics, Ft. Lauderdale, USA, 56-63.

31. Bunke H., Messmer B.T. (1993). Similarity measures for structured representations. First European Workshop on Case-Based Reasoning, Springer-Verlag LNAI 837, 106-118.

32. Cain T., Pazzani M.J. and Silverstein G. (1991). Using domain knowledge to influence similarity judgment. Proceedings Case-Based Reasoning Workshop, Washington Morgan Kaufmann, 191-202.

33. Carbonell J. (1983). Learning by analogy: Formulating and generalizing plans from past experience. In (Michalski, Carbonel and Mitchell, eds), Machine Learning: An Artificial Intelligence Approach, Tioga, Palo Alto, 137-161.

34. Carbonell J., Knoblock C.A. and Minton S. (1991). PRODIGY: An integrated architecture for planning and learning. In (Kurt Van Lehn ed.) Architectures for Intelligence, The Twenty-Second Carnegie Mellon Symposium on Cognition, Erlbaum Publ.

35. Chang L. and Harrison D. (1997). A case-based reasoning testbed for experiments in adaptive memory retrieval and indexing. In Proceedings of the AAAI Fall Symposium on Adaptation of Knowledge for Reuse, Menlo Park, AAAI Press.

36. Chatterjee N. and Campbell J. (1993). Adaptation through interpolation for time-critical case-based reasoning. First European Workshop on Case-Based Reasoning, Springer Verlag LNAI 837, 221-233.

37. Cheetham W. and Graf J. (1997) In Proceedings of the Second International Conference on Case-Based Reasoning (ICCBR-97). Lecture Notes in Artificial Intelligence 1266, Springer-Verlag, 1-12.

38. Clark P.E. (1989). Exemplar-based reasoning in geological prospect appraisal. Technical Report 89-034, University of Stratchclyde, Turing Institute.

39. Collins G. (1987). Plan creation: Using strategies as blueprints. Ph.D. Thesis. Yale University.

40. Connolly D. and Christey S. (1993). Learning representation by integrating case-based and inductive learning. Proceedings AAAI Case-Based Reasoning Workshop, Washington, 147-159.

41. Cost S. and Salzberg S. (1990). A weighted nearest neighbor algorithm for learning with symbolic features. Technical Report JHU-90/11, The John Hopkins University, Dept. of Computer Science.

42. Dave B., Schmitt G., Shih S.G., Bendel L., Faltings B., Smith I., Hua K., Bailey S., Ducret J.M., Jent K. (1994). Case-based spatial design reasoning. In (Haton, Keane, Manago eds.) Adavances in Case-Based Reasoning: Proceedings of the Second European Workshop (EWCBR-94). Lecture Notes in Artificial Intelligence 984, Springer Verlag, 198-210.

43. Deters R.D. (1994). CBR for maintenance of telecommunication networks. Preprints Second European Workshop on Case-Based Reasoning, AcknoSoft Press, 23-32.

44. Dubois D., Prade H. and Testemale C. (1988). Weighted fuzzy pattern matching. Fuzzy Sets and Systems, 28, 351-362.

45. Dubois D. and Prade H. (1992). Fuzzy rules in knowledge-based systems: Modelling gradedness, uncertainty and preference. In: An introduction to Fuzzy Logic Applications in Intelligent Systems (R.R. Yager and L.A. Zadeh, eds.), Kluwer. 45-68.

46. Dubois D. and Prade H (1995). Possibility theory as a basis for qualitative decision theory. In Proceedings IJCAI-95, Montreal, 1924-1930.

47. Dubois D., Esteva F., Garcia P., Godo L., Lopez de Mantaras R. and Prade H. (1997). Fuzzy modelling of case-based reasoning and decision. In Proceedings of the Second International Conference on Case-Based Reasoning (ICCBR-97). Lecture Notes in Artificial Intelligence 1266, Springer-Verlag, 599-610.

48. Dubois D., Esteva F., Garcia P., Godo L., Lopez de Mantaras R. and Prade H. (1998). Fuzzy set modelling in case-based reasoning. International Journal of Intelligent Systems 13, 345-373.

49. Faltings B. (1997). Probabilistic indexing for case-based prediction. In Proceedings of the Second International Conference on Case-Based Reasoning (ICCBR-97). Lecture Notes in Artificial Intelligence 1266, Springer-Verlag, 611-622.

50. Faltings B., Hua K., Schmitt G. and Shih S.G. (1991). Case-based representation of architectural design knowledge. Proceedings Case-Based Reasoning Workshop, Washington, Morgan Kaufmann, 307-316.

51. Finnie G.R., Wittig G.W. and Desharnais J.M. (1997). Estimating software development effort with case-based reasoning. In Proceedings of the Second International Conference on Case-Based Reasoning (ICCBR-97). Lecture Notes in Artificial Intelligence 1266, Springer-Verlag, 13-22.

52. Fox S. and Leake D.B. (1995). Learning to refine indexing by introspective reasoning. In (Veloso and Aamodt, eds.) Case-Based Reasoning Research and Development, Proceedings First Int. Conference on Case-Based Reasoning, ICCBR-95, LNAI 1010, Springer, 431-440.

53. Francis A.G. and Ram A. (1993). The utility problem in case-based reasoning. Proceedings AAAI Case-Based Reasoning Workshop, Washington, 160-167.

54. Goel A. and Chandrasekaran B. (1989). Use of device models in adaptation of design cases. In Proceedings Second Workshop on case-based reasoning, Pensacola Beach, Florida, Morgan-Kauffman, 100-109.

55. Goldweic P. and Hammond K.J. (1993). Multi-agent interactions: A vocabulary of engagement. Representation issues in multimedia case retrieval, In Proceedings AAAI Case-Based Reasoning Workshop, Washington, 48-56.
56. Gomes P. and Bento C. (1997). A case-based approach for elaboration of design requirements. In Proceedings of the Second International Conference on Case-Based Reasoning (ICCBR-97). Lecture Notes in Artificial Intelligence 1266, Springer-Verlag, 33-42.
57. Hammond K. (1986). CHEF: A model of case-based planning. Proceedings of AAAI-86. AAAI/Morgan Kaufmann. 267-271.
58. Hammond K. (1987). Explaining and repairing plans that fail. IJCAI-87, 109-114.
59. Hanney K. and Keane M.T. (1997). The adaptation knowledge bottleneck: How to easy it by learning from cases. In Proceedings of the Second International Conference on Case-Based Reasoning (ICCBR-97). Lecture Notes in Artificial Intelligence 1266, Springer-Verlag, 359-370.
60. Hinrichs T.R. (1988). Towards an architecture for open world problem solving. In Kolodner (ed.): Proceedings Case-Based Reasoning Workshop, Clearwater Beach, Florida, Morgan-Kaufman, 182-189.
61. Hinrichs T.R. (1989). Strategies for adaptation and recovery in a design problem solver. In Hammond (ed.): Proceedings Second Workshop on case-based reasoning, Pensacola Beach, Florida, Morgan-Kaufmann, 115-118.
62. Hinrichs T.R. and Kolodner J. (1991). The roles of adaptation in case-based design. Proceedings Case-Based Reasoning Workshop, Washington, 121-132.
63. Howe N. and Cardie C. (1997). Examining locally varying weights for nearest neighbor algorithms. In Proceedings of the Second International Conference on Case-Based Reasoning (ICCBR-97). Lecture Notes in Artificial Intelligence 1266, Springer-Verlag, 455-466.
64. Jabbour K., Riveros J.F., Landsbergen D. and Meyer W. (1987). ALFA : Automated load forecasting assistant. In Proceedings IEEE Power Engineering Society Summer Meeting. San Francisco.
65. Jaczynski M. and Trousse B. (1994). Fuzzy Logic for the retrieval step of a case-based reasoner. Preprints Second European Workshop on Case-Based Reasoning, AcknoSoft Press, 313-322.
66. Jarmulak J., Kerckhoffs J.H. and van't Veen P.P. (1997). Case-based reasoning in an ultrasonic rail-inspection system. In Proceedings of the Second International Conference on Case-Based Reasoning (ICCBR-97). Lecture Notes in Artificial Intelligence 1266, Springer-Verlag, 43-52.
67. Karacapilidis N., Trousse B. and Papadias D. (1997). Using case-based reasoning for argumentation with multiple viewpoints. In Proceedings of the Second International Conference on Case-Based Reasoning (ICCBR-97). Lecture Notes in Artificial Intelligence 1266, Springer-Verlag, 541-552.
68. Kibler D. and Aha D. (1988). Case-based classification. Proceedings of the AAAI Case-Based Reasoning Workshop, Minneapolis.
69. Kolodner J. (1983). Reconstructive memory, a computer model. Cognitive Science 7, 281-328.
70. Kolodner J., Sympson R.L. and Sycara K. (1985). A process model of case-based reasoning in problem solving. In IJCAI-85, 284-290.
71. Kolodner J. (1987). Capitalizing on failure through case-based inference. Proceedings Ninth Annual Conference of the Cognitive Science Society, Erlbaum.
72. Kolodner J. (1988). Retrieving events from a case memory: A parallel implementation. In Kolodner (ed.): Case-Based Reasoning. Proceedings from a Workshop, Clearwater Beach, Florida, Morgan-Kaufmann, 233-249.
73. Kolodner J. (1993). Case-based Reasoning. Morgan-Kauffman.
74. Koton P. (1988). Using experience in learning and problem solving. Ph.D. Thesis. Computer Science Dept. MIT.

75. Krampe D. and Lusti M. (1997). Case-based reasoning for information systems design. In Proceedings of the Second International Conference on Case-Based Reasoning (ICCBR-97). Lecture Notes in Artificial Intelligence 1266, Springer-Verlag, 63-73.

76. Leake D.B. (1996). Case-Based Reasoning: Experiences, Lessons and Future Directions. AAAI Press/ The MIT Press.

77. Leake D. B., Kinley A., and Wilson D. (1997). A case study of case-based CBR. In Proceedings of the Second International Conference on Case-Based Reasoning (ICCBR-97). Lecture Notes in Artificial Intelligence 1266, Springer-Verlag, 371-382.

78. Lebowitz M. (1987). Experiments with incremental concept formation: UNIMEM. Machine Learning 2, 103-138.

79. Lopez B. (1993). Reactive planning through the integration of a case-based system and a rule-based system. In (Sloman et al. ed.) Prospects for Artificial Intelligence, IOS Press, 189-198.

80. Lopez B. and Plaza E. (1993). Case-based learning of strategic knowledge. In (Kodratoff ed.) Machine Learning EWSL-91, Lecture Notes in Artificial Intelligence, Springer-Verlag, 398-411.

81. Macedo L., Pereira F.C., Grilo C. and Cardoso A. (1997). Experimental study of a similarity metric for retrieving pieces from structured plan cases: Its role in the originality of plan case solutions. In Proceedings of the Second International Conference on Case-Based Reasoning (ICCBR-97). Lecture Notes in Artificial Intelligence 1266, Springer-Verlag, 575-586.

82. Magaldi R. (1994). Maintaining airplanes using CBR. Preprints Second European Workshop on Case-Based Reasoning, AcknoSoft Press, 1-12.

83. Malek M. and Rialle V. (1994). A Case-based reasoning system applied to neuropathy diagnosis. Second European Workshop on Case-Based Reasoning. Springer Verlag LNAI 984. 255-265.

84. Manago M., Althoff K-D., Auriol E., Traphoner R., Wess S., Conruyt N. and Maurer F. (1993). Induction and reasoning from cases. In Preprints First European Workshop on Case-Based Reasoning, SEKI-Report SR-93-12, University of Kaiserslautern Press, 313-318.

85. Moore A.W. (1990). Acquisition of dynamic control knowledge for a robotic manipulator. Proceedings Seventh Int. Conference on Machine Learning, Austin , Morgan Kauffmann, 244-252.

86. Myllymäki P. and Tirri H. (1994). Massively parallel case-based reasoning with probabilistic similarity metrics. In (Althoff et al. eds.) Topics in Case-Based Reasoning, Lecture Notes in Artificial Intelligence 837, Springer-Verlag, 144-154.

87. Nakatani Y. and Israel D. (1993). Tuning rules by cases. In First European Workshop on Case-Based Reasoning, Springer-Verlag, LNAI 837, 313-324.

88. Osborne H. and Bridge D. (1997). Similarity metrics: A formal unification of cardinal and non-cardinal similarity measures. In Proceedings of the Second International Conference on Case-Based Reasoning (ICCBR-97). Lecture Notes in Artificial Intelligence 1266, Springer-Verlag, 235-244.

89. Pearce M., Ashok K.G., Kolodner J.L., Zimring C., Billington R. (1992). Case-based support - A case study in architectural design. IEEE Expert 7(5), 14-20

90. Pews G. and Wess S. (1993). Combining case-based and model-based approaches for diagnostic applications in technical domains. In (Richter, Wess, Althoff, Maurer, eds.) Preprints First European Workshop on Case-Based Reasoning, SEKI-Report SR-93-12, University of Kaiserslautern Press, Vol.2, 325-328.

91. Plaza E. and Arcos J-L. (1993). A reflective architecture for integrated memory-based learning and reasoning. In Proceedings First European Workshop on Case-Based Reasoning. Vol.2, 329-334.

92. Plaza E. and Lopez de Mantaras R. (1990). A case-based apprentice that learns from fuzzy examples. In (Ras, Zemankova and Emrich ed.) Methodologies for Intelligent Systems 5. Elsevier, 420-427.

93.   Poole J. (1993). Similarity in legal case-based reasoning as degree of matching between conceptual graphs: Work in progress. In (Richter, Wess, Althoff, Maurer, eds.) Preprints First European Workshop on Case-Based Reasoning, SEKI-Report SR-93-12, University of Kaiserslautern Press, Vol. 1, 54-58.

94.   Porter B. (1986). PROTOS: an experiment in knowledge acquisition for heuristic classification tasks. Proceedings First Int. Meeting on Advances in Learning, Les Arcs, France, 159-174.

95.   Portinale L., Torasso P., Ortalda C. and Giardino A. (1993). Using case-based reasoning to focus model-based diagnostic problem solving. In (Richter, Wess, Althoff, Maurer, eds.) Preprints First European Workshop on Case-Based Reasoning, SEKI-Report SR-93-12, University of Kaiserslautern Press, Vol.2, 335-340.

96.   Portinale L., Torasso P. and Magro D. (1997). Selecting most adaptable diagnostic solutions through pivoting-based retrieval. In Proceedings of the Second International Conference on Case-Based Reasoning (ICCBR-97). Lecture Notes in Artificial Intelligence 1266, Springer-Verlag, 393-402.

97.   Purvis L. and Athalye S. (1997). Towards improving case adaptability with a genetic algorithm. In Proceedings of the Second International Conference on Case-Based Reasoning (ICCBR-97). Lecture Notes in Artificial Intelligence 1266, Springer-Verlag, 403-412.

98.   Racine K. and Yang Q. (1997). Maintaining unstructured case bases. In Proceedings of the Second International Conference on Case-Based Reasoning (ICCBR-97). Lecture Notes in Artificial Intelligence 1266, Springer-Verlag, 553-564.

99.   Richards B.L. (1994). Qualitative models as a basis for case indices. In Second European Workshop on Case-Based Reasoning. Springer Verlag, LNAI 984, 126-135.

100.   Rissland E.L. and Skalak D.B. (1991). CABARET: Rule interpretation in a hybrid architecture. Int. J. of Man-Machine Studies 34, 839-887.

101.   Rissland E.L. and Ashley K.D. (1988). Credit assignment and the problem of competing factors in case-based reasoning. In Kolodner (ed.): Case-Based Reasoning. Proceedings from a Workshop, Clearwater Beach, Florida, Morgan-Kauffman Publ.

102.   Rissland E.L., Skalak D.B. and Timur Friedman M. (1993). Using heuristic search to retrieve cases that support arguments. Proceedings AAAI Case-Based Reasoning Workshop, Washington, 5-11.

103.   Rodriguez A.F., Vadera S. and Sucar L.E. (1997). A probabilistic model for case-based reasoning. In Proceedings of the Second International Conference on Case-Based Reasoning (ICCBR-97). Lecture Notes in Artificial Intelligence 1266, Springer-Verlag, 623-632.

104.   Rougerez S. (1993). A similarity-assessment algorithm based on comparisons between events. In (Richter, Wess, Althoff, Maurer, eds.) Preprints First European Workshop on Case-Based Reasoning, SEKI-Report SR-93-12, University of Kaiserslautern Press, Vol. 1, 59-64.

105.   Salotti S. (1992). Filtrage flou et representation centree objet pour raisonner par analogie: le systeme FLORAN. PhD thesis, University of Paris VI.

106.   Salzberg S. (1990). Learning with nested generalized exemplars. Kluwer.

107.   Sanders K.E., Kettler B.P. and Hendler J.A. (1997). The case for graph-structured representations. In Proceedings of the Second International Conference on Case-Based Reasoning (ICCBR-97). Lecture Notes in Artificial Intelligence 1266, Springer-Verlag, 245-254.

108.   Schank R. (1982). Dynamic Memory: A theory of learning in computers and people. Cambridge University Press.

109.   Schmidt-Belz B. and Voss A. (1993) Case-oriented knowledge acquisition for architectural design. Proceedings AAAI Case-Based Reasoning Workshop, 168-175.

110.   Schweizer B. and Sklar A. (1963). Associative functions and abstract semi-groups. Publicationes Mathematicae Debrecen, 10, 69-81.

111. Sebag M. and Schoenauer M. (1993). A rule-based similarity measure. In First European Workshop on Case-Based Reasoning, Springer Verlag, LNAI 837, 119-131.
112. Sharma S. and Sleeman D. (1988). REFINER: A case-based differential diagnosis aide for knowledge acquisition and knowledge refinement. Proceedings European Working Session on Learning.
113. Simina M. and Kolodner J. (1997). Creative design: Reasoning and understanding. In Proceedings of the Second International Conference on Case-Based Reasoning (ICCBR-97). Lecture Notes in Artificial Intelligence 1266, Springer-Verlag, 587-598.
114. Smyth B. and Keane M.T. (1993). Retrieving adaptable cases: The role of adaptation knowledge in case retrieval. In First European Workshop on Case-Based Reasoning, Springer Verlag, LNAI 837, 209-220.
115. Stanfill C. (1987). Memory-based reasoning applied to English pronunciation. Proceedings AAAI-87, Seattle, 577-581.
116. Surma J. (1994). Enhancing similarity measures with domain specific knowledge. Preprints Second European Workshop on Case-Based Reasoning, AcknoSoft Press, 365-372.
117. Sycara E.P. (1987). Resolving adversarial conflicts: an approach to integrating case-based and analytic methods. Ph. D. Thesis, Georgia Tech.
118. Sycara K. (1988). Using case-based reasoning for plan adaptation and repair. In Kolodner (ed.): Case-Based Reasoning. Proceedings from a Workshop, Clearwater Beach, Florida, Morgan-Kaufmann, 425-434.
119. Tautz C. and Althoff K-D. (1997). Using case-based reasoning for reusing software knowledge. In Proceedings of the Second International Conference on Case-Based Reasoning (ICCBR-97). Lecture Notes in Artificial Intelligence 1266, Springer-Verlag, 156-165.
120. Turner S.R. (1993). A case-based model of creativity. Proceedings AAAI Spring Symposium on Artificial Intelligence and Creativity. 137-144.
121. Veloso M. (1992). Learning by analogical reasoning in general problem solving. Ph.D. Thesis. Carnegie Mellon University.
122. Veloso M. and Carbonell J. (1991). Variable-precision case retrieval in analogical problem solving. Proceedings Case-Based Reasoning Workshop, Washington, Morgan Kaufmann, 93-108.
123. Watson I. (1997). Applying Case-Based Reasoning: Techniques for enterprise systems. Morgan Kaufmann.
124. Watson I. and Perera S. (1997). The evaluation of a hierarchical case representation using context guided retrieval. In Proceedings of the Second International Conference on Case-Based Reasoning (ICCBR-97). Lecture Notes in Artificial Intelligence 1266, Springer-Verlag, 255-266.
125. Weber-Lee R., Miranda-Barcia R., da Costa M.C., Rodrigues-Filho I.W., Hoeschl H.C., D'Agostini-Bueno T.C., Martins A. and Pacheco R.C. (1997). A large case-based reasoner for legal cases. In Proceedings of the Second International Conference on Case-Based Reasoning (ICCBR-97). Lecture Notes in Artificial Intelligence 1266, Springer-Verlag, 190-199.
126. Wettschereck D., Aha D. W. and Mohri T. (1997). A review and empirical evaluation of feature weighting methods for a class of lazy learning algorithms. Artificial Intelligence Review, 11 (1-5), 273-314.
127. Zeleznikow J., Hunter D. and Vossos G. (1993). Integrating rule-based and case-based reasoning with information retrieval: The IKBALS project. In (Richter, Wess, Althoff, Maurer, eds.) Preprints First European Workshop on Case-Based Reasoning. SEKI-Report SR-93-12 University of Kaiserslautern Press, Vol.2, 341-346.
128. Zeyer F. and Weiss M. (1993). Similarity-based adaptation and its application to the case-based redesign of local area networks. In Preprints First European Workshop on Case-Based Reasoning, SEKI-Report SR-93-12, University of Kaiserslautern Press, 125-130.

Genetic Algorithms in Machine Learning

Jonathan Shapiro

Department of Computer Science, University of Manchester, Manchester M13 9PL,
United Kingdom
jls@cs.man.ac.uk

1 Introduction

1.1 What Is a Genetic Algorithm

Genetic algorithms are stochastic search algorithms which act on a population
of possible solutions. They are loosely based on the mechanics of population
genetics and selection. The potential solutions are encoded as 'genes' — strings
of characters from some alphabet. New solutions can be produced by 'mutating'
members of the current population, and by 'mating' two solutions together to
form a new solution. The better solutions are selected to breed and mutate and
the worse ones are discarded. They are probabilistic search methods; this means
that the states which they explore are not determined solely by the properties of
the problems. A random process helps to guide the search. Genetic algorithms
are used in artificial intelligence like other search algorithms are used in artificial
intelligence — to search a space of potential solutions to find one which solves
the problem.

1.2 Genetic Algorithms in Machine Learning

In machine learning we are trying to create solutions to some problem by using
data or examples. There are essentially two ways to do this. Either the solution
is constructed from the data, or some search method is used to search over a
class of candidate solutions to find an effective one. Decision tree induction by
ID3 and nearest-neighbour classification are examples of creation of a solution by
construction. Use of a gradient-descent algorithm to search over a space of neural
network weights to find those which affect a particular input-output mapping
is an example of the use of search. Genetic algorithms are stochastic search
algorithms which are often used in machine learning applications.

This distinction might not be strict; ID3 might include a search over different
prunings, for example. Nonetheless, algorithms like ID3 are fast and computationally simple. In addition, there is usually an explicit simplifying assumption
about the nature of the solutions. For example, in ID3 the bias is towards independent attributes; in nearest neighbour methods it is towards similarity of
outputs being reflected in input similarity. Using search, however, a wide range
of complex potential solutions can be tested against the examples, and thus,
much more difficult problems can be tackled. The cost, of course, is in increased

G. Paliouras, V. Karkaletsis, and C.D. Spyropoulos (Eds.): ACAI'99, LNAI 2049, pp. 146–168, 2001.
© Springer-Verlag Berlin Heidelberg 2001

computational cost. In addition, any inductive bias is embedded in the algorithm and is thereby more difficult to control, although introducing explicit controls or regularizers is becoming increasingly important. In many respects, genetic algorithms are on the dumb and uncontrolled end of machine learning methods. They rely least on information and assumptions, and most on blind search to find solutions. However, they have been seen to be very effective in a range of problems.

Genetic algorithms are important in machine learning for three reasons. First, they act on discrete spaces, where gradient-based methods cannot be used. They can be used to search rule sets, neural network architectures, cellular automata computers, and so forth. In this respect, they can be used where stochastic hill-climbing and simulated annealing might also be considered. Second, they are essentially reinforcement learning algorithms. The performance of a learning system is determined by a single number, the *fitness*. This is unlike something like back-propagation, which gives different signals to different parts of a neural network based on its contribution to the error. Thus, they are widely used in situations where the only information is a measurement of performance. In that regard, its competitors are Q-learning, TD-learning and so forth. Finally, genetic algorithms involve a population and sometimes what one desires is not a single entity but a group. Learning in multi-agent systems is a prime example.

In artificial intelligence, search is used in reasoning as well as learning, and genetic algorithms are used in this context as well. To make the distinction clear, consider a chess-playing program. Machine learning could be used to acquire the competence of chess-playing. (Most chess-playing programs are not created that way; they are programmed.) However, when the program plays the game it also uses search to find a good move. Other examples include searching over a set of rules to evaluate a predicate. Genetic algorithms have been used for problems which have been in the domain of artificial intelligence, such as finding an effective timetable or schedule within a set of constraints.

1.3   History of Evolutionary Computing

Genetic algorithms are one of a class of approaches often called *evolutionary computation* methods used in adaptive aspects of computation — search, optimisation, machine learning, parameter adjustment, etc. These approaches are distinguished by the fact that they act on a population of potential solutions. Whereby most search algorithms take a single candidate solution and make small changes to that, attempting to improve it, evolutionary algorithms adapt an entire population of candidate solutions to the problem. These algorithms are based on biological populations and include selection operators which increase the number of better solutions in the population and decrease the number of the poorer ones; and other operators which generate new solutions. The algorithms differ in the standard representation of the problems and in the form and relative importance of the operations which introduce new solutions.

Genetic algorithms were first proposed by John Holland in his book "Adaptation in Natural and Artificial Systems" [14]. Holland guessed that an important feature which distinguished natural adaptive systems like the biological systems from artificial ones like perceptrons (this was the early 70's remember) was that in biological systems there is only an effective solution when all of the necessary elements are in place, a property which he deemed "epistatis". (In biology, genes encode proteins which catalyse reactions, and typically all of the reactants must be present. Epistatis is a biological term to describe the situation where many genes contributed to a single trait.) Holland tried to create an artificial procedure which simulated this, one component of which was what is now called a genetic algorithm with crossover. He emphasised crossover, because he believed that this was the ideal way to search over systems containing epistatis. During a similar period, L. Fogel and his collaborators [9] used selection and mutation to search over finite-state automata as solutions to a range of problems. These studies are described in the book, "Artificial Intelligence through Simulated Evolution". Around the same time, Richenberg [26] developed a method called Evolutionary Strategies in which solutions to a problem were represented as real numbers; these were selected and mutated with Gaussian noise. He applied this technique to engineering problems including the design of airfoils. More recently, John Koza [17,18] developed Genetic Programming, in which genetic algorithms are used to search parse trees of LISP expressions, essentially computer programs.

These are the four so-called evolutionary programming paradigms. Genetic algorithms and their extension to genetic programming are probably the most widely used and most important in machine learning. However, there are still proponents of evolutionary strategies, notably Schwefel, Back, Hoffmeister and others who have achieved interesting results.

2   The Basics of Genetic Algorithms

2.1   Elements of a Simple Genetic Algorithm

Representation. In order to use a genetic algorithm to search for solutions to a problem, potential solutions to the problem must be encoded as strings of characters drawn from some alphabet, $A = a_1 a_2 ... a_L$. Often the characters are binary, but it is also possible to draw them from larger alphabets, and real numbers are sometimes used.

In describing genetic algorithms, one often uses jargon taken from the population dynamics. The strings, A are called chromosomes. The components of the string, $a_1, a_2, ...$ are called genes. The values which each gene can take are called the alleles. In the most common case of binary strings, the two possible alleles are 0 and 1. So, for example, the chromosome $A = 11110000$ the first four genes take the allele 1 and the last four take the allele 0.

Fitness Function. It is the task of the genetic algorithm to find very good strings. The goodness of a string is represented in the GA by some function of the strings, which I will call the *objective function*, the quantity to be optimised. Another function which is needed is called the *fitness function*. This is a monotonic function of the objective function, and is what determines how the strings will be

multiplied or discarded during the algorithm. It is usual to define the fitness function so that the algorithm *increases* the fitness of the strings, so better solutions
correspond to more fit strings.

The *genotype* is the string representation. The *phenotype* is what the genotype
produces. Often in genetic algorithms, the two are not terribly different, although
there is a great difference between a biological organism (the phenotype) and
its DNA (the genotype). The objective function is a kind of phenotype. The
objective function and the fitness function are often used interchangeably in the
GA community, but it is useful to separate them. In the biological terminology,
the fitness is the increase due to selection. Thus, the fitness has to do with the
particular form of selection, whereas the objective function is a property of the
problem to be solved.

Population Dynamics. A genetic algorithm works on a population of strings. It
starts with a random population and evolves the population to one containing
(hopefully) good strings. At the heart of the algorithm are operations which
take the population at the present generation, and produce the population at
the next timestep in such a way that the overall fitness of the population is
increased. These operations are repeated until some stopping criterion is met,
such as a given number of strings been processed, a string of given quality has
been produced, etc. There are numerous ways of actually implementing a genetic
algorithm.

The simple genetic algorithm we will consider works with a population size,
N, which is held constant. Three operations take the population at generation
t and produce the new population at generation $t + 1$: selection, crossover, and
mutation. These are described below.

Selection: This operator selects strings from the current population such that
better strings are more likely to be chosen. Selection does not introduce any
new strings; if applied repeatedly it simply re-proportions the strings in the
population, increasing the number of fitter ones and decreasing the number
of less fit ones.

Recombination/Crossover: This operation produces two (or some other
number) of offspring from a pair of parents by combining parts of each parent. Each offspring contains parts of the strings of each parent.

Mutation: This operation simply changes characters in the offspring string at
random. Each character is changed with a small probability.

2.2 A Simple Genetic Algorithm

There are a number of different variations. Here I show the simplest form.

Dynamics. A simple realization is the following,

```
current_population=N random strings.
repeat
```

```
repeat
    Select 2 strings from current population using selection operator.
    Produce 2 offspring using recombination.
    Mutate those 2 offspring.
    Add the 2 offspring to new_population.
  until size_of(new_population) = N.
  current_population = new_population.
until (stopping criterion met)
```

Such an approach is called "generational" because it is divided into distinct generations during which the entire population changes. In addition, offspring do not compete with parents. Alternatives are to change just a few of the strings in each time step, or to generate a large "mating pool" using recombination, including parents, and select N from that to get the next generation.

Fitness Proportional Selection. The simplest implementation of selection is to select in proportion to the fitness. That is, the probability of selecting a string α is

$$p^\alpha = \frac{F^\alpha}{\sum_{\alpha'} F^{\alpha'}} \tag{1}$$

where F^α is the fitness of the string α. Often, this is taken to be the objective function E^α itself. This works if E is positive and is to be maximised. Another approach is called Boltzmann selection, where

$$F(E^\alpha) = \exp(sE^\alpha). \tag{2}$$

This has a selection strength parameter s.

Fitness proportional selection is also called "roulette wheel selection". This is in analogy with a biased roulette wheel, associated with each string is a wedge of the wheel, whose size is proportional to the fitness of the string. Selection is equivalent to a spin of the wheel.

There are are two problems with roulette wheel selection. First, the randomness does not introduce new individuals; it only removes individuals from the population. Although it is most likely that unfit members of the population are removed, it is also possible that fit members are removed by chance. It is often better to remove this randomness and put the strings into the next population deterministically in proportion to their fitness.

The second problem is that as the search evolves, the spread of fitnesses decreases. There is less diversity in the population. This means that selection has less effect later in the search. To counteract this, the fitness is often rescaled to keep the spread constant. For example, one can rescale the selection strength by dividing by the standard deviation of the fitness within the population at each generation [28].

Mutation. The mutation operation changes the value of each gene with a mutation probability p_m. I.e. each character is changed to some other character with probability p_m, and left unchanged with probability $1 - p_m$. The mutation probability is taken to be small, e.g. $1/L$, for strings of length L. This probability is small so that mutation can explore small changes in the solutions without disrupting good solutions too much.

Crossover. Crossover works on pairs of strings. For each pair crossover occurs with probability p_c and with probability $1 - p_c$ the offspring are identical to the parents. Typical value is $p_c \approx 0.6$.

A commonly used form is called single-point crossover. In this operation, a crossing site is chosen at random somewhere along the length of the strings. Two new strings are generated by swapping all of the components of the two strings on one side of the crossing site. For example, if the two strings are

$$A_1 = 1111111|1111111$$

$$A_2 = 0000000|0000000$$

and the crossover position is between the 7th and 8th position (as marked), the new strings would be

$$A_1' = 0000000|1111111$$
$$A_2' = 1111111|0000000$$

This operation effectively means that each offspring possesses features from both parents.

Likewise, multi-point crossover uses multiple crossover points. I.e.

$$A_1 = 111|111111|11111$$

$$A_2 = 000|000000|00000$$

would yield

$$A_1' = 000|111111|00000$$
$$A_2' = 111|000000|11111.$$

A most extreme form of crossover is uniform crossover, where each site is independently chosen from parent 1 or parent 2. This is a very effective search operator if the genes don't interact in producing the fitness, but is very disruptive when they do.

Other forms of crossover have been invented for use in specific problems or domains.

Expected behaviour. To see how the genetic algorithm can be useful, consider the effect of mutation and crossover. Mutation is clearly local random search, it takes a solution and generates a small, unguided change. Crossover is more complicated. It takes a pair of parents and produces two offspring between the parents (think of what it does to binary numbers). The two offspring can be near the two parents, or they can be far from them, in this sense it is said to be a global rather than local search algorithm.

One view of what crossover is meant to do is to combine partial solutions to form more complete solutions. To use a ridiculous example, if you are trying to produce a duck and one parent has developed wings, while the other has developed webbed feet, the crossover operation should combine these so that one offspring has *both* webbed feet and wings and the other offspring has neither. Goldberg [10] writes about the *the principle of meaningful building blocks* — the problem should be encoded in such a way that substrings or partial solutions with intermediate fitness can combine under crossover to produce fitter, more complete solutions. Whether this will actually occur depends upon the likelihood of both building blocks being in the population simultaneously, and the likelihood of combining them in that way. Others have argued that crossover is useful because it allows large moves.

One expects the mean fitness in the population to increase until some form of equilibrium is reached. Equilibrium is were there is a balance between the improving effect of selection and the (generally) deleterious effects of mutation and crossover. Selection tends to make the population better on average, but decreases the variation. The other operators tend to decrease the quality of the population on average, but restore diversity. Figure 1 shows histograms of the fitness distribution in a population during a GA evolution.

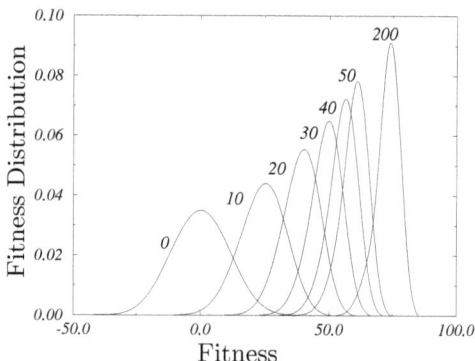

Fig. 1. The distribution of fitnesses in a population for different generations of a genetic algorithm. The x axis is the fitness value; the y axis is the fraction of the population with that value. Computed from histograms which have been averaged over many runs of the genetic algorithm. The decrease in variance as the algorithm runs is apparent. It is also the case that more of the variance is on the low fitness side; the distribution has positive skewness.

One thing that often happens is that a state is reached where there is very little diversity in the population. When this happens, improvement is very slow because crossover has little effect on very similar strings. This is called "premature convergence" and is one of the most important causes of failure of genetic

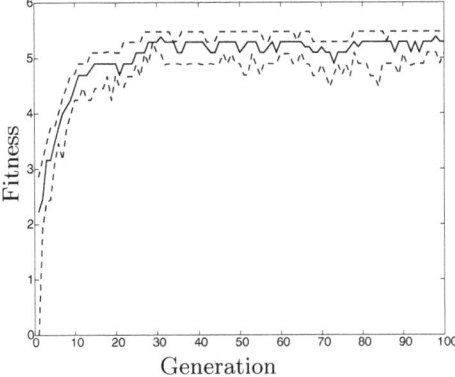

Fig. 2. Evolution of the mean fitness and the 10 and 90 percentile on a simple problem. An apparent stable population has been reached.

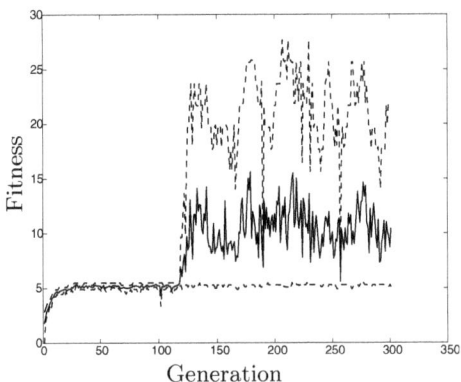

Fig. 3. The same as the previous figure for a longer run. Punctuated equilibrium is apparent. Had premature convergence occurred, the population would have been like in the previous figure.

algorithms. A population of very similar strings in the vicinity of a local minimum is very stable. Crossover has very little effect on populations of very similar strings and the time to leave a local minimum via selection and mutation alone can be very long. Exploration is inhibited by competition with strings in the vicinity of the minimum [29].

Figures 1 and 2 show examples of the increase in mean fitness in a population for a short and longer run. The improvements come in levels, or epoch. Had premature convergence occurred, the population would have remained stuck in the first level for a long time.

Example – Colouring a Map or Graph. Here is a simple example problem showing how a genetic algorithm is applied to a simple optimisation problem. Suppose you have a map that you want to colour with three colours. By this I mean that you want to assign one of three colours to each country such that adjacent countries are coloured with a different colour. A related problem is graph colouring - you assign colours to vertices of a graph so that adjacent vertices have a different colour. Say the colours are red, green, and blue.

In order to devise a genetic algorithm to solve a problem, there are basically three things you must do:

1. Encode possible solutions to the problem as strings
2. Devise a fitness function which determines how good a solution is. Generally, this should be positive and increasing with the quality of the solution.
3. Decide on the forms of the genetic search operators to be used, selection, mutation and crossover.

Encoding: Let each gene of the string represent one of the countries. Each gene can take three values: red, green, or blue. For example, one possible string might be

$$A = rbrgrbgg.$$

This would be a map in which the first country is coloured red, the second is blue, the third is red, and so forth.

Objective function: The obvious cost function is the number of times that two neighbouring countries have the same colour. This could be written,

$$E = \sum_{ij} W_{ij} d(a_i a_j)$$

where $W_{ij} = 1$ if country i neighbours country j and 0 otherwise; and $d(a_i a_j) = 1$ if $a_i = a_j$ and 0 otherwise.

Fitness Function: However, this does not work as a genetic algorithm fitness function, because we would want to minimise this, while genetic algorithm maximises the fitness function. We also could not use $-E$ since the fitness function should be positive. So, add to $-E$ the smallest value which insures that the fitness is always positive. What works as the fitness function is,

$$F = N(N - 1) - \sum_{ij} W_{ij} a_i a_j.$$

Another possibility is to use

$$F = \exp(-\beta E),$$

where β is a selection strength parameter. This works because $\exp(\text{anything})$ is always positive. This is called "Boltzmann selection". It has the advantage that it has a parameter, β which controls the strength of selection.

Genetic Operators: The usual selection, single-point crossover, and mutation could be used.

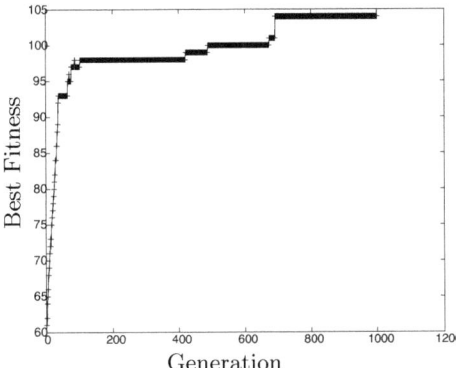

Fig. 4. Evolution of the best member of the population for a GA attempting to 2-colour a map. Premature convergence has occurred; the final population contains strings which differ by only a few mutations, are within a few mutations of a local optimum, and are many mutations away from the global optimum.

2.3   Extensions to the Basic Genetic Algorithm

There are many different ways of implementing a genetic algorithm, and researchers rarely use the simple form described above. Below some extensions are outlined.

Alternative Selection Schemes. Most alternative selection schemes are designed to avoid premature convergence. Here is a list:

Elitism: The best members of the population are put into the next generation at each timestep. The best individuals cannot be lost due to random sampling, and selection strength used to pick the other members of the population can be weaker to maintain diversity.

Tournament Selection: Two members of the population are chosen at random. The least fit is removed and replaced by a copy of the most fit.

Steady-state selection: Rather than changing all members of the population at each stage, only a few members of the population are changed at each timestep.

Fitness Sharing: In order to maintain diversity in the population, the fitness of an individual is shared among all other individuals which have similar genotypes. So a string which is very different from others in the population has its fitness enhanced, while strings which are very similar to many others have their fitness decreased.

A related method is called "implicit fitness sharing". This can only be applied in applications where the task is to perform well on a set of examples, such as in classification tasks. Fitness sharing is implemented by having the fitness shared among all of the solutions which classify a given example correctly, summed over all examples. Two strings which perform well on a overlapping set of examples would have their fitness reduced, while a string which performs well on examples not correctly dealt with by other strings would have a high fitness.

For a comparison of fitness sharing to implicit fitness sharing, see [7].

Niching and Island Models: This is similar to the previous; it is a method of maintaining diversity in a population and preventing premature convergence. Here a population is divided into several subpopulations, each evolving independently for periods of time. If the subpopulations converge, it is likely to be to different optima. Occasionally, some members of the subpopulations are exchanged. This injects diversity into the subpopulations. A useful feature of this approach is that it can be implemented on parallel computers. Different subpopulations evolve on different processors, and there is only occasional need for inter-processor communication.

Alternative Crossover Operators. Cutting the solutions up into chunks and recombining them may not be the best way of creating offspring. The method of recombination should reflect the structure of the problem. This has been discussed in a formal sense by [25]. A well-studied example is that of the Travelling Salesman Problem. In this case, a potential solution is a permutation, e.g. a potential solution might be 364521 which means visit city 3 first, 6 second, etc. Single point crossover between two such lists will fail to produce even a valid tour, much less a good one. To see more about special operators for the travelling salesman problem, see for example, [8].

Using the Entire Population. In most uses of genetic algorithms, the "answer" is the best member of the population; the other members of the population are used to help in the search but are discarded at the end. However, there are some exceptions.

In the early work on genetic algorithms in machine learning, Holland developed the Learning Classifier System [15]. In this, each string of the genetic algorithm was one "classifier", an if-then rule. The population was the system of classifiers. This approach is called the "Michigan" approach. The alternative approach, where each member of the population is a complete solution to the problem, as in DeJong et. al.'s GABIL system, is deemed the "Pittsburgh" approach.

Another approach in which the entire population is used rather as a solution is that proposed by Yao and Liu [34]. Here a genetic algorithm is used to train a neural network. It has been known in the neural network community for some time that if there exist a number of classifiers to solve the same problem, a classifier consisting of a committee of all of the classifiers can give better expected generalisation than any one of the classifiers taken alone (see, for example, subsection 9.6 of [6]). Yao and Liu propose using the final population of neural networks as the committee, and propose four different methods for combining the output of the neural networks. They use implicit fitness sharing, so that different learners are encouraged to learn different examples.

3 Examples of Genetic Algorithms in Machine Learning

3.1 Learning Rule Sets

A simple example of the use of a genetic algorithm to induce a set of rules was described by DeJong et. al. and is called GABIL. The genetic algorithm learns a boolean concept by searching for a disjunctive set of propositional rules. To represent a rule, a string contains a bit for each value that each variable can take, and a bit for the concept value. For example, if v_1 can take the values V_{11}, V_{12}, V_{13}, and v_2 takes the values V_{21}, V_{22}, and these are the only two variables, then the string

110 01 1

is used to denote the rule

$$\text{IF } (v_1 = V_{12}) \vee (v_1 = V_{13}) \wedge (v_2 = V_{21}) \text{ THEN } c = T, \tag{3}$$

where c is the concept. So if the substring associated with a particular variable is all 1's, that variable can take any value.

A set of rules is a long string of rules concatenated together. In order to allow for a variable number of rules, a modified form of crossover is used. Two crossover points are selected at random in the first parent. The crossover points in the second parent can be in any rule, but must be in the analogous place in the rule as in the rule of the first parent. For example, if parent one consists of three rules as represented by the following string and the crossover points are as shown,

```
v_1  v_2 c   v_1 v_2 c   v_1  v_2 c
00|1 11  1   111 0|1 0   110 10  1
```

then possible crossover points in the second parent must be between the first and second attribute bit in a substring associated with v_1 in any rule, and the first and second attribute bit in a substring associated with v_2 in any rule. For example,

```
v_1  v_2 c   v_1 v_2 c
10|1 1|1  1   001 01  0
```

would yield as offspring,

```
v_1  v_2 c   v_1 v_2 c
001  11  0   110 10  1
```

and

```
v_1  v_2 c   v_1 v_2 c   v_1  v_2 c
101  11  1   111 01  1   001  01 0
```

This allows varying lengths of rule sets to be explored, while preserving the structure of the rules.

It is worth noting that bits with more 1's are more general rules, and bits with more 0's are more specific. Thus, a mutation operator which is biased towards adding more 1's than 0's will generate more general rule sets. DeJong et. al. exploited this fact by experimenting with operators which changed a 0 to a 1 in a variable substring. An additional operator changed all of the bits to 1's in a substring associated with a variable in a rule (thereby exploring the possibility that that variable is irrelevant). The objective function was taken to be the square of the number of examples correctly classified by the rule set. In experiments comparing GABIL to over rule induction algorithms such as AQ14 and ID5R and C4.5, comparable results were achieved. Significant improvements were found by introducing the biased mutation operators mentioned in the previous paragraph.

Another example of use of genetic algorithms to evolve rule sets is Holland's Learning Classifier System [15].

3.2   Evolving Computer Programs

Genetic Programming. Genetic programming [17,18] is a form of evolutionary computation in which computer programs are evolved using a genetic algorithm. John Koza is credited with its invention. The representation of the program is in terms of trees rather than strings. Each tree represents the parse tree of a LISP expression. The leaves (or end nodes) of the tree represents terminals — objects which take no input. The other nodes represent functions which take a number of arguments, where each argument is either a terminal or another function. In order to apply this to any problem, the appropriate functions and terminals must be chosen. So, for example, in order to represent the absolute value function, the function set could be IF, which takes three arguments and evaluates the second (third) argument if the first argument evaluates to TRUE (FALSE), and GT, which takes two arguments and returns TRUE if the first argument is greater than the second. The terminal set would be real variables x and real constants. The LISP expression,

```
(IF (GT (x) (0))
    (x)
    (-x))
```

would be represented by the tree shown in figure 5.

As the representation is in terms of trees, a tree-based crossover and mutation operator is required. The crossover is done by replacing one randomly chosen subtree from one parent by a subtree from the other parent. This is shown in figure 6. Mutation occurs by taking a randomly chosen subtree and replacing it by a randomly generated subtree. Unlike standard genetic algorithms, this process generates varying sized structures. Some mechanisms might be required to regulate the size of the trees generated, and to insure that objects of the appropriate type go into the functions.

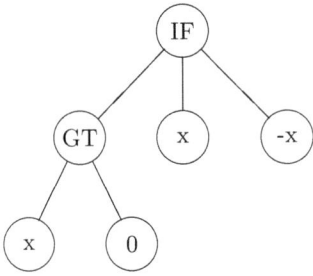

Fig. 5. A parse tree representation of the absolute value function.

Koza [17] uses fitness proportional selection with 90% of the trees generated from the crossover operator and the remaining unmodified from the previous generation. Koza considered mutation to be of minor importance and often did not use it.

Example - A simulated ant. A simple example described in [17]. A simulated ant can detect food directly in front of it and can move forward, or turn left or right on a square grid. There is a trail of food along the grid, with some gaps in the trail. The ant has to collect as much food as possible. Where the trail of food is continuous, the ant must learn to follow the trail. Since there are gaps in the trail, the ant must learn some exploration behaviour, so as to navigate past the gaps and find the trail again. The complexity of the exploration required depends upon the size of the gaps.

To solve this using genetic programming, Koza used three terminals corresponding to the actions of the ant, MOVE, LEFT, and RIGHT, meaning: move forward, turn left, and turn right respectively. IF-FOOD-AHEAD is a function with two arguments. The first is evaluated if food is detected ahead and the second is evaluated if food is not. For example, the program

(IF-FOOD-AHEAD (MOVE) (LEFT))

moves forward if food is detected and turns left if it is not. Two other functions were used. PROG2 takes two arguments, evaluates the first and then evaluates the second. So the program

(PROG2 (MOVE) (LEFT))

simply moves then turns left. A similar function, PROG3, takes three arguments and evaluates them in turn.

The fitness of a program is the number of pieces of food found by the ant in a given number of time steps (to prevent random exploration solutions). Each program is evaluated fully, then re-executed repeatedly until the maximum amount of time is used up. A population of 500 was used.

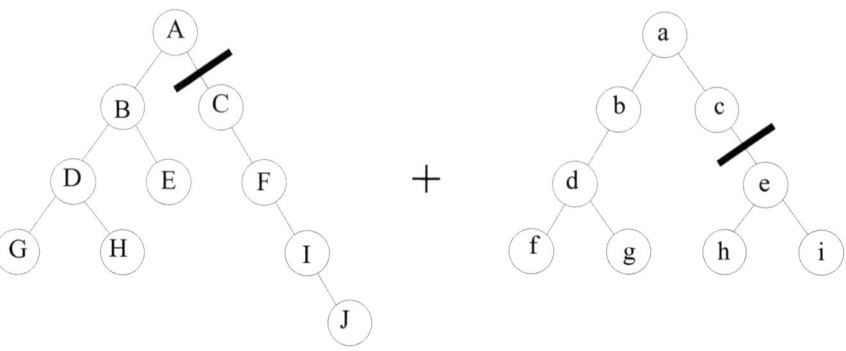

$+$

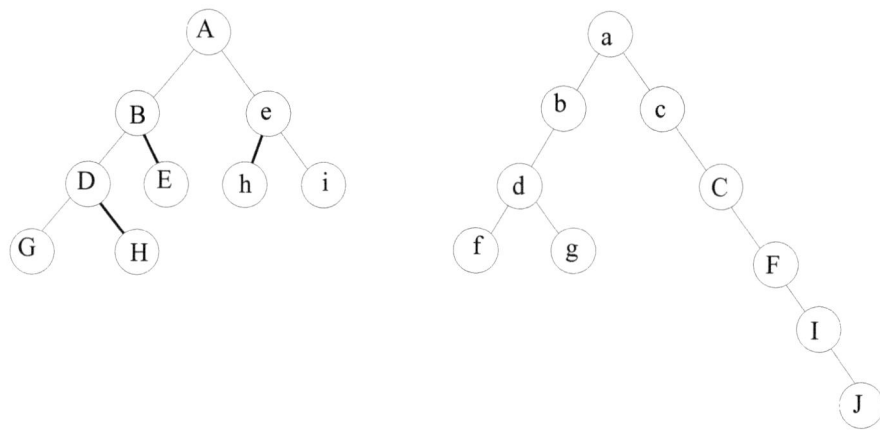

Fig. 6. An example of crossover on trees. The two parents are on the top of the figure; the dark line shows the crossover points. The two offspring are below.

Koza found a solution which worked perfectly on one particular trail used for training after 21 generations. It is

```
(IF-FOOD-AHEAD (MOVE)
               (PROGN3 (LEFT)
                       (PROGN2 (IF-FOOD-AHEAD (MOVE)
                                              (RIGHT))
                               (PROGN2 (RIGHT)
                                       (PROGN2 (LEFT)
                                               (RIGHT))))
                       (PROGN2 (IF-FOOD-AHEAD (MOVE)
                                              (LEFT))
                               (MOVE))))
```

If food is detected ahead the ant moves to it. Otherwise it turns left and looks for food. If no food is there, it turns back to the right and the right again, and so looks to the right of its original position. If no food is there, it just moves in the direction it was originally heading. There is also a pointless but harmless step in which it moves to the left and then to the right resulting in no change in heading. There is nothing about this rule induction system which prevents redundant rules like this.

Genetic programming has been used in a wide range of applications, including the design of circuits [19], and the prediction of complex time series.

3.3   Genetic Algorithms and Neural Networks

Artificial neural networks are very successful methods in machine learning. In their simplest form, they produce a mapping between an input space and an output space. This mapping is not represented in terms of rules, but in terms of non-linear functions of real-valued parameters called "weights". The mapping is determined by the structure of the non-linear functions, and given that structure by the values of the weight parameters. Two learning tasks are: find the structure of the neural network, and find the weight values of the neural network to make it perform a particular task.

Often neural networks are used for *supervised learning*. In this situation, the correct outputs are known for some example inputs. Then the learning problem is to find the best neural network given these examples. By "best neural network" we could mean the neural network which does the best job of producing the correct outputs on the example inputs, or some other criterion could be used. For example, one often wants to balance performance on the example set with other criteria, such as model simplicity, in order to improve generalisation performance. A standard approach is to choose the network structure by hand, and then use some real-valued optimisation method using gradient information (e.g. a conjugate gradient method) to search for the weights which optimise the chosen criterion.

Numerous authors have used genetic algorithms to search over the structure space and/or over the weight space to train neural networks to perform different tasks. For reviews, see Schaffer et. al. [27] or Yao [35].

Genetic Algorithms to Train Fixed Structures. A number of authors have explored replacing the standard, gradient-based, algorithm with a genetic algorithm to search for the weights which optimise neural network performance on an example set for a fixed structure neural network. This appears to be a questionable enterprise for several reasons. First, it is a long-held belief in the optimisation community that if you have gradient information you should use it [24]. Second, it is worth noting that genetic algorithms turn all learning problems into reinforcement learning tasks. The performance of the network is defined by a single number, the fitness (unless a multi-objective approach is used, which has not been tried to the best of my knowledge). If there are multiple outputs, a gradient-based approach can focus the search on those parameters which contribute to the outputs which are wrong, and if learning is done after each pattern, the changes can be made which are associated with the patterns which the network gets wrong. Experience with reinforcement learning as compared to supervised learning using standard algorithms supports the view that reinforcement learning requires longer search, so it seems questionable to turn the problem into a reinforcement learning problem.

The argument in favour of evolutionary algorithms over gradient-based ones is that evolutionary algorithms are global search algorithms, they can in principle search the entire space eventually. Local search algorithms can get stuck in local minima. Thus, in search problems dominated by many local minima, global search methods such as simulated annealing or evolutionary algorithms are used.

An early example of this approach was described by Montana and Davies [22]. They found that a genetic algorithm using simple mutation and uniform crossover on the weight vectors for an underwater sonar classification task outperformed the gradient descent algorithm. However, it did not outperform a simple modified algorithm (quickprop) [27], and it is likely to seriously underperform compared to more sophisticated versions of gradient descent.

Genetic Algorithms to Search for Neural Network Structure. A well known problem in using neural networks is that one does not know what structure to use. A structure which is too complex may easily perform well on the example set without giving good generalisation; a structure which is too simple may be unable to perform the desired task at all. Although methods of automatically growing or pruning network architectures have been known for some time [6], they are not widely used (cascade correlation may be an exception). A more standard approach is to train networks of different architectures, and use cross-validation to determine the expected generalisation of networks of different structures. Then one of the networks from the class with the best expected structure is tested and used. This evolves training an ensemble of networks of different structure (if cross-validation is used to estimate the expected generalisation, many networks of each structure are trained as well). Either only one of these is used, or a committee is formed from a set of them[6,30].

An alternative approach is to use an evolutionary algorithm to search over different network architectures. In this approach, the weight adaptation is done using a gradient method; the evolutionary search is adapting the structure of the network, either the number of neurons or the connection topology between them. A straight-forward approach is described in [35], and called EPNet. A population of neural networks learns weights using a hybrid adaptive gradient-descent/simulated annealing algorithm. The population undergoes mutations of various types; no crossover. The mutations grow and prune the network. Each generation consists of a fixed application of the hybrid algorithm for a fixed number of computation steps, and then one of four mutations — delete a node, delete a connection, add node, add connection. The mutations are all tried, the first one to lead to improvement is chosen. Deletions are tried first to bias the system towards simple networks. Three example sets are used. The first is used by the hybrid algorithm to train the weights; the second is a validation set used to compete the fitness of the neural networks in the population for selection. The final one is used to select the member of the final population to use as *the* network.

The above approach does not include crossover. Once crossover is included, a string representation of the network architecture is required. There are two approaches to this. The first is called *direct encoding*, where the structure of the neural network is represented directly in the strings. The alternative is to encode in the strings some dynamical process which produces the strings, such as a *grammatical encoding*, in which the genetic algorithm evolves a grammar which is then used to produce a network topology [16]. Another example is a genetic string which produces a set of developmental instructions [21]. These have been mostly applied to toy and test problems.

There is a problem to this approach, which is sometimes called the problem of competing conventions. There are a number of structures by which a neural network can solve a problem, many related by symmetries. For example permutation of the labels of the neurons in a layer of a neural network leaves the network functionally unchanged. A population can consist of networks which differ in the symmetry of the solution they are learning towards. Crossover between such neural networks is very disruptive.

3.4 Genetic Algorithms and Reinforcement Learning

Reinforcement learning deals with those situations when the information the learner gets about its performance is evaluative, rather then instructive. In other words, it only knows how well it is doing, not what it should or should not be doing, and perhaps the performance information is available only sometimes. Learning to talk might be an example of this. No teacher is available to instruct on how to move the muscles of the mouth to make a particular word, but if the child can successfully produce the word "up", it gets a reward (picked up by its mother). If it fails, it gets no information about which part of the sequence of movements it made was wrong. Reinforcement learning is important in adaptive control problems, such as learning to control a mobile robot, learning to play games, and modelling learning in biological systems. The simulated ant discussed in section 3.2 was an example of a reinforcement learning problem, since the only feedback provided to the ant is the amount of food picked up after a long sequence of actions.

As mentioned previously, genetic algorithms turn learning problems into reinforcement learning problems, and is perhaps one of the simplest ways to implement a reinforcement learning method. Thus, reinforcement learning is one of the most important applications of genetic algorithms in machine learning. Examples of this include studies of reinforcement learning in simulated agents [1], and training of robots using evolutionary algorithms.

4   Interaction of Evolution and Learning

4.1   Combining Genetic Algorithms with Local Search Algorithms

Many authors have used a local search algorithm combined with an evolutionary algorithm to improve search. The idea is that the evolutionary steps move members of the population near locally optimal solutions, and the local search algorithm takes it the rest of the way. See, for example Ackley and Littman [1] and Belew [4]. Alternatively, one could use the local algorithm as the main search element of the population, adding occasional crossovers as a global element to move individuals away from locally optimal states.

Once local search is added to the genetic algorithm a question arises, should the result of the local search change the strings or not. In other words, should evolution be Lamarckian or Darwinian? Lamarck believed in inheritance of acquired traits, e.g. the giraffe has a long neck because its ancestors stretched their necks to reach the tall leaves, and their offspring inherited the longer necks. Weismann [32] argued that this is impossible for biological organisms; there was no way for information to pass from the somatic cells which make up the body of the organism to the germ cells which carry the inheritable genetic material (Darwin argued that this was unnecessary to understand evolution, but did not rule it out).

Although it is impossible for biological organisms, computer programs can be Lamarckian. There is some evidence that they should be. Hart and Belew [11] used a genetic algorithm, a variety of local optimisation approaches, Lamarckian combinations of genetic algorithms with local optimisation and non-Lamarckian combinations of genetic algorithms with local search on a test optimisation problem containing a large number of local optima. They found that the Lamarckian methods were significantly better than all other methods in most of the trials.

Their interpretation of the results was that initially the GA population is distributed across the search space. A normal GA, however, would become centred around one good optimum as the population converged. Combining the GA with a high number of local search steps per generation prevents that, as all members of the population are centred around optima. The Lamarckian aspect enhances this. However, if the population starts to converge, the opposite is true, the Darwinian algorithm is better. Hart and Belew found that for infrequent local searches, the Darwinian algorithm performs better. Why this might be is shown in figure 7. When the population has converged around a local optimum, genetic algorithm search is particularly slow, as discussed in [29]. However, using local searches without modifying the genotype gives all of the points within a basin of attraction of an optimum effectively the same fitness. This allows a more diverse population which can move between optima much more readily. This idea has been explored for simulated annealing in the *basin hopping algorithm* and is discussed in [31].

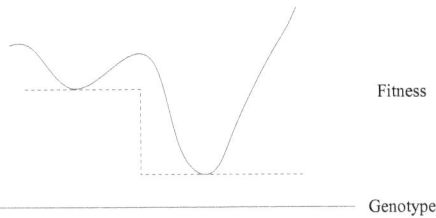

Fitness

Genotype

Fig. 7. A fitness function (solid line) and the effective fitness (dashed line) when a genetic algorithm is combined with local search in a Darwinian manner. Every point within the basin of attraction of a minimum has the same effective fitness.

Other studies of this effect are presented by Whitley et. al. [33].

4.2   The Baldwin Effect

One effect of the interaction of learning with evolution was first proposed by J. M. Baldwin in 1896 [3]. He argued that acquired characteristics could be indirectly inherited. This occurs in two steps. First, plasticity can increase fitness of partial mutation which is otherwise useless. For example, an organism which lives in a hot climate may be born with structures which protect it from the sun, or it could have skin pigments which can react by tanning. Likewise, an organism can be born with the ability to hunt, or it can be born with the ability to learn to hunt. The tanning reaction and learning are both examples of plasticity which impart increased fitness.

However, plasticity has a cost. While an organism is learning to hunt, it may go hungry or even die. So the second step of the Baldwin effect is genetic assimilation. The adaptation becomes genetically encoded and innate. Thus, through this two step process, acquired characteristics are inherited, but without violating the impossibility of information transfer back to the genetic material.

A model of this was proposed by Hinton and Howlan [13] The genotype is a string of 20 characters drawn from the alphabet, $\{0, 1, ?\}$. The phenotype is a neural network with weight values of 0 or 1 assigned from the genotype. The weights associated with the ?'s are plastic, random search assigns 1 or 0 to those over 1000 trials. The ideal phenotype has all weight values equal to 1, any other phenotype is not useful.

The fitness of the individual is

$$F = 20 - \frac{19}{1000} \min\left(\text{number of trials to find ideal}, 1000\right). \tag{4}$$

So if you are born with the ideal phenotype, the fitness is 20. The fitness decreases linearly with the time for learning to find the ideal phenotype, and is 1 if learning fails to find the solution in 1000 trials. Learning has a cost.

Without learning, the genetic search is a needle in a haystack problem, and a solution is never found. With learning, a solution is found and the fitness of the population increases over time. One also sees that the number of ?'s in the population decays slowly over time; genetic assimilation does occur, albeit slowly. Thus, learning guides evolution. With plasticity, evolution can work even where only a perfect solution imparts fitness advantage. This is important, because it was often hard to see how evolution could work otherwise to evolve structures which are useless unless complete. This model has been studied further by Harvey [12] and Mayley [20].

5   Conclusions

Genetic algorithms are general purpose search algorithms which act on a population of candidate solutions. They can be applied to search on discrete spaces, so can be used to search rule sets, representations of computer programs or computer structures, neural network architectures, and so forth. When applied to learning, genetic algorithms turn learning tasks into reinforcement learning problems; it is in this domain where they are often used. Genetic algorithms combine quite successfully with local search algorithms or local machine learning methods.

Good introductory texts on genetic algorithms include books by Goldberg [10] and Mitchell [23]. The standard introductory books on genetic programming are those by Koza [17,18].

References

1. D. Ackley and M. Littman, "Interaction between learning and evolution". In *Artificial Life II* C. Langton, editor, Addison-Wesley, 1991.
2. H. Adeli and S. Hung, *Machine Learning: Neural Networks, Genetic Algorithms and Fuzzy Systems* John Wiley and Sons, 1995.
3. J. Baldwin, "A new factor in evolution", *American Naturalist* 30: 441–451, 1896.
4. R. Belew, "When both individuals and populations search: adding simple learning to the genetic algorithm". In *Proceedings of the Third International Conference on Genetic Algorithms* J. D. Schaffer, editor. Morgan-Kaufmann, 1989.
5. R. Belew and M. Mitchell, *Adaptive Individuals in Evolving Populations* Santa Fe Institute Studies in the Sciences of Complexity Volume XXVI Addison-Wesley, 1996.
6. C. M. Bishop, *Neural Networks for Pattern Recognition* Oxford University Press, 1996.
7. P. Darwen and X. Yao, "Every Niching Method has its Niche: Fitness Sharing and Implicit Sharing Compared", preprint.
8. L. Davis, *Handbook of Genetic Algorithms*, Van Nostrand Reinhold, 1991.
9. L. Fogel, and A. Owens, and M. Walsh, *Artificial Intelligence through Simulated Evolution*, Wiley, 1966.

10. D. Goldberg, *Genetic Algorithms in Search, Optimization, and Machine Learning*, Addison-Wesley, 1989.

11. W. Hart and R. Belew, "Optimization of Genetic Algorithm Hybrids that Use Local Search". In [5].

12. I. Harvey, "The puzzle of the persistent question marks: a case study of genetic drift. " In *Proceedings of the fifth international conference on genetic algorithms*, S. Forrest, editor. 1993.

13. G. E. Hinton and S. J. Nowlan, "How learning can guide evolution". *Complex Systems* 1: 495–502, 1987.

14. J. H. Holland, *Adaptation in Natural and Artificial Systems*, University of Michigan Press, 1975. (Second edition: MIT Press, 1992.)

15. J. H. Holland, "Escaping brittleness: The possibilities of general purpose learning algorithms applied to parallel rule-based systems". In *Machine Learning II*, R. Michalski, J. Carbonell, T. M. Mitchell, editors, Morgan Kaufmann, 1986.

16. H. Kitano, "Designing neural networks using genetic algorithms with graph generation system". *Complex Systems* 4:461–476, 1990.

17. J. Koza, *Genetic Programming: On the Programming of Computers by Means of Natural Selection*, MIT Press, 1992.

18. J. Koza, *Genetic Programming II: Automatic Discovery of Reusable Programs*, MIT Press: 1994.

19. J. Koza and F. Bennett III, and D. Andre and M. Keane, "Four problems for which a computer program evolved by genetic programming is competitive with human performance", *Proceedings of the 1996 IEEE International Conference on Evolutionary Computation* IEEE Press, 1996.

20. G. Mayley, "Landscapes, Learning Costs, and Genetic Assimilation", *Evolutionary Computation* 4(3), 231–234, 1996.

21. O. Miglino and S. Nolfi, and D. Parisi, "Discontinuity in Evolution: How Different Levels of Organization Imply Preadaptation" In [5].

22. D. Montana and L. Davis, "Training feedforward networks using genetic algorithms", *Proceedings of International Joint Conference on Artificial Intelligence*, Morgan Kaufman, 1989.

23. M. Mitchell, *An Introduction to Genetic Algorithms*, MIT Press, 1996.

24. W. H. Press and S. A. Teukolsky and W. T. Vetterling and B. P. Flannery, *Numerical Recipes in C* Cambridge University Press, 1992.

25. N. J. Radcliffe, "Equivalent Class Analysis of Genetic Algorithms", *Complex Systems* 5(2) 183–205, 1991.

26. I. Richenberg, "Cybernetic Solution Path of an Experimental Problem. Ministry of Aviation, Royal Aircraft Establishment (U.K.), 1965.

27. J. D. Schaffer, D. Whitley, and L. J. Eshelman, "Combinations of genetic algorithms and neural networks: a survey of the state of the art" *Proceedings of the International Workshop on Combinations of Genetic Algorithms and Neural Networks*, (D. Whitley and J. D. Schaffer, editors), pp. 1–37. IEEE Computer Society Press, Los Alamitos, Ca. 1992.

28. J. L. Shapiro and A. Prügel-Bennett, "A Maximum Entropy Analysis of Genetic Algorithms", *Lecture Notes in Computer Science* 993, 14–24, 1995.

29. J. L. Shapiro and A. Prügel-Bennett, "Genetic Algorithm Dynamics in a Two-well Potential", in *Foundations of Genetic Algorithms 4* R. Belew and M. Vose, editors. Morgan Kaufmann, 1997.

30. L. Tarassenko, *A Guide to Neural Computing Applications* Arnold Publishers, 1998.

31. D. Wales and J. Doye, "Global Optimization by Basin-Hopping and the Lowest Energy Structures of Lenard-Jones Clusters Containing up to 110 Atoms", *J. Phys. Chem. A*. 101, 5111–5116, 1997.
32. A. Weismann, *The germ-plasm: A theory of heredity*, Scribners, 1893.
33. D. Whitley and V. Gordon, and K. Mathias, "Lamarckian Evolution, the Baldwin Effect, and function optimization", in *Parallel Problem Solving From Nature III*, Y. Davidor, H. Schwefel and R. Männer, editors. Springer-Verlag, 1994.
34. X. Yao and Y. Liu and P. Darwen, "How to Make Best Use of Evolutionary Learning" Published in *Complex Systems — From Local Interactions to Global Phenomena* R. Stocker (ed.) IOS Press, Amsterdam 229–242, 1996.
35. X. Yao, "Evolutionary artificial neural networks" Published in *Encyclopedia of Computer Science and Technology*, A. Kent and J. G. Williams, editors. Volume 33, pages 137–170, Marcel Dekker, Inc. 1995.

Pattern Recognition and Neural Networks

Sergios Theodoridis[1] and Konstantinos Koutroumbas[2]

[1] Department of Informatics, Division of Communications and Signal Processing,
University of Athens, Panepistimiopolis, T.Y.P.A. Buildings, 157 71 Athens, Greece
`stheodor@di.uoa.gr`
[2] National Observatory of Athens, Metaxa & V. Pavlou, 152 36 Palaia Penteli,
Athens, Greece
`koutroumbas@space.noa.gr`

1 Introduction

Pattern Recognition (PR) is a fast growing field with applications in many diverse areas such as optical character recognition (OCR), computer - aided diagnosis and speech recognition, to name but a few.

Pattern recognition deals with the automatic classification of a given object into one from a number of different *categories (classes)*. The goal of PR is the development of an *automatic classification system*, which will be used for the classification of objects relevant to the application at hand.

In order to illustrate how an automatic classification system works, let us consider a computer-aided diagnosis classification system. The purpose of such a system is to classify regions from an image (e.g. X-rays) in either of two classes, depending on whether this image corresponds to a benign or malignant lesion. Given the specific region of the image as input, the classification system will measure some prespecified quantities related to the image region (such as its perimeter, its area, etc.), known as *features*. In the sequel, each region is represented by the vector formed by the above features, which is called *feature vector*. Then, based on this vector, a new reduced order feature vector may be formed, each coordinate of which is either one of the coordinates of the original vector and/or a combination of them. This feature vector is then used for the classification of the corresponding lesion either to the benign or to the malignant class.

The vector space into which the selected feature vectors lie is known as *feature space*. The dimension of the space depends on the number of features, l, and it can be either continuous or discrete valued. Thus, if in an application the features used are discrete valued (i.e., they may take values only in a finite data set C), the feature space is C^l. If, on the other hand, the features can take values in a continuous real number interval, the feature space is R^l. In the case where the first l_1 features are continuous valued and the remaining $l - l_1$ are discrete valued, taking values in C, the feature space is $R^{l_1} \times C^{l-l_1}$.

Having given the basic definitions, let us now focus on the major design stages of a classification system.

G. Paliouras, V. Karkaletsis, and C.D. Spyropoulos (Eds.): ACAI'99, LNAI 2049, pp. 169–195, 2001.
© Springer-Verlag Berlin Heidelberg 2001

- *Feature generation:* This stage deals with the generation of the features that will be used to represent an object. These should be chosen so that their values vary significantly among the different classes. The choice is application dependent and they are ususally chosen in cooperation with experts in the field of application.
- *Feature selection:* This stage deals with the selection of features, from a larger number of generated ones, that are most representative for the problem. That is, they are rich in information concerning the classification task. Basically, their values must vary a lot for the different classes. This is an important task. If the selected features are poor in classification related information, the overall performance of the system will be poor.
- *Classifier design:* This stage can be considered as the heart of the classifica-tion system. The design of the vector classifier is usually carried out through the optimization of an optimality criterion. Speaking in geometrical terms, the task of a classifier is to divide the feature space into regions each of which corresponds to a class. Thus, for a given feature vector, the classifier identifies the region in the feature space where it belongs and assigns the vector to the corresponding class.
- *System Evaluation:* The final stage consists of the performance evaluation of the system, that is the estimation of the classification error probability. This is also an important task, since in the majority of cases this estimation is based on a limited number of test data. If the error probability turns to be higher than a prespecified threshold, the designer may have to redesign some or all the previous stages.

In the sequel, we will focus on the classfier design stage. Thus, we assume that appropriate features have been selected during the feature genereation and feature selection stage [1]. It is assumed that there is a one to one correspondence between objects and selected feature vectors. Also, unless otherwise stated, we assume that the feature vector consists of real valued coordinates and the feature space is R^l.

2   Bayes Decision Theory

Consider an m-class classification task, i.e., a problem where an object may belong to one out of m possible classes. Let ω_i denote the ith class. The problem that has to be solved by the classifier may be stated as: *"Given a feature vector x which is the most appropriate class to assign it?"*. The most reasonable solution is to assign it to the *most probable* class. Here is the point where probability theory enters into the scene. In this context, the feature vector x will be treated as a random vector, i.e., a vector whose coordinates (features) are treated as random variables.

Let $P(\omega_i|x)$ be the probability that x stems from the ω_i class. This is also known as *a posteriori probability*. In mathematical terms the notion of "most probable" is stated as:

---

[1] Techniques for feature generation and feature selection are discussed in [30]

Assign x to class ω_i if

$$P(\omega_i|\boldsymbol{x}) = \max_{j=1,\dots,m} P(\omega_j|\boldsymbol{x}) \,. \tag{1}$$

This is the well known *Bayes classification rule* [2].

Let $P(\omega_i)$ be the a priori probability for class ω_i and $p(\boldsymbol{x}|\omega_i)$ be the class conditional probability density function (pdf) for class ω_i, which describes the distribution of the feature vectors of the ith class, $i = 1,\dots,m$. Finally, let $p(\boldsymbol{x})$ denote the pdf of $\boldsymbol{x}$. Recalling that

$$P(\omega_i|\boldsymbol{x}) = \frac{P(\omega_i)p(\boldsymbol{x}|\omega_i)}{p(\boldsymbol{x})} \,, \tag{2}$$

the Bayes rule may be stated as

Assign x to class ω_i if

$$P(\omega_i)p(\boldsymbol{x}|\omega_i) = \max_{j=1,\dots,m} P(\omega_j)p(\boldsymbol{x}|\omega_j) \,. \tag{3}$$

$p(\boldsymbol{x})$ has been omitted since it is the same for all classes, i.e., independent of ω_i.

In the special case of equiprobable classes, i.e., if $P(\omega_j) = 1/m$, $j = 1,\dots,m$, the Bayes rule can simply be stated as

Assign x to class ω_i if

$$p(\boldsymbol{x}|\omega_i) = \max_{j=1,\dots,m} p(\boldsymbol{x}|\omega_j) \,. \tag{4}$$

That is, in this special case, the Bayes decision rule rests on the values of the class conditional probability densities evaluated at $\boldsymbol{x}$.

Let us consider now fig. 1, where the class conditional pdf's of an one-dimensional two class problem are depicted. The classes are assumed equiprobable. The points $\boldsymbol{x_0}$ and $\boldsymbol{x_1}$ correspond to thresholds that partition the feature space into three regions. Thus, according to the third version of the Bayes decision rule, all $\boldsymbol{x}$ that belong either to R_1 or to R_3 are assigned to class w_1, and all $\boldsymbol{x} \in R_2$ are assigned to class w_2.

The above example shows how the condition of the Bayes decision rule may be interpreted in terms of conditions in the feature space. Moreover, the above example indicates that classification errors are unavoidable. Speaking in terms of fig. 1, there is a finite probability for some $\boldsymbol{x}$ to stem from w_2 and lie in R_1. However, the classifier will assign it to class w_1.

The probability of a vector $\boldsymbol{x}$ from class ω_i to be wrongly assigned to a different class is

$$\sum_{j=1,j\neq i}^{m} \int_{R_j} p(\boldsymbol{x}|\omega_i)P(\omega_i)d\boldsymbol{x} = 1 - \int_{R_i} p(\boldsymbol{x}|\omega_i)P(\omega_i)d\boldsymbol{x}. \tag{5}$$

[2] In the case where two classes satisfy (1) we may choose arbitrarily one of the classes.

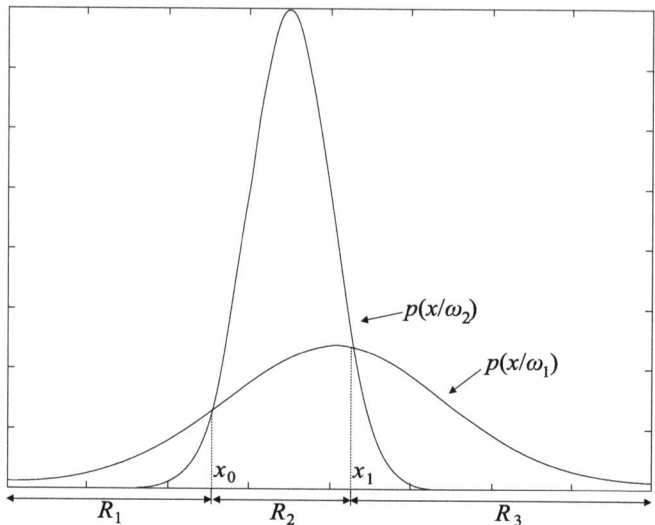

Fig. 1. The class conditional pdf's of a one dimensional two-class problem. The regions R_1 and R_3 are assigned to class ω_1, while R_3 is assigned to class ω_2

Thus, the total probability of committing a decision error P_e is defined as

$$P_e = \sum_{i=1}^{m}[1 - \int_{R_i} p(\boldsymbol{x}|\omega_i)P(\omega_i)d\boldsymbol{x}] \ . \tag{6}$$

It may be shown (see, eg., [30]) that *the Bayes decision rule minimizes the total probability of error.*

3 Discriminant Functions and Discriminant Surfaces

In some cases, instead of working directly with $P(\omega_i|\boldsymbol{x})$ it is more convenient to use $g_i(\boldsymbol{x}) = f(P(\omega_i|\boldsymbol{x}))$, where $f(.)$ is a monotonically increasing function. The $g_i(.)$'s are known as *discriminant functions*. In this case, the Bayes decision rule becomes

Assign $\boldsymbol{x}$ to class ω_i if

$$g_i(\boldsymbol{x}) = \max_{j=1,\dots,m} g_j(\boldsymbol{x}) \ . \tag{7}$$

In other words, the set of discriminant functions identifies a partition of the feature space into regions, each one corresponding to a class.

The contiguous regions of the feature space R^l that correspond to different classes are separated by continuous surfaces, known as *decision surfaces*. Thus, the decision surface separating the two regions R_i and R_j associated with classes ω_i and ω_j, respectively, is described by the following equation:

$$g_{ij}(\boldsymbol{x}) = g_i(\boldsymbol{x}) - g_j(\boldsymbol{x}) = 0, \qquad i,j = 1,2,\dots,m, \quad i \neq j \ . \tag{8}$$

In the sequel we focus on the case where $p(\boldsymbol{x}|\omega_i)$ are *normal (Gaussian) distributions*, i.e.,

$$p(\boldsymbol{x}|\omega_i) \equiv \mathcal{N}(\boldsymbol{\mu}_i, \Sigma_i) = \frac{1}{(2\pi)^{l/2}|\Sigma_i|^{1/2}} \exp(-\frac{1}{2}(\boldsymbol{x}-\boldsymbol{\mu}_i)^T \Sigma_i^{-1}(\boldsymbol{x}-\boldsymbol{\mu}_i)), , \quad (9)$$

$i = 1, 2, \ldots, m$, where $\boldsymbol{\mu}_i = E[\boldsymbol{x}|\boldsymbol{x} \in \omega_i]$ is the mean vector of the class ω_i, $\Sigma_i = E[(\boldsymbol{x}-\boldsymbol{\mu}_i)(\boldsymbol{x}-\boldsymbol{\mu}_i)^T]$ is the $l \times l$ covariance matrix for class ω_i and $|\Sigma_i|$ is the determinant of Σ_i. It is clear that only the vectors $\boldsymbol{x} \in \omega_i$ contribute Σ_i.

Our objective is to design a Bayesian classifier taking into account that each $p(\boldsymbol{x}|\omega_i)$ is a normal distribution. Having in mind the Bayesian rule given in (3), we define the discriminant functions

$$g_i(\boldsymbol{x}) = \ln(P(\omega_i)p(\boldsymbol{x}|\omega_i)) . \quad (10)$$

Substituting (9) into (10) we obtain

$$g_i(\boldsymbol{x}) = -\frac{1}{2}(\boldsymbol{x}-\boldsymbol{\mu}_i)^T \Sigma_i^{-1}(\boldsymbol{x}-\boldsymbol{\mu}_i) + \ln P(\omega_i) + c_i , \quad (11)$$

or, after some maninulations,

$$g_i(\boldsymbol{x}) = -\frac{1}{2}\boldsymbol{x}^T \Sigma_i^{-1}\boldsymbol{x} + \frac{1}{2}\boldsymbol{x}^T \Sigma_i^{-1}\boldsymbol{\mu}_i - \frac{1}{2}\boldsymbol{\mu}_i^T \Sigma_i^{-1}\boldsymbol{\mu}_i + \frac{1}{2}\boldsymbol{\mu}_i^T \Sigma_i^{-1}\boldsymbol{x} + \ln P(\omega_i) + c_i , \quad (12)$$

where c_i is a constant equal to $-\frac{l}{2}\ln(2\pi) - \frac{1}{2}\ln|\Sigma_i|$.

Clearly, the decision surfaces defined as $g_i(\boldsymbol{x}) - g_j(\boldsymbol{x}) = 0$ are *quadrics* (hyperellipsoids, hyperparaboloids, pairs of hyperplanes, etc.) and the resulting Bayesian classifier is a *quadric classifier*.

Special cases:

I: Assuming that the covariance matrices for all classes are equal to each other, i.e., $\Sigma_i = \Sigma$, $i = 1, 2, \ldots, m$, the terms $-\frac{1}{2}\boldsymbol{x}^T \Sigma_i^{-1}\boldsymbol{x}$ and c_i are the same in all g_i's, thus they can be omitted. In this case, $g_i(\boldsymbol{x})$ becomes a linear function of $\boldsymbol{x}$, and it can be rewritten as:

$$g_i(\boldsymbol{x}) = \boldsymbol{w}_i^T \boldsymbol{x} + w_{i0} , \quad (13)$$

where

$$\boldsymbol{w}_i = \Sigma^{-1} \boldsymbol{\mu}_i \quad (14)$$

and

$$w_{i0} = -\frac{1}{2}\boldsymbol{\mu}_i^T \Sigma^{-1}\boldsymbol{\mu}_i + \ln P(\omega_i) . \quad (15)$$

In this case, the decision surfaces $g_i(\boldsymbol{x}) - g_j(\boldsymbol{x}) = 0$ are hyperplanes and the Bayesian classifier is a *linear classifier*.

II: Assume, in addition, that all classes are equiprobable, i.e. $P(\omega_i) = 1/m$, $i = 1, 2, \ldots, m$. Then eq. (11) gives

$$g_i(\boldsymbol{x}) = -\frac{1}{2}(\boldsymbol{x}-\boldsymbol{\mu}_i)^T \Sigma^{-1}(\boldsymbol{x}-\boldsymbol{\mu}_i) \equiv -\frac{1}{2}d_m^2 , \quad (16)$$

The quantity d_m in the right hand side of the above equation, without the minus sign, is called *Mahalanobis distance*. Thus, in this case, instead of searching for the class with the maximum $g_i(\boldsymbol{x})$, we can equivalently search for the class for which the Mahalanobis distance between the respective mean vector and the input vector $\boldsymbol{x}$ is minimum.

III: In addition to the above asumptions, assume that $\Sigma = \sigma^2 I$, where I is the $l \times l$ identity matrix. In this case, eq. (16) gives

$$g_i(\boldsymbol{x}) = -\frac{1}{2\sigma^2}(\boldsymbol{x} - \boldsymbol{\mu_i})^T(\boldsymbol{x} - \boldsymbol{\mu_i}) , \qquad (17)$$

or, eliminating the factor $\frac{1}{2\sigma^2}$, which is common for all g_i's, we obtain:

$$g_i(\boldsymbol{x}) = -(\boldsymbol{x} - \boldsymbol{\mu_i})^T(\boldsymbol{x} - \boldsymbol{\mu_i}) \equiv -d_\varepsilon^2 . \qquad (18)$$

Clearly, searching for the class with the maximum $g_i(\boldsymbol{x})$ is equivalent to searching for the class for which the Euclidean distance, d_ε, between the respective mean vector and the input vector $\boldsymbol{x}$ becomes minimum.

In summary, in the case where each $p(\boldsymbol{x}|\omega_i)$ is a normal distribution, $g_i(\boldsymbol{x})$'s are quadratic functions of $\boldsymbol{x}$ and the decision surface between any two classes is a quadric. If, in addition, all the classes have equal covariance matrices, $g_i(\boldsymbol{x})$'s are linear functions of $\boldsymbol{x}$ and the decision surfaces are hyperplanes.

4 Estimation of Unknown Probability Density Functions

As we saw above, the Bayes decision rule requires the knowledge of $p(\boldsymbol{x}|\omega_i)$'s and $P(\omega_i)$'s, $i = 1, 2, \ldots, m$. However, in practice, this is rarely the case. In the majority of the cases, all we have at our disposal is a finite set of feature vectors from each class known as the *training set*, i.e.,

$$S = \{(\boldsymbol{x_i}, c_i), \boldsymbol{x_i} \in A(\subseteq R^l), c_i \in \{1, 2, \ldots, m\}, i = 1, 2, \ldots, N\} , \qquad (19)$$

where c_i is the index indicating the class to which $\boldsymbol{x_i}$ belongs.

A commonly used estimate for $P(\omega_i)$ ([30]) is

$$P(\omega_i) = \frac{n_i}{N} , \qquad (20)$$

where n_i is the number of vectors in the data set that belong to class ω_i.

However, the estimation of $p(\boldsymbol{x}|\omega_i)$ is not so straightforward. One way to attack the problem of estimating $p(\boldsymbol{x}|\omega_i)$ is to assume that it has a given parametric form and to establish certain optimality criteria, the optimization of which will give estimates for the unknmown parameters of the distribution, using only the feature vectors available for class ω_i. If, for example, we assume that $p(\boldsymbol{x}|\omega_i)$ is a normal distribution, the unknown parameters that have to be estimated, may be the mean vector and/or the covariance matrix.

Parametric methods that follow this philosophy are the Maximum Likelihood Parameter Estimation, the Maximum A Posteriori Probability Estimation and the Mixture models (see eg. [8], [22], [30]).

An alternative way for estimating $p(\boldsymbol{x}|\omega_i)$, using the feature vectors available for ω_i, requires no assumptions of parametric models for $p(\boldsymbol{x}|\omega_i)$. The basic idea relies on the approximation of the unknown pdf using the histogram method. Let us consider the one dimansional case ($l = 1$). In this case the data space is divided into intervals (bins) of size h. Then, the probability of x lying in a specific bin is approximated by the frequency ratio, i.e.,

$$P \simeq \frac{k_N}{N} , \tag{21}$$

where k_N is the number of data points lying in this bin. As $N \to +\infty$, the frequency ratio converges to the true P. The corresponding pdf value is assumed to be constant throughout the bin and is approximated by

$$\hat{p}(x) = \frac{1}{h}\frac{k_N}{N}, \quad |x - \hat{x}| \leq \frac{h}{2} , \tag{22}$$

where $\hat{x}$ is the center of the bin.

Generalizing to the l dimensional case, the bins become l dimensional hypercubes of edge h and $\hat{p}(\boldsymbol{x})$ becomes

$$\hat{p}(\boldsymbol{x}) = \frac{1}{h^l}\frac{k_N}{N} , \tag{23}$$

where now k_N is the number of feature vectors lying in the l dimensional hypercube where $\boldsymbol{x}$ belongs.

Let us define $\phi(\boldsymbol{x_i})$ as

$$\phi(\boldsymbol{x_i}) = \begin{cases} 1, if \ |x_{ij}| < \frac{1}{2}, \ for \ j = 1,\ldots,l \\ 0, otherwise \end{cases} , \tag{24}$$

where x_{ij} is the jth coordinate of the ith vector. In words, $\phi(\boldsymbol{x_i})$ equals to 1 if $\boldsymbol{x_i}$ lies in the l-dimensional unit hypercube centered at the origin $\boldsymbol{0}$ and 0 otherwise. Then, eq. (23) may be rewritten in the following more general form

$$\hat{p}(\boldsymbol{x}) = \frac{1}{h^l}(\frac{1}{N}\sum_{i=1}^{N}\phi(\frac{\boldsymbol{x_i} - \boldsymbol{x}}{h})) . \tag{25}$$

However, in the above equation, we try to approximate a continuous function ($\hat{p}(\boldsymbol{x})$) in terms of a linear combination of instances of a discontinuous one ($\phi(.)$). Parzen ([23]) generalized (25) by using smooth functions ϕ that satisfy

$$\phi(\boldsymbol{x}) \geq 0 ,$$

and

$$\int_{\boldsymbol{x}} \phi(\boldsymbol{x})d\boldsymbol{x} = 1 , \tag{26}$$

and showed that such choices of ϕ lead to legitimate estimates of pdf. A widely used form of ϕ is the Gaussian ([30]).

5   Nearest Neighbor Rules

A different kind of rules that are suboptimal in the sense that they lead to error P_e grater than that of the Bayesian clasifier, are the k-nearest neighbor (k-NN) rules. The general idea is the following: for a given vector x we determine the set A of the k closest neighbors of x among the feature vectors of S (see (19)), irrespective to the class where they belong. Let $k_j(A)$, $j = 1, 2, \ldots, m$ be the number of feature vectors in A that belong to class ω_j. We determine, among the $k_j(A)$'s the largest one, say $k_i(A)$, and we assign x to class ω_i. The Euclidean is the most frequently used distance between vectors although other distances may also be used.

A popular rule that belongs to this category is the nearest neighbor (NN) rule, which results from the above general scheme for $k = 1$. According to this rule, a vector x is assigned to the class where its closest vector in S belongs. It has been shown that the probability of error for the NN classifier is no greater than twice the probability of error of a Bayesian classifier, P_B ([8], [7]). Upper bounds for the probability of error are also available for the general case where $k > 1$. It is worth noting that as $k \to +\infty$, the probability of error of the k-NN classifier approaches P_B ([7], [30]).

Note that all the above schemes require at least $O(N)$ operations, which in cases where large data sets are to be utilized require excessive computational effort. One way to avoid this problem, at the cost of loss of information, is to cluster feature vectors of the same class that are close to each other and to use the mean vectors of the resulted clusters as data set. Such an approach reduces significantly the size of the data set.

6   Linear Classifiers

In the sequel, we consider the case of a two-class problem ($m = 2$) and we label the two classes ω_1 and ω_2 as 1 and 0, respectively. In the previous section we discussed how discriminant functions, that stem from pdf's, are related to decision surfaces. From now on we will emancipate from the notion of probability densities and our goal will be to design classifiers that divide the feature space into class regions, via appropriately chosen discriminant functions. These have not necessarily any relation to probability densities and the Bayesian rule. The aim is to estimate a set of unknown parameters of the discriminant function in a way that place the equivalent decision surfaces optimally in the feature space, according to an optimality criterion.

In this section we deal with linear classifiers, that is, with classifiers that implement linear decision surfaces, i.e. hyperplanes. A hyperplane is described as

$$g(x) = \sum_{i=1}^{l} w_i x_i + w_0 = w^T x + w_0 = 0 , \qquad (27)$$

where $w = [w_1, w_2, \ldots, w_l]^T$ are the parameters specifying the hyperplane. Note that (w, w_0) define uniquely a single hyperplane.

For the compactness of notation, we embed w_0 into $\boldsymbol{w}$ and we augment the feature vector $\boldsymbol{x}$ with one more coordinate which is equal to 1, i.e., $\boldsymbol{w} = [w_0, w_1, w_2, \ldots, w_l]^T$ and $\boldsymbol{x} = [1, x_1, x_2, \ldots, x_l]^T$. Thus the last equation becomes

$$g(\boldsymbol{x}) = \boldsymbol{w}^T \boldsymbol{x} = 0 . \tag{28}$$

Our aim is to determine the optimal hyperplane that separates the two classes. Let us define

$$\delta_{\boldsymbol{x}} = \begin{cases} 1, & if\ \boldsymbol{x} \in \omega_2 \\ -1, & if\ \boldsymbol{x} \in \omega_1 \end{cases} . \tag{29}$$

Then a vector $\boldsymbol{x}$ is *miclassified (correctly classified)* by the hyperplane $\boldsymbol{w}$ if

$$\delta_{\boldsymbol{x}}(\boldsymbol{w}^T \boldsymbol{x}) > (<)0. \tag{30}$$

Let us now assume that the feature vectors of the two classes that belong to S are lineraly separable, i.e., there exists a hyperplane $\boldsymbol{w}^*$ that leaves all feature vectors of S that belong to class 1 (0) in its positive (negative) half-space. An algorithm that is appropriate for the determination of such a hyperplane that classifies correctly the feature vectors of S, is the *perceptron algorithm* (e.g [26], [8], [20], [30]). This may be viewed as an optimization task as described below. Let us define the following optimization function

$$J(\boldsymbol{w}) = \sum_{\boldsymbol{x} \in \mathcal{Y}_{\boldsymbol{w}}} \delta_{\boldsymbol{x}}(\boldsymbol{w}^T \boldsymbol{x}) , \tag{31}$$

where $\mathcal{Y}_{\boldsymbol{w}}$ is the set of all misclassified feature vectors of S by $\boldsymbol{w}$. Clearly, $J(\boldsymbol{w})$ is a non-negative function taking its minimum value when $\mathcal{Y}_{\boldsymbol{w}} = \emptyset$ [3]. Then, the perceptron algorithm may be written as a gradient descent like method that minimizes $J(\boldsymbol{w})$ as follows

$$\boldsymbol{w}(t+1) = \boldsymbol{w}(t) - \rho_t \frac{\partial J(\boldsymbol{w})}{\partial \boldsymbol{w}}|_{\boldsymbol{w}=\boldsymbol{w}(t)} . \tag{32}$$

Note, however, that this is not a true gradient descent scheme since $J(\boldsymbol{w})$ is piecewise linear, thus, non differentiable at the points of discontinuity. For the points where $\partial J(\boldsymbol{w})/\partial \boldsymbol{w}$ is defined we can write

$$\frac{\partial J(\boldsymbol{w})}{\partial \boldsymbol{w}} = \sum_{\boldsymbol{x} \in \mathcal{Y}_{\boldsymbol{w}}} \delta_{\boldsymbol{x}} \boldsymbol{x} . \tag{33}$$

Substituting the above result to eq. (32), we obtain

$$\boldsymbol{w}(t+1) = \boldsymbol{w}(t) - \rho_t \sum_{\boldsymbol{x} \in \mathcal{Y}_{\boldsymbol{w}(t)}} \delta_{\boldsymbol{x}} \boldsymbol{x} . \tag{34}$$

This is the updating equation of the perceptron algorithm. Note that this equation is defined at all points. Typical choices for ρ_t are $\rho_t = c/t$, where c is a constant and $\rho_t = \rho < 2$.

---

[3] Or in the trivial case where $\boldsymbol{w} = \boldsymbol{0}$.

It can be shown that *if the available feature vectors of the two classes are linearly separable, then the perceptron algorithm converges in a finite number of steps to a* w^* *that separates perfectly these vectors.* However, when the available feature vectors of the two classes are not linearly separable the perceptron algorithm does not converge. A variant of this algorithm that converges (under certain conditions) to an optimal solution (i.e., to a solution with the minimum possible number of misclassified feature vectors) is the *pocket algorithm* ([10]).

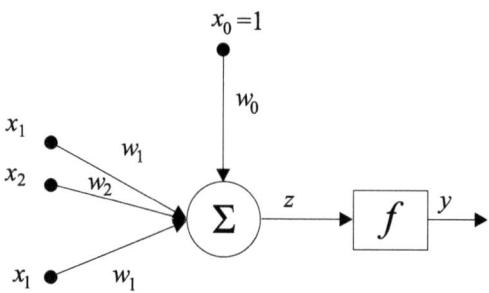

Fig. 2. The perceptron

Let us consider now the structuring element shown in fig. 2, with parameters $w_0, w_1, \ldots, w_l$. Let also $f(z)$ be the *hard limiter function* defined as

$$f(z) = \begin{cases} 1, & if\ z \geq 0 \\ 0, & otherwise \end{cases} . \tag{35}$$

The operation of this element is the following: Once $x_1, x_2, \ldots, x_l$ are applied to the input nodes, they are weighted by $w_1, w_2, \ldots, w_l$, respectively, and the results are summed , i.e.,

$$z = \sum_{i=1}^{l} w_i x_i + w_0 = w^T x , \tag{36}$$

where $w = [w_0, w_1, \ldots, w_l]^T$ and $x = [1, x_1, \ldots, x_l]^T$. Then, the output of this element is 1 if $z \geq 0$ and 0 otherwise. The w_i's are known as *synaptic weights* or simply *weights*. Also, w and w_0 are called *weight vector* and *threshold*, respectively. Finally, the function f is called *activation function*.

The above structuring element is known as *percepton*. Clearly, *it implements the separation of the feature space by the hyperplane H defined by the parameters* $w_i, i = 0, \ldots, l$. That is, the perceptron will output 1 if the vector applied to its input nodes lies in the positive side of H and 0 otherwise.

The perceptron, with a generalized activation function f, will be the basic structuring element for most of the more complicated structures, known as *neural networks* that will be discussed next. In this context, it will be known as *neuron* or *node*.

7   Neural Network Classifiers

As it was discussed in the previous section, the perceptron structure can deal
with two-class problems, provided that the classes are linearly separable. Two
well known linearly separable problems are the AND and OR problems (see fig.
3(a)-(b)). The question that arises now is how often linear separability is met in
practice. One has not to go very far to see that even well known simple problems
are not linearly separable. Consider for example the XOR problem, where $(0,0)$
and $(1,1)$ are assigned to class 0 and $(0,1)$ and $(1,0)$ are assigned to class 1 (see
fig. 3(c)). Clearly, this problem cannot be solved by a single perceptron, since
a single perceptron realizes a single hyperplane and there is no hyperplane that
separates perfectly the vectors of the two classes.

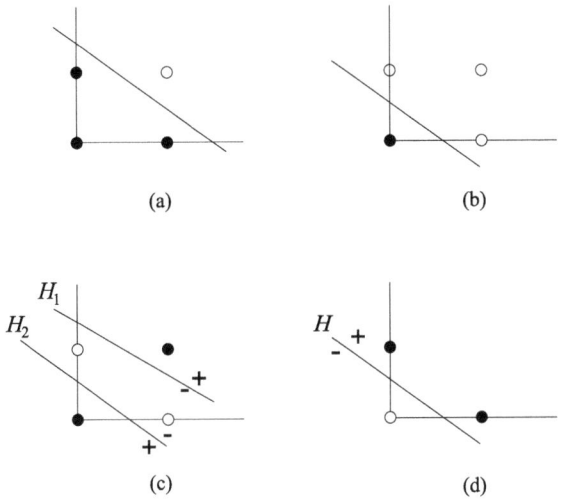

Fig. 3. (a) The AND problem. (b) The OR problem. (c) The XOR problem. (d) The
transformed space for the XOR problem. The open (fiiled) circles correspond to class
1 (0)

Table 1. The XOR problem

x_1	x_2	y_1	y_2	y
0	0	0	1	0
0	1	0	0	1
1	0	0	0	1
1	1	1	0	0

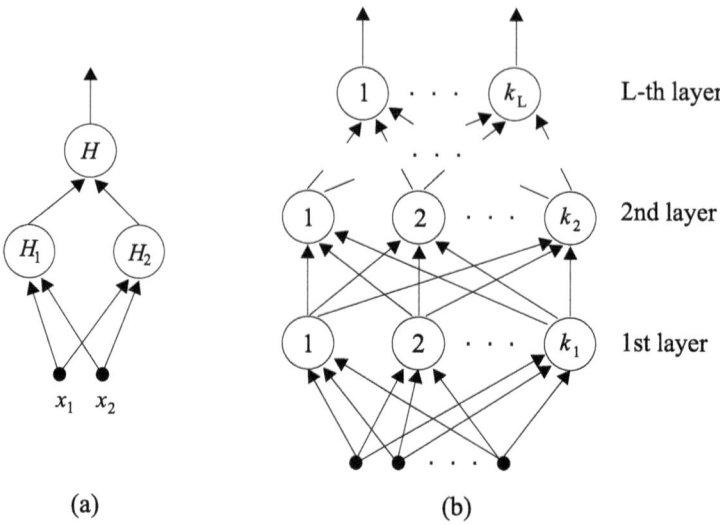

(a)   (b)

Fig. 4. (a) The network that solves the XOR problem. (b) A generalized neural network architecture

In order to solve this problem two hyperplanes are needed, as shown in fig. 3(c). Taking into account the relative position of each point with respect to each hyperplane, we achieve the transformation of the problem as shown in fig. 3(d) and table 1. That is, y_1 and y_2 take the values 0 or 1 depending on the relative position $(+$ or $-)$ of the point (x_1, x_2) with respect to the respective hyperplane. Basically, this is a transformation of the original space into the vertices of the unit square. Clearly, a single hyperplane now suffices to separate the two classes in the transformed space (y_1, y_2). Speaking in terms of neurons, we need two neurons to realize the two hyperplanes H_1 and H_2 and a single neuron that combines the outputs of the previous two neurons and realizes a third hyperplane in the (y_1, y_2) space. Thus, the structure shown in fig. 4(a) results, where each neuron has the structure shown in fig. 2 (For simplicity, the neuron thresholds are not shown explicitly). This is known as a *two-layer perceptron*. It consists of two layers of neurons. The first layer consists of two neurons and the second layer of a single neuron. The input layer has as many input neurons as the dimensionality of the input space. This is a special type of a neural network architecture.

In general, a Neural Network consists of L layers of neurons (excluding the input layer) and the rth layer consists of k_r neurons (see fig. 4(b)). The Lth (final) layer is known as the *output layer* and its neurons *output neurons*. All the other layers are called *hidden layers* and the respective neurons *hidden neurons*.

So far we have seen how a two layer neural network can be used to solve the XOR problem. The natural question that now arises is whether there are partitions of the feature space into classes, via hyperplanes, that cannot be solved by a two-layer architecture. Let us consider the example of fig. 5(a), where the shaded regions correspond to class 1 (ω_1) and the rest to class 0 (ω_2). Clearly, a two layer network that will tackle this problem must have in its first layer as many neurons as the hyperplanes that define the regions in the feature space. Thus, speaking in the spirit of the solution of the XOR problem, each of these neurons realizes one of the hyperplanes and at the same time perform a transformation of the original x space into the (y_1, y_2, y_3) H_3 hypercube space, depending on the position (1 or 0) of x with respect to the respective plane (fig. 5(b)). However, no single hyperplane, realized by the output neuron in the 3-dimensional (y_1, y_2, y_3) space, can separate the vertices of the hypercube that correspond to class 1 from those that correspond to class 0. Thus, this problem cannot be solved by a two-layer network.

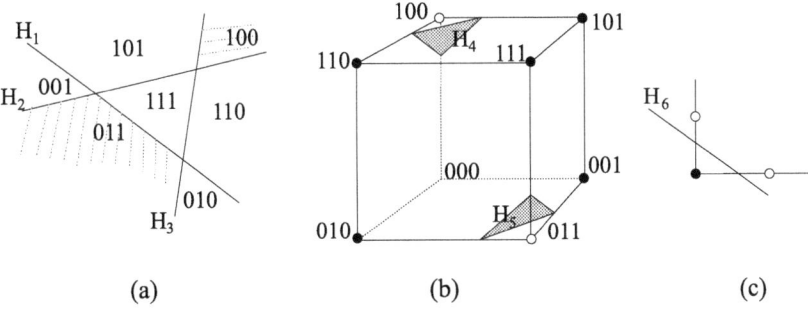

(a)   (b)   (c)

Fig. 5. (a) Classes separated by hyperplanes. (b)-(c) The transformed spaces (see text for explanation). The open (filled) circles correspond to class 1 (0)

However, this problem can be solved by a three layer network as follows. Having transformed the original problem to that of fig. 5(b), we can use two neurons to realize the hyperplanes H_4 and H_5 in the transformed 3-dimensional space. H_4 (H_5) leaves the vertex $(1, 0, 0)$ $((0, 1, 1))$ to its positive side and all the others to its negative side. Thus, we achieve a further transformation as shown in fig. 5(c), where class 0 (ω_2) is represented by a single vertex in the two-dimensional hypercube (square). Clearly, the problem now in this transformed space (fig. 5(c)) is linearly separable. The network that implements the given partition is shown in fig. 6.

The above construction (which by no means is optimal with respect to the number of neurons used) can be applied to any partition of the input space in two classes, where each class is a union of polyhedral sets. A *polyhedral set* is a union of half-spaces. For example, in fig. 5(a) we have three hyperplanes (lines in R^2) that form seven non-intersected polyhedral sets.

In summary, we can say that *the first layer neurons form hyperplanes, the second layer neurons form regions, and the third layer neurons form classes.*

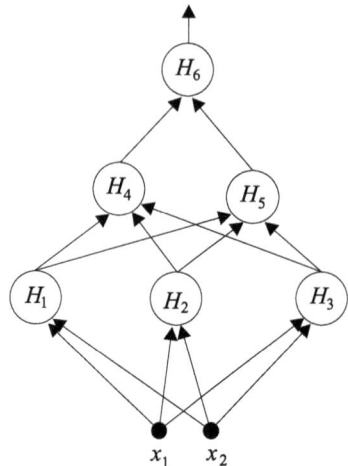

Fig. 6. The network implementing the partition shown in fig. 5(a)

7.1 Choosing the Size of the Network

Having established the capabilities of neural networks in a more theoretical context, one has to find ways for utilizing them in real world situations, where, in most of the times, the only available information is a finite set of training vectors S. More specifically, we need to determine the right size of a network, as well as all the values of the weights connecting its neurons and the neuron thresholds. The size of the network plays a very important role. *The right size for the network should be large enough to be able to learn the differences between the different classes and small enough to be unable to distinguish the differences between the feature vectors of the same class.*

There are three basic directions to approach this problem.

- *Constructive techniques:* The idea here is to begin with a small neural network architecture (often unable to solve the problem at hand) and to augment it, utilizing the available training data set, until a specific criterion is satisfied. One such criterion (not necessarily the best one) is the resulting architecture to classify correctly *all* the available training vectors.

  In this case, the size of the network as well as the values of its weights are adjusted simultaneously. Some algorithms of this category are the Divide and Conquer algorithm ([5], [17]), the Cascade Correlation algorithm ([9]), the Constructive Learning by Specialization algorithm([25]), the Tilling algorihm ([19]) etc.
- *Prunning techniques:* Here one begins with a very large architecture and gradually reduces it by prunning weights or even neurons when certain predefined criteria are met. This procedure is repeated until a specific termination criterion is satisfied (see eg., [18], [11], [25], [28], [30]).

- *Analytical methods:* In this case, the size of the network is estimated a priori, using statistical or algebraic methods, and then, an appropriate algorithm is employed in order to determine the values of the weights and the thresholds of the network. Note that the network structure is kept unaltered when esitmation of the weights and the thresholds takes place.

7.2   The Back Propagation Algorithm

By far, the most well known and widely used learning algorithm to estimate the values of the synaptic weights and the thresholds, is the so called *Back Propagation (BP) algorithm* and its variants ([33], [27], [30]). According to this training method, the size (number of layers and number of nodes in each layer) of the network remains fixed. In general, the procedure of determining the values of the unknown parameters of a network is known as *training of the network*.

The BP algorithm relies on a training data set S (see (19)). Note that we can use various representations for labeling the respective class of each vector of the training set. One representation that is frequently used in practice is the following:

$$y(i) = [\overbrace{0,\dots,0,\ \underbrace{1}_{c_i},\ 0,\dots,0}^{m}]\ ,\tag{37}$$

where $y(i)$ is the vector having zeros everywhere except at position c_i, that corresponds to the class to which the ith training vector belongs, where it has 1.

The BP algorithm is a gradient descent scheme that determines a local minimum of the cost function which is adopted. The most popular cost function is the following:

$$J = \sum_{i=1}^{N} \mathcal{E}(i)\ ,\tag{38}$$

where

$$\mathcal{E}(i) = \frac{1}{2}\sum_{p=1}^{k} e_p^2(i) = \frac{1}{2}\sum_{p=1}^{k}(\hat{y}_p(i) - y_p(i))^2\ ,\tag{39}$$

with $\hat{y}_p(i)$ being the true output of the pth output node of the network when the ith feature vector is fed to the network and k is the number of neurons of the output layer. Note that, in general, y_p and $\hat{y}_p$ are different and are known as the desired and true outputs, respectively.

In the sequel we adopt the representation of classes described above. Thus, we have $k = m$.

The gradient descent optimization procedure requires the computation of the gradient of the cost function with respect to the unknown parameters. However, differentiation of J is not possible, since $\hat{y}_p(i)$ is expressed via the hard limiter function, which is not a differentiable function. One way to overcome this difficulty is to use a smooth function that approximates the hard limiter function, which will be continuous and differentiable. One such function is the *logistic function*, shown in fig. 7, which is defined as

$$f(x) = \frac{1}{1 + \exp(-ax)} \, , \tag{40}$$

where a is the slope parameter. The larger the value of a, the more the logistic function approaches the hard limiter. Clearly, this function takes values between 0 and 1. This function belongs to a broader class of functions known as *squashing functions*, whose output is limited in a continuous real number interval. Other such functions are also possible (e.g., [30]).

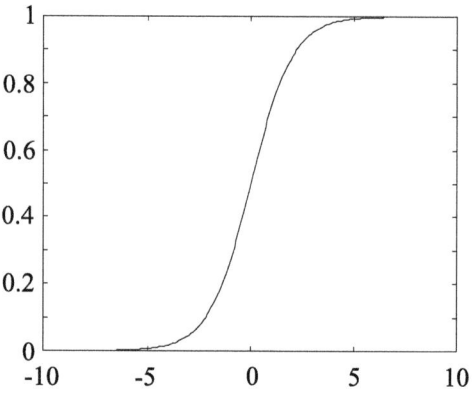

Fig. 7. The logistic function

An important property of a neuron with sigmoid activation function is that *it gives the same output for all points lying on a hyperplane parallel to the hyperplane implemented by the neuron*. This can be easily verified as follows. Let H be the hyperplane $z = \boldsymbol{w}^T \boldsymbol{x}$ implemented by the neuron with $\boldsymbol{w} = [w_0, \ w_1, \ \dots, w_l]^T$, and H_1 be the hyperplane $z = \boldsymbol{w_1}^T \boldsymbol{x}$, parallel to H at distance d. Let $\boldsymbol{x}'$ be a point on H_1. Then, the distance between $\boldsymbol{x}'$ and H is

$$d(\boldsymbol{x}', H) = d = \frac{\boldsymbol{w}^T \boldsymbol{x}'}{\sqrt{\sum_{i=1}^{l} w_i}} {}^4 \, . \tag{41}$$

or

$$\boldsymbol{w}^T \boldsymbol{x}' = d \sqrt{\sum_{i=1}^{l} w_i} \, . \tag{42}$$

---

[4] A negative distance means that the input vector $\boldsymbol{x}$ lies in the negative half-space of H.

Since the right hand side term of the last equality is constant, for all points in H_1, and taking into account that the output of the node is equal to $1/(1 + \exp(-a(\boldsymbol{w}^T\boldsymbol{x}')))$, the claim follows.

Because of the above property, we say that the output of such a neuron is of *global nature*.

Note that what has been said, concerning the classification capabilities of neural networks consisted of neurons with hard limiter activation functions, in the case of neurons with logistic activation functions is valid only approximately for large values of a.

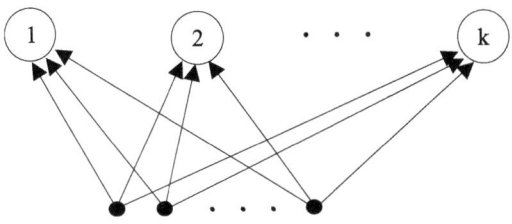

Fig. 8. A one-layer network

Let us now return to the BP algorithm. First, we will derive it for a one layer network (see fig. 8). In this case, $\hat{y}_p(i)$ is given as

$$\hat{y}_p(i) = f(z_p(i)) = f(\sum_{j=0}^{l} w_{pj}x_j(i)) = f(\boldsymbol{w_p}^T\boldsymbol{x}(i)) , \qquad (43)$$

where w_{pj} denotes the weight from the jth input neuron to the pth output neuron, w_{p0} is the threshold of the pth neuron, $\boldsymbol{w_p} = [w_{p0},\ w_{p1}, \ldots, w_{pl}]^T$ is the weight vector of the pth neuron, $x_j(i)$ is the jth coordinate of the ith input vector and $\boldsymbol{x}(i) = [1,\ x_1(i), \ldots, x_l(i)]^T$ is the input vector. Also, $z_p(i)$ is the weighed sum of the inputs to the pth output neuron.

The basic equation of the BP algorithm, at the tth iteration step, is

$$\boldsymbol{w_p}(t+1) = \boldsymbol{w_p}(t) + \Delta\boldsymbol{w_p}(t+1), \qquad p = 1, \ldots, k , \qquad (44)$$

where

$$\Delta\boldsymbol{w_p}(t+1) = -\rho\frac{\partial J(\boldsymbol{w_p})}{\partial \boldsymbol{w_p}}\Big|_{\boldsymbol{w_p}=\boldsymbol{w_p}(t)} . \qquad (45)$$

Let us define

$$\delta_p(i) = \frac{\partial \mathcal{E}(i)}{\partial z_p(i)} \qquad (46)$$

and

$$e_p(i) = \hat{y}_p(i) - y_p(i) . \qquad (47)$$

It is easy to see that

$$\delta_p(i) = \frac{\partial \mathcal{E}(i)}{\partial z_p(i)} = (\hat{y}_p(i) - y_p(i))f'(z_p(i)) = e_p(i)f'(z_p(i)) \ . \tag{48}$$

Also

$$\frac{\partial z_p(i)}{\partial \boldsymbol{w_p}} = \boldsymbol{x}(i) \ . \tag{49}$$

Combining eqs. (44), (45), (38), (46), (49) we finally obtain

$$\boldsymbol{w_p}(t+1) = \boldsymbol{w_p}(t) - \rho[\sum_{i=1}^{N} \delta_p(i)\boldsymbol{x}(i)] \ , \tag{50}$$

where $\delta_p(i)$ is given by eq. (48).

Let us now state explicitly the steps of the BP algorithm for the one layer case.

- Initialize the weight vectors $\boldsymbol{w_p}$, $p = 1, \ldots, k$
- Repeat
  - For $i = 1$ to N
    * Present $\boldsymbol{x}(i)$ to the network
    * For each neuron compute $\hat{y}_p(i)$, $e_p(i)$ and $\delta_p(i)$, $p = 1, \ldots, k$
  - End { For }
  - Use eq. (50) to update the weight vectors $\boldsymbol{w_p}$, $p = 1, \ldots, k$
- Until a specific termination criteron is met

The above algorithm is also known as the *delta rule* [Rummelhart]. Moreover, if $f(.)$ is the identity function, the delta rule coincides with the well known LMS rule [31], [32].

Let us now move to the more general case of multilayer neural networks, i.e., networks with more than one layers. In this framework we adopt the following notation: L is the number of layers of the network (excluding, of course, the input layer), k_q is the number of neurons in the qth layer, $q = 1, \ldots, L$, $\boldsymbol{w_j^q}$ is the weight vector for the jth neuron in the qth layer, w_{ji}^q is the weight connecting the jth neuron of the qth layer with the ith neuron of the previous layer, $y_j^q(i)$ is the output of the jth neuron in the qth layer, when $\boldsymbol{x}(i)$ is the input to the network, $\boldsymbol{y^q}(i)$ is the output vector of the qth layer. Here, the convention that $\boldsymbol{y^0}(i) = \boldsymbol{x}(i)$ has been adopted. Also, we define

$$z_j^q(i) = \boldsymbol{w_j^q}^T \boldsymbol{y^{q-1}}(i) \tag{51}$$

and

$$e_j^L = \hat{y}_j^L(i) - y_j^L(i) \ . \tag{52}$$

Note that the threshold w_{j0}^q of each neuron in any layer is embedded in $\boldsymbol{w_j^q}$, i.e., we define $\boldsymbol{w_j^q} = [w_{j0}^q, w_{j1}^q, \ldots, w_{jk_{q-1}}^q]^T$ and $\boldsymbol{y^{q-1}}(i) = [1, y_1^{q-1}(i), \ldots, y_{k_{q-1}}^{q-1}(i)]^T$.

Using the above notation, the updating equation (50) is written as

$$\boldsymbol{w_p^q}(t+1) = \boldsymbol{w_p^q}(t) - \rho[\sum_{i=1}^{N} \delta_p^q(i)\boldsymbol{y^{q-1}}(i)] \ . \tag{53}$$

The terms $\delta_m^L(i)$ for the output layer neurons are computed as in the one layer case and in this context we can write

$$\delta_p^L(i) = (\hat{y}_p^L(i) - y_p(i))f'(z_p^L(i)) = e_p^L(i)f'(z_p^L(i)) \ . \tag{54}$$

The problem now is the computation of the terms $\delta_m^q(i)$ for $q < L$. In this case we use the chain rule in differentiation, which, after some manipulations, gives (see e.g. [30])

$$\delta_p^q(i) = e_p^q(i)f'(z_p^q(i)) \ , \tag{55}$$

with

$$e_p^q(i) = \sum_{s=1}^{k_{q+1}} \delta_s^{q+1}(i)w_{sp}^{q+1} \ . \tag{56}$$

Note that $e_p^q(i)$ for $q < L$ is not a true error, as the one given in eq. (52), but it is defined as such for notational uniformity.

The above two equations provide the term $\delta_p^q(i)$ in terms of all $\delta_p^{q+1}(i)$'s of the next layer. Thus, for a given input vector $\boldsymbol{x}(i)$, we compute the output vector $\boldsymbol{y^L}(i)$ and the terms $\delta_p^L(i)$'s. Then we move one layer back, in order to compute $\delta_p^{L-1}(i)$'s in terms of $\delta_p^L(i)$'s, through eqs. (55) and (56). Continuing this process backwards we can compute the terms $\delta_p^q(i)$ for all neurons and then we use eq. (53) to update the weight vectors. It is this way of moving backwards, in order to compute the terms $\delta_p^q(i)$, that gives to the Back Propagation algorithm its name.

Let us state now explicitly the BP algorithm

- Initialize the weight vectors $\boldsymbol{w_p^q} = \boldsymbol{w_p^q}(0)$, $p = 1, \ldots, k_q$, $q = 1, \ldots, L$.
- Repeat
  - For $i = 1$ to N
    * Present the vector $\boldsymbol{x}(i)$ to the network
    * Compute $\hat{y}_p^L(i)$, $p = 1, \ldots, k_L$
    * Compute $\delta_p^L(i)$, $p = 1, \ldots, k_L$, using eq. (54)
    * For $q = L - 1$ to 1
      · Compute $\delta_p^q(i)$, $p = 1, \ldots, k_q$ using eqs. (55) and (56)
    * End
  - End
  - Update the weight vectors of the network using eq. (53)
- Until a specific termination criterion is met

The time needed for the presentation of all training feature vectors to the network and the computation of the $\delta_p^q(i)$'s, $i = 1, \ldots, N$, i.e., the time required for the execution of the statements in the for - loop once, is known as an *epoch*. Some comments about the BP algorithm are now in order.

- Usually, the number of the output neurons in a neural network, used for classification, equals to the number of classes involved in the problem at hand, i.e. each neuron corresponds to a class. This implies that the representation given in (37) for the class indices is employed.
- The BP algorithm is a nonlinear optimization task due to the nonlinearity of the activation functions of the neurons of the network. This implies that the cost function J has local minima and the algorithm may converge to one of them. However, a local minimum is not necessarily a bad solution as we will see soon.
- As a termination criterion we may require that the value of J falls below a prespecified threshold or that the gradient of J is close enough to zero. The last criterion indicates convergence to a local minimum.
- The quantity ρ, which is known as *learning rate*, plays a very important part to the convergence of the algorithm. It should be sufficiently small, in order to guarantee convergence, but not very small, so that to slow down the convergence procedure. In regions of the weight space where broad minima (A in fig. 9) are encountered, ρ should be larger in order to accelerate convergence. On the other hand, in regions with very narrow minima (B in fig. 9), small ρ should be used in order to avoid oscillation around the local minimum.

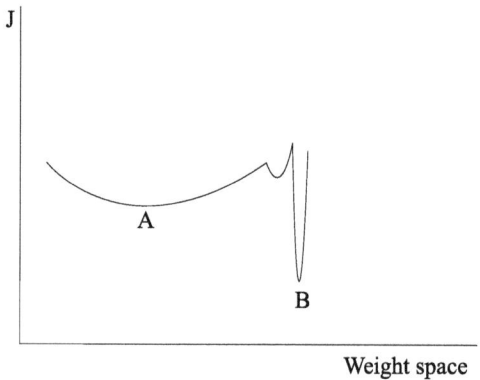

Fig. 9. A broad minimum (A) and a narrow minimum (B)

- In the BP version presented above, the updating of the network weights takes place once all feature vectors have been presented to the network. This mode of learning is called *batch mode*. A different mode arises if we update the weights of the network each time a new vector is presented to the network. This mode is called *pattern mode* of operation. In practice, in the pattern mode of operation, for each epoch, the sequence of vectors in which they are presented to the network is randomized.

Training in the batch mode exhibits a smoother convergence behavior. On the other hand, training in the pattern mode offers the algorithm the possibility of escaping from a local minimum ([30]).

– In practice, it is common that the change of the cost function gradient between successive iteration steps is not smooth but oscillatory, which results in slow convergence. One way to speed up convergence is to use a momentum term that smooths out the oscillatory behavior and speeds up convergence. Then, the correction term Δw_p^q is no more a function of the $\partial J/\partial w_p^q$ only, but it also depends on the correction term of the previous step via the following relation

$$\Delta w_p^q(new) = a \Delta w_p^q(old) - \rho \sum_{i=1}^{N} \delta_p^q(i) y^{q-1}(i) \, , \qquad (57)$$

where a is a constant called *momentum factor*, which usually takes values between 0.1 and 0.8.

It is worth noting that due to the above relation, the whole history of the correction steps is accumulated into $\Delta w_p^q(old)$.

It can be shown (see [30]) that the use of the momentum term is equivalent to the increase of the learning rate at regions in the weight space where the gradient of J is close to zero.

– An alternative way to accelerate convergence of the BP algorithm is to adapt the learning rate ρ using heuristic rules (see e.g. [30]). One set of such rules is the following: if $J(t)/J(t-1) < 1(> c > 1)$ then increase (decrease) ρ by a factor r_i (r_d). Otherwise, if $1 \leq J(t)/J(t-1) \leq c$, we leave ρ unchanged. Typical values for the constants r_i, r_d and c are 1.05, 0.7 and 1.04, respectively. Other acceleration schemes are also possible (see e.g. [6], [12])

– After the completion of the training phase, the parameters of the network are frozen to their converged values and the network is now ready for classification. Adopting the repesentation given in (37), the classification of an unknown vector x into one of the m classes, depends on which output neuron gets the maximum value (this is expected to be close to one and all the others close to zero).

– An important aspect of the type of training discusssed above, i.e., using the representation given in eq. (37) and the cost function given by (38) and (39), is that the outputs $\hat{y}_p$ of the network, *corresponding to the optimal weights*, are estimates, in the least square sense, of $P(\omega_p|x)$.

– More complex training algorithms, such as Newton type schemes, which involve the computation of the Hessian matrix of J with respect to w_p^q's, have also been suggested in order to speed up convergence (see e.g. [16], [2], [14], [3], [21], [4]).

– Different cost function choices are also possible. If for example we assume that y_p take binary values (0 or 1) and they are independent to each other, and $\hat{y}_p$ are interpreted as estimates of the a posteriori probabilites $P(\omega_p|\boldsymbol{x})$, we may define the so called *cross-entropy function* as

$$J = -\sum_{i=1}^{N}\sum_{p=1}^{k_L}(y_p(i)\ln\hat{y}_p(i) + (1-y_p(i))\ln(1-\hat{y}_p(i))) \ . \qquad (58)$$

Computation of the δ terms is independent of the cost function used and is performed in the BP spirit.
- It can be shown that if we adopt the cross-entropy cost function and binary values for $y_p^L(i)$'s, the outputs $\hat{y}_p$ of the network, corresponding to the optimal weights, are also estimates of $P(\omega_p|\boldsymbol{x})$.

7.3   Training Aspects

In the last section we commented on the termination criteria of the BP algorithm. However, a problem that may arise in practice is that of *overtraining*. If this happens, the network learns the peculiarities of the specific training data set very well and fails to capture the underlying general structure of the problem. As a consequence, the behavior of the network is expected to be rather poor on new data, "unknown" to the network.

A way out of the problem of overtraining is to use apart from the training set at hand, an additional data set, known as *test set*, which will be used to measure the performance of the trained neural network. Thus, we split the set of all available data into two sets, the training set and the test set. Then, we plot the evolution of the error on the training and the test set, during the training phase, versus the number of epochs. The point where overtraining becomes noticeable is the one where the error on the test set starts to increase [5] (see fig. 10). However, it must be pointed out that this method requires the existence of a large data set, which is not available for all applications.

Avoiding overtraining is one prerequisite for good *generalization*, i.e., for good performance to feature vectors that do not belong to the training set. Another factor affecting the generalization properties is the size of the network. Small networks (with respect to the number of parameters) are often unable to solve the problem at hand, while large networks tend to learn the details of the training data set leading to poor generalization performance.

7.4   Radial Basis Function (RBF) Networks

Up to now we considered only neurons of the structure shown in fig. 2, that implement the function $y = f(\boldsymbol{w}^T\boldsymbol{x})$, where f may be a hard limiter or a sigmoid function. In this section we consider networks whose neurons implement functions of the form

$$y = f(||\boldsymbol{x} - \boldsymbol{c_i}||) \ , \qquad (59)$$

---

[5] Of course, we do not compute the error on the test set at each epoch but after the completion of a predetermined number of epochs.

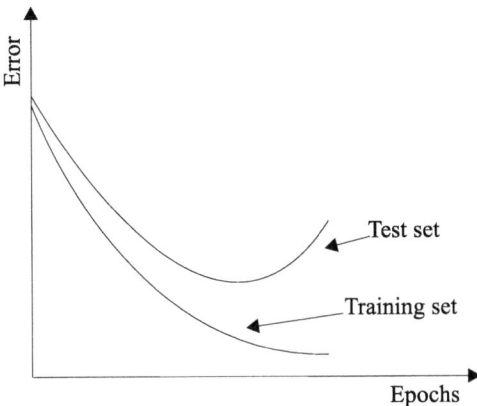

Fig. 10. Plot of the error on the training and the test set versus the number of epochs. The point where the test error starts to increase, indicates the beginning of overtraining

where c_i is a vector in R^l. Typical choices for f are

$$f(x) = \exp(-\frac{1}{2\sigma_i^2}||x - c_i||^2) ,$$ (60)

and

$$f(x) = \frac{\sigma^2}{\sigma^2 + ||x - c_i||^2} ,$$ (61)

with the Gaussian being the most commonly used form in practice.

In words, the output of each neuron is determined by the distance between the input vector x and the vector c_i, associated with the corresponding node. Clearly, a neuron of this kind gives the same response for all the points lying on a hypersphere centered at c_i. This is the reason why these neurons are called *radial basis function neurons*. Moreover, note that for the above choices of f, the output of the neuron decreases as $||x - c_i||$ increases. Thus the action of such nodes is of a *local nature*.

Radial Basis Function Networks usually consist of two layers of neurons. The first layer consists of k RBF neurons and the second layer of linear output neurons, i.e., neurons as those shown in fig. 2, with f being the identity function. A typical architecture of an RBF network is shown in fig. 11.

Let us now see how an RBF network works through an example. Consider the data set shown in fig. 12(a). The points denoted by open circles belong to class w_1, while the rest belong to class w_2. Let us choose $k = 2$ and RBF neurons with centers $c_1 = (0, 0)$ and $c_2 = (1, 1)$. The activation function of these neurons is the one given in eq. (60). Also, let $\sigma_i = 1/2$, $i = 1, 2$. Then $y = [\exp(-||x - c_1||^2), \exp(-||x - c_2||^2)]^T$ denotes the mapping implemented by the above choice of RBF neurons. Thus, the data points are mapped to a two-dimensional space as follows: the points $(0, 0)$ and $(1, 1)$ are mapped to the points $(1, 0.135)$ and $(0.135, 1)$, respectively, the points $(0, 1)$ and $(1, 0)$ are

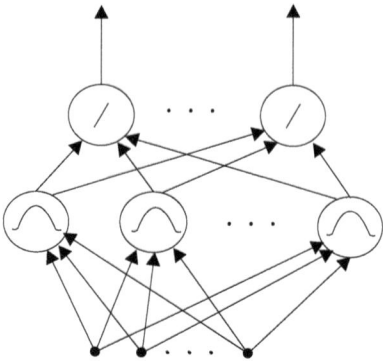

Fig. 11. A typical architecture of an RBF network

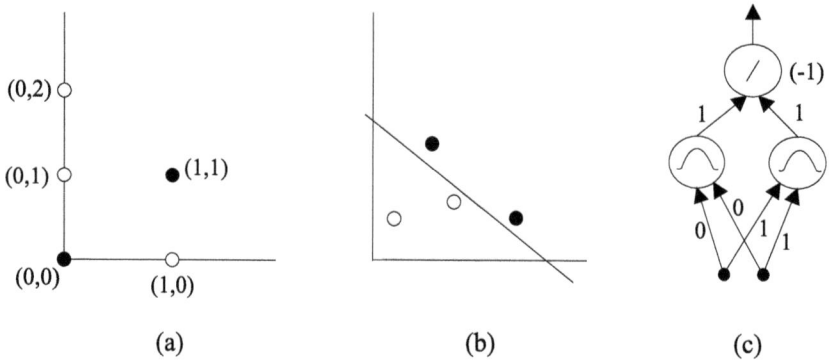

Fig. 12. (a) Set up of the example. The open (filled) circles correspond to class 1 (0). (b) The transformed space. (c) The RBF network implementing the desired partition. The threshold of the output node is shown in parenthesis

both mapped to the point (0.368, 0.368) and, finally, the point (0, 2) is mapped to the point (0.018, 0.136). This mapping is shown in fig. 12(b). Note that the two classes are linearly separable in the transformed space and the straight line

$$g(\boldsymbol{y}) = y_1 + y_2 - 1 = 0 \ , \tag{62}$$

is one possible solution. The corresponding RBF network is shown in fig. 12(c).

Training of the RBF Networks. In the above toy example, we chose arbitrarily the parameters of the RBF network, i.e., the centers c_i and the variances σ_i for each hidden layer neuron and the weights w_j for the output layer neuron. The question that arises now is how can we estimate these parameters in a real world problem. In the sequel we consider the case where we have a single output neuron.

Let $\hat{y}(i)$ be the output of the network and $y(i)$ the desired output, when $\boldsymbol{x}(i)$ is the input and $\phi(.)$ a differentiable function (for example $\phi(z) = z^2$). One way to determine the parameters of the network is to define a cost function of the form

$$J = \sum_{i=1}^{N} \phi(e(i)) \ , \tag{63}$$

where $e(i) = \hat{y}(i) - y(i)$, and to use a gradient descent method to determine the above parameters, i.e.,

$$w_j(t + 1) = w_j(t) - \rho_1 \frac{\partial J}{\partial w_j}|_t \ , \quad j = 0, 1, \ldots, k \tag{64}$$

$$c_i(t + 1) = c_i(t) - \rho_2 \frac{\partial J}{\partial c_i}|_t \ , \quad j = 1, \ldots, k \tag{65}$$

$$\sigma_i(t + 1) = \sigma_i(t) - \rho_3 \frac{\partial J}{\partial \sigma_i}|_t \ , \quad j = 1, \ldots, k \ , \tag{66}$$

where t is the current iteration step. However, the computational complexity of such an approach is excessively high. To overcome this problem other ways have been suggested. One such way is to select the centers corresponding to the hidden layer neurons in a way representative of the distribution of the data set. This can be achieved by assigning a center to every region in the feature space which is dense in feature vectors. These regions may be unravelled using appropriate clustering algorithms (see e.g., [13], [8], [1], [30]). Then, we assign a center to each one of these regions [6] and we compute the variance σ_i of each such region.

After the parameters of the first layer neurons have been determined, we define the following data set

$$S' = \{(\boldsymbol{z}_j, y_j), \ \boldsymbol{z}_j = [f^1(\boldsymbol{x}_j), \ldots, f^k(\boldsymbol{x}_j)]^T, \ \boldsymbol{x}_j \in S, \ j = 1, \ldots, N\} \ , \tag{67}$$

where $f^i(\boldsymbol{x}_j)$ is the output of the ith first layer neuron of the network. Then, based on the new S', we determine w_j's using the delta rule for one layer networks described above.

Alternative ways for the training of RBF networks have also been suggested (e.g., [29], [24], [34], [15], [30]).

8   Concluding Remarks

In this chapter a number of basic classifiers were considered and discussed, such as the Bayesian classifier, classifers based on Parzen windows and nearest neighbor concepts, the perceptron and neural networks. The goal was to present these methods in a way appropriate for the newcomer in the field.

---

[6] In most of the cases, the center is computed as the mean of the data vectors in the corresponding region.

References

1. Anderberg M. R., *Cluster Analysis for Applications*, Academic Press, 1973.
2. Barnard E., "Optimization for training neural networks", *IEEE Transactions on Neural Networks*, Vol. 3(2), pp. 232-240, 1992.
3. Battiti R., "First and second order methods for learning: Between steepest descent and Newton's method", *Neural Computation*, Vol. 4, pp. 141-166, 1992.
4. Bishop C. M., *Neural Networks for Pattern Recognition*, Oxford University Press, 1995.
5. Bose N. K., Lianf P., *Neural Network Fundamentals with Graphs, Algorithms and Applications*, McGraw-Hill, 1996.
6. Cichocki A., Unbehauen R., *Neural Networks for Optimization and Signal Processing*, John Wiley, 1993.
7. Devroye L., Gyorfi L., Lugosi G. A., *A Probabilistic Theory of Pattern Recognition*, Springer-Verlag, 1996.
8. Duda R., Hart P. E., *Pattern Classification and Scene Analysis*, John Wiley, 1973.
9. Fahlman S. E., Lebiere C., "The cascade-correlation learning architecture", in *Advances in Neural Information Processing Systems, 2* (Touretzky D. S., ed.), pp. 524-532, Morgan Kaufmann, San Mateo, CA, 1990.
10. Gallant S. I., "Perceptron based learning algorithms", *IEEE Transactions on Neural Networks*, Vol., 1(2), pp. 179-191, 1990.
11. Hassibi B., Stork D. G., Woff G. J., "Optimal brain surgeon and general network pruning", *Proceedings IEEE Conference in Neural Networks*, Vol. 1, pp. 293-299, Sna Francisco, 1993.
12. Jacobs R. A., "Increased rates of convergence through learning rate of adaptation", *Neural Networks*, Vol. 2, pp. 359-366, 1988.
13. Jain A. K., Dubes R. C., *Algorithms for Clustering Data*, Prentice Hall, 1998.
14. Johansson E. M., Dowla F. U., Goodman D.M., "Backpropagation learning for multilayer feedforward neural networks using conjugate gradient method", *International Journal of Neural Systems*, Vol. 2(4), pp. 291-301,1992.
15. Karayiannis N. B., Mi G. W., "Growing radial basis neural networks. Merging supervisedand unsupervised learning with network growth techniques", *IEEE Transactions on Neural Networks*, Vol. 8(6) pp. 1492-1506, 1997.
16. Kramer A. H., Sangiovanni-Vincentelli A., "Efficient parallel learning algorithms for neural networks", in *Advances in Neural Information Processing Systems 3* (Lippmann R. P., Moody J., Touretzky D. S., eds.), pp. 684-692, Morgan Kaufmann, San Mateo, CA, 1991.
17. Koutroumbas K., Pouliakis A., Kalouptsidis N., "Divide and conquer algorithms for constructing neural network architectures", EUCIPCO '98, Rhodes, 1998.
18. Le Cun Y., Denker J. S., Solla S. A., "Optimal brain damage", in *Advances in Neural Information Systems 2* (Touretzky D. S. ed.), pp. 598-605, Morgan Kaufmann, San Mateo, CA, 1990.
19. Mezard M., Nadal J. P., "Learning in feedforward layered networks: The tilling algorithm", *Journal of Physics*, Vol. A 22, pp. 2191-2203,1989.
20. Minsky M. L., Papert S.A., *Perceptrons*, expanded edition, MIT Press, Cambridge, MA, 1988.
21. Palmieri F., Datum M., Shah A., Moiseff A., "Sound localization with a neural network trained with the multiple extended Kalman algorithm", *International JointConference on Neural Networks*, Vol. 1, pp. 125-131, Seattle, 1991.

22. Papoulis A., *Probability, Random Variables and Stochastic Processes*, 3rd ed., McGraw-Hill, 1991.
23. Parzen E., "On the estimation of a probability density function and mode", *Ann. Math.m Stat.*, Vol. 33, pp. 1065-1076, 1962.
24. Platt J., "A resource allocating network for function interpolation", *Neural Computation*, Vol. 3, pp. 213-225, 1991.
25. Refenes A., Chen L., "Analysis of methods for optimal network construction", *University College London Report*, CC30/080:DCN, 1991.
26. Rosenblatt F., "The perceptron: A probabilistic model for information storage and organization in the brain", *Psychological Review*, Vol. 65, pp. 386-408, 1958.
27. Rumelhart D. E., McLelland J. L., *Parallel Distributed Processing*, Cambridge MA: MIT Press, 1986.
28. Russell R., "Pruning algorithms: A survey", *IEEE Transactions on Neural Networks*, Vol. 4(5), pp. 740-747, 1993.
29. Scholkopf B., Sung K.-K., Burges C. J. C., Girosi F., Niyogi P., Poggio T., Vapnik V., "Comparing support vector machnies with Gaussian kernels to RBF classifiers", *IEEE Transactions on Signal Processing*, Vol. 45(11), pp. 2758-2766, 1997.
30. Theodoridis S., Koutroumbas K., *Pattern Recognition*, Academic Press, 1998.
31. Widrow B., Hoff M. E. Jr, "Adaptive switching circuits", *IREWESCON Convention Record*, pp. 96-104, 1960.
32. Widrow B., Lehr M. A., "30 years of adaptive neural networks: Perceptron, madaline and backpropagation", *Proceedings of the IEEE*, Vol. 78(9), pp. 1415-1442, 1990.
33. Werbos P.J., "Beyond regression: New tools for prediction and analysis in the behavioral sciences", Ph.D. Thesis, Harvard University, Cambridge, MA, 1974.
34. Yingwei L., Sundarajan N., Saratihandram P., "Performance evaluation of a sequential minimal RBF network learning algorithm", *IEEE Transactions on Leural Networks*, Vol. 9(2), pp. 308-318, 1998.

Model Class Selection and Construction: Beyond the Procrustean Approach to Machine Learning Applications

Maarten van Someren

Department of Social Science Informatics, University of Amsterdam, Roetersstraat 15,
1018 WB Amsterdam, The Netherlands
maarten@swi.psy.uva.nl

1   Introduction

Machine Learning was primarily inspired by human learning. In a branch of Artificial Intelligence scientists tried to build systems that reproduce forms of human learning. Currently the methods that were discovered in this way have been elaborated and are applied to tasks that are not performed by humans at all. For example, one of the most popular applications is the analysis of consumer data to predict buying behaviour. This has not traditionally been viewed as an interesting form of human intelligence.

The result of learning is what we shall call a "model". A model can be a software system or "knowledge" in the sense of symbolic descriptions (or diagrams) that are inspected by human users. The requirements for a "system" are often different from the requirements on "knowledge". For example, "knowledge" must be communicated to people and therefore it must be expressed in comprehensible vocabulary and split into small parts that can be "digested" by people.   A system must often satisfy different requirements such as efficiency, modularity or compatibility with other software. Another dimension along which learning tasks vary is if learning takes place in a single pass or "sustained", "continuously". In the latter case, the learning task is to update the acquired model (system or knowledge) all the time. After each update the model should be usable. Table 1 summarises the main types of learning tasks.

Table 1. Types of tasks.

	Learn once	**Learn sustained**
System	learning system	adaptive system
Knowledge	data analysis	"dynamic knowledge"

The task of "dynamic knowledge" or sustained acquisition of knowledge is not studied very often. Most applications and research in machine learning address tasks of the other three types. A special case is knowledge acquisition for knowledge based systems. In this case, the result of learning is "system" and "knowledge" in one: it can be run on a computer to perform a task and it can also be understood by a human user.

Constructing a model in general is not a matter of simply applying a technique. In *learn once* tasks this involves the following steps (e.g. [19]):

G. Paliouras, V. Karkaletsis, and C.D. Spyropoulos (Eds.): ACAI '99, LNAI 2049, pp. 196-217, 2001.
© Springer-Verlag Berlin Heidelberg 2001

1. Select a model class. This involves defining a language for representing models. This language consists of a structure and a vocabulary and an interpretation from a model to the examples.
2. Collect the data.
3. Clean the data by removing examples or values that violate certain constraints and estimating missing values.
4. Transform the data and formulate these so that models can be constructed.
5. Apply an induction method to construct a model.
6. Interpret the model and/or use the model to make predictions about new data.

This general methodology applies to the use of symbolic machine learning methods but also neural network methods or evolutionary algorithms for model construction. In fact, an important aspect of the choice between such "paradigms" is the model class. The most important criterion for a model is usually that the model must be consistent with the data and also with the wider domain from which the data were sampled. Because this domain is not known, the model must be a good estimate for the unknown part. Different learning methods produce different models from the same data. One of the problems in the application of machine learning systems is therefore the selection of a tool for a particular problem. Many tools include more than one method. The choice of a tool includes the choice of methods that are included in the tool. At a more detailed level, many tools have parameters that need to be tuned to the dataset. Selecting an appropriate tool and selecting appropriate settings for the parameters are difficult problems. Experiments in which the results of different methods were compared show that for many datasets the differences are relatively small but sometimes the differences can be quite large: a method may detect regularities that other tools do not find at all. This raises the problem of finding a method that is appropriate for a problem. A dual to this problem is that of transforming the problem data such that a particular method can be applied. Practitioners have often been observed to have a favourite method and to be able to transform a wide range of problems into a form that allows the method to be applied. Selecting a method and transforming a problem is considered an art. Running a tool that implements a method is considered the actual machine learning part.

We may call this the Procrustean approach, after the giant robber Procrustes. According to the myths around the ancient Greek hero Theseus, travellers who reached Procrustes' house after a long journey through the wild mountains were kindly invited to spend the night there. However, Procrustes would allow them to sleep only in his special bed for guests. Guests who were too tall for this bed would be fitted by cutting their feet and if necessary their hands. Guests who were actually too short he would stretch to make them fit, which many of them did not survive. Theseus visited Procrustes and when the robber tried to bind him on the bed Theseus managed to win the struggle and killed Procrustes. In the rest of this paper we try to follow Theseus and analyse the role of selecting a learning method with an emphasis on the selection of a class of models or the actual models that are considered by the method. The goal is to find a way to assign each learning problem to a comfortable rather than a Procrustean bed. We include a brief discussion of transformations of the data, and illustrate these with an example. This paper does not present a solution but rather articulates the issues involved and proposes that selection and construction of model classes and data transformation can be guided by the principle of minimising the expected size per accuracy of a model class or data transformation. Section 2 motivates the problem with observations from the practice of data mining, section 3 reviews popular learning methods and their model classes, section 4 illustrates the problem of model selection and problem transformation and sections 5 and 6 discuss current approaches to these problems.

2   Selection of a Machine Learning Method

As was shown in a survey by Verdenius and Van Someren [17], the issue of selecting a tool and method is often not addressed. A survey in the Netherlands provided an almost complete overview of the applications of inductive techniques around 1995, when this technology was still at an early stage of development. They identified 93 applications of computational induction methods, including symbolic machine learning, neural networks, genetic algorithms and case-based reasoning. Table 2 gives an overview:

Table 2. Overview of how frequently each method is used.

Neural nets	58
Symbolic learning	12
Genetic algorithms	12
Case-Based Reasoning	4
Statistics[1]	4
Other	3
Total	*93*

The survey asked why a particular technique was selected. The answers were categorised by the type of reason that the user gave for using a particular technique. Table 3 shows the result:

Table 3. Reasons for using a particular method.

Reason type	Number
Pragmatic: flexibility, costs, simplicity, availability, speed, experience present	25
Empirical evidence: best on similar tasks, best tested for task	8
Rational motivation: insight in representation	11
Other: no alternatives, robustness, fixed in advance, suitable	34

This shows that few of the arguments were rational in the sense that they gave an actual reason why one method is arguably better than another. As Table 4 illustrates, very few even considered other approaches as an alternative.

---

[1] Obviously the study did not aim to give an overview of applications of statistics. It only included applications of statistics in the context of learning systems.

Table 4. Alternative considered for application.

Applied:	Most frequent alternative:	N
Neural nets (44)	other neural net	19
	statistical	13
	symbolic	3
	other	9
Symbolic learning (8)	neural nets	2
	other symbolic	2
	statistical	2
	other	2
GA (11)	neural nets	6
	other	4
	statistical	1

This table shows that alternatives considered are mostly within the same paradigm. Neural nets are also considered as an alternative. Together with the previous tables this suggests that the selection of a paradigm is motivated mostly by pragmatic reasons and that these tend to limit the choice to a single paradigm. If we consider the state of the art, this is not surprising. Not much is known about the conditions under which one paradigm is better than another and therefore a "rational choice" is hard to make.

At a more fine-grained level we encounter the same problem when selecting a particular technique within a paradigm. Consider the following (very incomplete!) list of model classes, each with the form of models and the geometric shapes:

Table 5. Model classes.

Model class	Form	Geometry
threshold function	**IF** F(interval values) > threshold **THEN** X	hyperplane
decision tree	Tree with tests at branches and classes at leaves	nested hyperrectangles
linear function	$g_1 {}^* w_1 + g_2 {}^* w_2 + \ldots =$	hyperplane
prototype	Prototype feature vector for each class	sphere
N-prototypes	Set of feature vectors for each class	Voronoi tesselation
decision list	nested **IF - THEN - ELSE IF - ELSE IF -** ... **ELSE** ...	nested hyperrectangles
relational rules	as above but with relations	?
m-of-n rules	**IF** m **OF** condition$_1$, condition$_2$ ... condition$_n$ **THEN** ...	?

We illustrate the variety of model classes with two examples taken from real applications.

Example 1: a medical domain with symptoms, complaints and risk factors

This domain involves the relation between information about patients and their diseases. The goal of learning is to acquire knowledge that can be used to predict the disease of future patients. Information about patients consists of *complaints* (presented by the patient when they come to see a doctor), *signs and symptoms* (observations on the patient made by the doctor) and *risk factors* (properties of patients that are not directly visible but that may be relevant for the diagnosis). Some examples of complaints, signs and symptoms are:

Complaints:	• pain in chest: yes/no
	• felt this pain before: yes/no
	• resting / body exercise
Symptoms:	• heavy breathing
	• pale
Risk factors:	• age
	• frequency of heart disease in family
	• prior diagnoses of heart disease
	• certain medication
	• habits like smoking, eating too much, lack of body movement, etc.
Relevant possible diseases:	• heart infarction
	• angina pectoris
	• psychosomatic disorder
	• hyperventilation
	• lung embolia

Consider some possible models for this domain. Even without real medical knowledge we can invent some possible models:

• *Threshold functions.* These models consist of a function evaluating to a number and a threshold. If the value is above the threshold then a class is assigned to the object. The function is either a weighted sum of numerically valued attributes or a count of boolean functions over categorical attributes. A special form of the latter case are m-of-n rules: if m of the values specified in the n conditions of rule are satisfied by the attribute values of an object then a certain class is assigned to the object. Constructing a *threshold function* model involves finding the value for the threshold and the values for the weights or the boolean functions. Consider the class "heart infarction" in the medical example. The attributes are a mixture of numerical and categorical ones. For the complaints and symptoms the number of indications of heart disease can be counted and we get c. For the attributes *felt this pain before* and *resting/body exercise* it is not clear if these are by themselves indicators of heart infarction. It is the combination of *pain in chest, not had this before* and *rest* that is indicative. This situation cannot be expressed well as an additive function. An approximation would assign a heavy weight to *pain in chest* and a small weight to the other two properties. The weights of the observed values are added and if the resulting sum is above a threshold then the class is heart infarction. The same applies to the categorical risk factors. The numerical risk factor values can be multiplied with a weight factor (possibly after standardising the values).

• *Decision trees and decision lists.* These are both well known from the literature on Machine Learning. The main problem of these methods in the diagnosis of heart disease concerns the numerical risk factors. In this case it makes no sense to use the precise values of these attributes as tests in a decision tree or a decision list. The standard solution is to use a method for constructing intervals as a subroutine in decision tree learning. A small example illustrates this:

> **IF** *pain in chest* =
>   yes : *age*
>   >50: *felt this pain before* =
>   no : *resting* =
>   yes: heart infarction
>   no: angina pectoris
>   yes: angina pectoris
>   =<50 ....
>   no: ....

An example of a decision list is:

> **IF** *pain in chest* = yes **AND** *age*>50 **AND** *felt pain before*=yes
>   **AND** resting=yes **THEN** heart infarction
> **ELSE IF** pain in chest = no **THEN OK**
> **ELSE IF** age=<50 **AND** resting=no **THEN OK**
> **ELSE IF** ...
>
> ...
> **ELSE OK**

- *Prototype and N-prototypes.* A model of this class consists of one or more prototypical "exemplars" of patients with heart infarction. The prototypical patient could be:

  Complaints:
  - *pain in chest*: yes
  - *felt this pain before*: no
  - *resting*

  Symptoms:
  - *heavy breathing*: yes
  - *pale*: <any>

  Risk factors:
  - *age*: over 55
  - *frequency of heart disease in family*: over 2
  - *prior diagnoses of heart disease*: yes
  - *certain medication*: no
  - *habits like smoking, eating too much, lack of body movement*: yes

In this domain it is not clear if more prototypes are useful.

Example 2: relational vs. propositional representations
This example involves two alternative representations of "shopping events": customers in a shop see objects on display and decide on whether to buy them or not. Below, there is a situation in which a customer of age around 35, who has already bought coffee, sees the milk. The milk is below the cheese and above the sugar. When we observe such an event, the low level image consists of colour and intensity values

of pixels. However, combinations of low level units can be described as relations between objects. Although initially this may appear an irrelevant difference, it becomes important when different generalisation methods are used. Consider the following example in which we describe a single underlying event in two different forms. One form uses only attributes with values and the second uses relations:

Table 6. Relational and propositional representations.

Attribute/value	Relational
buys-milk: yes / no	*buys*(client-1, milk)
age: 35	*age*(client-1, 35)
buys-cheese: yes/no	*buys*(client-1, cheese)
above-milk: cheese	*above*(milk, cheese)
below-milk: sugar	*above*(cheese, sugar)
above-cheese: milk	*above*(milk, sugar)
bought-coffee: yes	*bought*(client-1, coffee)

This learning problem has several interesting properties. One is that some information is not specific to some examples but is true for any example. Here the positions of milk, cheese and sugar are always the same, at least for a single shop. This seems to make them irrelevant for classification but in combination with another property of this learning problem they may be very relevant. Suppose that a number of shopping events have been collected and that an attempt is made to induce a general relation between properties of the client and his or her buying behaviour. Suppose that the actual relation here is that a client who buys something will also buy a product on the shelf above the first product.

$$above(X, Y) \ \& \ bought(P, X) \rightarrow buys(P, Y)$$

The actual rules will be probabilistic but that can be represented by adding probabilities. Here we focus on the structure of the rules. In this case the generalisation is over "clients" but also over "products" because the relation holds for any product. Only its properties (in this case "*buys*(P, X)") and its relations with other products (*above*) matter. The propositional representation must express all combinations of products, their attributes and their relations as separate attributes. In the attribute-based representation this rule would be represented as a collection of rules, like:

$$bought\text{-}cheese = \text{yes} \rightarrow buys\text{-}milk = \text{yes}$$
$$bought\text{-}milk = \text{yes} \rightarrow buys\text{-}sugar = \text{yes}$$

This makes models as the one above much more complex in the propositional representation. The example illustrates that in a relational model class the actual model is much more compact and simpler to express than in a propositional model class.

It will become clear from our discussion of model classes that there are many more model classes. In fact, it is not hard to define new model classes. We consider this below. First we review some of the main learning methods.

3   Learning Methods

Table 7 summarises the main methods for constructing models of the model classes in Table 5.

Table 7. Learning methods.

Model class	Learning method
threshold function; m-of-n rules	discriminant analysis; m-of-n methods
decision tree	top-down induction of decision trees
linear function	multiple regression
prototype	matching
N-prototypes	competitive learning
N-nearest neighbour	storing data and matching
decision list	rule learning methods
relational rules	ILP methods

Details about most of these methods are easily found in the Machine Learning literature and we shall summarise only a few below for further reference. Although there is a large variety in the methods, most learning methods have the character of heuristic approximations. They use the language for the models as starting point and generate models from compact to complex. Models are evaluated by the extent to which they explain the data. The approximation has the form of a search process. Search stops when some function that trades off size of the model against the extent to which the data are explained is either minimal or satisfies a condition. Because the search space is usually too large to search exhaustively, heuristic methods are used that do not guarantee that a global optimum is found.

A typical ML method exploits an ordering of simplicity on the possible models to construct candidate models from simple to complex. The parameters of a method that determine the result of the learning process can be characterised as follows:

- representation language for the models,
- model evaluation function (involving simplicity and explanatory power),
- search method and
- actual structure of the dataset.

One prototypical example of a method, and actually the one that has been applied most to practical problems is *top-down induction of decision trees*. This has been discussed widely in the literature. A very good systematic overview can be found in Langley [7]. Here we summarise the method for further reference. The data are descriptions of objects in the form of attribute vectors associated with a class label. An attribute is selected that is the best predictor of the classes for the dataset. The data are then split by their value for this attribute and the attribute with its values become the root and the first branches of the decision tree. For each subset of data generated by the split the same process is applied recursively and each resulting tree is attached to the initial branches. The process stops when all data have the same class (or earlier, according to a statistical criterion). The method contains two important parameters: a criterion for deciding when to stop building the tree and a criterion for selecting the best attribute test to add to the decision tree. The decision tree can be viewed as comprehensible "knowledge" but it can also be viewed as a system (if complemented with a procedure that classifies new objects).

The basic form involves only tests on the values of attributes but there are many other possibilities. The C4.5 system [16] includes operators that construct intervals of continuous attributes and group nominal values. The introduction of intervals for defining tests that are associated with branches of decision trees let C4.5 search different model classes from the basic decision tree learning method, which only allows values of attributes as tests.

Another method is *top-down induction of rules*. This method constructs rules that classify subsets of the data. Unlike decision tree learning the rules are not structured in a tree. The method starts with a set of examples and selects the attribute-value combination that "covers" most examples of the most frequent class. Next it considers the subset of data that satisfy this condition and again selects the attribute/value combination that for this subset keeps most examples of the largest class and excludes most examples of other classes. This continues until all examples that satisfy the rule belong to one class or until a statistical criterion is reached. Next the method considers all examples that are not satisfied by the first rule and continues with these. The rules are similar to trees but the search strategy and the structure of the knowledge can cause this method to find different rules.

A method with a probabilistic model is the *"naive bayesian classifier"*. This method uses Bayes' rule:

$$P(Class|Observation) = (P(Observation|Class) * P(Class)) / P(Observation)$$

interpreted as follows: an example is a set of attribute-value pairs. In probabilistic terms this is interpreted as an "event": Obs1 ^ Obs2 ^ ... Obsj. From the data we get:

Table 8. Concepts, notation and measurement of the Bayesian view.

Concept	Notation	Measured as
prob. observation	$P(Observation)$	#Observation / #cases
prior probability	$P(Class_j)$	#Class_j / #cases
conditional prob.	$P(Observation_i|Class_j)$	#(Observation_i AND Class_j) / #Class_j

Using this interpretation we can find $P(Class)$, $P(Observation_i)$ and $P(Observation_i|Class)$. For a new observation we can compute for each class the posterior probability $P(Class_j|Observations)$:

$$(P(Observation_1|Class_j) *...* P(Class_j)) / P(Observation_1) *...* P(Observation_n)$$

The prediction is the *Class* with highest posterior probability. A problem is that an example is viewed as a compound event. The naive bayesian classifier assumes conditional independence. Details of this method can be found in most textbooks on machine learning.

We complete this summary with a method for learning threshold functions: *N-of-M learning*. The basic method for this (see for example [14]) involves two steps: collecting a set of (M) conditions (in general attribute-value pairs) and optimising the threshold (N). The standard method is to search for N-of-M rules one by one. Search is organised by systematically increasing M (the set of conditions) and N, evaluating the resulting rules on the data. This is combined with a pruning procedure using a statistical criterion.

4   The Role of Model Class Selection in Learning

In general the task for machine learning methods such as those sketched above is the following:

Given: *Data + initial or current model* + prior knowledge* + a set of possible models,*

Find a model satisfying the following constraints:
- *It belongs in the given set of possible models.*
- *It is the most compact model.*
- *It provides the best explanation of the data.*
- *It is the most consistent model with the given prior knowledge.*
- *It is close to the initial or current model.*

The justification for finding a *compact* model is that in general a simple model is better than a more complex model if both explain the same data ("Occam's razor"). This does not refer to models that are semantically the same in the sense that they make the same predictions but that are expressed in two ways, one of which is more compact: these are obviously equally good in predictive accuracy, although we may prefer one over the other for reasons of comprehensibility. From the perspective of generalisation and predictive accuracy, we should compare the most compact expression of each hypothesis and prefer the most compact of these. Intuitively the justification for using compactness as a criterion is that, if we look at parts of the model that say something about the domain, parts of a simpler model "say more" about the data and so, vice versa, are supported by more data. In the context of top-down decision tree learning and top-down rule learning, splitting the data during learning reduces at each step the amount of data on which extensions of the tree or the rule can be based. Consider the following example:

Table 9. Example data.

noise level	colour	class
low	blue	positive
low	brown	positive
live music	brown	positive
low	red	positive
low	orange	negative

For this table, consider the following models:

(A) **IF** *noise level* = any **AND** *colour* = any **THEN** *class* = positive
(B) (B1) **IF** *colour* = (blue **OR** brown **OR** red) **THEN** *class* = positive
      (B2) **IF** *colour* = orange **THEN** *class* = negative

Model (B) consists of two submodels about parts of the domain. Now consider the evidence for each model:

Table 10. Evidence for models in example.

Model	Sample size	Proportion correct in sample
(A)	5	0.8
(B1)	4	1
(B2)	1	1

Which is better: (A) or (B) (= (B1) + (B2))? Although (A) and (B1) involve the same statements about part of the examples, (A) and (B2) have different implications for all objects that are "orange". The evidence for B2 is so weak compared with the evidence for A that A seems a better model. Top-down learning methods construct candidate models by focusing on ever smaller subsets of the data. At some point this causes overfitting and therefore a form of pruning or a cut-off is needed. Methods that during learning recursively decompose the data into subsets all suffer from this problem of reducing available data for the next learning step. This problem is called the "data fragmentation problem". In the case of fitting polynomials or regression models on data a similar problem occurs. Higher order polynomials and in general more complex functions are "longer" and therefore a particular part of the function models fewer data than a simpler, lower order or linear function and therefore receives support from less data, giving rise to overfitting when the evidence becomes too weak. Compare fitting a first-degree polynomial and a second-degree polynomial to a dataset. The second-degree polynomial can approximate the data better but the function is also "longer" in the sense of being more complex. Thus, if we look at two parts of the function of equal length then the part of the first-degree polynomial predicts more observations and is supported by more observations than the part of the second-degree polynomial. For a formal analysis, see the literature on Minimal Description Length [8].

The standard approaches to avoiding overfitting are the use of cross validation to find the optimal complexity of a model and the use of a statistical criterion to decide if a more complex model class results in a model that is not only better in the sense that it predicts better for the available data but that it is also *significantly* (in the statistical sense) different from a model constructed earlier in the process. In our example above, this means that there is a (statistically significant) difference between models (A) and (B). This method avoids models that are based on limited data because then a difference must be quite large to be significant. Without going further into the merits and problems of this approach, we can consider the effect of model class selection on the risk of overfitting. For model classes, Occam's razor implies that a model class MC1 is better than another model class MC2 if for the models in MC1 the ratio of complexity of a model per data supporting it (or being predicted by it) is lower than in MC2.[2] This makes a priori selection of a good model class useful because it increases the probability of finding a simple model that explains the data.

---

[2] In fact this analysis should take the search strategy of the learning method into account: it is also important that the simple model is actually found.

5   Methods for Model Class Selection

Existing methods construct an optimal model within a particular model class. As illustrated with the examples in the previous sections, the model class of each individual method does not include the optimal model for every application, that is, for every underlying actual structure in the domain. Thus, we face the problem of selecting an optimal model class and the corresponding method(s). There are several lines of attack to this problem. One limitation is set by the No Free Lunch theorem. This states that there is no effective method for finding the optimal (e.g. the minimal) model in the general case without exponentially complex computation. This is usually prohibitive. However, if prior knowledge is available then this can be used to achieve effective induction. Using prior knowledge a class of models can be selected or constructed that includes the optimal model. A learning method can then be selected, which finds (or approximates) the optimal model. An alternative approach is to select a learning method that searches a specific class of models and transform the *data* in a way that facilitates the formulation of a model that subsumes the assumed model set. We have illustrated this approach with the examples above.

Model class selection method 1: *The monkey and the toolbox.*
This method consists of selecting all (or as many as resources of time, money and computers allow) possible model classes, learning within each model class and then evaluating the result using a form of cross validation. This method can be supported by the use of a "toolbox" of learning systems, making it less expensive than finding, buying or obtaining otherwise, understanding and installing many different systems. Although for some problems this may be feasible, and although this method is often used, it is both a practical and a scientific challenge to improve over it. Also, for problems for which no existing model class (that is: no model class for an existing learning method) leads to an optimal solution, it will not find a good solution. In our two examples in section 2, this approach would involve applying all available methods to the medical data and to the shopping event data, using cross validation to find the best predicting method and apply this.

Model class selection method 2: *Using prior knowledge about the model class.* [3]
If some properties of the data or of possible models or even of the target model are known in advance then it may be possible to use these to select or construct the desired model class. Ideally, the model class should minimise the number of candidate models and include the actual model. The model class should include a relatively simple model that is adequate for the data. If this is the case then the learning methods have a good chance of finding it. Using prior knowledge about possible models involves the mapping of properties of the learning problem to model classes. At the moment this is largely an art rather than a science. It exists in the form of expertise of the data analysts. Below is a list of some fragments of this expertise:

- *Linear separability.* This is one of the best known examples of this principle. The proof by Minsky and Papert [12] that one layer neural networks can only learn

---

[3] This is also known as "declarative bias" (e.g. [15]).

models that are "linearly separable" is a prime example of relating the model class of a learning method (one level neural networks) to a property of the domain and the data. This is an extreme case in which a method actually excludes a class of models. The rule that this gives is:

IF the classes are linearly separable by the attributes THEN a single layer neural network model (architecture) is sufficient ELSE a multi-layer model is needed.

- *Differences between classes in "polymorphy", "variance", "number of peaks".* Good examples of this are medical domains. The persons who suffer from a particular disease may be quite similar but those who do not will vary widely. The more compact and uniform class will be captured by a relatively compact rule but for the other class a very complex rule may be needed. This can be solved by using the class with the largest variance or number of peaks as default class and learn to recognise the other class (or classes). So the heuristic that we get is:

  IF there are two classes and one class is much more homogeneous than the other THEN learn to recognise the homogeneous class and use the other as default class.

- *Exceptions.* Usually, there is a relatively simple part of the model that explains most of the data but there are a few situations that need small and very specific additional model parts. These special parts are likely to be represented by few examples in the training set. This requires a model class that allows fine-grained decomposition of the domain. Model classes with model parts for subsets of cases (decision trees, rule-based models, instance-based models) are more appropriate than other model classes.

- *Relevance and local relevance.* Some learning problems involve many attributes, many of which may not be relevant. Although all learning methods can handle irrelevant attributes, some methods (e.g. the naïve bayesian learner above) include by definition all attributes in a model. A more complicated case is when attributes are *locally relevant*: these attributes are not always relevant but only for certain subsets of the total domain; their relevance depends on the values of other attributes. For such domains, model classes that allow locally relevant attributes are obviously more suitable than others. In our collection above, these include TDIDT and TDIR but not the naïve bayesian classifier and regression methods. These methods can only assign a *global* role to an attribute and therefore they cannot adequately express local relevance. If there is prior knowledge about (local) relevance an appropriate learning method can be selected. It is not clear that it is possible to detect this more efficiently than just by experimenting with different methods.

- *Noise and associated or correlated attributes.* The data may contain much "random noise", errors in the data that are caused by poor data collection (measurement errors, transcription and typing errors). In general this should be counteracted by using redundancy in the data and applying a form of averaging. Suppose that in a medical domain we have two ways to measure blood pressure. Both measures involve errors and therefore they are not perfectly correlated. However, because the errors are random, they will on average cancel each other if the two attributes are averaged. This means that, although the attributes are correlated it is better to include the average of the two as predictor than a single attribute. If the attributes are numerical then error-cancelling is achieved in models that allow a form of addition. If symbolic attributes are associated (like for example medication of a patient and chronic disease) then attributes can be combined in N-of-M or other rules that define new attributes. Learning methods with model classes that include a form of averaging of attributes are multiple regression and bayesian methods. Decision tree learning and rule learning are less suitable because they do not exploit this type of redundancy in attributes. Models that add or average attributes are better able to explore the redundancy in the attributes to counter the effect of noise. The heuristic that we get is:

IF the domain structure involves both noise and attributes that are correlated THEN use a method that includes (weighted) sums of these attributes in the models in its model class.

- *Conditional independence* of attributes with respect to the criterion (in classification or prediction). Two attributes are conditionally independent if P(prediction|attribute = value) does not depend on the values of other attributes. Intuitively, the effect of an attribute on the predicted class does not depend on the values of other attributes. Some learning methods only give optimal results if this holds. For example, in the models constructed by the naïve bayesian classifier and regression analysis the role of an attribute in predicting a class should not depend on the values of other attributes. In decision tree learning, this is no problem. The effect of an attribute may be very different in different branches of the tree. The heuristic that we get is:

IF the relation between attributes and class can be factored into independent effects of all separate attributes THEN use a model class with independent effects.

The properties of learning problems listed so far are relevant for categorical data, the focus of most machine learning methods. If we broaden the scope to mathematical modelling techniques in general then the range of model classes and of problem properties becomes very wide. Also in the area of discrete categories there are more properties of the underlying structure in the data than these summarised here. The purpose of the heuristics presented above is to demonstrate that it is possible to identify problem properties that can be used to define heuristics that can be justified from underlying principles.

Model class selection method 3: *Selection based on "cheap" properties of the data.*
If properties of the data distribution such as the ones we discussed above are not known as prior knowledge, a possibility is to compute them. However, in terms of computational costs this would take us back to *the monkey and the typewriter*: measuring properties such as the number of peaks, linear separability and the existence of exceptions amounts to applying complete learning methods. A number of studies have been conducted that try to relate "cheaper" (in the computational sense) properties of the distribution of data to the performance of learning techniques. Examples of "cheap" statistical properties are properties of the distribution of classes or a continuous criterion such as number of classes or skewness, number of predictors, average association between predictors or scale type of predictors (numerical / nominal / ordinal). It is also possible to include properties that may indirectly predict the effectiveness of learning methods. For example, the content of the domain or the provider of the data. If the relation between such properties and the

effectiveness of methods is known then this can be used to follow a three-step approach to learning problems:
1. Measure properties of the dataset.
2. Select an appropriate induction method.
3. Apply the method.

A number of studies have been conducted to obtain knowledge that relates properties of datasets to the performance of induction methods. We can distinguish three types of studies:

Type 1 study: Method evaluation.
Type 1 studies relate individual datasets to the performance of individual methods. The result of a type 1 study is a table of Dataset * Technique * Performance. A typical type 1 study using our examples would select representative induction methods and apply these to a number of datasets without data transformation, using the default settings for parameters, where possible. Performance would be measured empirically as the average accuracy using a single cross-validation testing suite. A more refined version of type 1 includes variations in the parameters of techniques and possibly some standard data transformations. Many type 1 studies are a mere justification for developing a new technique, which is compared with a number of existing techniques. The main limitation of type 1 studies is that the results are difficult to interpret and generalise. Since each induction method involves a search bias, it is usually possible to find a dataset on which the technique outperforms comparable methods. Type 1 studies do not give an indication of why and when this is the case.

Type 2 study: Relating properties of data to the effect of learning methods.
Studies of type 2 improve generalisability of the results by measuring *properties* of datasets instead of individual datasets and relating these properties to the performance of learning techniques. Some large scale type 2 studies on many datasets using a relatively wide range of techniques have been done in the STATLOG project [11], but there have been many comparisons between methods reported in the literature.

Type 2 studies tend to produce typical patterns of results:

- On most problems performance of all methods is similar.
- On some problems there are significant differences in performance.
- There are large differences in speed (several orders of magnitude).
- Some problems need manual "encoding" or re-formulation.

Type 2 studies have several limitations:

- They do not generalise over techniques. If one technique is found to work bad for certain properties of the data this means nothing for a somewhat modified version of the technique. The modification may remove the problem, make it worse, or not affect it at all.
- It does not explain why techniques work well with some datasets but not with others. There is no abstraction that justifies the observed relation.
- It is difficult to select relevant and predictive attributes of datasets. There are many parameters to describe datasets and there is no way to know if a particular selection of parameters includes the relevant ones.

These problems are due to the purely empirical, a-theoretical character of this type of study.

Type 3 study: Relating properties of datasets and methods to the effectiveness of types of learning methods.

Type 3 studies resolve the problems of the above two types, by relating both properties of datasets and properties of methods to the performance of the methods on the domain. This brings the results closer to the factors identified above in section 2 and makes it possible to generalise over methods in terms of their characteristics. Type 3 studies are the ultimate goal. The main difficulty of this approach is to define relevant properties of methods. These must be somewhere between those that we reviewed under the use of prior knowledge and those used in empirical studies. The examples that we gave above under the use of prior knowledge illustrate this approach.

Model class selection method 4: Divide the data and conquer.

A frequently occurring problem is that a model class is appropriate for only part of the data: part of the examples or part of the attributes. In this case a problem can be decomposed into subproblems that are solved with different methods after which the results are combined. Brodley [3] gives a method for partitioning the data into subsets that are then modelled using different model classes. In our medical example an elegant approach is to use decision tree or rule learning for (categorical) symptoms and complaints and bayesian learning or regression for (numerical) risk factors. A complete solution then needs a way to combine the predictions from both partial models. At this point we consider the two partial models as attributes and look for a model class able to combine the models. The final model is then constructed by learning a model that combines the two partial models using the original dataset.

Model class selection method 5: Propose and revise, using feedback.

Another approach is a variation of the monkey with the toolkit that uses information from the application of a method as feedback to select a new model class (or transformation). This is largely an art. How to do this in a principled way remains an open problem.

6   Data Transformation and Construction of New Learning Methods

For many problems there is no single model class and method will produce an adequate solution. For example, our medical domain involves a mixture of "nominal" and numerical data which corresponds to a model class for which few techniques are available. A crude "Procrustean" solution is to select a technique that is appropriate for at least part of the data (in this case part of the attributes) and forget about the rest. This loses much information, however. There are two other possibilities: data transformation and method construction. Data transformation can be guided by the need to apply a learning method or it can be "unsupervised".

If a model class has been selected from prior knowledge or from "cheap" attributes of the data, there may still be remaining problems that will prevent the discovery of a compact model. If these problems are associated with certain attributes then it is sometimes possible to apply a transformation to the data that produces new attributes to describe examples. This is also known as "constructive induction" (e.g. [20]) or "term invention" (e.g. [13]). These new attributes either replace the original attributes or are added to the descriptions of the examples, if a learning method is used that can select only relevant features. As with model classes, a new attribute set is better than the original one if it allows a model to be found that has a better size per accuracy/error ratio. When considering the compactness of models that use the new attribute, the definition of the new attribute should also be taken into account. Data transformations can also affect the complexity of the learning process. If new attributes replace the original attributes then the size of the space of possible models decreases but if new attributes are added to the original attributes the size of this space increases. In other words, replacing attributes introduces bias into the learning process but adding attributes increases the computational cost of learning.

In our medical example we had both numerical and nominal methods. Many model classes include models with either numerical or nominal (or categorical) attributes and these will not be appropriate for this problem. Yet, if for lack of alternatives, it is decided to use one of these model classes then part of the attribute set cannot be used or must be transformed into a different type. In our medical example, the risk factors can be transformed into nominal values so that a symbolic method can be applied or the symbolic values can be transformed into numerical values:

1. *numerical properties* → *nominal properties*. This is called *"discretisation"*. A numerical scale is divided into two or more intervals and these intervals are used as nominal values. The main problem is to find a minimal number of intervals that gives good accuracy in the final model. A number of methods have been proposed for constructing such intervals. The basic idea is to exploit the distribution of examples over the numerical scale (to make intervals coincide with high-density clusters of examples) and the association between attribute values and the attribute selection criterion.

2. "nominal properties" → "numerical properties". For this there are several possibilities:

   • *Scaling.* Applied to nominal values of property P with respect to the selection criterion. The principle is that a range of items, in this case nominal values, are ordered to create a scale. Scaling methods include the possibility of constructing numerical (interval) scales and multidimensional scales. Consider the following example. Suppose that possible colours of a patient are normal, white, red, blue, grey, yellow. Suppose that the data show that the probability of a particular disease for patients with these colours is:

normal	.01
white	.01
red	.03
blue	.02
grey	.05
yellow	.08

These probabilities can be used to define a scale for the attribute colour, transforming a nominal attribute into an attribute with an ordinal or interval scale. A discussion of methods for constructing scales can be found in the literature on psychophysical measurement methods, for example Birnbaum [1].

- *Counting.* A different approach is to construct numerical properties from more than one nominal property. For example, in our medical example, some attributes are "risk factors". If more risk factors hold for a person, the probability of a disease increases. For this problem we can introduce a new property such as the count of the number of positive risk factors.
- *Flattening and structure introduction.* A structured description can be transformed into a less structured description or to a name. The inverse of Flattening is introducing structure. Examples of this are the transformations between relations and propositions in the descriptions of buying events in section 2 above. Above we also illustrated the effect that these operations have on the learning process and the result.

Table 11 lists some examples of attribute transformations that are frequently used.

Table 11. Some examples of transformations.

Transformation	Meaning
counting	count the number of occurrences of values for given attributes
grouping	group values of an attribute into sets, interpreted as disjunctions; can be hierarchical
interval construction / discretisation	define interval on numerical attribute
scaling	map nominal/categorical values to an ordered or numerical scale by their association with the selection criterion [1]
flattening	transform a structured description to a "flat" description
structure introduction	the inverse of flattening: introduce new structured objects
(weighted) sum of attributes	compute a new value as a (weighted sum) of original numerical values
normalisation (of numerical values)	normalise the values on a numerical attribute to a distribution, usually with a mean of 0 and a standard deviation of 1
term invention	defining a new term based on existing terms such that the new term can be used for further learning; the new term can be a symbolic (e.g. boolean) or numerical function
multi-valued attributes to boolean attributes	define a boolean attribute for each value
boolean attributes into multi-valued attributes	inverse of above
clustering	variables or objects are clustered and clusters are defined as new attributes
principal component analysis	the dimensionality of the (numerical) domain is reduced by defining new attributes and removing the attributes on which there is little variation

The range of possible transformations is of course very large and in the end includes all mathematical functions. In practice, however, a relatively small set of transformations is effective for many problems. As indicated above, these transformations are often used to complement model class selection.

How can transformations be selected? The main reason for transforming the data is that the model class of the learning method that will be applied does not include models for some of the attributes. This means that the initial attributes must be transformed into new, constructed attributes, such that the new attributes can be computed from the initial ones and the model class of the learning method does include the possible relation between the new attributes and the target class or criterion. This guides the selection of transformations from the list above.

Some data transformations are not aimed at adapting the data to the model class of the selected technique but at avoiding statistical problems, in particular overfitting. For example, learning methods that (recursively) partition the data into subsets to construct models for the subsets may not exploit weak global structures in the data because locally there is not enough data to detect the pattern. Consider data with *noise and correlated attributes*. A decision tree learner will select one of the correlated attributes and split the data. In the resulting subsets the remaining small additional effect of the other attribute is likely to remain undetected. However, a global analysis could have shown that the attributes were correlated and both were predictive. A better solution would have been to first cluster attributes, define strong clusters as new attributes, define the scores on the cluster-attribute as a (weighted) sum of the original attributes and replace the attributes in the cluster with the new cluster-attribute. The reason that this results in more compact models per accuracy level is that in the cluster-attribute random errors can cancel out and therefore the relation between a cluster-attribute and a selection criterion becomes more compact. The advantage of this method is that it can be combined with methods that construct local models, such as decision tree learning.

This example suggests two interesting points: (1) data transformations can themselves involve inductive learning and (2) by combining (inductive) data transformation operations with learning methods creates new learning methods. In the example above, we effectively defined a new learning method: first apply clustering and then apply decision tree learning to the clustered (and unclustered) attributes. The new method can be viewed as an old method "wrapped" in a data transformation.

In fact, if we consider other inductive learning methods to construct "data transformers" there are suddenly very many ways to define new "hybrid" model classes in terms of old classes. Some examples in the recent machine learning literature are:

- *Linear additive combination of models.* The idea is to construct several models using one or more learning methods and combine the predictions of these by a weighting scheme. The models can all be of the same kind, e.g. decision trees, neural networks, etc. but it is also possible to use more than one model class. Using a linear combination is likely to help if the component models include random errors that cancel each other in a linear combination. Examples are bagging and boosting (e.g. [4]). Boosting combines this with overweighting misclassified examples.

- *Decision trees of models.* Just as the terms in a linear (threshold) function, the terms in a decision tree can be replaced by "submodels" constructed by other methods: this leads to a range of new methods: discrimination trees [5], regression trees [18], decision trees with relational terms [2], and so on.

Another attractive possibility, suggested by the observations above, is to integrate model selection or model construction into learning methods. For many methods this is relatively easy. Operators that modify the model class (or that transform the data) are added to the learning method. In methods based on heuristic search such operators can be added to the actual learning algorithm. Another principle is to increase the model class when normal learning operators cannot solve the problem. Michalski proposed this under the heading "constructive induction". The famous C4.5 decision tree learner includes operators that construct intervals and group nominal values into value groups, thus dynamically increasing the space of possible models. Several of Michalski's AQ systems include operators that construct new terms [9], [10]. Several learning systems based on inverted resolution include inverted resolution operators that construct new terms and use these for further learning (e.g. [13]).

7   Conclusions and Further Issues

One of the differences between learning methods is the model class that they consider. The choice of a model class for a particular learning problem is important because for a particular dataset one model class may allow a simpler model to be found than another model class. A simpler model is better than a complex one because parts of a simple model receive support from more data than parts of a longer, more complex model. We distinguish the following possibilities for dealing with the problem of representation (or model class misfit), in terms of our Procrustean metaphor:

- transform your data to make them fit better into the procrustean bed of a learning method or
- increase the range of available beds and find out how to allow problem-specific bed construction.

On one hand, we have the certainty that there is No Free Lunch: without prior information about the structures in the data no learning method will systematically, for each domain, dominate all others in terms of accuracy. However, in some cases we do have prior knowledge and frequently we consider only a particular set of learning methods. In these cases, choice of a model class is possible. In other cases we can apply "cheap" steps that tell us which class of methods will be applicable. Our understanding of the selection or construction of model classes and learning methods is still in an early stage. What we have at this moment are some examples of rational model class selection, some ideas and pieces of methods but it looks as if this is only the surface of a whole range of new methods. What we need most are more concepts for relating properties of data distributions to properties of model classes for learning methods. In this chapter we reviewed an unstructured collection of these concepts, but structuring them and constructing effective procedures clearly requires more work.

Further reading. Most of this paper is based on ideas that appear in the literature under the headings "bias selection", "bias evaluation", "declarative bias" and Minimal Description Length. Useful further reading is a special issue of the Machine Learning journal edited by Diana Gordon and Marie DesJardins [6]. As we mentioned above, many authors have explored the possibilities of extending or restructuring a model class by constructing new concepts and vocabulary. More global model selection is less well understood although most authors mention this as a key problem. A good source on the empirical approach to this issue is the book by Michie et al. [11]. Li and Vitanyi [8] includes a formal discussion of the Minimal Description Length principle.

The recent research literature includes many examples of hybrid methods that can be viewed as extending or modifying the model class of the basic component methods. Especially conferences and journals on Data Mining and Knowledge Discovery in Databases publish studies that address more global model class selection. The METAL project (see www.cs.bris.ac.uk/~cgc/METAL/) studies the method selection problem.

Acknowledgements. The author thanks Floor Verdenius for his contributions to the study of users of Machine Learning and many discussions on Machine Learning methodology, the organisers of the ACAI Summer School on Machine Learning Applications for the opportunity to work on this paper and Edwin de Jong, Floor Verdenius, Arnold Kraakman and Georgios Paliouras for their comments on an earlier version.

References

1. Birnbaum, M. H. (ed.) (1997) *Measurement, Judgement, and Decision Making*, London:Academic Press.
2. Blockeel, H., and De Raedt, L. (1998). Top-down Induction of First Order Logical Decision Trees. *Artificial Intelligence, 101*, pp. 285-297.
3. Brodley, C.E. (1995) Recursive bias selection for classifier construction. *Machine Learning, 20*, pp. 63-94.
4. Freund, Y. and Schapire, R.E. (1996) Experiments with a new boosting algorithm. In: *Machine Learning: Proceedings of the Thirteenth International Conference*, San Francisco:Morgan Kaufmann, pp.148-156.
5. Gama, J. (1999) Discriminant Trees, in:*Proceedings of the* Sixteen International Conference on Machine Learning, ICML99, pp.134-142, San Francisco:Morgan Kaufmann.
6. Gordon, D.F. and desJardins, M. (1995) Evaluation and selection of biases in machine learning, *Machine Learning, 20*, p.5-22.
7. Langley, P. (1997) *Elements of Machine Learning*, San Francisco:Morgan Kaufmann.
8. Li, M. and Vitanyi, P. (1997). *An introduction to Kolmogorov complexity and its applications,* Berlin:Springer.
9. Michalski, R. S. (1983) A Theory and Methodology of Inductive Learning, in: Michalski, R.S., Carbonell, J. and Mitchell, T. (Eds.): *Machine Learning: An Artificial Intelligence Approach*, Palo Alto:TIOGA Publishing Co., , pp. 83-134.
10. Michalski, R.S. (1993) *Inferential Theory of Learning as a Conceptual Basis for Multistrategy Learning, Machine Learning, 11*, pp. 111-151.
11. Michie, D., Spiegelhalter, D. J. and Taylor, C. C. (Eds.) (1994). *Machine Learning, Neural and Statistical Classification*. London:Ellis Horwood.
12. Minsky, M. and Papert, S. (1969) *Perceptrons: an introduction to computational geometry*. Boston:MIT Press.
13. Muggleton, S. and Buntine, W. (1992) Inventing first-order predicates by inverting resolution, In: Muggleton, S., editor, *Inductive logic programming*, pp. 261-280, London:Academic Press.

14. Murphy, P., & Pazzani, M. (1991). ID2-of-3: Constructive induction of m-of-n discriminators for decision trees, in: Proceedings of the Eighth International Workshop on Machine Learning, pp. 183-187, San Francisco:Morgan Kaufmann.
15. Nedellec, C., Rouveirol, C., Ade, H., Bergadano, F. and Tausend, B. (1996) Declarative Bias in ILP,in: L. De Raedt (ed.) Advances in Inductive Logic Programming, pp.82-103, Amsterdam:IOS.
16. Quinlan, J.R. (1993) *C4.5: Programs for Empirical Learning*. Morgan Kaufmann.
17. Verdenius, F., and Someren, M.W. van (1997), Applications of Inductive Techniques: a Survey in the Netherlands, *AI Communications*, *10*, pp. 3-20.
18. Torgo, L. and Gama, J. (1997) Regression using Classification Algorithms, *Intelligent Data Analysis*, *1*, pp. 275-292.
19. Weiss, S.M. and Indhurkya, N. (1998) *Predictive data mining*, San Francisco:Morgan Kaufmann.
20. Wnek, J. and Michalski, R.S., "Hypothesis-driven Constructive Induction in AQ17-HCI: A Method and Experiments (1994) *Machine Learning*, 14, pp. 139-168.

Integrated Architectures for Machine Learning

Lorenza Saitta

Università del Piemonte Orientale,
Dipartimento di Scienze e Tecnologie Avanzate,
Corso Borsalino 54, 15100 Alessandria, Italy
saitta@di.unito.it

1   Introduction

With the growing complexity of Machine Learning applications, the need for using integrated or hybrid (or multistrategy) approaches becomes more and more imperative, and an increasing amount of research effort is devoted to this issue. The increasing complexity of applications is not the only reason making multistrategic approaches appealing: as it is well known, no single approach/system can claim to be uniformly superior to any other, so that hybridisation seems a natural and viable way of compensating drawbacks and enhancing advantages. Even though there is no common agreement on what *integration* exactly means in Machine Learning, in a broad sense an integrated architecture can be defined as one which is *organised or structured so that its constituent units function co-operatively.*

Some effort has also been made to define "multistrategy" learning. For example Michalski [36] proposes to classify learning methods as a set of "knowledge transmutation" processes. Kodratoff [32], and Console and Saitta [13] try to systematise the definitions of several reasoning methods used in learning so far. Other contributions to theory come from Plaza and Arcos [47], who propose that learning requires a "self-model" of the learner to work in parallel with the learner itself, and from Altmann [2].

Hybrid systems can be analysed from several perspectives. We have mainly used the following two dimensions: a "syntactic" one, i.e., *type of co-operation* among system components, independently of their nature and content, and a "semantic" one, which, instead, takes into account the nature of the components.

2   Type of Interaction

At the highest architectural level, a Machine Learning (ML) program can be simply viewed as one among a complex system's components, as represented in Figure 1. Other components possibly include performance modules, human experts, Knowledge Acquisition interfaces, databases, traditional software or simulators.

G. Paliouras, V. Karkaletsis, and C.D. Spyropoulos (Eds.): ACAI '99, LNAI 2049, pp. 218-229, 2001.
© Springer-Verlag Berlin Heidelberg 2001

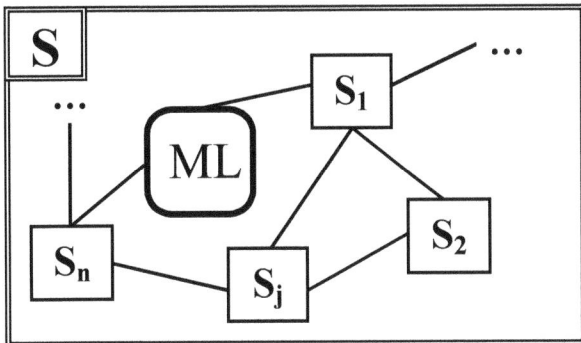

Fig. 1. A ML module can be included in a complex system S, whose component units S_j are usually functionally differentiated.

In this case, each module is devoted to its own specific task, and the co-operation with ML reduces to an exchange of input/output information. However, mutual dependencies among modules may occur: for instance, a given performance module, or a database may impose constraints on the ML module's content. This type of interaction actually characterises Knowledge Discovery in Databases (KDD) systems, in which the Data Mining (DM) module contains the learning component in the whole process, as it is described in Figure 2.

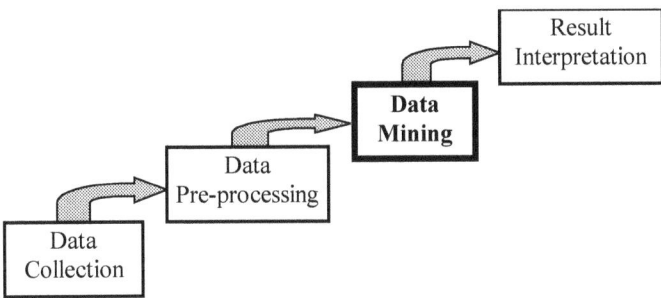

Fig. 2. Scheme of the KDD process [21], in which modules with different functions interact. Data Mining represents the learning component.

Even though the architecture in Figure 1 can be further elaborated upon, in this overview we are more interested in a type of co-operation that takes place inside the ML component, as presented in Figure 3.

The architecture in Figure 3 is very abstract, and may represent a large variety of hybrid learning systems, differing in the topology, in the meaning of the internal links, and in the content of the components C_i. For instance, integration of alternative systems, devoted to specific learning tasks, is achieved in the MOBAL system [41]. This system introduces the idea of "balanced co-operation" between human expert and learning algorithms, and includes automated tools for rule discovery, concept formation, model acquisition, sort taxonomy handling, predicate structuring, knowledge revision and a control and inference engine module.

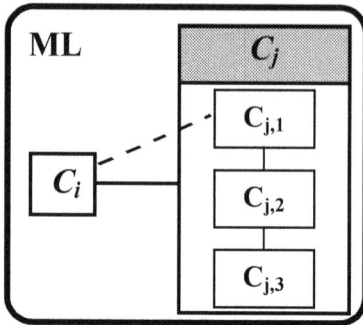

Fig. 3. The hybridisation that we are interested in occurs inside the ML component of a possibly more complex system.

In the following, we will first consider variations in the topology of the connections [48]. Generally, the topologies can be broadly grouped into three classes:

1. Toolbox.
2. Co-operative (sequential/functional).
3. Tightly Integrated.

A *Toolbox* is one of the simplest ways to achieve co-operation, and can be realised among modules designed to perform the same task but with different means. The toolbox architecture has two variants, according to the specific policy of interaction: *Toolbox with Selection* and *Toolbox with Integration*. In the first variant, which is presented in Figure 4, a number of "strategies" S_i ($1 \bullet i \bullet M$) work on (or are related to) the same learning problem P independently. Each strategy tends to achieve the common goal by itself, and all of them could be possibly run in parallel. In this case, the strategies correspond to algorithms/systems. The result R_j is the "best", according to some predetermined criterion, among the results provided by each one of the strategies. The choice can be done before using the various S_i's (*ex-ante* selection), if a-priori information is available, or after using the S_i's (*ex-post* selection).

This idea of a toolbox with selection has been the basis of the MLT Project [33], which offers a number of choices related to knowledge representation (from tables to FOL expressions), learning tasks (classification and clustering, for instance) and systems, oriented towards the learning of new rules, new concepts, or new classes, or combinations of these.

The choice among alternative systems is based, among other parameters, on the type of knowledge representation that is used and on the target learning task. The problem of strategy selection has been alleviated by means of a Consultant [15], [52], which is a classification expert system, where the user is interrogated about features of the learning task and the Consultant suggests the use of one of the available algorithms. As a continuation of the MLToolbox project, the system MUSKRAT [26] has been built, which helps the user to select a knowledge refinement tool among a number of systems.

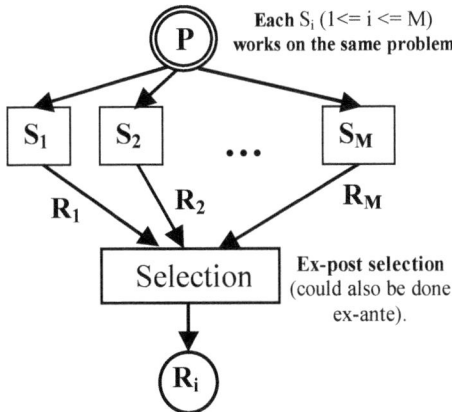

Fig. 4. *Toolbox with Selection.* Only one among the strategies S_i ($1 \leq i \leq M$) has to be chosen. This selection can be done before or after the strategies have been used.

For a toolbox to be effective, it is important to provide the user with a homogeneous interface between the problem/data and the data types required by any single algorithm. This goal can be addressed by designing a common language, as it has been done with the Common Knowledge Representation Language (CKRL) [42]. CKRL allows uniform access to all tools, each having its own internal reasoning and learning approaches.

A modification of the schema in Figure 4 is the *Toolbox with Integration,* presented in Figure 5. The "strategies" S_i ($1 \cdot i \cdot M$) again work on (or are related to) the same learning problem P, but the result R is a function $f(R_1,..., R_M)$ of the results obtained by all the strategies.

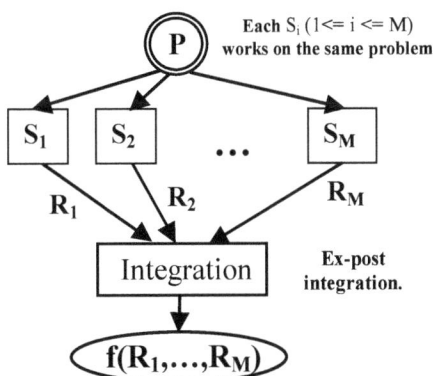

Fig. 5. *Toolbox with Integration.* The global result is a combination of the results obtained by all the strategies S_i ($1 \leq i \leq M$).

An early example of this kind of toolbox with integration is given by Drobnic and Gams [19], who try to combine the results of alternative classification systems to obtain a single final decision. Similar ideas are suggested by Heath, Kasif and Salzberg [27], who generate decision trees with alternative methods and then combine the resulting classifications with a majority voting strategy, and by Chan and Stolfo [12], who propose to use meta-learning strategies for combining the results of several classification systems, no matter how learned.

More recently, this type of algorithm combination has been proposed in the *Bagging* [10] or *Boosting* [22] approaches to ML. The basic idea behind boosting is that combining different classification models is better than selecting one. In boosting, the "strategies" of Figure 5 are different runs of the same "weak" learning algorithm. In each run, the probability distribution over the examples in the learning set changes. Combination consists in applying a function to the outputs obtained at each run from the classifiers, in order to get a single decision. As an example, the function may be majority voting. The utility of boosting consists in the fact that even though the performance of a classifier learned in any single run may be affected by a large error ε_t(provided that ε_t is less than 1/2), the global error δ tends to zero when T goes to infinity.

Another scheme of hybridisation is *Sequential Co-operation,* presented in Figure 6, in which each strategy works (possibly iteratively) during a different phase Ph_i of the problem solution, according to a fixed temporal/logical order. The final result is the result provided by the last strategy in the chain.

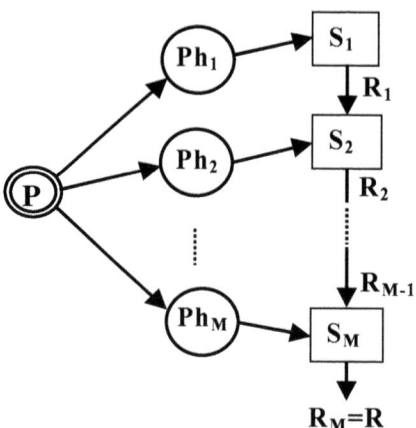

Fig. 6. *Sequential Cooperation.* S_M outputs the global result. Each component works during a different phase of the learning process.

An example of sequential co-operation is provided by Botta, Giordana and Piola [8], and by Botta and Piola [9]. According to this approach, a symbolic learner acquires the structural part of a rule base, whereas a subsequent connectionist algorithm adjusts the numerical parameters occurring in the rules. The components of a system based on sequential co-operation may be functionally differentiated.

Another type of co-operation is *Functional Co-operation,* presented in Figure 7, in which components devoted to different tasks work on subproblems of a given problem. The components work independently and only their results are merged.

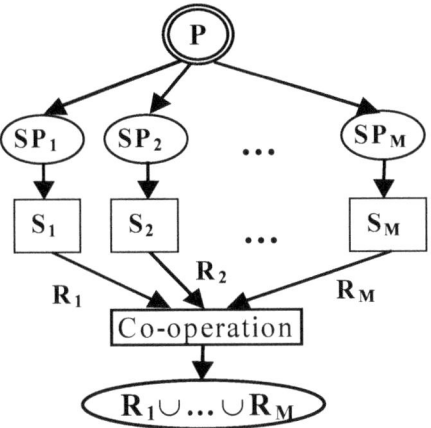

Fig. 7. *Functional Co-operation.* The global result is produced by the union of the outputs of components devoted to different tasks.

Finally, in the *Tight Integration* scheme, represented in Figure 8, different phases or aspects of subproblems cannot be isolated, and all the strategies must work together.

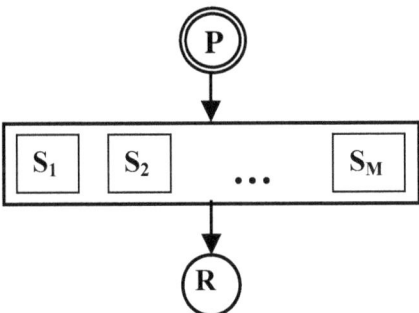

Fig. 8. *Tight Integration.* The global result is produced by the joint work of all system components.

Tight integration is the most difficult scheme to design, because it requires both a meaningful partition of the problem into subproblems, and an effective way of recombining the results.

3   Level of Interaction

Integration, according to any of the schemes described in Section 2, can occur at many levels in a ML system. The most abstract one is the system level, in which the S_j components, introduced in Section 2, are alternative ML systems. A typical example of this type of integration is MOBAL [41], whose idea of *balanced co-operation* considers also the human user as part of the global system.

Most instances of integration, in ML systems, occur at the paradigm level. In particular, the symbolic, connectionist, and evolutionary paradigms have been combined in various ways to improve system performance or scope.

The integration of connectionist with symbolic methods has received a lot of attention, in the effort of exploiting both the powerful learning rules used in neural nets, and the comprehensibility of symbolic knowledge. Towel and Shavlik [56], and Craven and Shavlik [14] transform a rule base into a neural net; then, the network weights are updated and the final network is transformed again into a set of rules. Bayesian classification, neural nets and symbolic learning are combined in the approach proposed by Tchoumatchenko and Ganascia [53]. Mitchell and Thrun [39] have proposed the use EBNN (explanation-based neural nets) to encode task-independent knowledge, which is used to supply a kind of explanation. Integration of connectionist and symbolic approaches in First Order Logic has been proposed by Botta and Piola [9].

Genetic algorithms have been used in connection with symbolic learning for acquiring concepts both in propositional calculus [59], [57], [17], [31] and in First Order Logic [23], [24], [1]. Recent approaches have been proposed by Michalski [37], who suggests the exploitation of the symbolic approach to guide evolutionary learning, and Burns and Danyluk [11], who propose the integration of an evolutionary and a connectionist approach for feature selection. An alternative type of integration between symbolic and stochastic learning is suggested by Sebag and Rouveirol [50], who suggest reducing the complexity of learning in FOL by means of stochastic sampling.

There are also systems that try to integrate several paradigms in the same learning system. For instance, Hunter [30] suggests exploiting statistics, symbolic and connectionist learning for the prediction of the secondary structure of proteins. In this respect, a classic system is PRODIGY, which integrates induction, deduction, analogy and CBR [58]. Considering the nature of the available data, instead of the type of target knowledge, various approaches have been proposed to handle both categorical and numerical data in the training instances, combining statistics, artificial neural networks or genetic algorithms with symbolic learning methods, as done, for instance, by Giordana et al. [25].

Within the same paradigm, there may exist hybrid systems integrating different inference types for learning. This happens mostly in the symbolic approach, which allows hypotheses to be searched for not only inductively, but also through deduction, abduction and analogy. The first combined approaches of this type, appeared after the introduction of EBL [38], [16]. Examples appear in Pazzani [45], Lebowitz [35], and Bergadano and Giordana [4]. More recently, besides the combination of induction and deduction [46], [6], other approaches have been proposed combining more complex inference methods. In particular, Tecuci [54] proposes the refinement of a knowledge base using induction, deduction, abduction and analogy. He also proposes the introduction of active experimentation and interaction with the user for more effective learning [55]. Induction, deduction and abduction on a causal theory are also used in the systems WHY [49], SMART+ [7], CLINT [18], and Esposito et al. [20] to build and/or refine a FOL classification knowledge base. The system EITHER [40] uses the same types of inference for refining a propositional rule base. Another logic-based multistrategy approach to learning is proposed by Lamma, Pereira and Riguzzi [34]. Finally, Zucker [60] has proposed a novel approach to multiple levels of knowledge representation via abstraction.

On the application side, the field of robotics seems particularly well suited to support a variety of learning approaches, due to the complexity and diversity of the tasks involved in robot learning. In particular, Baroglio et al. [3] use symbolic learning, neural networks and reinforcement learning to build fuzzy controllers for an industrial manipulation robot. Other interesting fields of application are medicine [43], and modelling of human learning [20], [44], [51]. In this last field, multistrategy learning seems particular promising, given the complexity and variety of human learning mechanisms. Other recent applications of hybrid learning systems have been presented by Hekanaho et al. [28], and by Hsu et al. [29]. The first one refers to bankrupt analysis, whereas the second one concerns learning heterogeneous time series for crisis monitoring. Multistrategy learning fits also well the metaphor of agents, as proposed by Bergen and Bock [5].

4   Conclusions

Multistrategy or hybrid learning is proving increasingly useful and far-reaching for learning in complex domains. On the other hand, there are still several conceptual and technical difficulties that need to be addressed and overcome. Among the most important conceptual difficulties, there is the problem of evaluation. According to what parameters can the improvement of a multistrategy system be evaluated? How should the increased system complexity weighted vis-à-vis of improvements? Examples of important technical difficulties are the problem of computational complexity and the difficulty of control.

Notwithstanding the above still unsolved problems, trying to proceed along the route of integration seems fundamental to face real-world problems. An example is the new field of knowledge discovery in data bases, in which components from several disciplines naturally cooperate: for instance, statistics, machine learning, and data base management, each contributing a variety of methods and approaches.

References

1. Anglano C., Giordana A., Lo Bello G. and Saitta L. (1998). "An Experimental Evaluation of Coevolutive Concept Learning". In *Proeedings of the 5th International Conference in Machine Learning* (Madison, WS), Morgan Kaufman, pp. 19-27.
2. Altmann E. (1993). "Learning Scope, Task Analysis and Sharable Components". In *Proc. 2nd Int. Workshop on Multistrategy Learning* (Harpers Ferry, WV), Publ. Center for Artificial Intelligence, George Mason University, pp. 50-57.

3.   Baroglio C., Giordana A., Kaiser. M., Nuttin M., Piola R. (1996): "Learning Controllers for Industrial Robots". *Machine Learning, 23,* 221-250.
4.   Bergadano F. and Giordana A. (1988). "A knowledge intensive approach to concept induction". In *Proceedings of 5th International Conference in Machine Learning* (Ann Harbor, MI), Morgan Kaufman pp. 350-317.
5.   Bergen D.E. and Bock P. (1998). "Applying Collective Learning Systems Theory to Reactive Actor Design and Control". In *Proc. of the 4th Int. Workshop on Multistrategy Learning* (Desenzano del Garda, Italy), pp. 38-46.
6.   Bloedorn E., Michalski R.S., & Wnek J. (1993). "Multistrategy Constructive Induction: AQ17-MCI". In *Proc. of the 2nd Int. Workshop on Multistrategy Learning* (Harpers Ferry, WV), Publ. Center for Artificial Intelligence, George Mason University, pp. 188-203.
7.   Botta M. and Giordana A. (1993). "Smart+: a Multi Strategy Learning Tool". In *Proc. 13th Int. Joint Conference on Artificial Intelligence* (Chambéry, France), pp. 937-943.
8.   Botta M., Giordana A. and Piola R. (1997). "FONN: Combining First Order Logic with Connectionist Learning". In *Proceedings of the 14th International Conferenceon Machine Learning* (Nashville, USA), Morgan Kaufmann, pp. 48-56.
9.   Botta M. and Piola R. (2000). "Refining Numerical Concepts in First Order Logic Theories". *Machine Learning, 38:1-2,* 109-131.
10. Breiman L. (1996). "Bagging predictors". *Machine Learning, 24,* 123-140.
11. Burns B.D. and Danyluk A.P. (2000). "Feature Selection vs. Theory Reformulation: A Study of Genetic Refinement of Knowledge-Based Neural Networks ". *Machine Learning, 38:1-2,* 89-107.
12. Chan P.K. and Stolfo S.J. (1993). "Meta-Learning for Multistrategy and Parallel Learning". In *Proc. of the 2nd Int. Workshop on Multistrategy Learning* (Harpers Ferry, WV), Publ. Center for Artificial Intelligence, George Mason University, pp. 150-165.
13. Console L. and Saitta L. (1999). " On the relations between Abduction and Inductive Explanations". In P. Flach and A. Kakas (Eds.), *Abduction and Induction:Essays on their Relation and Integration, Applied Logic Series, Vol. 18, Kluwer Academic Publishers, Dordrecht.*
14. Craven M. and Shavlik J (1995). "Investigating the Value of a Good Input Representation". In T. Petsche, S. Judd & S. Hanson (Eds.), *Computational Learning Theory and Natural Learning Systems, Vol. 3,* MIT Press, Cambridge, MA, pp.102-127.
15. Craw S., Sleeman D., Graner N., Rissakis M and Sharma S. (1992). "CONSULTANT: Providing Advice for the Machine Learning Toolbox". In M. Bramer (Ed.), *Proc. of the BCS Expert Systems Conference,* Cambridge Univ. Press, Cambridge, UK, pp 5 - 23.
16. DeJong G., Mooney R. (1986). "Explanation-based learning: An alternative view". *Machine Learning, 1,* 145-176.
17. De Jong K. A., Spears W. M. and Gordon F. D. (1993). "Using Genetic Algorithms for Concept Learning", *Machine Learning, 13* , 161-188.
18. De Raedt L. and Bruynooghe M. (1991): "CLINT: A Multistrategy Interactive Concept-Learner and Theory Revision System". In *Proc. of the First Multistrategy Learning Workshop* (Harpers Ferry, WV), Publ. Center for Artificial Intelligence, George Mason University, pp. 175-190.
19. Drobnic M. and Gams M. (1993). "Multistrategy Learning: An Analytical Approach". In *Proc. of the 2nd Int. Workshop on Multistrategy Learning* (Harpers Ferry, WV), Publ. Center for Artificial Intelligence, George Mason University, pp. 31-41.
20. Esposito F., Semeraro G., Fanizzi N. and Ferilli S. (2000). "Multistrategy Theory Revision: Induction and Abduction in INTHELEX". *Machine Learning, 38:1-2,* 133-156.
21. Fayyad, U. (1996). "Data mining & knowledge discovery: Making sense out of data". *IEEE Expert, 11 (5),* 20-25.

22. Freund Y. and Schapire R. E. (1996). "Experiments with a New Boosting Algorithm". In *Proceedings of the 13th International Conference in Machine Learning* (Bari, Italy), San Francisco: Morgan Kaufmann, pp. 149-156.

23. Giordana A. and Sale C. (1992). "Genetic Algorithms for Learning Relations". In *Proceedings. 9th International Conference in Machine Learning* (Aberdeen, UK), San Francisco: Morgan Kaufmann, pp. 169-178.

24. Giordana A. and Neri F. (1995). "Search Intensive Concept Induction". *Evolutionary Computation, 3*, 375-416.

25. Giordana A., Neri F., Saitta L. and Botta M. (1997). "Integrating Multiple Learning Straegies in First Order Logics". *Machine Learning, 27*, 209-240.

26. Graner M.   and Sleeman D. (1993). "MUSKRAT: A Multistrategy Knowledge Refinement and Acquisition Toolbox". In *Proc. 2nd Int. Workshop on Multistrategy Learning* (Harpers Ferry, WV), Publ. Center for Artificial Intelligence, George Mason University, pp. 107-119.

27. Heath D., Kasif S. and Salzberg S. (1993). "k-DT: A Multi-Tree Learning Method". In *Proc. of the 2nd Int. Workshop on Multistrategy Learning* (Harpers Ferry, WV), Publ. Center for Artificial Intelligence, George Mason University, pp. 138-149.

28. Hekanaho J., Sere K., Back B. and Laitinen T. (1998). "Analysing Bankruptcy Data with Multiple Methods". In *Proc. 4th International Workshop on Multistrategy Learning* (Desenzano del Garda, Italy), pp. 75-81.

29. Hsu W.H., Gettings N.D., Lease V.E., Pan Y. and Wilkins D.C. (1998). "Heterogeneous Time Series Learning for Crisis Monitoring". In *Proc. 4th International Workshop on Multistrategy Learning* (Desenzano del Garda, Italy), pp.82-89.

30. Hunter L. (1991). "Classifying for Prediction: A Multistrategy Approach to Predicting Protein Structure". In *Proc. of the 1st Int. Workshop on Multistrategy Learning* (Harpers Ferry, WV), Publ. Center for Artificial Intelligence, George Mason University, pp. 394-402.

31. Janikow C. Z. (1993). "A Knowledge Intensive Genetic Algorithm for Supervised Learning". *Machine Learning, 13*, 198-228.

32. Kodratoff Y. (1991): "Induction and the Organization of Knowledge". In *Proceedings of the First Multistrategy Learning Workshop* (Harpers Ferry, WV), Publ. Center for Artificial Intelligence, George Mason University, pp. 34-48.

33. Kodratoff, Y., Sleeman, D., Uszynski, M., Causse, K. and Craw, S. (1992). "Building a Machine Learning Toolbox". In L. Steels and B. Lepape (Eds.), *Enhancing the Knowledge-Engineering Process - Contributions from Esprit,* Elsevier Publ. Co., pp. 81-108.

34. Lamma E., Pereira L.M. and Riguzzi F. (2000). "Strategies in Combined Learning via Logic Programs". *Machine Learning, 38:1-2,* 63-87.

35. Lebowitz M. (1986). "Integrated Learning: Controlling Explanation". *Cognitive Science, 10,* 219-240.

36. Michalski R. (1991): "Inferential Learning Theory as a Basis for Multistrategy Task-Adaptive Learning". In *Proc. First Int. Workshop on Multistrategy Learning* (Harpers Ferry, WV), Publ. Center for Artificial Intelligence, George Mason University, pp. 3-18.

37. Michalski R. S. (2000). "Learnable Evolution Model: Evolutionary Processes Guided by Machine Learning". *Machine Learning, 38:1-2,* 9-40.

38. Mitchell T., Keller R.M., Kedar-Cabelli S. (1986): "Explanation-Based Generalization: A Unifying View". *Machine Learning, 1,* 47-80.

39. Mitchell T. and Thrun S. (1993). "Explanation Based Learning: A Comparison of Symbolic and Neural Network Approaches". In *Proceedings of the 10th International Conference in Machine Learning* (Amehrst, MA), San Francisco: Morgan Kaufmann, pp. 197-204.

40. Mooney R.J. and Ourston D. (1991): "A Multistrategy Approach to Theory Refinement". In *Proc. First International Workshop on Multistrategy Learning* (Harpers Ferry, WV), Publ. Center for Artificial Intelligence, George Mason University, pp. 115-131.

41. Morik K. (1991). "Balanced Cooperative Modeling". In *Proc. First Int. Workshop on Multistrategy Learning* (Harpers Ferry, WV), Publ. Center for Artificial Intelligence, George Mason University, pp. 65-80.

42. Morik K., Causse K. and Boswell R. (1991). "A Common Knowledge Representation Integrating Learning Tools". In *Proc. 1st Int. Workshop on Multistrategy Learning* (Harpers Ferry, WV), Publ. Center for Artificial Intelligence, George Mason University, pp. 81-96.

43. Morik K. (1998). "Multistrategy Learning in Intensive Care – Knowledge Discovery for Protocol Development and Control". In *Proc. 4th International Workshop on Multistrategy Learning* (Desenzano del Garda, Italy), pp. 21.

44. Neri F. (2000). "Multiple Representations in Modelling Qualitative Physics Learning". *Machine Learning, 38:1-2,* 181-211.

45. Pazzani M.J. (1988). "Integrating explanation-based and empirical learning methods in OCCAM". In *Proc. of the Third European Working Session on Learning* (Glasgow, UK), pp.147-165.

46. Pazzani M. and Kibler D. (1992). "The Utility of Knowledge in Inductive Learning". *Machine Learning, 9,* 57-94.

47. Plaza E. and J.L. Arcos (1993). "Reflection and Analogy in Memory-Based Learning". In *Proc. 2nd Int. Workshop on Multistrategy Learning* (Harpers Ferry, WV), Publ. Center for Artificial Intelligence, George Mason University, pp. 42-49.

48. Saitta L. (1996). "Multistrategy Learning: When, How and Why". In *Proc. 3rd Int. Workshop on Multistrategy Learning* (Harpers Ferry, WV), Publ. Center for Artificial Intelligence, George Mason University, pp. 3-9.

49. Saitta L., Botta M., Neri F. (1993): "Multistrategy Learning and Theory Revision", *Machine Learning, 11,* 153-172.

50. Sebag M. and Rouveirol C. (2000). "Resource-bounded Relational Reasoning: Induction and Deduction Through Stochastic Matching". *Machine Learning, 38:1-2,* 41-62.

51. Sison R., Numao M. and Shimura M. (2000). "Multistrategy Discovery and Detection of Novice Programmer Errors". *Machine Learning, 38:1-2,* 157-180.

52. Sleeman, D., Rissakis, M., Craw, S., Graner, N., & Sharma, S. (1995). "Consultant-2: Pre- and post-processing of machine learning applications". *International Journal of Human-Computer Studies, 43,* 43-63.

53. Tchoumatchenko I. and Ganascia J-G. (1994). "A Bayesian Framework to Integrate Symbolic and Neural Learning". In *Proceedings of the 11th International Conference in Machine Learning* (New Brunswick, NJ), San Francisco: Morgan Kaufmann, pp. 302-308.

54. Tecuci G. (1991). "Learning as Understanding the External World". In *Proc. First International Workshop on Multistrategy Learning* (Harpers Ferry, WV), Publ. Center for Artificial Intelligence, George Mason University, pp. 49-64.

55. Tecuci G. and Duff D. (1993). "Knowledge Base Refinement Through a Supervised Validation of Plausible Reasoning". In *Proc. of 2nd International Workshop on Multistrategy Learning* (Harpers Ferry, WV), Publ. Center for Artificial Intelligence, George Mason University, pp. 76-91.

56. Towell G.G. and Shavlik J.W. (1994). "Knowledge-Based Artificial Neural Networks". *Artificial Intelligence, 70,* 119-165.

57. Vafaie H. and De Jong K.A. (1991). "Improving the Performance of Rule Induction System Using Genetic Algorithms". In *Proc. of the First International Workshop on Multistrategy Learning* (Harpers Ferry, WV), Publ. Center for Artificial Intelligence, George Mason University, pp. 305-315.

58. Veloso M. and Carbonell J. (1991). "Learning by Analogical Replay in PRODIGY: First Results". In *Proc. European Working Session on Learning* (Oporto, Portugal), pp. 375-390.

59. Venturini G. (1993). "SIA: a Supervised Inductive Algorithm with Genetic Search for Learning Attribute Based Concepts". In *Proceedings of the European Conference on Machine Learning* (Vienna, Austria), pp. 280-296.

60. Zucker J-D. (1998). "Semantic Abstraction for Concept Representation and Learning". In *Proc. 4th International Workshop on Multistrategy Learning* (Desenzano del Garda, Italy), pp. 157-164.

The Computational Support of Scientific Discovery

Pat Langley

DaimlerChrysler Research and Technology Center, 1510 Page Mill Road, Palo Alto,
CA 94304 USA
langley@rtna.daimlerchrysler.com

1 Introduction

The process of scientific discovery has long been viewed as the pinnacle of creative thought. Thus, to many people, including some scientists themselves, it seems an unlikely candidate for automation by computer. However, over the past two decades, researchers in artificial intelligence have repeatedly questioned this attitude and attempted to develop intelligent artifacts that replicate the act of discovery. The computational study of scientific discovery has made important strides in its short history, some of which we review in this paper.

Artificial intelligence often gets its initial ideas from observing human behavior and attempting to model these activities. Computational scientific discovery is no exception, as early research focused on replicating discoveries from the history of disciplines as diverse as mathematics [27], physics [21], chemistry [44], and biology [20]. As the collection by Shrager and Langley [34] reveals, these efforts also had considerable breadth in the range of scientific activities they attempted to model, though most work aimed to replicate the historical record only at the most abstract level. Despite the explicit goals of this early research, some critics (e.g., [13]) have questioned progress in the area because it dealt with scientific laws and theories already known to the developers.

Although many researchers have continued their attempts to reproduce historical discoveries, others have turned their energies toward the computational discovery of new scientific knowledge. As with the historical research, this applied work covers a broad range of disciplines, including mathematics, astronomy, metallurgy, physical chemistry, biochemistry, medicine, and ecology. Many of these efforts have led to refereed publications in the relevant scientific literature, which seems a convincing measure of their accomplishment.

Our aim here is to examine some recent applications of computational scientific discovery and to analyze the reasons for their success. We set the background by reviewing the major forms that discovery takes in scientific domains, giving a framework to organize the later discussion. After this, we consider steps in the larger discovery process at which humans can influence the behavior of a computational discovery system. We then turn to seven examples of computer-aided discoveries that have produced scientific publications. In each case, we examine briefly the role played by the developer or user, then discuss the interactions

G. Paliouras, V. Karkaletsis, and C.D. Spyropoulos (Eds.): ACAI'99, LNAI 2049, pp. 230–248, 2001.
© Springer-Verlag Berlin Heidelberg 2001

with one such system at greater length. In closing, we consider directions for future work, emphasizing the need for discovery aids that explicitly encourage interaction with humans.

2   Stages of the Discovery Process

The history of science reveals a variety of distinct types of discovery activity, ranging from the detection of empirical regularities to the formation of deeper theoretical accounts. Generally speaking, these activities tend to occur in a given order within a field, in that the products of one process influence or constrain the behavior of successors. Of course, science is not a strictly linear process, so that earlier stages may be revisited in the light of results from a later stage, but the logical relation provides a convenient framework for discussion.

Perhaps the earliest discovery activity involves the formation of *taxonomies*. Before one can formulate laws or theories, one must first establish the basic concepts or categories one hopes to relate. An example comes from the early history of chemistry, when scientists agreed to classify some chemicals as acids, some as alkalis, and still others as salts based on observable properties like taste. Similar groupings have emerged in other fields like astronomy and physics, but the best known taxonomies come from biology, which groups living entities into categories and subcategories in a hierarchical manner.

Once they have identified a set of entities, scientists can begin to discover *qualitative laws* that characterize their behavior or that relate them to each other. For example, early chemists found that acids tended to react with alkalis to form salts, along with similar connections among other classes of chemicals. Some qualitative laws describe static relations, whereas others summarize events like reactions that happen over time. Again, this process can occur only after a field has settled on the basic classes of entities under consideration.

A third scientific activity aims to discover *quantitative laws* that state mathematical relations among numeric variables. For instance, early chemists identified the relative masses of hydrochloric acid and sodium hydrochloride that combine to form a unit mass of sodium chloride. This process can also involve postulating the existence of an *intrinsic property* like density or specific heat, as well as estimating the property's value for specific entities. Such numeric laws are typically stated in the context of some qualitative relationship that places constraints on their operation.

Scientists in most fields are not content with empirical summaries and so try to explain such regularities, with the most typical first step involving the creation of *structural models* that incorporate unobserved entities. Thus, nineteenth century chemists like Dalton and Avogadro postulated atomic and molecular models of chemicals to account for the numeric proportions observed in reactions. Initial models of this sort are typically qualitative in nature, stating only the components and their generic relations, but later models often incorporate numeric descriptions that provide further constraints. Both types of models are closely tied to the empirical phenomena they are designed to explain.

Eventually, most scientific disciplines move beyond structural models to *process models*, which explain phenomena in terms of hypothesized mechanisms that involve change over time. One well-known process account is the kinetic theory of gases, which explains the empirical relations among gas volume, pressure, and temperature in terms of interactions among molecules. Again, some process models (like those in geology) are mainly qualitative, while others (like the kinetic theory) include numeric components, but both types make contact with empirical laws that one can derive from them.

In the past two decades, research in automated scientific discovery has addressed each of these five stages. Clustering systems like CLUSTER/2 [29], AUTO-CLASS [4], and RETAX [1] deal with the task of taxonomy formation, whereas systems like NGLAUBER [16] search for qualitative relations. Starting with BACON [21], [23], researchers have developed a great variety of systems that discover numeric laws. Systems like DALTON [23], STAHLP [33], and GELL-MANN [43] formulate structural models, whereas a smaller group, like MECHEM [39] and ASTRA [19], instead construct process models.

A few systems, such as Lenat's [27] AM, Nordhausen and Langley's IDS [31], and Kulkarni and Simon's [20] KEKADA, deal with more than one of these facets, but most contributions have focused on one stage to the exclusion of others. Although the work to date has emphasized rediscovering laws and models from the history of science, we will see that a similar bias holds for efforts at finding new scientific knowledge. We suspect that integrated discovery applications will be developed, but only once the focused efforts that already exist have become more widely known.

This framework is not the only way to categorize scientific activity, but it appears to have general applicability across different fields, so we will use it to organize our presentation of applied discovery work. The scheme does favor methods that generate the types of formalisms reported in the scientific literature, and thus downplays the role of mainstream techniques from machine learning. For example, decision-tree induction, neural networks, and nearest neighbor have produced quite accurate predictors in scientific domains like molecular biology [15], but they employ quite different notations from those used normally to characterize scientific laws and models. For this reason, we will not focus on their application to scientific problems here.

3   The Developer's Role in Computational Discovery

Although the term *computational discovery* suggests an automated process, close inspection of the literature reveals that the human developer or user plays an important role in any successful project. Early computational research on scientific discovery downplayed this fact and emphasized the automation aspect, in general keeping with the goals of artificial intelligence at the time. However, the new climate in AI favors systems that advise humans rather than replace them, and recent analyses of machine learning applications (e.g., [22]) suggest an important role for the developer. Such analyses carry over directly to discovery

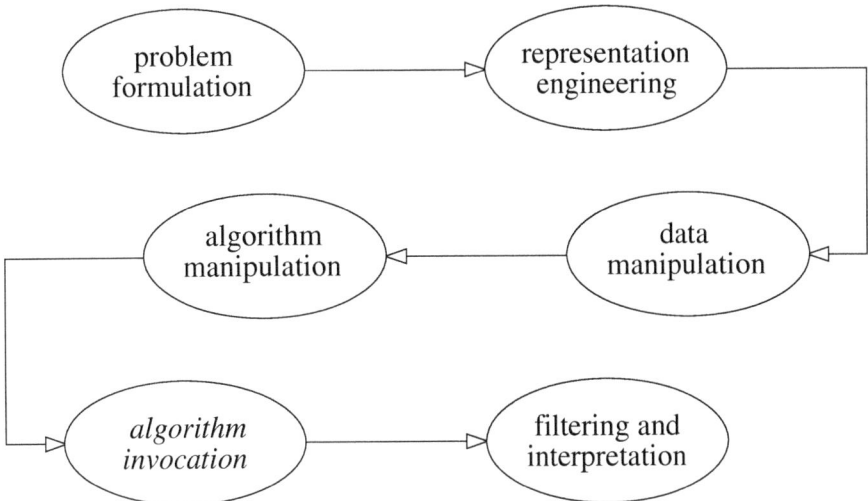

Fig. 1. Steps in the computational discovery process at which the developer or user can influence system behavior.

in scientific domains, and here we review the major ways in which developers can influence the behavior of discovery systems.

As Figure 1 depicts, the first step in using computational discovery methods is to formulate the discovery problem in terms that can be solved using existing techniques. The developer must first cast the task as one that involves forming taxonomies, finding qualitative laws, detecting numeric relations, forming structural models, or constructing process accounts. For most methods, he must also specify the dependent variables that laws should predict or indicate the phenomena that models should explain. Informed and careful *problem formulation* can greatly increase the chances of a successful discovery.

The second step in applying discovery techniques is to settle on an effective representation.[1] The developer must state the variables or predicates used to describe the data or phenomena to be explained, along with the output representation used for taxonomies, laws, or models. The latter must include the operations allowed when combining variables into laws and the component structures or processes used in explanatory models. The developer may also need to encode background knowledge about the domain in terms of an initial theory or results from earlier stages of the discovery process. Such *representational engineering* plays an essential role in successful applications of computational scientific discovery.

Another important activity of the developer concerns preparing the data or phenomena on which the discovery system will operate. Data collected by

---

[1] We are not referring here to the representational formalism, such as decision trees or neural networks, but rather to the domain features encoded in a formalism.

scientists may be quite sparse, lack certain values, be very noisy, or include outliers, and the system user can improve the quality of these data manually or using techniques for interpolation, inference, or smoothing. Similarly, scientists' statements of empirical phenomena may omit hidden assumptions that the user can make explicit or include irrelevant statements that he can remove. Such *data manipulation* can also improve the results obtained through computational discovery.

Research papers on machine discovery typically give the algorithm center stage, but they pay little attention to the developer's efforts to modulate the algorithm's behavior for given inputs. This can involve activities like the manual setting of system parameters (e.g., for evidence thresholds, noise tolerance, and halting criteria) and the interactive control of heuristic search by rejecting bad candidates or attending to good ones. Some systems are designed with this interaction in mind, whereas others support the process more surreptitiously. But in either case, such *algorithm manipulation* is another important way that developers and users can improve their chances for successful discoveries.

A final step in the application process involves transforming the discovery system's output into results that are meaningful to the scientific community. This stage can include manual filtering of interesting results from the overall output, recasting these results in comprehensible terms or notations, and interpreting the relevance of these results for the scientific field. Thus, such *postprocessing* subsumes both the human user's evaluation of scientific results and their communication to scientists who will find them interesting. Since evaluation and communication are central activities in science, they play a crucial role in computational discovery as well.

The literature on computational scientific discovery reveals, though often between the lines, that developers' intervention plays an important role even in historical models of discovery. Indeed, early critiques of machine discovery research frowned on these activities, since both developers and critics assumed the aim was to completely automate the discovery process. However, this view has changed in recent years, and the more common perspective is that discovery systems should aid scientists rather than replace them. In this light, human intervention is perfectly acceptable, especially if the goal is to discover new scientific knowledge and not to assign credit.

4   Some Computer-Aided Scientific Discoveries

Now that we have set the stage, we are ready to report some successful applications of AI methods to the discovery of new scientific knowledge. We organize the presentation in terms of the basic scientific activities described earlier, starting with examples of taxonomy formation, then moving on to law discovery and finally to model construction. In each case, we review the basic scientific problem, describe the discovery system, and present the novel discovery that it has produced. We also examine the role that the developer played in each application, drawing on the five steps outlined in the previous section.

Although we have not attempted to be exhaustive, we did select examples that meet certain criteria. Valdés-Pérez [40] suggests that scientific discovery involves the "generation of novel, interesting, plausible, and intelligible knowledge about objects of scientific study", and reviews four computer-aided discoveries that he argues meet this definition. Rather than repeating his analysis, we have chosen instead to use publication of the result in the relevant scientific literature as our main criterion for success, though we suspect that publication is highly correlated with his factors.

4.1 Stellar Taxonomies from Infrared Spectra

Existing taxonomies of stars are based primarily on characteristics from the visible spectrum. However, artificial satellites provide an opportunity to make measurements of types that are not possible from the Earth's surface, and the resulting data could suggest new groupings of known stellar objects. One such source of new data is the Infrared Astronomical Satellite, which has produced a database that describes the intensity of some 5425 stars at 94 wavelengths throughout the infrared spectrum.

Cheeseman et al. [5] applied their AutoClass system to these infrared data. They designed this program to form one-level taxonomies, that is, to group objects into meaningful classes or clusters based on similar attribute values. For this domain, they chose to represent each cluster in terms of a mean and variance for each attribute, thus specifying a Gaussian distribution. The system carries out a gradient descent search through the space of such descriptions, starting with random initial descriptions for a specified number of clusters. On each step, the search process uses the current descriptions to probabilistically assign each training object to each class, and then uses the observed values for each object to update class descriptions, repeating this process until only minor changes occur. At a higher level, AutoClass iterates through different numbers of clusters to determine the best taxonomy, starting with a user-specified number of classes and increasing this count until it produces classes with negligible probabilities.

Application of AutoClass to the infrared data on stars produced 77 stellar classes, which the developers organized into nine higher-level clusters by running the system on the cluster descriptions themselves. The resulting taxonomy differed significantly from the one then used in astronomy, and the collaborating astronomers felt that it reflected some important results. These included a new class of blackbody stars with significant infrared excess, presumably due to surrounding dust, and a very weak spectral 'bump' at 13 microns in some classes that was undetectable in individual spectra. Goebel et al. [14] recount these and other discoveries, along with their physical interpretation; thus, the results were deemed important enough to justify their publication in an refereed astrophysical journal.

Although AutoClass clearly contributed greatly to these discoveries, the developers acknowledge that they also played an important role [6]. Casting the basic problem in terms of clustering was straightforward, but the team quickly encountered problems with the basic infrared spectra, which had been normalized to ensure that all had the same peak height. To obtain reasonable results, they renormalized the data so that all curves had the same area. They also had to correct for some negative spectral intensities, which earlier software used by the astronomers had caused by subtracting out a background value. The developers' decision to run AUTOCLASS on its own output to produce a two-level taxonomy constituted another intervention. Finally, the collaborating astronomers did considerable interpretation of the system outputs before presenting them to the scientific community.

4.2 Qualitative Factors in Carcinogenesis

Over 80,000 chemicals are available commercially, yet the long-term health effects are known for only about 15 percent of them. Even fewer definitive results are available about whether chemicals cause cancer, since the standard tests for carcinogens involve two-year animal bioassays that cost $2 million per chemical. As a result, there is great demand for predictive laws that would let one predict carcinogenicity from more rapid and less expensive measurements.

Lee, Buchanan, and Aronis [24] have applied the rule-induction system RL to the problem of discovering such qualitative laws. The program constructs a set of conjunctive rules, each of which states the conditions under which some result occurs. Like many other rule-induction methods, RL invokes a general-to-specific search to generate each rule, selecting conditions to add that increase the rule's ability to discriminate among classes and halting when there is no improvement in accuracy. The system also lets the user bias this search by specifying desirable properties of the learned rules.

The developers ran RL on three databases for which carcinogenicity results were available, including 301, 108, and 1300 chemical compounds, respectively. Chemicals were described in terms of physical properties, structural features, short-term effects, and values on potency measures produced by another system. Experiments revealed that the induced rules were substantially more accurate than existing prediction schemes, which justified publication in the scientific literature [26]. They also tested the rules' ability to classify 24 new chemicals for which the status was unknown at development time; these results were also positive and led to another scientific publication [25].

The authors recount a number of ways in which they intervened in the discovery process to obtain these results. For example, they reduced the 496 attributes for one database to only 75 features by grouping values about lesions on various organs. The developers also constrained the induction process by specifying that RL should favor some attributes over others when constructing rules and telling it to consider only certain values of a symbolic attribute for a given class, as well as certain types of tests on numeric attributes. These constraints, which they developed through interaction with domain scientists, took precedence over accuracy-oriented measures in deciding what conditions to select, and it seems likely that they helped account for the effort's success.

4.3   Chemical Predictors of Mutagens

Another area of biochemistry with important social implications aims to understand the factors that determine whether a chemical will cause mutations in genetic material. One data set that contains results of this sort involves 230 aromatic and heteroaromatic nitro compounds, which can be divided into 138 chemicals that have high mutagenicity and 92 chemicals that are low on this dimension. Qualitative relations that characterize these two classes could prove useful in predicting whether new compounds pose a danger of causing mutation.

King, Muggleton, Srinivasan, and Sternberg [17] report an application of their PROGOL system to this problem. The program operates along lines similar to other rule-induction methods, in that it carries out a general-to-specific search for a conjunctive rule that covers some of the data, then repeats this process to find additional rules that cover the rest. The system also lets the user specify background knowledge, stated in the same form, which it takes into account in measuring the quality of induced rules. Unlike most rule-induction techniques, PROGOL assumes a predicate logic formalism that can represent relations among objects, rather than just attribute values.

This support for relational descriptions led to revealing structural descriptions of mutation factors. For example, for the data set mentioned above, the system found one rule predicting that a compound is mutagenic if it has "a highly aliphatic carbon atom attached by a single bond to a carbon atom that is in a six-membered aromatic ring". Combined with four similar rules, this characterization gave 81% correct predictions, which is comparable to the accuracy of other computational methods. However, alternative techniques do not produce a structural description that one can use to visualize spatial relations and thus to posit the deeper causes of mutation, so that the results justified publication in the chemistry literature [17].

As in other applications, the developers aided the discovery process in a number of ways. They chose to formulate the task in terms of finding a classifier that labels chemicals as causing mutation or not, rather than predicting levels of mutagenicity. King et al. also presented their system with background knowledge about methyl and nitro groups, the length and connectivity of rings, and other concepts. In addition, they manipulated the data by dividing them into two groups with different characteristics, as done earlier by others working in the area. Although the induced rules were understandable in that they made clear contact with chemical concepts, the authors aided their interpretation by presenting graphical depictions of their structural claims. Similar interventions have been used by the developers on related scientific problems, including prediction of carcinogenicity [18] and pharmacophore discovery [11].

4.4   Quantitative Laws of Metallic Behavior

A central process in the manufacture of iron and steel involves the removal of impurities from molten slag. Qualitatively, the chemical reactions that are responsible for this removal process increase in effectiveness when the slag contains more free oxide (O^{2-}) ions. However, metallurgists have only imperfect quantitative laws that relate the oxide amount, known as the *basicity* of the slag, to dependent variables of interest, such as the slag's sulfur capacity. Moreover, basicity cannot always be measured accurately, so there is a need for improved ways to estimate this intrinsic property.

Mitchell, Sleeman, Duffy, Ingram, and Young [30] applied computational discovery techniques to these scientific problems. Their DAVICCAND system includes operations for selecting pairs of numeric variables to relate, specifying qualitative conditions that focus attention on some of the data, and finding numeric laws that relate variables within a given region. The program also includes mechanisms for identifying outliers that violate these numeric laws and for using the laws to infer the values of intrinsic properties when one cannot measure them more directly.

The developers report two new discoveries in which DAVICCAND played a central role. The first involves the quantitative relation between basicity and sulfur capacity. Previous accounts modeled this relation using a single polynomial that held across all temperature ranges. The new results involve three simpler, linear laws that relate these two variables under different temperature ranges. The second contribution concerns improved estimates for the basicity of slags that contain TiO_2 and FeO, which DAVICCAND inferred using the numeric laws it induced from data, and the conclusion that FeO has quite different basicity values for sulphur and phosphorus slags. These results were deemed important enough to appear in a respected metallurgical journal [30].

Unlike most discovery systems, DAVICCAND encourages users to take part in the search process and provides explicit control points where they can influence choices. Thus, they formulate the problem by specifying what dependent variable the laws should predict and what region of the space to consider. Users also affect representational choices by selecting what independent variables to use when looking for numeric laws, and they can manipulate the data by selecting what points to treat as outliers. DAVICCAND presents its results in terms of graphical displays and functional forms that are familiar to metallurgists, and, given the user's role in the discovery process, there remains little need for postprocessing to filter results.

4.5   Quantitative Conjectures in Graph Theory

A recurring theme in graph theory involves proving theorems about relations among quantitative properties of graphs. However, before a mathematician can prove that such a relation always holds, someone must first formulate it as a conjecture. Although mathematical publications tend to emphasize proofs of theorems, the process of finding interesting conjectures is equally important and has much in common with discovery in the natural sciences.

Fajtlowicz [8] and colleagues have developed GRAFFITI, a system that generates conjectures in graph theory and other areas of discrete mathematics. The system carries out search through a space of quantitative relations like $\sum x_i \geq \sum y_i$, where each x_i and y_i is some numerical feature of a graph (e.g., its diameter or its largest eigenvalue), the product of such elementary features, or their ratio. GRAFFITI ensures that its conjectures are novel by maintaining a record of previous hypotheses, and filters many uninteresting conjectures by noting that they seem to be implied by earlier, more general, candidates.

GRAFFITI has generated hundreds of novel conjectures in graph theory, many of which have spurred mathematicians to attempt their proof or refutation, which in turn has produced numerous publications. One example involves a conjecture that the 'average distance' of a graph is no greater than its 'independence number', which resulted in a proof that appeared in the refereed mathematical literature [7]. Although GRAFFITI was designed as an automated discovery system, its developers have clearly constrained its behavior by specifying the primitive graph features and the types of relations it should consider. Data manipulation occurs through a file that contains qualitatively different graphs, against which the system tests its conjectures empirically, and postprocessing occurs when mathematicians filter the system output for interesting results.

4.6   Temporal Laws of Ecological Behavior

One major concern in ecology is the effect of pollution on the plant and animal populations. Ecologists regularly develop quantitative models that are stated as sets of differential equations. Each such equation describes changes in one variable (its derivative) as a function of other variables, typically ones that can be directly observed. For example, Lake Glumsoe is a shallow lake in Denmark with high concentrations of nitrogen and phosphorus from waste water, and ecologists would like to model the effect of these variables on the concentration of phytoplankton and zooplankton in the lake.

Todorovski, Džeroski, and Kompare [37] have applied techniques for numeric discovery to this problem. Their LAGRAMGE system carries out search through a space of differential equations, looking for the equation set that gives the smallest error on the observed data. The system uses two constraints to make this search process tractable. First, LAGRAMGE incorporates background knowledge about the domain in the form of a context-free grammar that it uses to generate plausible equations. Second, it places a limit on the allowed depth of the derivations used to produce equations. For each candidate set of equations, the system uses numerical integration to estimate the error and thus the quality of the proposed model.

The developers report a new set of equations, discovered by LAGRAMGE, that model accurately the relation between the pollution and plankton concentrations in Lake Glumsoe. This revealed that phosphorus and temperature are the limiting factors on the growth of phytoplankton in the lake. We can infer Todorovski et al.'s role in the discovery process from their paper. They formulated the problem in terms of the variables to be predicted, and they engineered the representation both by specifying the predictive variables and by providing the grammar used to generate candidate equations. Because the data were sparse (from only 14 time points over two months), they convinced three experts to draw curves that filled in the gaps, used splines to smooth these curves, and sampled from these ten times per day. They also manipulated LAGRAMGE by telling it to consider derivations that were no more than four levels deep. However, little postprocessing or interpretation was needed, since the system produces output in a form familiar to ecologists.

4.7   Structural Models of Organic Molecules

A central task in organic chemistry involves determining the molecular structure of a new substance. The chemist typically knows the substance's chemical formula, such as $C_{18}H_{24}O_2$, and frequently knows its mass spectrum, which maps the masses of fragments (obtained by fracturing the chemical in a mass spectrometer) against their frequency of occurrence. The goal is to infer the structure of the compound in terms of the molecular connections among its elementary constituents. For reasonably complex compounds, there can be hundreds of millions of possible structures, suggesting the need for computational aids to search this space effectively.

In perhaps the earliest effort to use AI techniques for scientific reasoning, Feigenbaum, Buchanan, and Lederberg [10] developed DENDRAL to address this task. The system operates in three stages, first using the mass spectrum to infer likely substructures of the molecule that could explain major peaks in the data.[2] Next, DENDRAL considers different combinations of these substructures, plus the residual atoms, that produce the known chemical formula, using knowledge of chemical stability to generate all (and only) chemical structure graphs consistent with these constraints. Finally, the system ranks these candidate structural models in terms of their abilities to predict the observed spectrum, using knowledge of mass spectrometry for this purpose.

The DENDRAL effort led to a variety of chemical structures that were published in organic chemistry journals. For instance, Cheer et al. [3] report new structural models for terpenoids, that is, C_{15} and C_{20} compounds isolated from plants, as well as for sterol compounds that could be metabolic precursors of known sterols in marine organisms. Similarly, Varkony, Carhart, and Smith [41] report system-generated models for compounds that result from chemical and photochemical rearrangements of cyclic hydrocarbons, whereas Fitch, Anderson, Smith, and Djerassi [12] describe models for chemicals found in the body fluids of patients suspected of inherited metabolic disorders. Lindsay, Buchanan, Feigenbaum, and Lederberg [28] give a fuller list of scientific publications that resulted from the project, including results on gaseous ions, compounds that display pharmacological activity, and secretions used by insects for defense.

Although the early DENDRAL work emphasized automating the structural-modeling process, the system's developers influenced its behavior by encoding considerable knowledge about chemical stability into its search constraints. They presented spectrograms to DENDRAL without any special preprocessing, but they

---

[2] At this step, the system can also accept input from chemists about likely or unlikely substructures.

did select the structural-modeling tasks and thus the spectrograms that it encountered. Later versions of the system were more interactive, letting chemists impose additional constraints based on their own knowledge and data sources. Also, it seems likely that users filtered the structural inferences included in their publications, although the output itself required little interpretation, being cast in a formalism familiar to organic chemists.

4.8   Reaction Pathways in Catalytic Chemistry

For a century, chemists have known that many reactions involve, not a single step, but rather a sequence of primitive interactions. Thus, a recurring problem has been to formulate the sequence of steps, known as the *reaction pathway*, for a given chemical reaction. In addition to the reactants and products of the reaction, this inference may also be constrained by information about intermediate products, concentrations over time, relative quantities, and many other factors. Even so, the great number of possible pathways makes it possible that scientists will overlook some viable alternatives, so there exists a need for computational assistance on this task.

Valdés-Pérez [39] developed MECHEM with this end in mind. The system accepts as input the reactants and products for a chemical reaction, along with other experimental evidence and considerable background knowledge about the domain of catalytic chemistry. MECHEM lets the user specify interactively which of these constraints to incorporate when generating pathways, giving him control over its global behavior. The system carries out a search through the space of reaction pathways, generating the elementary steps from scratch using special graph algorithms. Search always proceeds from simpler pathways (fewer substances and steps) to more complex ones. MECHEM uses its constraints to eliminate pathways that are not viable and also to identify any intermediate products it hypothesizes in the process. The final output is a comprehensive set of the simplest pathways that explain the evidence and that are consistent with the system's background knowledge.

This approach has produced a number of novel reaction pathways that have appeared in the chemical literature. For example, Valdés-Pérez [38] reports a new explanation for the catalytic reaction $ethane + H_2 \rightarrow 2\ methane$, which chemists had viewed as largely solved, whereas Zeigarnik et al. [42] present another novel result on acrylic acid. Bruk et al. [2] describe a third application of MECHEM that produced 41 novel pathways, which prompted experimental studies that reduced this to a small set consistent with the new data. The human's role in this process is explicit, with users formulating the problem through stating the reaction of interest and manipulating the algorithm's behavior by invoking domain constraints. Because MECHEM produces pathways in a notation familiar to chemists, its outputs require little interpretation.

4.9   Other Computational Aids for Scientific Research

We have focused on the examples above because they cover a broad range of scientific problems and illustrate the importance of human interaction with the discovery system, but they do not exhaust the list of successful applications. For example, Pericliev and Valdés-Pérez [32] have used their KINSHIP program to generate minimal sets of features that distinguish kinship terms, like *son* and *uncle*, given genealogical and matrimonial relations that hold for each. They have applied their system to characterize kinship terms in both English and Bulgarian, and the results have found acceptance in anthropological linguistics because they are stated in that field's conventional notation.

Another instance comes from Swanson and Smalheiser [36], who have used their ARROWSMITH program to discover unsuspected relations in the medical literature. The system searches through online papers, looking for an entry in which some relation $B \Rightarrow C$ occurs along with some other relation $A \Rightarrow B$. ARROWSMITH constrains its search by requiring that C be a physiological state (like a disease) and that A be a possible intervention (like a drug or dietary factor). For example, the system noted that magnesium can inhibit spreading depression, and that spreading depression has been implicated in migraine attacks. The resulting hypothesis, that magnesium could alleviate migraines, appeared in the medical literature [35] and has since been supported repeatedly in clinical tests.

We should also consider the relation between computational scientific discovery and the kindred topic of data mining, which also aims to uncover novel, interesting, plausible, and intelligible knowledge. One difference is that data mining typically focuses on commercial applications, though Fayyad, Haussler, and Stolorz [9] review some impressive examples of mining scientific data from astronomy (for classifying stars and galaxies in sky photographs) and planetology (for recognizing volcanoes on Venus). However, these efforts and related ones invoke induction algorithms primarily to automate tedious recognition tasks in support of cataloguing and statistical analysis, rather than to discover publishable scientific knowledge in its own right.[3] Moreover, such work seldom produces knowledge in any standard scientific notation, since they typically rely on representations from supervised machine learning like decision trees or probabilistic summaries.

A similar relation holds between computational scientific discovery and computational approaches to molecular biology. One major goal here, which Fayyad et al. also review, is to predict the qualitative structure of proteins from their nucleotide sequence. This paradigm has led to many publications in the biology and biochemistry literature, but most studies emphasize predictive accuracy, with low priority given to expressing the predictors in some common scientific notation. A similar trend has occurred in work on learning structure-activity relations in biochemistry, though the work by King, Muggleton, Srinivasan, and Sternberg [17] constitutes an exception, in that they focus on presenting discovered relations in chemical notation. Within computational molecular biology,

---

[3] The classifiers learned by such methods, when applied to images, can 'discover' new stars or volcanoes, but we would be unlikely to use that term if a human carried out the same task.

the main exceptions deal with the discovery of structural motifs, which are simple taxonomies that describe configurations of nucleotides or other components that tend to recur in biological sequences. However, most research in the area has been less concerned with discovering new knowledge than with showing that their predictors give slight improvements in accuracy over other methods, which has led us to discuss them here only in passing.

5   An Illustration of Interactive Discovery

Since we have emphasized the interaction between humans and computational discovery methods, we should illustrate the nature of such interactions in more detail. Table 1 presents a sample trace of DAVICCAND, a system that provides explicit support for such interaction. Recall that DAVICCAND deals with the discovery of quantitative relations among variables that describe the behavior of the irons slags central to steelmaking. In this case, the metallurgist communicated verbally with one of the program's developers, who in turn entered commands to the system.

The first step involves the user selecting a data set from those available in the online library, in this case one known as the 'Strathclyde data set'. The user can also focus the system's attention on certain groups of data points, in this case those that contain less than 10% silicon dioxide. This process can rely on predefined groups or, as in this trace, the definition of entirely new groups based on ranges of values. DAVICCAND also lets the user define groups in terms of conjunctions of ranges, ratios of quantities, and distance from a specified line, though here the definition is univariate.

In this trace, having specified a group, the scientist asks the system to display a straight line through the data contained in that group. Since this appears to give a close fit, he redirects attention to another group of cases that contain more than 10% silicon dioxide, then changes his mind and displays instead those with more than 20% silicon. Because neither group seems easy to characterize, the user asks DAVICCAND to search for group definitions in terms of silicon dioxide percentages, specifying the region within which to search. The system displays the resulting groups and transition between them, which the user deems interesting. He focuses especially on one cluster, defined as having less than 44% silicon, that he thinks requires more analysis. The scientist notes that a straight line does not describe these data, and so asks the system to fit and display a higher-order curve for his inspection.

Later interactions with the same scientist led DAVICCAND to define new groups based on temperature ranges and percentage of titanium dioxide. These in turn led him to focus on regions in which values for optical basicity were uncertain, and finally to invoke a module that estimated new values from experimental data. Interactions with this user ignored some of DAVICCAND's features, such as the ability to label some observations as outliers. However, this fact supports our view that both humans and machines have an important role to play in computational scientific discovery.

Table 1. A trace interaction between a metallurgist (M) and system developer (S) jointly using DAVICCAND to analyze data about the behavior of iron slags.

M: Okay, can you bring up the Strathclyde data set?*

S: [Loads and displays the data set.]

M: Can you highlight all those points that contain less than 10% silicon [actually SiO_2]?

S: [Creates and displays the new group.]

M: Can you draw a line through those points?

S: Straight line or curve?

M: A straight line.

S: [Invokes module that fits and dispays a line.]

M: What about those points with more than 10% silicon?

S: [Creates and displays the new group.]

M: That doesn't look quite right. Can you change the value to 20%?

S: [Removes old groups from display, then creates and displays the new groups and lines.]

M: Still not quite right.

S: Do you want to try a curve? Or we could try searching for the two lines.

M: Let's try searching.

S: Where abouts in the data set do you want to search for the lines?

M: From 10% to 70% silicon?

S: We're currently looking at log sulphur vs optical basicity. To do that I need to change the visualization or, if you can say roughly where on the screen you want to search from, I can do that without changing the visualization.

M: [Points at screen, showing start and stop points.] From here to here.

S: [Invokes the search process.]

M: That looks interesting. Can you show me what the groups look like?

S: [Displays the group definitions.]

M: It looks like the bottom group [silicon less than 44%] is not a straight line. Can you draw a curve through that?

S: What degree of polynomial?

M: Two or three.

S: [Invokes curve-fitting module.]

---

* This data set has two slightly different groups that more or less fall on a line, but the fits are better if each   group is treated separately.

6 Progress and Prospects

As the above examples show, work in computational scientific discovery no longer focuses solely on historical models, but also contributes novel knowledge to a range of scientific disciplines. To date, such applications remain the exception rather than the rule, but the breadth of successful computer-aided discoveries provides convincing evidence that these methods have great potential for aiding the scientific process. The clear influence of humans in each of these applications does not diminish the equally important contribution of the discovery system; each has a role to play in a complex and challenging endeavor.

One recurring theme in applied discovery work has been the difficulty in finding collaborators from the relevant scientific field. Presumably, scientists in many disciplines are satisfied with their existing methods and see little advantage to moving beyond the statistical aids they currently use. This attitude seems less common in fields like molecular biology, which have taken the computational metaphor to heart, but often there are social obstacles to overcome. The obvious response is to emphasize that we do not intend our computational tools to replace scientists but rather to aid them, just as simpler software already aids them in carrying out statistical analyses.

However, making this argument convincing will require some changes in our systems to better reflect the position. As noted, existing discovery software already supports intervention by humans in a variety of ways, from initial problem formulation to final interpretation. But in most cases this activity happens in spite of the software design rather than because the developer intended it. If we want to encourage synergy between human and artificial scientists, then we must modify our discovery systems to support their interaction more directly. This means we must install interfaces with explicit hooks that let users state or revise their problem formulation and representational choices, manipulate the data and system parameters, and recast outputs in understandable terms. The MECHEM and DAVICCAND systems already include such facilities and thus constitute good role models, but we need more efforts along these lines.

Naturally, explicit inclusion of users in the computational discovery process raises a host of issues that are absent from the autonomous approach. These include questions about which decisions should be automated and which placed under human control, the granularity at which interaction should occur, and the type of interface that is best suited to a particular scientific domain. The discipline of human-computer interaction regularly addresses such matters, and though its lessons and design criteria have not yet been applied to computer-aided discovery, many of them should carry over directly from other domains. Interactive discovery systems also pose challenges in evaluation, since human variability makes experimentation more difficult than for autonomous systems. Yet experimental studies are not essential if one's main goal is to develop computational tools that aid users in discovering new scientific knowledge.

Clearly, we are only beginning to develop effective ways to combine the strengths of human cognition with those of computational discovery systems. But even our initial efforts have produced some convincing examples of computer-aided discovery that have led to publications in the scientific literature. We predict that, as more developers realize the need to provide explicit support for human intervention, we will see even more productive systems and even more impressive discoveries that advance the state of scientific knowledge.

Acknowledgements. Thanks to Bruce Buchanan, Saso Džeroski, Fraser Mitchell, Steve Muggleton, Derek Sleeman, John Stutz, and Raul Valdés-Pérez for providing information about both their discovery systems and their use. An earlier version of this paper appeared in the *Proceedings of the First International Conference on Discovery Science* and in the *International Journal of Human-Computer Studies*.

References

1. Alberdi, E., & Sleeman, D. (1997). RETAX: A step in the automation of taxonomic revision. *Artificial Intelligence, 91*, 257–279.
2. Bruk, L. G., Gorodskii, S. N., Zeigarnik, A. V., Valdés-Pérez, R. E., & Temkin, O. N. (1998). Oxidative carbonylation of phenylacetylene catalyzed by Pd(II) and Cu(I): Experimental tests of forty-one computer-generated mechanistic hypotheses. *Journal of Molecular Catalysis A: Chemical, 130*, 29–40.
3. Cheer, C., Smith, D. H., Djerassi, C., Tursch, B., Braekman, J. C., & Daloze, D. (1976). Applications of artificial intelligence for chemical inference, XXI: The computer-assisted identification of [+]- palustrol in the marine organism cespitularia ap., aff. subvirdis. *Tetrahedron, 32*, 1807.
4. Cheeseman, P., Freeman, D., Kelly, J., Self, M., Stutz, J., & Taylor, W. (1988). AUTOCLASS: A Bayesian classificiation system. *Proceedings of the Fifth International Conference on Machine Learning* (pp. 54–64). Ann Arbor, MI: Morgan Kaufmann.
5. Cheeseman, P., Goebel, J., Self, M., Stutz, M., Volk, K., Taylor, W., & Walker, H. (1989). *Automatic classification of the spectra from the infrared astronomical satellite (IRAS)* (Reference Publication 1217). Washington, DC: National Aeronautics and Space Administration.
6. Cheeseman, P., & Stutz, J. (1996). Bayesian classification (AUTOCLASS): Theory and results. In U. M. Fayyad, G. Piatetsky-Shapiro, P. Smyth, & R. Uthurusamy (Eds.), *Advances in knowledge discovery and data mining*. Cambridge, MA: MIT Press.
7. Chung, F. (1988). The average distance is not more than the independence number. *Journal of Graph Theory, 12*, 229–235.
8. Fajtlowicz, S. (1988). On conjectures of GRAFFITI. *Discrete Mathematics, 72*, 113–118.
9. Fayyad, U., Haussler, D., & Stolorz, P. (1996). KDD for science data analysis: Issues and examples. *Proceedings of the Second International Conference of Knowledge Discovery and Data Mining* (pp. 50–56). Portland, OR: AAAI Press.
10. Feigenbaum, E. A., Buchanan, B. G., Lederberg, J. (1971). On generality and problem solving: A case study using the DENDRAL program. In *Machine intelligence* (Vol. 6). Edinburgh: Edinburgh University Press.
11. Finn, P., Muggleton, S., Page, D., & Srinivasan, A. (1998). Pharmacophore discovery using the inductive logic programming system PROGOL. *Machine Learning, 30*, 241–270.

12. Fitch, W. L., Anderson, P. J., Smith, D. H., & Djerassi, C. (1979). Isolation, identification and quantitation of urinary organic acids. *Journal of Chromatography*, *162*, 249–59.

13. Gillies, D. (1996). *Artificial intelligence and scientific method*. Oxford: Oxford Univerity Press.

14. Goebel, J., Volk, K., Walker, H., Gerbault, F., Cheeseman, P., Self, M., Stutz, J., & Taylor, W. (1989). A Bayesian classification of the IRAS LRS Atlas. *Astronomy and Astrophysics*, *222*, L5–L8.

15. Hunter, L. (1993). (Ed.). *Artificial intelligence and molecular biology*. Cambridge, MA: MIT Press.

16. Jones, R. (1986). Generating predictions to aid the scientific discovery process. *Proceedings of the Fifth National Conference on Artificial Intelligence* (pp. 513–517). Philadelphia: Morgan Kaufmann.

17. King, R. D., Muggleton, S. H., Srinivasan, A., & Sternberg, M. E. J. (1996). Structure-activity relationships derived by machine learning: The use of atoms and their bond connectives to predict mutagenicity by inductive logic programming. *Proceedings of the National Academy of Sciences*, *93*, 438–442.

18. King, R. D., & Srinivasan, A. (1996). Prediction of rodent carcinogenicity bioassays from molecular structure using inductive logic programming. *Environmental Health Perspectives*, *104* (Supplement 5), 1031–1040.

19. Kocabas, S., & Langley, P. (1998). Generating process explanations in nuclear astrophysics. *Proceedings of the ECAI-98 Workshop on Machine Discovery* (pp. 4–9). Brighton, England.

20. Kulkarni, D., & Simon, H. A. (1990). Experimentation in machine discovery. In J. Shrager & P. Langley (Eds.), *Computational models of scientific discovery and theory formation*. San Mateo, CA: Morgan Kaufmann.

21. Langley, P. (1981). Data-driven discovery of physical laws. *Cognitive Science*, *5*, 31–54.

22. Langley, P., & Simon, H. A. (1995). Applications of machine learning and rule induction. *Communications of the ACM*, *38*, November, 55–64.

23. Langley, P., Simon, H. A., Bradshaw, G. L., & Żytkow, J. M. (1987). *Scientific discovery: Computational explorations of the creative processes*. Cambridge, MA: MIT Press.

24. Lee, Y., Buchanan, B. G., & Aronis, J. M. (1998). Knowledge-based learning in exploratory science: Learning rules to predict rodent carcinogenicity. *Machine Learning*, *30*, 217–240.

25. Lee, Y., Buchanan, B. G., Mattison, D. R., Klopman, G., & Rosenkranz, H. S. (1995). Learning rules to predict rodent carcinogenicity of non-genotoxic chemicals. *Mutation Research*, *328*, 127–149.

26. Lee, Y., Buchanan, B. G., & Rosenkranz, H. S. (1996). Carcinogenicity predictions for a group of 30 chemicals undergoing rodent cancer bioassays based on rules derived from subchronic organ toxicities. *Environmental Health Perspectives*, *104* (Supplement 5), 1059–1063.

27. Lenat, D. B. (1977). Automated theory formation in mathematics. *Proceedings of the Fifth International Joint Conference on Artificial Intelligence* (pp. 833–842). Cambridge, MA: Morgan Kaufmann.

28. Lindsay, R. K., Buchanan, B. G., Feigenbaum, E. A., & Lederberg, J. (1980). *Applications of artificial intelligence for organic chemistry: The DENDRAL project*. New York: McGraw-Hill.

29. Michalski, R. S., & Stepp, R. (1983). Learning from observation: Conceptual clustering. In R. S. Michalski, J. G. Carbonell, & T. M. Mitchell (Eds.), *Machine learning: An artificial intelligence approach*. San Francisco: Morgan Kaufmann.
30. Mitchell, F., Sleeman, D., Duffy, J. A., Ingram, M. D., & Young, R. W. (1997). Optical basicity of metallurgical slags: A new computer-based system for data visualisation and analysis. *Ironmaking and Steelmaking*, *24*, 306–320.
31. Nordhausen, B., & Langley, P. (1993). An integrated framework for empirical discovery. *Machine Learning*, *12*, 17–47.
32. Pericliev, V., & Valdés-Pérez, R. E. (1998). Automatic componential analysis of kinship semantics with a proposed structural solution to the problem of multiple models. *Anthropological Linguistics*, *40*, 272–317.
33. Rose, D., & Langley, P. (1986). Chemical discovery as belief revision. *Machine Learning*, *1*, 423–451.
34. Shrager, J., & Langley, P. (Eds.) (1990). *Computational models of scientific discovery and theory formation*. San Francisco: Morgan Kaufmann.
35. Swanson, D. R. (1988). Migraine and magnesium: Eleven neglected connections. *Perspectives in Biology and Medicine*, *31*, 526–557.
36. Swanson, D. R., & Smalheiser, N. R. (1997). An interactive system for finding complementary literatures: A stimulus to scientific discovery. *Artificial Intelligence*, *91*, 183–203.
37. Todorovski, L., Džeroski, S., & Kompare, B. (1998). Modeling and prediction of phytoplankton growth with equation discovery. *Ecological Modelling*, *113*, 71–81.
38. Valdés-Pérez, R. E. (1994). Human/computer interactive elucidation of reaction mechanisms: Application to catalyzed hydrogenolysis of ethane. *Catalysis Letters*, *28*, 79–87.
39. Valdés-Pérez, R. E. (1995). Machine discovery in chemistry: New results. *Artificial Intelligence*, *74*, 191–201.
40. Valdés-Pérez, R. E. (1999). Principles of human-computer collaboration for knowledge discovery in science. *Artificial Intelligence*, *107*, 335–346.
41. Varkony, T. H., Carhart, R. E., & Smith, D. H. (1977). Applications of artificial intelligence for chemical inference, XXIII: Computer-assisted structure elucidation. Modelling chemical reaction sequences used in molecular structure problems. In W. T. Wipke (Ed.), *Computer-assisted organic synthesis*. Washington, DC: American Chemical Society.
42. Zeigarnik, A. V., Valdés-Pérez, R. E., Temkin, O. N., Bruk, L. G., & Shalgunov, S. I. (1997). Computer-aided mechanism elucidation of acetylene hydrocarboxylation to acrylic acid based on a novel union of empirical and formal methods. *Organometallics*, *16*, 3114–3127.
43. Żytkow, J. M. (1996). Incremental discovery of hidden structure: Applications in theory of elementary particles. *Proceedings of the Thirteenth National Conference on Artificial Intelligence* (pp. 750–756). Portland, OR: AAAI Press.
44. Żytkow, J. M., & Simon, H. A. (1986). A theory of historical discovery: The construction of componential models. *Machine Learning*, *1*, 107–137.

Support Vector Machines: Theory and Applications

Theodoros Evgeniou[1] and Massimiliano Pontil[2]

[1] Technology Management, INSEAD, 77305 Fontainebleau, France
theodoros.evgeniou@insead.fr
[2] Center for Biological and Computational Learning, MIT, E25-201, 45 Carleton St.,
Cambridge MA 02139, USA
pontil@ai.mit.edu

1 Introduction

This chapter presents a summary of the issues discussed during the one day workshop on "Support Vector Machines (SVM) Theory and Applications" organized as part of the Advanced Course on Artificial Intelligence (ACAI '99) in Chania, Greece [19]. The goal of the chapter is twofold: to present an overview of the background theory and current understanding of SVM, and to discuss the papers presented as well as the issues that arose during the workshop.

Support Vector Machines (SVM) have been recently developed in the framework of statistical learning theory [14], [4], and have been successfully applied to a number of applications, ranging from time series prediction [7], to face recognition [12], to biological data processing for medical diagnosis [17]. Their theoretical foundations and their experimental success encourage further research on their characteristics, as well as their further use.

In this chapter we present a brief introduction to the theory and implementation of SVM, and we discuss the five papers presented during the workshop. The chapter is organized as follows: section 2 presents the theoretical foundations of SVM. A brief overview of statistical learning theory also using the discussion in [16] is given. The mathematical formulation of SVM is presented, and theory for the implementation of SVM, as in [13], is briefly discussed. Section 3 summarizes the experimental work of [17], [7] and [12] and the variations of the standard SVM proposed in these papers. Finally section 4 presents some conclusions and suggestions for future research.

2 A Brief Overview of the SVM Theory

Support Vector Machines have been developed in the framework of Statistical Learning Theory - see for example [14]. We first briefly discuss some basic ideas of the theory.

2.1 Statistical Learning Theory: A Primer

In statistical learning theory (SLT) the problem of supervised learning is formulated as follows. We are given a set of l training data $\{(\mathbf{x}_1, y_1)...(\mathbf{x}_l, y_l)\}$ in $R^n \times R$ sampled

G. Paliouras, V. Karkaletsis, and C.D. Spyropoulos (Eds.): ACAI '99, LNAI 2049, pp. 249-257, 2001.
© Springer-Verlag Berlin Heidelberg 2001

according to unknown probability distribution $P(\mathbf{x},y)$, and a loss function $V(y,f(\mathbf{x}))$ that measures the error done when, for a given $\mathbf{x}$, $f(\mathbf{x})$ is "predicted" instead of the actual value y. The problem consists in finding a function f that minimizes the expectation of the error on new data, that is, find a function f that minimizes the expected error:

$$\int V(y,f(\mathbf{x}))\, P(\mathbf{x},y)\, d\mathbf{x}\, dy$$

Since $P(\mathbf{x},y)$ in unknown, we need to use some induction principle in order to infer from the l available training examples a function that minimizes the expected error. The principle used is Empirical Risk Minimization (ERM) over a set of possible functions, called hypothesis space. Formally this can be written as minimizing the empirical error:

$$\frac{1}{l}\sum_{i=1}^{l} V(y_i, f(\mathbf{x}_i))$$

with f being restricted to be in a space of functions - hypothesis space - say H. An important question is how close the empirical error of the solution (minimizer of the empirical error) is to the minimum of the expected error that can be achieved with functions from H. A central result of the theory states the conditions under which the two errors are close to each other, and provides probabilistic bounds on the distance between empirical and expected errors (see theorem 1 below). These bounds are given in terms of a measure of complexity of the hypothesis space H: the more "complex" H is, the larger the distance between the empirical and expected errors is in probability (see theorem 1 below).

From the bounds that the theory provides, it occurs that it is possible to improve the ERM inductive principle by considering a structure of hypothesis spaces $H_1 \subset H_2 \subset ... \subset H_m$, with ordered "complexity" (i.e. H_{i+1} is more "complex" than H_i). ERM is performed in each of these spaces, and the choice of the final solution can be done using the aforementioned bounds. This principle of performing ERM over a structure (sequence) of nested hypothesis spaces is known as Structural Risk Minimization (SRM) [14].

An important question that arises in SLT is that of measuring the "complexity" of a hypothesis space - which, as we discussed, we need in order to choose the final optimal solution to the learning problem. In [16] quantities measuring this "complexity" of a hypothesis space are discussed, and suggestions for how to measure such quantities experimentally are made. We briefly describe the "complexity" quantities discussed in [16].

The first quantity discussed is a standard one in SLT [14], and is called the VC dimension of a set of functions. This is a combinatorial quantity that characterizes the capacity of the set of functions to shatter a set of points (for more information we refer the reader to the literature). Using the VC dimension of a hypothesis spaces H, the aforementioned distance between empirical and expected errors can be bound as follows:

Theorem 1 [15] If h is the VC-dimension of a hypothesis space H, then   with probability $1-\eta$, the minimum of the expected error that can be achieved with functions from H, say L, and the minimum empirical error, say L_{emp}, satisfy the constraint:

$$L_{emp} - 4\sqrt{2}\sqrt{\frac{h\left(1+\log\left(\frac{2l}{h}\right)\right)-\log\left(\frac{\eta}{4}\right)}{l}} \le L \le L_{emp} + 4\sqrt{2}\sqrt{\frac{h\left(1+\log\left(\frac{2l}{h}\right)\right)-\log\left(\frac{\eta}{4}\right)}{l}}$$

*independent of the distribution of the data P(**x**,y).*

Theorem 1 holds independently of the probability distribution of the data P(**x**,y). In [16] the distribution P(**x**,y) is also taken into account (similar work has already been done in the past - for example see [14] and references therein), and the distance between empirical and expected error is bounded using a "complexity" quantity that takes P(**x**,y) into account. The bounds presented are tighter than that of theorem 1, but require the knowledge of the distribution dependent complexity quantity. The goal of Vayatis and Azencott [16] was to introduce a possible experimental setup to compute the distribution-depended complexity quantity they suggest. To summarize, Vayatis and Azencott [16] discuss the basic theoretical framework in which learning machines such as SVM have been developed, and suggest possible directions of research that can lead to improvements of the theory and so possibly to improvements of SVM (for example the theory can be used to choose the parameters of an SVM, such as the kernel and the regularization parameter C - see below).

We now discuss how SVM emerge from the theoretical framework we outlined.

2.2   Support Vector Machines Formulation

Support Vector machines realize the ideas outlined above. To see why, we need to specify two things: the hypothesis spaces used by SVM, and the loss functions used. The folklore view of SVM is that they find an "optimal" hyperplane as the solution to the learning problem. The simplest formulation of SVM is the linear one, where the hyperplane lies on the space of the input data **x**. In this case the hypothesis space is a subset of all hyperplanes of the form:

$$f(\mathbf{x}) = \mathbf{w}\cdot\mathbf{x} +b.$$

In their most general formulation, SVM find a hyperplane in a space different from that of the input data **x**. It is a hyperplane in a feature space induced by a kernel K (the kernel defines a dot product in that space [18]). Through the kernel K the hypothesis space is defined as a set of "hyperplanes" in the feature space induced by K. This can also be seen as a set of functions in a Reproducing Kernel Hilbert Space (RKHS) defined by K [18], [14]. We do not discuss RKHS here and refer the reader to the literature.

So to summarize, the hypothesis space used by SVM is a subset of the set of hyperplanes defined in some space - an RKHS. This space can be formally written as

$$\left\{ f : \|f\|_K^2 < \infty \right\}$$

where K is the kernel that defines the RKHS, and $\|f\|_K^2$ is the RKHS norm of the function [18]. For example, for the linear case mentioned above, K is the kernel $K(\mathbf{x}_1, \mathbf{x}_2) = \mathbf{x}_1\cdot\mathbf{x}_2$, the functions considered are of the form $f(\mathbf{x}) = \mathbf{w}\cdot\mathbf{x} + b$, and the RKHS norm of these functions is simply the norm of **w**, namely $\|f\|_K^2 = \|\mathbf{w}\|^2$.

In fact SVM consider subsets of this space, namely sets of the form

$$\left\{ f : \|f\|_K^2 \le A^2 \right\}$$

for some constant A. In the SLT framework discussed above, the constant A is used to define a structure of hypothesis spaces (the larger A is, the more complex the hypothesis space is). The goal of SVM is to find the solution with the "optimal" RKHS norm, that is, to find the optimal A.

Instead of searching many hypothesis spaces one by one by performing ERM for each choice of A, SVM search for an A (or the optimal RKHS norm $\|f\|_K^2$) in a different way, as it will become obvious from the SVM formulation presented below. This "search method" for the optimal $\|f\|_K^2$ has been extensively discussed in the literature (see for example [1], [3], [6]), and we do not discuss it here any further.

The second choice is that of the loss function. For this we have to distinguish between SVM classifiers and SVM regressors. For classification ideally the misclassification error needs to be minimized, so a loss function of the form sign(-yf($\mathbf{x}$)) should be used (in classification y takes binary values ±1, and classification is done by taking the sign of function f($\mathbf{x}$)). However because of scaling as well as computational reasons [14], the actual loss function used for SVM classification is |1-yf($\mathbf{x}$)|_+ (that is, 0 if 1-yf($\mathbf{x}$) < 0, and 1-yf($\mathbf{x}$) otherwise). This is also called the "soft margin" loss function because of its standard "margin" interpretation: the points for which the loss function is zero are the ones that have "margin"

$$yf(\mathbf{x})\big/ \|f\|_K^2$$

at least $1\big/\|f\|_K^2$ (that is $1 - yf(\mathbf{x}) \le 0 \Rightarrow yf(\mathbf{x})/\|f\|_K^2 \ge 1/\|f\|_K^2$). The margin is an important geometric quantity associated with SVM classification. For every point (x,y) its margin is its Euclidean distance from the hyperplane, with positive sign if the point is correctly classified by the hyperplane f, and negative sign otherwise. The margin of the hyperplane f is defined to be the distance of the closest correctly classified point from the hyperplane f. For more information we refer the reader to the literature.

For regression the loss function used is the so-called epsilon-insensitive loss function |y-f($\mathbf{x}$)|_ε which is equal to |y-f($\mathbf{x}$)|-ε if |y-f($\mathbf{x}$)| > ε, and 0 otherwise.

To summarize, following the SLT ideas outlined above for the given choices of the loss function and the hypothesis spaces, SVM are learning machines that minimize the empirical error while taking into account the "complexity" of the hypothesis space used by also minimizing the RKHS norm of the solution $\|f\|_K^2$. SVM in practice minimize a trade off between empirical error and complexity of hypothesis space. Formally this is done by solving the following minimization problems:

SVM classification $$\min_f \|f\|_K^2 + C\sum_{i=1}^{l}|1 - y_i f(\mathbf{x}_i)|_+ \tag{1}$$

SVM regression $$\min_f \|f\|_K^2 + C\sum_{i=1}^{l}|y_i - f(\mathbf{x}_i)|_\varepsilon \tag{2}$$

where C is a so called "regularization parameter" that controls the trade off between empirical error and complexity of the hypothesis space used.

Having discussed how SVM stem out of the theory outlined above, we now turn to their actual implementation. The next section briefly discusses how the minimization problems (1) and (2) can be done, taking also into account [13].

2.3   SVM Implementation

As mentioned above, training an SVM means solving problems (1) or (2). It turns out that both problems can be rewritten as constrained quadratic programming (QP) problems. We present the QP formulation for SVM classification, and regarding regression we refer the reader to the literature [14].

Problem (1) can be rewritten as follows:

SV classification:
$$\min_{f,\xi_i} \|f\|_K^2 + C \sum_{i=1}^{l} \xi_i \tag{3}$$

subject to: $y_i f(\mathbf{x}_i) \geq 1 - \xi_i$, for all i, $\xi_i \geq 0$.

Variables ξ_i are called slack variables and they measure the error made at point $(\mathbf{x}_i, y_i)$. We see that the number of constraints is equal to the number of training data, l. Training SVM, that is, solving constrained QP problem (3), becomes quite challenging when the number of training points is large. A number of methods for fast SVM training have been proposed in the literature. Decomposing the QP problem into a number of smaller ones through chunking or decomposition algorithms is one approach suggested (for example see [8], [14]). A sequential optimization method has also recently been proposed [9].

In [13] the approach suggested to solve the QP problem (3) was that of Interior Point Methods (IPM). Trafalis [13] presents an overview of IPM, concentrating on primal-dual optimization methods. These methods consist of solving iteratively the QP problem by moving between the formulation (3) (called the "primal" formulation) and its dual formulation, which can be found to be (see [14], [13]):
SVM classification, Dual formulation:

$$\min_{\alpha_i} \sum_{i=1}^{l} \alpha_i - \frac{1}{2} \sum_{i=1}^{l} \sum_{j=1}^{l} \alpha_i \alpha_j y_i y_j K(\mathbf{x}_i, \mathbf{x}_j) \tag{4}$$

subject to: $0 \leq \alpha_i \leq C$, for all i,

$$\sum_{i=1}^{l} \alpha_i y_i = 0$$

Typically in the literature SVM are trained by solving the dual optimization problem (4) (e.g. [8], [14], [3]). Trafalis [13] proposes primal-dual IPM methods for SVM training which differ from the ones typically used.

In [13] the IPM discussed are also used to train learning machines other than SVM. In particular, Trafalis [13] shows how the proposed primal-dual IPM can be used to train Artificial Neural Networks (ANN) typically trained using backpropagation. One of the main differences between ANN and SVM is that, as mentioned in [13], while for ANN there can be many local optimal solutions, for SVM there is only one optimal solution for problem (3), since SVM are trained by solving a QP problem which has one global optimal solution. This is one practical "advantage" of SVM when compared with ANN.

3   Experiments with SVM and Some Variations

3.1   Application of SVM to Medical Decision Support

Veropoulos et al. [17] proposed an application of SVM classifiers to medical diagnosis of Tuberculosis from photomicrographs of Sputum smears. Except the fact that this is the first time that SVMs are used in a medical problem, another interesting point was the introduction of two methods that can be used for controlling the performance of the system on a particular class of the data (that is, force the SVM to better classify the data from one of the two classes of the classification task). In most medical problems, medical experts must have the ability to put more weight on one of the classes of the problem (usually the class on which the diagnosis is 'heavily' based). Another common problem in a wider area of applications is the presence of unbalanced data sets (the set of examples from one class is significantly larger than the set of examples from the other class). For these reasons, controlling the performance of a system on a particular class of the data is practically very useful. To do so, Veropoulos et al. [17] used a slightly modified version of the standard SVM formulation (3) – the same idea was suggested in [8]. The idea is to use different regularization parameter C for each of the two classes. This translates in the following SVM formulation:

$$\min_{f, \xi_i} \|f\|_K^2 + C_1 \sum_{i \in class_1} \xi_i + C_2 \sum_{i \in class_2} \xi_i \qquad (5)$$

subject to: $y_i f(x_i) \geq 1 - \xi_i$, for all i, $\xi_i \geq 0$.

By changing the ratio C_1/C_2, Veropoulos et al. [17] showed how to influence the performance of the SVM on one of the classes, therefore altering the false negative vs false positive ratio for one of the classes.

A different approach to dealing with the problem of unbalanced data or to putting more weight on one of the classes is also discussed in [17]. This second approach is based on a version of SVM slightly different from the one described above, so we do not discuss it here and refer the reader to [17].

3.2   Time Series Prediction Using Local SVM

An application of SVM regression was discussed in [7]. The problem was time series prediction. The approach taken was the use of SVM regression to model the dynamics of the time series and subsequently predict future values of the series using the constructed model. Instead of using the standard SVM regression formulation described above, a variation developed in [11] was used. Using this variation the ε parameter of the SVM regression loss function (see above) is automatically estimated. Furthermore, Fernandez [7] used an approach to learning which is different from the standard one: instead of developing one global regression model from all the available training data, Fernandez [7] develops a number of SVM regression models, each one trained using only part of the initial training data. The idea, which has been suggested in [2], is to split the initial training data set into parts, each part consisting only of training data that are close to each other (in a Euclidean distance sense). Then a "local" SVM is trained for each subset of the data. The claim in [2] is that such an approach can lead to a number of simple (low complexity, in the SLT sense outlined above) learning machines, instead of a single machine that is required to fit all data.

In [7] each of the individual SVM machines had its ε parameter estimated independently. The ε parameter of the SVM loss function is known to be related to the noise of the data [10]. So, in a sense, the approach of Fernandez [7] leads to local SVMs each having an ε parameter that depends on the noise of the data in particular regions of the space (instead of a single ε that needs to "model" the noise of all the data).

The experiments described in [7] show that training many local SVMs instead of one global learning machine leads to significant improvements in performance. In fact, this was also the finding of [2] who first showed experiments with local learning machines.

3.3   An Application of SVM to Face Authentication

Starting from Fisher Linear Discriminant (FLT) [5], [12] develop variations of this standard classification method, and compare them with SVM classification. In [12] ideas behind the formulation of FLT are used to, effectively, choose a kernel for SVM classification. We briefly review FLT, and we then show the SVM used in [12].

Given data from two classes, FLT leads to a hyperplane separating the two classes using the following criterion: the projections of the data on the hyperplane are such that the between-class variance of the projections is maximized, while the within-class variance is minimized [5]. If $\mathbf{m}_1$ and $\mathbf{m}_2$ are the means of the two classes, and S_b and S_w are the between-class and within class scatter matrices, then FLT yields the hyperplane $\mathbf{w}$ that maximizes the so called Fisher discriminant ratio $\mathbf{w}^T S_b \mathbf{w} / \mathbf{w}^T S_w \mathbf{w}$.

In [12] the solution $\mathbf{w}^{FLT}$ of FLT is also shown to be the optimal solution of a constrained QP optimization problem. It is noted in [12] that SVM are also formulated as constrained QP problems (as we discussed in the previous section), and a comparison between the SVM formulation with the one yielding $\mathbf{w}^{FLT}$ is made.

Furthermore, Tefas et al [12] use the idea of FLT of maximizing the within class variance in order to design a kernel K for SVM classification. To see how this is done, we state again the SVM formulation for linear kernels, in which case, as discussed above, the RKHS norm of the functions $f(\mathbf{x}) = \mathbf{w} \cdot \mathbf{x} + f$ is simply $\|\mathbf{w}\|^2$. In this case SVM is formulated as:

SV linear classification $\min\limits_{\mathbf{w},\xi_i} \|\mathbf{w}\|^2 + C \sum\limits_{i=1}^{l} \xi_i$

subject to: $y_i(\mathbf{w} \cdot \mathbf{x}_i + b) \geq 1 - \xi_i$, for all i, $\xi_i \geq 0$.

Instead of using this linear SVM machine, Tefas et al. [12] use the following machine:

SV classification with "FLT" kernel: $\min\limits_{\mathbf{w},\xi_i} \mathbf{w}^T S_w \mathbf{w} + C \sum\limits_{i=1}^{l} \xi_i$ (6)

subject to: $y_i(\mathbf{w} \cdot \mathbf{x}_i + b) \geq 1 - \xi_i$, for all i, $\xi_i \geq 0$.

It turns out that Tefas et al. [12] use an SVM classifier with kernel $K(\mathbf{x}_1, \mathbf{x}_2) = \mathbf{x}_1^T S_w^{-1} \mathbf{x}_2$ (this can be seen through the dual formulation of problem (6)). In [12] the "FLT kernel" SVM was compared with the standard linear SVM for the task of face recognition from images. They show that the "FLT" SVM outperforms the standard SVM. On the other hand, they mention than using non-liner SVMs they can further improve performance.

4   Conclusions

The chapter presented an overview of the theory of SVM in parallel with a summary of the papers presented in the ACAI '99 workshop on "Support Vector Machines: theory and applications". Some of the important conclusions of this chapter as well as of the workshop are summarized below:

1. SVM are motivated through statistical learning theory. The theory characterizes the performance of learning machines using bounds on their ability to predict future data. One of the papers in the workshop [16] presented new bounds on the performance of learning machines, and suggested a method to use them experimentally in order to better understand the learning machines (including SVM).
2. SVM are trained by solving a constrained quadratic optimization problem. Among others, this implies that there is a unique optimal solution for each choice of the SVM parameters. This is unlike other learning machines, such as standard Neural Networks trained using backpropagation.
3. Primal dual interior point optimization methods may be used to efficiently train SVM with large data sets, as described in [13].
4. Training many local SVMs instead of a single global one can lead to significant improvement in the performance of a learning machine, as shown in [7].
5. SVM has been successfully used for medical diagnosis [17]. Methods for dealing with unbalanced training data, or for biasing the performance of an SVM towards one of the classes during classification were suggested and used in [17].
6. An SVM using a kernel motivated from Fisher Linear Discriminant was shown to outperform the standard linear SVM for a face recognition task in [12].

The ideas presented in the papers and discussed in the workshop suggest a number of future research directions: from tuning the basic statistical learning theory results, to developing efficient training methods for SVM, to designing variations of the standard SVM for practical usage. Some of the main issues regarding the design and use of SVMs are, among others, the choice of the kernel of the SVM (as Tefas et al. [12] showed), and the choice of the regularization parameter (as Veropoulos et al. [17] discussed). On the other hand, significant improvements in the performance of SVM may be achieved if ensembles of SVMs are used (like in [7]).

Acknowledgements. The authors would like to thank the organizers of ACAI '99, and the co-organizers of the workshop: Constantine Papageorgiou, Tomaso Poggio, and Ioannis Pitas.

References

1. Bartlett P. and Shawe-Taylor J., "Generalization performance of support vector machine and other pattern classifiers", In C.~Burges B.~Scholkopf, editor, "Advances in Kernel Methods-Support Vector Learning", pp. 43-55, MIT press, 1998.
2. Bottou L. and Vapnik V., "Local learning algorithms", Neural Computation, 4(6): 888-900, November 1992.
3. Burges C., "A tutorial on support vector machines for pattern recognition", In "Data Mining and Knowledge Discovery". Kluwer Academic Publishers, Boston, 1998, (Vol. 2), pp. 1-43.
4. Cortes C. and Vapnik V., "Support vector networks", Machine Learning, 20:1-25, 1995.
5. Duda R. and Hart P., "Pattern Classification and Scene Analysis", Wiley, New York 1973.
6. Evgeniou T., Pontil M., and Poggio T., "A unified framework for regularization networks and support vector machines" A.I. Memo No. 1654, AI Laboratory, MIT, 1999.
7. Fernandez R., "Predicting time series with a local support vector regression machine", In [19].
8. Osuna E., Freund R., and Girosi F., "Support Vector Machines: Training and Applications", A.I. Memo No. 1602, Artificial Intelligence Laboratory, MIT, 1997.
9. Platt J., "Fast training of Support Vector Machines using sequential minimal optimization", In C. Burges and B. Scholkopf, editor, "Advances in Kernel Methods-Support Vector Learning", pp.185-208, MIT press, 1998.
10. Pontil M., Mukherjee S., and Girosi F., "On the noise model of Support Vector Machine regression" A.I. Memo 1651, MIT Artificial Intelligence Laboratory, 1998.
11. B. Scholkopf, P. Bartlett, A. Smola, and R. Williamson. Support vector regression with automatic accuracy control. In L. Niklasson, M. Boden, and T. Ziemke, editors, Proceedings of ICANN'98, Perspectives in Neural Computing, pages 111-116, Berlin, 1998.
12. Tefas A., Kotropoulos C., and Pitas I., "Enhancing the performance of elastic graph matching for face authentications by using Support Vector Machines", In [19].
13. Trafalis T., "Primal-dual optimization methods in neural networks and support vector machines training", In [19].
14. Vapnik V., "Statistical Learning Theory", Wiley, New York, 1998.
15. Vapnik V. and Chervonenkis A., "On the uniform convergence of relative frequencies of events to their probabilities", in "Th. Prob. and its Applications", 17(2): 264-280, 1971.
16. Vayatis N. and Azencott R., "How to estimate the Vapnik-Chervonenkis Dimension of Support Vector Machines through simulations", In [19].
17. Veropoulos K., Cristianini N., and Campbell C., "The Application of Support Vector Machines to Medical Decision Support: A Case Study", In [19].
18. Wahba G., "Splines Models for Observational Data", Series in Applied Mathematics, Vol. 59, SIAM.
19. Proceedings of the Workshop on Support Vector Machines Theory and Applications, Advanced Course on Artificial Intelligence (ACAI '99), Chania, Greece, 1999 (http://www.iit.demokritos.gr/skel/eetn/acai99/Workshops.htm).

Pre- and Post-processing in Machine Learning and Data Mining

Ivan Bruha

McMaster University, Dept. Computing & Software, Hamilton, Ont., Canada L8S4L7
bruha@mcmaster.ca

1 Introduction: Knowledge Discovery and Machine Learning

Knowledge discovery in databases (KDD) has become a very attractive discipline both for research and industry within the last few years. Its goal is to extract "pieces" of knowledge or "patterns" from usually very large databases. It portrays a robust sequence of procedures or steps that have to be carried out so as to derive reasonable and understandable results. One of its components is the process which induces the above "pieces" of knowledge; usually this is a *machine learning (ML)* algorithm. However, most of the machine learning algorithms require perfect data in a specific format. The data that are to be processed by a knowledge acquisition (inductive) algorithm are usually noisy and often inconsistent. Many steps are involved before the actual data analysis starts. Moreover, many ML systems do not easily allow processing of numerical attributes as well as numerical (continuous) classes. Therefore, certain procedures have to precede the actual data analysis process. Next, a result of an ML algorithm, such as a decision tree, a set of decision rules, or weights and topology of a neural net, may not be appropriate from the view of custom or commercial applications. As a result, a concept description (model, knowledge base) produced by an inductive process has to be usually postprocessed. Postprocessing procedures usually include various pruning routines, rule quality processing, rule filtering, rule combination, model combination, or even knowledge integration. All these procedures provide a kind of symbolic filter for noisy, imprecise, or non-user-friendly knowledge derived by an inductive algorithm. Therefore, some *preprocessing* routines as well as *postprocessing* ones should fill up the entire chain of data processing. The pre- and post-processing tools always help to investigate databases as well as to refine the acquired knowledge. Usually, these tools exploit techniques that are not genuinely symbolic/logical, e.g., statistics, neural nets, and others.

Historically, different names have been used for the process of extracting useful knowledge from databases, e.g., knowledge extraction, data analysis, information discovery, knowledge discovery in databases, data mining. Especially the last term is used quite often and its connection to knowledge discovery is discussed at many papers and conferences. Some researchers claim that data mining is a subset of KDD (see e.g. [12]), others declare that it is the opposite way [20]. In this survey we use the first interpretation.

Research in knowledge discovery is supposed to develop methods and techniques to process large databases in order to acquire knowledge (which is "hidden" in these databases) that is compact, more or less abstract, but understandable, and useful for

G. Paliouras, V. Karkaletsis, and C.D. Spyropoulos (Eds.): ACAI '99, LNAI 2049, pp. 258-266, 2001.
© Springer-Verlag Berlin Heidelberg 2001

further applications. Agrawal and Psaila [1] define knowledge discovery as a nontrivial process of identifying valid, novel, and ultimately understandable knowledge in data.

In our understanding, knowledge discovery refers to the overall process of determining useful knowledge from databases, i.e. extracting high-level knowledge from low-level data in the context of large databases. Knowledge discovery can be viewed as a multidisciplinary activity because it exploits several research disciplines of artificial intelligence such as machine learning, pattern recognition, expert systems, knowledge acquisition, as well as mathematical disciplines such as statistics, theory of information, uncertainty processing.

The input to a knowledge discovery process is a *database*, i.e. a collection (a set) of objects. An *object* (also called *case, event, evidence, fact, instance, manifestation, record, observation, statement*) is a unit of the given problem. A formal description of an object is then formed by a suitable collection of so-called elementary descriptions. They can be of either quantitative (numerical) or qualitative (symbolic) character. Their collections can be of various forms, too, e.g. numerical vectors, lists of attribute values, strings, graphs, ground facts.

The output of the knowledge discovery process is a collection of "pieces" of knowledge "dug" from a database. They should exhibit a high-level description in a particular language. Such a *knowledge base* (*model, concept description*) is usually represented by a set of production (decision) rules, decision trees, collection of prototypes (representative exemplars), etc.

The entire chain of knowledge discovery consists of the following steps:

1. *Selecting the problem area.* Prior to any processing, we first have to find and specify an application domain, and to identify the goal of the knowledge discovery process from the customer's viewpoint. Also, we need to choose a suitable representation for this goal.

2. *Collecting the data.* Next, we have to choose the object representation and collect data as formally represented objects. If a domain expert is available, then he/she could suggest what fields (attributes, features) are the most informative. If not, then the simplest method is a 'brute-force' which indicates that we measure everything available and only hope that the right (informative, relevant) attributes are among them.

3. *Preprocessing of the data.* A data set collected by the 'brute-force' method or by following advices of a domain expert is not directly suitable for induction (knowledge acquisition); it comprises in most cases noise and missing values, the data are not consistent, the data set is too large, there are too many attributes that describe each object of the database and so on. Therefore, we need to minimize the noise in the data, and choose a strategy for handling missing (unknown) attribute values. Also, we should use any suitable method for selecting and ordering attributes (features) according to their informativity. In this step, we also discretize and/or fuzzify numerical (continuous) attributes, and eventually, process continuous classes.

4. *Data mining: Extracting pieces of knowledge.* Now, we reach the stage of selecting a paradigm for extracting pieces of knowledge (e.g., statistical methods, neural net approach, symbolic/logical learning, genetic algorithms). First, we have to realize that there is no optimal algorithm which would be able to process correctly any database.

Second, we are to follow the criteria of the end-user; e.g., he/she might be more interested in understanding the model extracted rather than its predictive capabilities. Afterwards, we apply the selected algorithm and derive (extract) new knowledge.

5. *Postprocessing of the knowledge derived.* The pieces of knowledge extracted in the previous step could be further processed. One option is to simplify the extracted knowledge. Also, we can evaluate the extracted knowledge, visualize it, or merely document it for the end user. They are various techniques to do that. Next, we may interpret the knowledge and incorporate it into an existing system, and check for potential conflicts with previously induced knowledge.

It is worth mentioning here that we may return from any step of the knowledge discovery process to any previous step and change our decisions. Thus, this process involves significant iteration and represents a time-consuming mechanism with many loops. Most previous work has been done in step 4. However, the other steps are also important for the successful application of knowledge discovery in practice.

2   Description of Workshop Papers

This section presents an overview of the papers presented during the workshop on "Pre- and Post-Processing in Machine Learning and Data Mining" organized as part of the Advanced Course on Artificial Intelligence (ACAI '99) [23].

The survey paper by Bruha [5] focuses on collecting and preprocessing the data, and postprocessing the extracted knowledge. It describes in detail all the essential steps for each of the three processes. The paper was motivated by several other papers, among them [1], [3], [12]. Here we will only introduce in brief the steps of collecting and preprocessing the data, and postprocessing extracted knowledge.

Collecting and Preprocessing of Data

1. *Choosing the object representation.* The input to a knowledge discovery process is a database, i.e. a set of objects. An object as a unit of the given problem must be formally described by a collection of elementary descriptions. Therefore, we have to choose the appropriate object representation. The most common choice is the attribute representation of objects. Elementary properties, called *attributes*, are selected on actual objects. An object is thus represented by a list of attributes and their values. Each attribute has its domain of possible values. Depending on the organization of the attribute's domain, we distinguish three basic types of attributes: symbolic (discrete, nominal, categorial), continuous (numerical), and structured.

2. *Mapping and collecting data.* After selecting a proper representation, we choose the attributes to be measured on objects (either following a suggestion of a domain expert or using the 'brute-force' method). Also, we have to determine the attribute names and the names of their values. The data collected are thus mapped into a single naming convention and uniformly represented.

3. *Scaling large datasets.* Practically all learning algorithms assume that data are in the main memory and pay no attention to how the algorithm could deal with extremely large databases when only a limited number of data can be viewed. There are several possibilities of solving this problem, e.g. windowing, batch-incremental mode.

4. *Handling noise and errors.* There are generally two sources of error. *External* errors are introduced from the world outside the system itself (random errors and noise, an imperfect teacher, etc.). *Internal* errors are caused by poor properties of the learning (data mining) system itself, e.g. poor search heuristics or preference criteria.

5. *Processing unknown attribute values.* When processing real-world data, one important aspect in particular is the processing of *unknown* (*missing*) attribute values. This topic has been discussed and analyzed by several researchers in the field of machine learning; see e.g. [18], [8], [6]. There are a few important factors to be taken into account when processing unknown attribute values. One of the most important ones is the *source of 'unknownness'*: (i) a value is *missing* because it was forgotten or lost; (ii) a certain attribute is *not applicable* for a given object, e.g., it does not exist for a given object; (iii) an attribute value is *irrelevant* in a given context; (iv) for a given observation, the designer of a training database does not care about the value of a certain attribute (so-called *dont-care* value).

6. *Discretization/fuzzification of numerical attributes.* The symbolic, logical learning algorithms are able to process symbolic, categorial data only. However, real-world problems involve both symbolic and numerical attributes. Therefore, there is an important issue to discretize numerical (continuous) attributes. It could be performed either off-line (preprocessor) or on-line (dynamic discretization). A natural extension of this procedure is fuzzification of numerical attributes.

7. *Processing of continuous classes.* Similar problem to the above issue is processing of continuous classes. Most inductive symbolic algorithms require discretized (symbolic) classes. In some applications, however, we are faced by continuous (numerical) classes. Similarly to the problem above, there are two approaches: either off-line or on-line splitting.

8. *Grouping of values of symbolic attributes.* It is a known problem that attributes with too many values are overestimated in the process of selecting the most informative attributes, both for inducing decision trees and for deriving decision rules. To overcome this overestimation problem, the values of multivalued attributes can be grouped into two or more subsets.

9. *Attribute selection and ordering.* We cannot be definitely sure that all attributes are informative for the given target. In real-world data, the representation of data often uses too many attributes, but only a few of them may be related to the target concept. Attribute selection and ordering procedures help to solve the above problem. They order the set of input attributes according to their informativity, and then select a relatively small subset of the most informative attributes.

10. *Attribute construction and transformation.* As we stated earlier, finding suitable attributes for problem representation could be a difficult and time-consuming task. If the attributes are inappropriate for the target concept, data mining (learning) could be difficult or impossible. To overcome this problem a system needs to be capable

of generating (constructing) new appropriate attributes. There are two different methods for doing that: attribute construction and attribute transformation.

11. *Consistency checking.* As for inconsistency in a database, it may not be eliminated by the previous steps of preprocessing. There are two general approaches to handle inconsistency in the data. The first one is done 'off-line', i.e. by a preprocessor or within the data mining process itself. Another possibility is to utilize the loop facility of the knowledge discovery process, i.e. to return to one of the previous steps and perform it again for different parameters.

Postprocessing

1. *Knowledge filtering: Rule truncation and postpruning.* If the training data is noisy then the learning algorithm generates leaves of a decision tree or decision rules that cover a very small number of training objects. This happens because the learning algorithm tries to split subsets of training objects to even smaller subsets that would be genuinely consistent. To overcome this problem a tree or a decision rule set must be shrunk, by either postpruning (decision trees) or truncation (decision rules).

2. *Interpretation and explanation.* Now, we may use the acquired knowledge directly for prediction or in an expert system shell as a knowledge base. If the knowledge discovery process is performed for an end-user, we usually document the derived results. Another possibility is to visualize the knowledge, or to transform it to an understandable form for the user-end. Also, we may check the new knowledge for potential conflicts with previously induced knowledge. In this step, we can also summarize the rules and combine them with a domain-specific knowledge provided for the given task.

3. *Evaluation.* After a learning system induces concept hypotheses (models) from the training set, their evaluation (or testing) should take place. There are several widely used criteria for this purpose: classification accuracy, comprehensibility, computational complexity, and so on.

4. *Knowledge integration.* The traditional decision-making systems have been dependant on a single technique, strategy, model. New sophisticated decision-supporting systems combine or refine results obtained from several models, produced usually by different methods. This process increases accuracy and successfulness.

The paper by Brijs et al. [4] deals with large sets of decision rules discovered during the mining process. Control of a large set of decision rules is extremely costly and difficult. Moreover, a set of rules is usually incomplete, i.e., some objects (instances) are not covered by any rule, and the rules are mutually inclusive, i.e., some objects may be covered by more than one rule. Therefore, the authors propose a postprocessing, knowledge-filtering procedure to solve the problem of selecting the most promising subset of decision (characteristic) rules. Their method also influences the pruning process in a sense that some overall measure of quality of the reduced decision set can be produced. In fact, it allows controlling a user-defined level of overall quality of the model in combination with a maximum reduction of the redundancy in the original decision set.

The paper discusses two integer-programming (IP) techniques developed by the authors, namely the *"Maximum redundancy reduction"* technique and the *"Incorporating noise and discriminant power"* one. The first technique searches for an optimal selection of rules that is able to maximally reduce redundancy under the constraint of covering all positive objects (instances) that are covered by the original set of rules. In the latter technique, the first technique has been adapted to account for noise in the data and to impose a quality criterion on the final set of decision rules. Both techniques have been empirically tested on real-world data and compared with the well-known *RuleCover* heuristic [22] as a method for redundancy reduction. It has been found that the integer-programming techniques are able to produce significantly better results than the RuleCover heuristic; in terms of the number of rules that remain in the final set of rules, in terms of the discriminant power of the final set of rules, and also in terms of the total redundancy.

The paper by Kalles and Papagelis [14] introduces a project on discretization of numerical attributes (as a preprocessor) for decision-tree induction. The authors prefer descriptions that make the grouping of objects easier rather than those that allow fuzzification. This bias can be captured by the observation that entropy gain is maximized at the class boundaries for numerical attributes [11]. The method splits the range of each numerical attribute to a small number of non-overlapping intervals; each interval is assigned to a bucket. Then the buckets are merged utilizing the χ^2 metric, which leads to a simple prepruning technique. The experiments on various datasets have revealed that the greater the confidence level that is required, the better the classification occurrence is achieved. The only drawback is the size of a decision tree constructed using this method for handling numerical attributes. On the other hand, an interesting aspect of the method is that it naturally paves the way for deploying more effective postprocessing schemes. The authors investigated the postprocessing technique for character recognition setting.

The paper by Kontkanen et al. [15] utilizes Bayesian networks for visualization as an important step in postprocessing for visual inspection of the rationality of the learned models (classifiers, knowledge bases). The authors have designed a model-based visualization scheme which utilizes a Bayesian network representing the problem domain probability distribution, and producing two- or three-dimensional (2D or 3D) images of the problem domain. To display high-dimensional data on a 2D or 3D device, each data vector has to be provided with the corresponding 2D or 3D coordinates that determine its visual location. The traditional statistical data analysis provides so-called multidimensional scaling [10]. The authors of the paper have developed a model-based visualization scheme with the motto 'Two vectors are considered similar if they lead to similar predictions'. This idea follows from a Bayesian distance metric [16].

The authors also discuss methods for validating the goodness of different visualizations, and suggest a simple scheme based on estimating the prediction accuracy that can be obtained by using reduced, low-dimensional data. Experiments have been performed on UCI benchmark databases. Examples of the 2D visualizations for some databases demonstrate that the proposed scheme produces visualizations that are much better (with respect to the validation scheme suggested) than those obtained by classical Euclidean multidimensional scaling.

The paper by Kralik and Bruha [17] introduces an off-line discretization procedure (as a preprocessor) for genetic learning algorithms. The genetic algorithms are usually developed in such a way that they are capable of processing symbolic data only, not continuous ones. There exist quite a few discretization procedures in the machine learning field. The paper introduces a version of a new algorithm for discretization of continuous attributes [2], which has been applied to a learning system based on genetic algorithms.

The induction stage of a learning process consists in searching usually a huge space of possible concept descriptions. There exist several paradigms on how to control this search. One of the promising and efficient paradigms is genetic algorithms. Several approaches have been proposed concerning the application of genetic algorithms to learning. The paper describes an efficient composite of the discretization preprocessor and a genetic algorithm in an attribute-based rule-inducing ML algorithm. Actually, a domain-independent genetic algorithm has been incorporated into the covering machine learning algorithm CN4 [7], a large extension of the well-known algorithm CN2. The induction procedure of CN4 (beam search methodology) has been replaced by the genetic algorithm.

The paper by Smid et al. [19] deals with the attribute selection problem. Modelling an input response system is an immense problem of great complexity. A good model typically requires insight from an engineer or a scientist. With the World Wide Web (WWW), engineers and scientists can use data mining techniques to understand better patterns and relationships among data. The authors discuss the selection of significant (informative) attributes. The set of input attributes sometimes is not sufficient and new attributes have to be derived (constructed). The project designed by the authors employs visual analysis [9] for discovering new attributes (in addition to the set of the input attributes). The set of new attributes also includes operators such as standard deviation, difference, delay. The authors utilize WebGraph, a data visualization and analysis tool. WebGraph provides algorithms and functions that allow users to preview patterns in selected data sets. The users need to use only a standard web browser. Two case studies are presented to demonstrate the use of the system for building an efficient model.

The paper by Talavera [21] presents an unsupervised feature (attribute) selection method aimed to reduce the dimensionality of a symbolic database prior to a clustering process. The author's method is based on the assumption that features which are not correlated with other features in the database are likely to be irrelevant. The author has applied a feature dependency measure proposed by [13]. Feature selection is viewed as a heuristic search in a feature space in which several characteristics such as an evaluation function, stopping criterion, or a generation procedure has to be determined. The author's method represents a greedy search that only performs one step at a time in the feature space to select the final feature set. In his experiments the author has utilized COBWEB, the well-known symbolic probabilistic clustering algorithm. The method has been evaluated on UCI databases. Despite a close relationship of the dependency measure used to rank the importance of features and the clustering system employed in the experiments, the method developed can be applied to any symbolic clustering algorithm. The experiments have demonstrated evidence that the dependency measure can identify completely irrelevant features. Thus, removal of these features should improve the performance of various clustering algorithms.

3   Conclusion

The discussion that followed the presentation of the papers first focused on the specification of the fields and methodologies of KDD. The conclusion of the discussion was that there are two main streams in KDD, namely: methodology and applications. In both streams, the following issues arise:

- selection of a problem and its representation;
- selection of a description language;
- data collection;
- data preprocessing (discretization, grouping, attribute selection, construction of new attributes, etc.);
- knowledge extracting;
- postprocessing the knowledge base (rule filtering, rule quality, etc.);
- evaluation, interpretation, visualization, combination, etc. of the derived knowledge.

The results of the fruitful discussion could be summarized as follows:

- There is work that combines the above mentioned streams in KDD, i.e. methodology and real-world applications. However, there is a 'gap' of terminology between these two streams. Methodologists use traditional terms common in KDD and ML. On the other hand, the specialists who apply KDD and ML methods to real problem use terminology common for the given discipline (medicine, financing, insurance, car manufacturing, etc.) which, however, is not understandable to KDD specialists.
- Preprocessing is a favourite topic in KDD, in contrast to postprocessing. There is much more work on preprocessing than on postprocessing. There are many algorithms for 'attribute mining', but only a few for postprocessing. Nevertheless, the visual interpretation and evaluation is now getting a great spirit in the field of KDD.
- Knowledge integration (i.e., model combination, merging, and modification) should not concentrate solely on boosting and bagging.
- Last but not least, a question arose about the difference between machine learning (ML) and data mining (DM). The general consensus was that ML and DM overlap and one is to observe ML as a *scientific* discipline, whereas DM as an *engineering* one.

References

1. R. Agrawal and G. Psaila: *Active data mining.* 1st International Conference on Knowledge Discovery and Data Mining, Menlo Park, Calif. (1995), 3-8
2. P. Berka, I. Bruha: *Empirical comparison of various discretization procedures.* International Journal of Pattern Recognition and Artificial Intelligence, 12, 7 (1998), 1017-1032
3. P. Brazdil and P. Clark: *Learning from imperfect data.* In: P. Brazdil, K. Konolige (eds.): Machine Learning, Meta-Reasoning, and Logics, Kluwer (1990), 207-232
4. T. Brijs, K. Vanhoof, G. Wets: Reducing redundancy in characteristic rule discovery by using IP-techniques. In [23]

5. Bruha: From machine learning to knowledge discovery: Preprocessing and postprocessing. In [23]
6. Bruha and F. Franek: *Comparison of various routines for unknown attribute value processing: covering paradigm*. International Journal of Pattern Recognition and Artificial Intelligence, 10, 8 (1996), 939-955
7. Bruha, S. Kockova: *A support for decision making: cost-sensitive learning system*, Artificial Intelligence in Medicine, 6 (1994), 67-82
8. B. Cestnik, I. Kononenko, I. Bratko: *ASSISTANT 86: a knowledge-elicitation tool for sophisticated users*. In: I. Bratko and N. Lavrac (eds.): Progress in Machine Learning: EWSL'87, Sigma Press (1987)
9. K. Cox, S. Eick, G. Wills: *Visual data mining: recognizing telephone calling fraud*. Data Mining and Knowledge Discovery, 1, 2 (1997)
10. R. Duda, P. Hart: *Pattern classification and scene analysis*. John Wiley (1973)
11. U. Fayyad, K.B. Irani: *On the handling of continuous-valued attributes on decision tree generation*. Machine Learning, 8 (1992), 87-102
12. U. Fayyad, G. Piatetsky-Shapiro, P. Smyth: *From data mining to knowledge discovery in databases*. Artificial Intelligence Magazine (1996), 37-53
13. D.H. Fisher: *Knowledge acquisition via incremental conceptual clustering*. Machine Learning, 2 (1987), 139-172
14. D. Kalles, A. Papagelis: Induction of decision trees in numeric domains using set-valued attributes. In [23]
15. P. Kontkanen, J. Lahtinen, P. Myllymaki, T. Silander, H. Tirri: Using Bayesian networks for visualizing high-dimensional data. In [23]
16. P. Kontkanen et al.: *On Bayesian case matching*. In: B. Smyth, P. Cunningham (eds.): Advances in Case-based Reasoning, EWCBR-98, Springer-Verlag (1998), 13-24
17. P. Kralik, I. Bruha: Discretizing numerical attributes in a genetic attribute-based learning algorithm. In [23]
18. J.R. Quinlan: *Unknown attribute values in ID3*. International Conference ML (1989), 164-168
19. J. Smid, P. Svacek, P. Volf, E. Levine, L. Kurz, I. Glucksmann, M. Smid: Web based data analysis tools. In [23]
20. P. Stolorz et al.: *Fast spatio-temporal data mining of large geophysical datasets*. 1st International Conference on Knowledge Discovery and Data Mining, Menlo Park, Calif. (1995), 300-305
21. L. Talavera: Dependency-based dimensionality reduction for clustering symbolic data. In [23]
22. H. Toivonen et al.: *Pruning and grouping of discovered association rules*. ECML-99, Workshop Statistics, Machine Learning, and Discovery in Databases, Heraclion, Greece (1995)
23. Proceedings of the Workshop on Pre- and Post-Processing in Machine Learning and Data Mining, Advanced Course on Artificial Intelligence (ACAI '99), Chania, Greece, 1999 (http://www.iit.demokritos.gr/skel/eetn/acai99/Workshops.htm).

Machine Learning in Human Language Technology

Nikos D. Fakotakis and Kyriakos N. Sgarbas

Wire Communications Laboratory, Electrical and Computer Engineering Department,
University of Patras, GR-265 00 Rio, Greece
{fakotaki,sgarbas}@wcl.ee.upatras.gr

1 Introduction

The undoubted usefulness of present-day information systems is only moderated by the fact that people have to invest substantial effort and training time in order to learn how to use them. Even modern applications with Graphical-User Interfaces (which are considered user-friendly), built-in wizards and on-line context-sensitive help, require a considerable self-training period, thus discouraging most people from fully exploiting their capabilities. In the years to come we expect that information systems will gradually become more and more complex and since the training period is usually proportional to the system complexity, with the usual Human Computer Interaction methods less and less people will have the time to learn how to use a new piece of software.

The obvious solution to the aforementioned problem is to make the Human Computer Interface intelligent enough to understand human language. That is one vital objective of Human Language Technology (HLT). HLT is an emerging field, which is expected not only to facilitate future applications as the natural improvement of today's Graphical User Interfaces, but also to provide applications of significant importance like machine translation systems and tele-services. HLT will enable casual, not technically inclined users to benefit from modern information technology. HLT will also enable the retrieval of information from resources, which are not organized for computer access, like newspapers and audio recordings.

HLT is further subdivided into Speech Processing (SP) and Natural Language Processing (NLP). SP covers all tasks concerning spoken language input and output, including speech recognition and synthesis, signal representation, speaker identification/verification and several performance issues, like robustness, adaptation and real-time response. NLP covers grammars and parsing techniques, lexicon representations, syntax, semantics and dialogues. The two areas (SP and NLP) are generally complementary to each other although some "gray areas" do exist, in which overlaps occur frequently, e.g. SP systems may have a language model independent of any NLP module that may follow, or NLP systems may consider phonetic transcriptions in order to become more versatile.

HLT is an intriguing field of research where some very interesting problems arise; problems that researchers in the Machine Learning (ML) field would like to try solving using their own methods. In fact, HLT researchers already use some well known machine learning techniques like hidden Markov models (HMMs), neural

G. Paliouras, V. Karkaletsis, and C.D. Spyropoulos (Eds.): ACAI ' 99, LNAI 2049, pp. 267-273, 2001.
© Springer-Verlag Berlin Heidelberg 2001

networks (NNs), probabilistic context-free grammars (PCFGs), etc., although they prefer the term "training" instead of "learning" to denote the adaptation of their systems. But most of the HLT systems, especially in the NLP area, are built by handcrafted rules derived from linguistic theories and syntax textbooks. There is nothing wrong about that of course, especially if the systems perform acceptably in practice, except that systems produced by this method are highly language dependent and very likely application dependent too. Considering the time and effort needed to build such systems for several languages and different applications, the need of language independent and application independent methods of language representation becomes imperative. Thus one of the most promising subfields of NLP is the so-called "corpus-based NLP" which aims to extract lexicons, linguistic rules and related knowledge from large text corpora automatically, usually by statistic methods.

We believe that if the communication between the HLT community and the ML community becomes stronger, then even more sophisticated ML methods will be applied to HLT systems and new ML techniques will be devised having the HLT requirements in mind. The use and evaluation of existing and innovative machine learning techniques in the field of HLT will affect significantly the overall performance of HLT systems and will indicate new directions for research and development. The ML field is mature enough to provide solutions and methodologies from which an emerging technology like HLT will certainly benefit. Fortunately, the scientific community has realized the importance of the cooperation between ML and HLT [8]. It remains to see to what extent these two fields can cooperate and what promises lie towards this direction.

This chapter stresses the importance for cooperation in research between the field of Machine Learning and the field of Human Language Technology, arguing that this cooperation can be of benefit to both scientific areas in terms of trends, aims and methods used. This argument is backed up by the results of the *Workshop on Machine Learning in Human Language Technology* (held on July 7-8, 1999, Chania, Greece, in the framework of ACAI '99), by introducing the papers presented in the Workshop and pointing out how these papers advance the research status of both fields.

2   Brief History

Although ML-oriented ideas like training the system to a set of rules (grammar) have been researched quite early in the SP field (see for example [1]), analogous attempts in NLP have flourished mostly in the nineties with a renewed interest towards corpus-based research, after the rule-based techniques used so far proved inefficient to confront real-world texts [3]. The new techniques were first applied as enhancements to rule-based methods (like [17]) thus producing hybrid components, and later were applied as stand-alone methods with satisfactory robust results. The applied ML-techniques varied from statistical/probabilistic methods [9], [23] to transformation-based learning [5] and n-gram models [7]. The good news with the statistical/corpus-based/ML methods was that they were mainly language independent [11], robust [4] and application independent [6]. The new techniques have also indicated new interesting directions for research, for example adaptation of existing systems to different domains [26]. For a thorough historic review on the subject see [21], [12] and [10].

3   The ACAI '99 Workshop on ML in HLT

The *Workshop on Machine Learning in Human Language Technology* was intended to promote the cooperation between the two scientific fields. The Workshop was held on July 7-8, 1999, at Chania, Greece, in the framework of the ECCAI Advanced Course on Artificial Intelligence for 1999 (ACAI '99), whose goal was to present the current state-of-the-art in Machine Learning, and to show the potential of Machine Learning in a variety of problems. The aim of the Workshop was the presentation of the current Machine Learning research activities in the area of Human Language Technology (i.e. Written and Spoken Language Recognition, Understanding, Generation, etc.).

The papers presented in the Workshop [27] addressed several HLT issues, like *Part-of-Speech Tagging, Word Sense Disambiguation, Unknown Word Acquisition, Sentence Boundary Disambiguation, etc.*, using a wide range of ML techniques, like *Decision Tree Induction, Transformation-Based Learning, Self-Organization, Memory-Based Learning, etc.* Descriptions of these papers are presented in the following section.

4   Overview of the Papers

The invited talk by Kodratoff [14] examined the potential of Knowledge Discovery in Texts (KDT) as a new scientific topic emerging from Knowledge Discovery in Databases (KDD or Data Mining, as often called). The author compared KDT with classical Natural Language Processing (NLP) and explained the different nature of the KDT-extracted knowledge arguing that the knowledge obtained by KDT, since it is extracted from a large number of texts, constitutes an absolutely new type of knowledge, often complementary to the knowledge obtained by NLP. The author provided a detailed example which presented the different types of knowledge that the NLP system TROPES and the KDD system CLEMENTINE extract from the same text corpus. Since Data Mining is an always-hot topic with a very broad range of applications, we can expect that KDT techniques will certainly develop and flourish in the years to come.

The paper by Orphanos et al. [18] presented a machine learning approach to the problems of disambiguation and unknown word guessing based on decision trees. Three induction algorithms were introduced; two producing generalized trees and one producing binary trees. All three algorithms use set value attributes in decision tree induction in a linguistic context obtained by some extensions to the basic model. The authors used a Modern Greek corpus of more than 130,000 tokens with wide thematic coverage to obtain performance results for the aforementioned three algorithms in POS disambiguation and POS guessing. The results were very positive: the authors reported 93-95% accuracy in POS disambiguation and 82-88% in guessing the POS of unknown words. These results are presented in detail in the paper and compared to each other, according to the algorithms used.

Megyesi [16] presented the implementation of a Brill tagger for Hungarian. The author has adapted and tested the tagger for the particular language, by automatically acquiring rules from a training corpus. The method used was based on Transformation-Based Error-Driven Learning, but the results obtained at first did not reach the high accuracy levels of the English implementation. Due to the rich morphology, high inflectionality and free word order of the Hungarian language, the method obtained only 83% accuracy. In order to improve the overall performance of the system, the author explained how she augmented the tagger's rule generating mechanism with extended lexical templates, obtaining an impressive 14% increase in accuracy for a final 97%.

Another method to enhance the performance of a Brill tagger was presented in the paper by Petasis et al. [19]. The authors used Transformation-Based Error-Driven Learning to resolve the POS ambiguity in Modern Greek texts. They presented experimental results from two different test cases, one based on a 65,000-word corpus on "management succession events" and the other based on a 125,000-word general-purpose corpus, obtaining 95% accuracy. One additional interesting result of these experiments was evidence that the performance of the method is independent of the thematic domain of the corpus used in the training process. The authors have also estimated the optimal size for the training corpus with respect to performance over training effort, i.e. the size after which the increase in performance is too small to justify further training. This optimal size was measured to 18,000 words for the Greek language.

On the task of word sense disambiguation, Levinson [15] presented a fully unsupervised method based on pairwise similarity clustering. The proposed method needs just a sufficiently large monolingual corpus in order to be applied and it can be used for both morphological disambiguation and for discrimination between different meanings of the same part of speech. Since it does not rely on any linguistic characteristics but only on the manner in which information is organized and conveyed, the method proves to be language independent. The author presented the successful application of his method to English and Hebrew, two languages with very different structures, and examined several variations of the main method.

The paper by Basili et al. [2] presented a conceptual clustering method for learning subcategorisation frames from a corpus and described an original architecture for tuning the lexicon to a specific sublanguage in order to improve syntactic analysis. A lexicalised shallow parser was used for the evaluation of the proposed techniques. The authors described RGL, a conceptual clustering system for learning verb subcategorisation frames, and CHAOS, a robust parser for information extraction, combined in a bootstrap architecture tested with a collection of tagged trees from a large newspaper corpus.

On the issue of unknown word acquisition, Kameda et al. [13] presented a rule-based method applied to Japanese language. The authors defined three classes of unknown words: heterographs, compound words and out-of-dictionary words. Especially for compound words, which are characterised by an underlying syntactic structure, the authors defined a surface layer and a deep layer utilizing a four-stage acquisition process. The paper described the corresponding algorithms for each class of unknown words and presented evaluation results for a system implementing the proposed method. The reported results were 96.8% for class-1 (heterographs), 76.4% (words) and 73.4% (lexemes) for class-2 (compound words).

In the paper by Thomas [24] an inductive machine learning method was presented for the construction of wrappers from semi-structured documents (such as WEB-pages). The proposed method learns how to construct T-wrappers for multi-slot extraction in an automatic way from positive examples, which consist of text-tuples occurring in the document. The technique is based on a modified version of least general generalization (TD-Anti-Unification) for a subset of feature structures (tokens). The author has tested the method on web pages with various types of structured information.

Using a "house design" task as an example, the paper by Sakurai et al. [20] described an algorithm for self-organization of a task model from word sequences. The proposed algorithm uses six basic rules and two types of background knowledge: "sequence changeable words knowledge" and "identical words knowledge". The authors described a structure called an Extended Object Automaton and they defined an inference method for constructing automatically Extended Object Automata based on a self-organization procedure. The proposed method has been successfully applied to a multi-modal system performing a house design task. The authors report 90% acceptance ratio for 175 sequences, 90% activity ratio and negative acceptance ratio less than 0.1%.

The problem of sentence boundary disambiguation was addressed by Stamatatos et al. [22]. The authors proposed a variation of Transformation-Based Learning (TBL) applied to the observation of preceding and following words and punctuation marks in order to automatically extract sentence boundary disambiguation rules from real-world texts. The proposed method has been tested for Modern Greek texts downloaded from the World Wide Web consisting of more than 165,000 words for the training corpus and more than 200,000 words for the test corpus and achieved high accuracy results (99.4%). The authors have also performed a test comparing their method to the traditional TBL, reporting a 3.7% increase in accuracy, in favor of their method.

Text chunking as an approach to data reduction in computational linguistics was the subject of the paper by Veenstra [25]. The author used Memory-Based Learning in the context of subject/object identification to perform efficient NP, VP and PP chunking. The method has been tested on an annotated and POS-tagged newspaper corpus of more than one million words and presented high precision and recall scores (94-95%).

5   Conclusion

It seems that the cooperation and exchange of ideas between the field of Machine Learning and the field of Human Language Technology provides many benefits for both fields. Some ML techniques have direct impact to HLT applications and HLT has some very interesting problems that require specially designed or augmented ML techniques. The papers presented in the ACAI '99 Workshop on Machine Learning in Human Language Technology give substantial evidence that research in this direction is promising and worthwhile.

Acknowledgments. We are grateful to all who have contributed to make this Workshop possible: the ACAI '99 Organisers, the Workshops Chair Dr. V. Karkaletsis, the Workshop Committee, the invited speaker Prof. Yves Kodratoff, the authors who submitted and presented their papers and all the participants.

References

1.   Baker, J. (1979). "Trainable Grammars for Speech Recognition", in Speech Communication Papers for the 97th Meeting of the Acoustical Society of America, June 1979,Cambridge, MA, New York, pp.547-550.
2.   Basili R., Pazienza M. T., Vindigni M. (1999). "Lexical Learning for Improving Syntactic Analysis". In [27].
3.   Black E., Garside R., Leech G. (eds.) (1993). "Statistically-Driven Computer Grammars of English: The IBM/Lancaster Approach", Language and Computers: Studies in Practical Linguistics 8, Rodopi, Amsterdam.
4.   Brent M. (1993). "From Grammar to Lexicon: Unsupervised Learning of Lexical Syntax", Computational Linguistics: Special Report on Using Large Corpora: II, Vol.19, pp.243-262.
5.   Brill E., (1993). "Automatic Grammar Induction and Parsing Free Text: A Transformation-Based Approach", in Proc. of the 31st Annual Meeting of ACL, June 1993, Columbus, OH, pp.259-265.
6.   Briscoe E., Carroll J. (1991). "Generalized Probabilistic LR Parsing of Natural Language (Corpora) with Unification-Based Grammars", Cambridge University, Technical Report 224.
7.   Brown P., Della Pietra V., deSouza P., Lai J., Mercer R. (1992). "Class-Based n-Gram Models of Natural Language", Computational Linguistics, Vol.18, pp.467-479.
8.   Cardie C., Mooney R.J. (1999). "Guest Editor's Introduction: Machine Learning and Natural Language", Machine Learning, Vol.34 (Special Issue on Natural Language Learning), pp.5-9, Kluwer Academic Publishers.
9.   Charniak E. (1993). "Statistical Language Learning", Cambridge, MA, MIT Press.
10.   Cole R. A., Mariani J., Uszkoreit H., Zaenen A., Zue V., Varile G. B., Zampolli A. (eds.). (1996). "Survey of the State of the Art in Human Language Technology", (http://cslu.cse.ogi.edu/HLTsurvey/).
11.   Dermatas E., Kokkinakis G. (1995). "Automatic Stochastic Tagging of Natural Language Texts", Computational Linguistics, Vol.21, pp.137-164.

12. Joshi A. (1995). "Some Recent Trends in Natural Language Processing", in Zampoli A., Calzolari N., Palmer M. (eds.) *Current Issues in Computational Linguistics: In Honor of Don Walker*, Kluwer Academic Publishers, pp.491-501.

13. Kameda H., Sakurai T., Kubomura C. (1999). "Unknown Word Acquisition System for Japanese Written-Language Document". In [27].

14. Kodratoff Y. (1999). "About Knowledge Discovery in Texts: A Definition and an Example". In [27].

15. Levinson D. (1999). "Corpus-Based Method for Unsupervised Word Sense Disambiguation". In [27].

16. Megyesi B. (1999). "Brill's PoS Tagger with Extended Lexical Templates for Hungarian". In [27].

17. Nagao M., Nakamura J. (1982). "A Parser which Learns the Application Order of Rewriting Rules", in Proc. of the 9th International Conference on Computational Linguistics (COLING), Prague, 1982, North-Holland Publishing Co., pp.253-258.

18. Orphanos G., Kalles D., Papagelis T., Christodoulakis D. (1999). "Decision Trees and NLP: A Case Study in POS Tagging". In [27].

19. Petasis G., Paliouras G., Karkaletsis V., Spyropoulos C. D., Androutsopoulos I. (1999). "Resolving Part-of-Speech Ambiguity in the Greek Language Using Learning Techniques". In [27].

20. Sakurai S., Endo T., Mukai T., Oka R. (1999). "Automatic Task Modeling for Realizing a Multi-modal Interface System". In [27].

21. Sparck-Jones K. (1994). "Natural Language Processing: A Historical Review", in Zampoli A., Calzolari N., Palmer M. (eds.) *Current Issues in Computational Linguistics: In Honor of Don Walker*, Kluwer Academic Publishers, pp.3-15.

22. Stamatatos E., Fakotakis N., Kokkinakis G. (1999). "Automatic Extraction of Rules for Sentence Boundary Disambiguation". In [27].

23. Stolcke A. (1995). "Efficient Probabilistic Context-Free Parsing", Computational Linguistics, Vol.21, pp.165-202.

24. Thomas B. (1999). "Learning T-Wrappers for Information Extraction". In [27].

25. Veenstra J. (1999). "Memory-Based Text Chunking". In [27].

26. Wilms G. J. (1995). "Automated Induction of a Lexical Sublanguage Grammar using a Hybrid System of Corpus- and Knowledge-Based Techniques", Ph.D. Dissertation, Mississippi State University, Department of Computer Science.

27. Proceedings of the Workshop on Machine Learning in Human Language Technology, Advanced Course on Artificial Intelligence (ACAI '99), Chania, Greece, 1999 (http://www.iit.demokritos.gr/skel/eetn/acai99/Workshops.htm).

Machine Learning for Intelligent Information Access

Grigoris Karakoulas[1] and Giovanni Semeraro[2]

[1]Department of Global Analytics, Canadian Imperial Bank of Commerce, 161 Bay St.,
Toronto, Ontario, Canada M5J 2S8
karakoul@cibc.ca
[2]Dipartimento di Informatica, Università di Bari, Via E. Orabona, 4, I-70126 BARI Italy
semeraro@di.uniba.it

1   Introduction

As the volume of electronically stored information continues to expand across computer networks, the need for intelligent access to on-line collections of multimedia documents becomes imperative. Examples of such collections are the World Wide Web, digital libraries and enterprise-wide information repositories. Machine learning offers an invaluable *corpus* of techniques, tools and systems that can help to solve effectively related problems, such as semantic indexing, content-based search, semantic querying, integration of ontologies/knowledge bases into Internet search technologies, in order to develop a new generation of *intelligent* search engines. There has been a growing interest in augmenting or replacing traditional information filtering and retrieval approaches with machine learning techniques in order to build systems that can scale to the intrinsic complexity of the task. This issue was addressed in the workshop on "Machine Learning for Intelligent Information Access", which was organized as part of the Advanced Course on Artificial Intelligence (ACAI '99).

Important themes of work in the application of machine learning techniques to intelligent information access problems include: (i) filtering of relevant information from distributed, heterogeneous sources that differ in type, form and content, (ii) text topic categorization, (iii) enterprise-wide dissemination of information and (iv) multi-agent information markets. In particular, state-of-the-art research topics that are also relevant to the workshop include:

- Text classification [6].
- Adaptive filtering [15].
- Query expansion [14].
- Clustering of documents [13].
- Scalability over very large datasets [15].
- Ensemble and multi-strategy learning [9].
- Knowledge representation for information retrieval [13].
- Architectures and protocols for electronic information markets [2].

The goal of this workshop was to promote discussion and interaction among researchers and practitioners from various related communities on how machine learning, which offers an invaluable *corpus* of techniques, tools and systems, can be used to augment or replace traditional information filtering and retrieval approaches for intelligent information access. The workshop consisted of an invited talk and five

G. Paliouras, V. Karkaletsis, and C.D. Spyropoulos (Eds.): ACAI '99, LNAI 2049, pp. 274-280, 2001.
© Springer-Verlag Berlin Heidelberg 2001

papers that presented machine learning techniques for various types of information access tasks, i.e.

- hypertext information extraction,
- development of web knowledge bases,
- automatic query expansion in document ranking systems,
- change detection in adaptive information filtering,
- information capture in digital libraries,
- information agents for learning user profiles,
- multi-agent engines that learn user models for searching the web.

The next section presents an overview of the workshop papers [16] and invited talk, followed by a summary of the discussion from the workshop and a list of references for suggested reading.

2   Overview of the Workshop Papers

In his invited talk Tom Mitchell [8] first addressed the topic of integrating knowledge bases/ontologies into Internet search technologies. The goal of his research is to develop a knowledge base that mirrors the content of the WWW, in order to make text information on the Web available in computer-understandable form. Specifically, Mitchell investigated the problem of what kind of knowledge base (KB) should be built and used for a specific task. He also gave an overview of what currently available systems do. Then, he presented the description of a KB that was automatically extracted. This KB was extracted at CMU in the first week of July 1999 and is about companies on the Web. It consists of about 50000 axioms and facts. The instances of the KB can be used as training examples for learning to classify Web pages.

In this context, a central role is played by the concept of "contiguous segment of text", which can be a Web page taken as a whole, or a fragment of text in a Web page, or a hyperlinked fragment of text in a Web page. The problem of the automatic extraction of KBs from the Web can be cast as a problem of *hypertext information extraction*, which involves/implies the analysis of a hypertext at three levels of resolution, namely:

- individual web pages (e.g., in a University Web site, these might be pages concerning Faculty, Student, etc),
- groups of interconnected Web pages (e.g., the Web pages concerning a course and the person who teaches that course, represented by a predicate teaches-courses(person, course)),
- individual sentences and fragments.

Another problem involved in the automatic extraction of KBs is that of recognizing the class of the extracted instances. Bag-of-words classification is usually used to cope with this problem. Results from applying a Naive-Bayes classifier to University Web sites, show that extracted instances are correctly classified with an accuracy that ranges from a minimum of 42% to a maximum of 100%, according to the class of instances, and with an overall average accuracy close to 80%. In this domain, the top learned word weights are "Faculty", "Student", "Courses", "Department", "Research Groups", by using a training set of 400 Web pages. Standard bag-of-words classifiers turn out to be useful for flat text, but not for hypertext. Therefore, the main idea is to learn rules expressed in First Order Logic for classifying Web pages. Results from this approach show a classification accuracy of greater than 90%.

Recent themes in the research about *web knowledge bases* are:

- learning to extract useful information, where the focus is about the linguistic structure of a "contiguous segment of text", and about the possibility of training a system with minimal effort,
- learning with unlabelled and labelled training data [1], [11].

In the last theme, a relevant concept is that of "redundantly sufficient attributes". Examples of redundantly sufficient attributes are:

- page and incoming anchor text for Web page classification [12],
- noun phrase and surrounding context for text information extraction,
- lips and voice for speech recognition,
- video, audio and close caption for classifying multimedia segments,
- local contexts for word sense disambiguation.

The algorithms that turn out to be effective for learning from unlabelled and labelled training data are called *co-training algorithms*. Given a (small) set of labelled training examples and a set of unlabelled ones, co-training algorithms are able to learn both hyperlink-based classifiers and full-text classifiers from the labelled training examples. Moreover, these classifiers are used to iteratively label a certain number of positive and negative examples taken from the set of unlabelled ones. Then, these newly labelled examples are added to the set of the labelled training examples and this leads to a new cycle of the algorithm. The approach based on co-training algorithms showed the best performance when compared to results based on supervised learning (overall predictive accuracy of 95%).

The paper by Carpineto and Romano [3] presented an empirical evaluation of term weighting and retrieval feedback schemes for automatic query expansion on the TREC-7 text collection. Their purpose was to identify potential differences in the distribution of term weights and relevant documents that could lead to performance gains by combining those schemes. In particular, they compare Rocchio's weighting scheme with three schemes that are based on the Chi-square statistic and Kullback-Lieber distance of term distributions. The results showed that the latter three techniques outperformed Rocchio's technique over all 50 queries (TREC topics 351-400). Furthermore, they found significant variations in both term ranking and retrieval effectiveness amongst these techniques. Because of this, they applied a simple approach for combining the term ranking from the three techniques. The evaluation of this combined weighting technique yielded improved mean retrieval performance on the above dataset. These experiments suggest that there is potential in studying methods for combining existing techniques for automatic query expansion, and adding to the growing literature of research on ensemble learning for information retrieval.

Lanquillon [7] looked at one of the key issues in adaptive information filtering, namely detecting changes in the content of a text stream. These changes occur because new topics may arise, existing topics may disappear, or the content of existing topics may change. The purpose of detecting such changes is to make the information filter adaptive to them so that, when due to changes documents start becoming relevant, these documents make their way to the user. Lanquillon considered two types of change indicators, those based on classification properties (e.g. error rate) and those on text properties (e.g. word frequencies). He proposed an indicator that uses intermediate classification results without additional user feedback for the true class labels. In particular, the indicator is defined as the average number of documents in the collection that are classified as irrelevant with a confidence below some threshold. The latter is empirically set. To make the information filter adaptive to changes he applied a rather simplistic approach of relearning from scratch once changes in the average value of the indicator were more than three times the standard deviation. For his experiments he used a dataset of Usenet articles and a similarity based classifier. The experiments showed that his approach for detecting changes and relearning the classifier scales to changes and compares well with a benchmark that requires complete knowledge of the true class labels. A shortcoming of this approach is that the proposed indicator may not be sensitive to changes in the content of a text stream when the irrelevance class consists of many diverse topics. Text clustering or learning multiple models of relevance could be ways for overcoming this problem.

The paper by Esposito et al. [5] applies learning techniques to the task of information capture within IDL (Intelligent Digital Library), a prototypical digital library service. Information capture denotes the task of converting data from the medium on which they are stored into a digital format. The main features of IDL are: (i) support for information capture, (ii) support for semantic indexing and (iii) support for content understanding and interface adaptivity. Prior to being stored in IDL, each document is transformed into a symbolic representation through the following steps: segmentation, document analysis, classification and understanding. The paper describes various techniques that have been applied for learning associations between layout components and the corresponding logical components of a document, such as document class, title, authors and sections of a paper. For learning document classifications, the layout of documents is represented in first-order descriptions. A supervised learning algorithm was initially developed for this task that combined two classifiers, one from the numeric features of the layout and one from the symbolic ones. More recently, research in this project has focused on applying incremental rule-based induction techniques to the problem of classifying scientific documents. The results from the application of these techniques indicate that the incrementally learned theories compare well with the batch learned theories in terms of predictive accuracy.

D'Aloisi and Giannini [4] presented a new approach to learning user profiles for searching on the Internet using an intelligent agent, named Abis (Agent Based Information System). Abis purports to predict the action a user might choose to apply to a document – i.e. store in a folder, delete, print – or the relevance value of a document – i.e. interesting/not interesting – based on past training examples. Once a user query is submitted to the system, Harvest, a public-domain search engine, is invoked for finding relevant documents. Harvest represents documents and queries using SOIF (Summary Object Interchange Format) that extracts relevant attributes from their structure. In Abis, documents, queries and profiles are represented as lists of attribute/value pairs through a modified version of SOIF. The documents retrieved by the search engine are processed by Abis in two stages. First, they are compared with the user profile for refining the results of the search. Then, the documents selected from the first stage are compared against the set of past situations to predict a relevance value or an action to perform on a document. A typical similarity metric is adopted for this comparison. Documents evaluated by the user are added as situations to the memory of the agent. The evaluation of the system is currently in a preliminary phase.

Muller [10] presented an abstract prototype, OySTER, for intelligent search on the Internet, based on user models that are learned with respect to an ontology that describes document contents in a multi-agent environment. The latter is structured as a blackboard system where different classes of agents are reading and writing requests. Search requests are submitted via interface agents. Search agents perform query refinement based on user models for generating a set of meta-search queries that are passed onto search engines. User models are represented as a disjunctive list of expressions where literals describe membership of document classes. A user model is initialized and continuously refined by several agents. Initially, the user's homepage and bookmarks are processed by URL updating daemon plans to derive user specific keyword lists and document categories of interest. For each result delivered by a search engine and evaluated by the user the model is updated. Since document categories form a lattice, machine learning techniques can be used for learning specific and general category descriptions of documents as well as user models on such categories. Database maintenance agents are used to organize the documents returned by the search engines into a hierarchy of document types. Classification of document types is currently done via a simple handcrafted grammar.

3   Discussion

The workshop ended with a discussion that addressed the following questions:

- What are the challenges that Information Retrieval (IR), Information Filtering (IF) and Information Extraction (IE) pose to the Machine Learning (ML) community?
- How ML can help IR/IF/IE?
- Which ML techniques are more appropriate for IR/IF/IE?
- What is the impact of ML technology on the IT market?
- How can we develop effective adaptive software systems?

The conclusions from this discussion can be summarised into a list of topics for future research as follows:

1. There is a growing attention of the ML community towards Information Retrieval, and in particular towards

- retrieval feedback methods (automatic query expansion and reweighting),
- adaptive information filtering or information filtering in dynamic environments (document classification on the ground of user interests and concept drift),
- intelligent/learning agents for information retrieval/filtering.

The three topics listed above are facets of the same area, namely multi-agent learning for information filtering and retrieval from distributed and heterogeneous information sources (Web, archives, etc).

2. There is a growing need of Meta-Search services, which poses the following challenges:

- integration of ontologies into Web search engines for personalized content-based retrieval,
- information capture and semantic indexing of documents in digital libraries.

Both of these challenges require ML techniques for:

- conceptual/knowledge-based/intelligent/content-based indexing,
- querying and retrieval of unstructured or semi-structured documents,
- on-line learning,
- adaptive information filtering.

These techniques should be able to:

- combine with symbolic knowledge (inductive logic programming),
- scale to deal with very large collections of textual/unstructured/semi-structured data.

If the ML community is able to provide answers to the above research topics then it is foreseeable that, the impact of ML technology on the IT market will grow as soon as role-based access to Internet services becomes common practice. In terms of the possibility of developing effective adaptive software systems, useful hints could come from systems that are able to measure the satisfaction of users (on-line user satisfaction) and perform some form of user analysis.

References

1. A. Blum and T. Mitchell. Combining Labeled and Unlabeled Data with Co-Training. Proceedings of the 11th Annual Conference on Computational Learning Theory (COLT-98), 1998.
2. J. Bradsaw. Software Agents. MIT Press, 1998.
3. C. Carpineto and G. Romano. Comparing and Combining Retrieval Feedback Methods: First results. In [16].
4. D. D'Aloisi and V. Giannini. Predicting Relevance of Documents with a Memory-Based Information Agent. In [16].
5. F. Esposito, N. Fanizzi, S. Ferilli and G. Semeraro. Supporting Document Acquisition and Organization in a Digital Library Service through ML techniques. In [16].
6. Proceedings of the 3rd Symposium on Intelligent Data Analysis, Amsterdam, Springer-Verlag, 1999.

7.   C. Lanquillon: Dynamic Aspects in Information Filtering: Detecting changes in text streams. In [16].
8.   T. M. Mitchell: Mining the Web. In [16].
9.   Proceedings of the 4th International Workshop on Multistrategy Learning, F. Esposito, R.S. Michalski and L. Saitta (Eds.), 1998.
10.   M. Muller: Intelligent Information Access in the Web: ML based user modeling for high precision meta-search. In [16].
11.   K. Nigam, A. McCallum, S. Thrun and T. Mitchell. Learning to Classify Text from Labeled and Unlabeled Documents. Proceedings of the 15th National Conference on Artificial Intelligence (AAAI-98), 1998.
12.   E. Riloff and R. Jones. Learning Dictionaries for Information Extraction by Multi-Level Bootstrapping. Proceedings of the 16th National Conference on Artificial Intelligence (AAAI-99), 1999.
13.   Proceedings of 21st International Conference on Research and Development in Information Retrieval. ACM Press, 1998.
14.   Proceedings of the Eighth Text Retrieval Conference (TREC-8). NIST Publication, 1998.
15.   Proceedings of the Ninth Text Retrieval Conference (TREC-9). NIST Publication, 1999.
16.   Proceedings of the Workshop on Machine Learning for Intelligent Information Access, Advanced Course on Artificial Intelligence (ACAI '99), Chania, Greece, 1999 (http://www.iit.demokritos.gr/skel/eetn/acai99/Workshops.htm).

Machine Learning and Intelligent Agents

Themis Panayiotopoulos and Nick Z. Zacharis

Knowledge Engineering Laboratory, Department of Computer Science
University of Piraeus, Karaoli & Dimitriou 80, Piraeus 18534,Greece
{themisp,nzach}@unipi.gr

1   Introduction

The purpose of this chapter is to provide an introduction to the field of machine learning techniques for intelligent agents based on the contributions in the workshop of 'Machine Learning and Intelligent Agents' [20], which was held in conjunction with the Advanced Course on Artificial Intelligence (ACAI '99) on Machine Learning & Applications, at Chania, Greece.

Machine Learning in single and multi-agent systems is a relatively new but significant and promising topic in Artificial Intelligence. Intelligent agents and agent-based computer systems represent an important, fundamentally new way of dealing with many important software application problems for which mainstream computer science techniques offer no obvious solution. Many of these new problems are due to the recent dynamic and distributed nature of both data and applications.

Topics covered in this chapter concern the development of intelligent agent architectures which exhibit machine learning capabilities. These architectures apply some learning strategy, learning from examples, evolutionary learning etc. and some learning feedback method, supervised, reward and punishment, unsupervised learning, etc. Various approaches and algorithms with comparative studies have also been concerned for classification problems such as k-nearest neighbor, naive bayes artificial neural networks with back propagation learning, Kohonen maps, decision rulesets, genetic algorithms, etc.

There are also many interesting agent-based applications from the areas of robotics, ship damage control, personalised information filtering and collection from the Web as well as natural language interfaces. We will give a brief overview of the main methods and techniques used in each field, summarize the presented work and provide some additional references. We highlight the important issues and trends based on the workshop discussions.

2   Overview of the Workshop Papers

2.1   Intelligent Agents for the Web

In the face of the constant change and explosive growth of information that is available through the World Wide Web, it is becoming increasingly difficult for the users to find the information of interest. Searching the Web efficiently is not an easy task and a number of search services have been developed for this purpose. Each of

G. Paliouras, V. Karkaletsis, and C.D. Spyropoulos (Eds.): ACAI '99, LNAI 2049, pp. 281-285, 2001.
© Springer-Verlag Berlin Heidelberg 2001

these search services works very differently and no one provides the best index for all the topics.

However, even though most of the search engines contain links to an overwhelming number of documents they are still the best place for a user to start a search. Thus, search services are valuable tools for searching the Web, they have several unsolved problems for the novice users. For example, which strategy a user should follow in order to find the information which interests him/her, which keywords describe a concept, how to combine the keywords with the logic operators, or what he/she should do with a huge list of hits.

Researchers in the field of Artificial Intelligence have proposed the development of intelligent software aiming to collect information from large, complex, unstructured and heterogeneous information spaces like the WWW, where information source may appear and disappear unpredictably. Furthermore, advanced applications such as electronic commerce and auctions, information filtering, workflow management etc., need flexible and adaptive mechanisms in order to manage and use the information available on the Web. During the past few years, the notion of a software agent [11], [5] has become increasingly popular, as a means for realizing intelligent systems that help their users in the discovery of useful information. The first two papers in the workshop, which are summarized below describe a personalized intelligent assistant aiming to support a single user's informational needs. A main variation among applications in this problem domain is when the agent collects documents from an index which has been constructed by recommendations from other users with similar interests. In such a case, the term collaborative filtering describes the task. Other practical Web applications based on agent systems fall into the following categories: WEB browsing [1], [2], [10], [13], filtering net news and email messages [9], [15], [14], shopping [4] and lifestyle [7]

The paper by Mladenic [12] presents a personal browsing assistant that suggests interesting hyperlinks on the requested Web documents. Personal WebWatcher consists of two main parts: a proxy server and a machine learning module. The system learns user interests from the pages requested by the user. Hyperlinks whose documents were visited by the user are considered to be positive examples and all the other to be negative examples of user interests. Experimental results show the classification accuracy of two algorithms, k-Nearest Neighbor and Naive Bayes.

Zacharis and Panayiotopoulos [19] presented the architecture and the main components of a intelligent agent that uses a meta-genetic algorithm to filter and collect information from the WWW. The meta-genetic algorithm operates in two stages and creates two interacting populations. The first population contains keyword sets from the user's profile and the second population contains sets of logic operators. The combination of keywords and logic operators creates queries for five popular Web search engines. The user's feedback on the agent's recommendations drives the learning process. Experimental results show that this learning algorithm can be used quite successfully to produce learning agents.

2.2   Learning Interface Agents

In the last few years, there has been a lot of interest and activity in the area of Intelligent User Interfaces. Various methods and techniques have been used to design and realize interfaces that make human-computer interaction easier and more effective. As the applications are getting more and more complex, it is necessary to build more flexible, portable, adaptive and collaborative interface systems in order to support the human-computer interaction. Furthermore, using Artificial Intelligence techniques and intelligent architectures for the interface is very important especially in a multi-user environment where the interface must adapt to the needs of different users, provide explanations of its actions, take initiative and make recommendations to the user etc.

Designing and building general-purpose Natural Language Processing systems for text understanding and information extraction is a very difficult task. Domain-specific semantics and vocabulary are necessary for a system in order to understand information relevant to a specific domain. Also, domain-specific linguistic patterns are used as references to domain objects. Thus, if an agent acts in a virtual environment it will need a set of rules that identify references to various objects in the virtual world and the possible types of interactions.

The paper by Kontos and Malagardi [6] describes the design of a motion command understanding system that could be applied to the communication between a user and an intelligent agent. The agent accepts commands and knowledge about the objects and the actions possible in a virtual environment. Commands are phrased in Greek or English Natural Language and express different kinds of actions. Moreover, the proposed system has the ability to learn from its user to understand and execute correctly motion commands that go beyond its initial capabilities. This learning takes place in cases when the system faces the problem of unknown words, of unknown senses of words or underspecified positions of objects.

2.3   Learning to Build Robot Maps

In the process of robot map building, many different aspects of the problem must be taken into account, like the environment the robot moves in, the type of sensors it uses, the dimensionality of the measurements, etc. Feature-extraction from the raw measurements for self-localization of the robot becomes therefore a fundamental issue, [18].

Sensor technology provides high-dimensional and highly correlated data vectors, which need an appropriate feature extraction method to be applied on these data, before the modeling step [16]. The principal component analysis, (PCA), projection method has been applied to extract linear features from a range sensor profile. The same method has also been applied to images. Non-linear feature extraction methods are the landmark-based approaches, as well as some direct nonlinear mapping using feed-forward neural networks. Recent research proposes a Bayesian localisation error formula in a neural network based non-linear feature extraction scheme as an optimization criterion [16].

The paper by Vlassis et al. [17] concerns the task of autonomous navigation of mobile robots, that requires precise localization of the robot within the workspace, and proposes an alternative criterion that is based on information-theoretic concepts. The paper presented an analysis of the method, comparison with other work and presentation of experimental results by a real robot in a typical office environment.

2.4   Learning to Take Decisions in a Real-Time Crisis

A typical problem-solving cycle within the blackboard framework consists of three steps: the deliberation step, during which a set of proposed actions is posted on the blackboard, a scheduling step, during which the best action is selected, and finally the execution step, during which the selected action is passed to the actuators and the environment changes.

Bulitko and Wilkins [3] described an Intelligent Agent for real-time crisis decision making. The agent is blackboard-based and uses envisionment to schedule its actions as the complexity associated with ship damage control does not allow to capture every behavior in a reasonably sized set of rules. Although, the procedure of simulating fire and flood spread is slow, the learning module compiles the generated knowledge and thus allows for real-time performance. A novel scheduling approach is proposed and the environment is represented as an Extended Petri Net model.

2.5   Inductive Concept Learning in a Three-Valued Logical Setting

It is often the case that we are confident about the truth or falsity of only a limited number of facts as the available information is too scarce. An agent gathering information from a surrounding world needs to distinguish what is true, what is false and what is unknown, in a three-valued setting.

Lamma et al. [8] presented an approach for inductive concept learning adopting a three-valued setting. The definition of a concept as well as its opposite can be derived considering positive and negative examples as instances of two disjoint classes. Extended logic programs under a well-founded semantics with explicit negation have been adopted as the representation formalism. The issue of strategic combination of possibly contradictory definitions was also considered.

3   Conclusions

During the last years, the topic of developing learning and adaptation mechanisms within Intelligent Agent systems has gained increasing attention in Artificial Intelligence. Intelligent agent theories, languages and systems can use all the research done in the area of machine learning, as the latter provides tools for dynamic adaptation in unknown environments. The dimensionality as well as the complexity of the modeled environments becomes an additional reason for developing machine learning intelligent agent systems.

During the Machine Learning and Intelligent Agents workshop, work was presented that applied machine learning to many different problems such as, searching the Web, adaptive and collaborative NLP interfaces, robot map building, and taking real-time decisions in crisis situations. All these domains can be successfully challenged if we select an appropriate machine learning strategy. We believe that the time is near, when hybrid intelligent agent systems will be provided, using alternative or unified machine learning techniques for solving the challenges of the future. One of these challenges is the development of an intelligent agent with learning capabilities from the Web. The Web suggests new problems and new constrains on existing techniques. Also, intelligent Web agents will provide tangible evidence of the power and utility of Artificial Intelligence techniques.

References

1. R. Armstrong, D. Freitag, T. Joachims, T. Mitchell, WebWatcher : A Learning Apprentice for the WWW, Proceedings of the AAAI Symposium on Information Gathering from Heterogeneous, Distributed Environments, Menlo Park, 1995, AAAI Technical Report SS-95-08, 6-12.
2. M. Balavanovic, Y. Shoham, Learning Information Retrieval Agents: Experiments with Automated Web Browsing, Proceedings of the AAAI Symposium on Information Gathering from Heterogeneous, Distributed Environments, Menlo Park, 1995, AAAI Technical Report SS-95-08, 1995, 13-18.
3. V.V. Bulitko and D.C. Wilkins: Learning to Envision: An Intelligent Agent for Ship Damage Control. In [20].
4. R.B. Doorendos, O. Etzioni, D.S. Weld, A Scalable Comparison-Shopping Agent for the WWW, Proceedings of the First International Conference on Autonomous Agents, Marina del Rey, CA, ACM, 1997, 39-48.
5. O. Etzioni, Moving Up the information Food Chain, AI Magazine, 18(2), AAAI, 1997, 11-18.
6. J. Kontos and I. Malagardi: A Learning Natural Language Interface to an Agent. In [20].
7. Krulwich, LifeStyle Finder - Intelligent User Profiling, AI Magazine, 18 (2), AAAI, 1997, 37-45.
8. E. Lamma, F. Riguzzi and L.Moniz Pereira: Agents Learning in a Three-Valued Logical Setting. In [20].
9. K. Lang, NewsWeeder: Learning to filter netnews, Proceedings of the 12th International Machine Learning Conference, Lake Taho, CA, Morgan Kaufmann, 1995, 331-339.
10. H. Lieberman, Letitzia: An Agent That Assists Web Browsing, Proceedings 14th International Joined Conference on AI, Montreal, Canada, Morgan Kaufmann, 1995, 924-929.
11. P. Maes, Agents that reduce work and Information Overload, Communications of ACM, 37 (7), ACM, 1994, 30-40.
12. D. Mladenic: Machine learning used by Personal WebWatcher. In [20].
13. A. Moukas, Information Discovery and Filtering using a Multiagent Evolving Ecosystem, Master Thesis, MIT Media Laboratory, Massachusetts Institute of Technology, 1997.
14. T.R Payne, P. Edwards, C.L. Green, Experience with Rule Induction and k-Nearest Neighbour Methods for Interface Agents that Learn, IEEE Transactions on Knowledge and Data Engineering, 9(2), IEEE, 1997, 329-335.
15. Sheth, A Learning Approach to Personalized Information Filtering, Master Thesis, MIT Media Laboratory, Massachusetts Institute of Technology, 1994.
16. S. Thrun, Bayesian landmark learning for mobile robot localization, Machine Learning, 33(1), Kluwer Academic Publishers, 1998, 41-76.
17. N. Vlassis, Y. Motomura and B. Krose: An information-theoretic localisation criterion for robot map building. In [20].
18. N. Vlassis, G. Papakonstantinou and P. Tsanakas, Dynamic sensory probabilistic maps for mobile robot localization, IROS'98, IEEE/RSJ International Confrence on Intelligent Robots and Systems, Victoria, B.C., Canada, IEEE, 1998, 718-723.
19. N. Zacharis and T. Panayiotopoulos: A Learning personalized information agent for the WWW. In [20].
20. Proceedings of the Workshop on Machine Learning and Intelligent Agents, Advanced Course on Artificial Intelligence (ACAI '99), Chania, Greece, 1999 (http://www.iit.demokritos.gr/skel/eetn/acai99/Workshops.htm).

Machine Learning in User Modeling

Christos Papatheodorou

Division of Applied Technologies, NCSR "Demokritos", 15310 Athens, Greece
papatheodor@lib.demokritos.gr

1   Introduction

It is generally recognized that information systems are becoming more complex and, therefore, intelligent user interfaces are needed to improve user interaction with these systems. Furthermore, the exponential growth of the Internet makes it difficult for the users to cope with the huge amount of available on-line information. The challenge that information providers and system engineers face is the creation of adaptive (Web-based) applications, as well as the development of "personalized" retrieval and filtering mechanisms. Responses to this challenge come from various disciplines including machine learning and data mining, intelligent agents and multi-agent systems, intelligent tutoring, information retrieval, etc.

User modeling (UM) aims to make information systems really user-friendly, by adapting the behaviour of the system to the needs of the individual. The importance of adding this capability to information systems is proven by the variety of areas in which user modeling has already been applied: information retrieval, filtering and extraction systems, adaptive user interfaces, educational software.

Machine learning (ML) techniques have been applied to user modeling problems for acquiring models of individual users interacting with an information system and grouping them into communities or stereotypes with common interests. This functionality is essential in order to have a useful and usable system that can modify its behavior over time and for different users. ML techniques are promising in cases where very large sets of usage data are available, like WWW sites, and other Internet applications (news filtering, digital libraries, search engines, etc.). In such applications, the information providers need a tool to help users in selecting useful information from the plethora of information on the Net.

This chapter is based on the work presented in the Workshop on "Machine Learning in User Modeling", which was organised in conjunction with the ECCAI Advanced Course on Artificial Intelligence for 1999 (ACAI '99). The aim of the Workshop was the presentation of the current trends and activities in exploiting Machine Learning techniques for the creation of adaptive user interfaces, the construction of user communities and stereotypes, the customized web usage and for the development of educational hypermedia. Pat Langley was invited speaker and the rest of the Workshop consisted of seven papers, which could be grouped in "clusters" corresponding to the topics: *Adaptive User Interfaces, Agent-based systems, Student Modeling and Web Mining*.

G. Paliouras, V. Karkaletsis, and C.D. Spyropoulos (Eds.): ACAI '99, LNAI 2049, pp. 286-294, 2001.
© Springer-Verlag Berlin Heidelberg 2001

The following section presents an overview of UM and describes the general contribution of ML in UM. Section 3 discusses the current research efforts in the above-mentioned topics, as they were presented in the workshop. Finally section 4 presents some conclusions and suggestions for future research.

2   Machine Learning in User Modeling

A user model consists mainly of knowledge about the individual preferences which determine the user's behaviour. As in the most knowledge based approaches, two are the main issues that user modelling faces: The user model representation and acquisition.

User models could be represented as preferences sets, first order predicates or groups of predicates, plans, decision trees, etc. Furthermore, a user model may contain personal information about the user, such as his/her age, occupation, etc. The latter type of information is not directly necessary for the adaptation of the system to the user, but may be used to categorise the user into a *stereotype*, which in turn allows the system to anticipate some of the user's behaviour. Stereotypes have been introduced by Rich [34], as a means of organising the users of the system with common behaviour, into meaningful groups. Personal information about the users of a system is not always available and therefore the construction of user stereotypes may not be possible. This is especially true of visitors to a Web site. In that case, the organisation of users into groups with common interests can still be useful. Such a group of users is termed by Orwant [26] a *user community* and corresponds to a stereotype missing the personal information.

Many user model acquisition methods have been presented in the literature. These methods depend on the user model definition and representation and vice versa. For example plan recognition methods are used when user models are represented as plan hierarchies or libraries. In general, the user model acquisition methods could be grouped in two families: The explicit and the implicit (non-invasive) methods. The first family creates the user models by asking the users directly about their interests and preferences or by allowing them to specify and modify their own model. These preference setting methods could be found in many modern software packages. The implicit methods estimate and infer user models by tracking the user behaviour and interaction.

Educational software uses student modelling techniques to personilise the learning process, i.e., to make it adaptive to the student skills and background knowledge, as well as to predict the student's actions [40], [17]. Student modeling precedes historically user modeling and thus one could argue that it was one of the "causes" for the development of UM technology.

On the other hand, information retrieval and filtering systems aim to deliver to the user those documents that are relevant to his/her information requirements, whereas information extraction systems aim to deliver specific facts from those documents. NewT is a system that helps the user filter Usenet Netnews [22] according to his/her interests. Brajnik and Tasso [8], [9] present the exploitation of the user modelling shell UMT in the prototype information-providing system Tourist Advisor (TA). Kay [19] describes the Movie Advisor project, which operates on a database of movie descriptions, suggesting movies that should appeal to a specific user. Doppelgänger [26] is a user modelling system that gathers sensor data about users, draws inferences on those data and makes the results available to applications. Firefly's agent software groups users' interests based on their similarities in order to suggest buying opportunities to specific customers based on their similarity to other customers. UMIE [5] is a Web-based prototype user modelling component (see http://www.iit.demo-kritos.gr/UMIE), that filters the data extracted from an information extraction system according to the users' models.

Machine learning (ML) methods have been applied to user modeling problems, mainly for acquiring models of individual users interacting with an information system, e.g. [7], [33], [32], [3]. In such situations, the use of the system by an individual is monitored and the collected data are used to construct the model of the user, i.e., his/her individual requirements. By definition, the development of intelligent and adaptive user interfaces presupposes the design of specific modules, responsible for learning user models by tracing the interaction of the system with the users [20], [10], [11].

Moreover, ML techniques have been used in many agent-based and multiagent systems which aim to discover and recommend information from Web sites like FAB [2], Syskill & Webert [29], WebWatcher [18], Amalthea [23] and Oyster [25]. Perkowitz and Etzioni [30], [31] deal with the development of adaptive Web-sites, which recommend (on the fly) pages relevant to the interests of their visitors. Specifically, they provide a conceptual cluster mining method that analyses the Web server usage data (logs).

Furthermore, ML for UM has been used in digital library services, like IDL [15], [14], and in news filtering systems, like News Dude [6]. The main goal of these systems is to learn and revise user profiles as well as to propose which information on a given topic would be interesting to a user.

Most of this work "revolves" around the World Wide Web, which provides a wealth of information to filter, as well as a famous interaction mechanism. We could classify the filtering methods into two families. The first one is *content-based* filtering in which the system accepts information describing the items, and learn to predict which items fit to the user models. Syskill & Webert and IDL are representatives of this family. The other family is the *collaborative* or *social* filtering, in which the system updates the user models and predicts items that fit to them, based on feedback from many different users. Typical representatives of this approach are FAB, Firefly and amazon.com. The works dealing with the formulation of user communities [26], [27] have similarities to the latter family. However there are systems (e.g. [3]), which adopt a hybrid philosophy in recommending items based on user models.

Apart from information discovery and filtering systems, Langley [20] refers to a variety of systems that use ML in order to adapt to particular situations that a user faces, such as travel assistance, routing in an area, emergencies reaction and scheduling. Furthermore, such techniques have been applied in intelligent tutoring systems [37], [12]. Finally, ML techniques have been applied succesfully to the prediction of a users' actions. Significant research efforts on intelligent assistance and/or tutoring view the user behaviour as a plan and learn the patterns of users' actions which achieve particular states [4]. Specifically, there are significant contributions concerning the usage of decision theory and Bayesian belief networks in plan recognition [1], [39].

3   Overview of the Workshop Papers

The workshop consisted of the invited talk of Pat Langley and seven papers [41], presenting Machine Learning applications for the development of adaptive user inerfaces, agent-based information discovery, student modeling systems, as well as for analyzing the behaviour of Web users.

3.1   Adaptive User Interfaces

Pat Langley in his invited talk [21] defined adaptive interfaces as "software artifacts that improve their ability to interact with users by constructing user models based on partial experience with each of them". Furthermore, he considered information filtering and recommendation systems as typical examples of adaptive interfaces and he presented a review of "content-based" and "collaborative" filtering systems as well as efforts, which combine the two approaches. Moreover, he described innovative applications of recommendation systems such as an Adaptive Route Advisor, which suggests alternative routes between a driver's current location and his destination. This system takes into account a weighted combination of parameters like the distance, the estimated driving time, the number of turns and intersections, etc. and proposes the routes that best fit to the current user model. Another application that was presented is INCA, which helps persons who are responsible in allocating resources in response to emergencies that involve hazardous materials. Finally, Prof. Langley compared the domain of adaptive user interfaces with other paradigms. He argued that the main difference between adaptive user interfaces and other cognition computational models, is that the former deal primarily with the content of human decision, while the latter focus on the process of human thought and decision making. He closed his talk providing a list of challenges and open questions that Machine Learning faces in creating Adaptive Interfaces.

The paper by Schwab and Pohl [35] described LaboUr, a recommendation system, which learns user profiles from ELFI, a Web-based system that provides information concerning research funds. In particular ELFI is organized into hierarchies of research topics, e.g. mathematics, computer science, etc., and funding types, such as grant, fellowship. The system displays the contents of a topic by listing links to so-called detailed views (DVs) of relevant funding programs. A DV consists of the available data about a research program, i.e. an abstract, the covered topics, the funding type, etc. The authors implemented a simple Bayessian classifier and they modified the known k-Nearest Neighbor algorithm to classify the set of information objects (DVs), selected by the users. Most probable or close DVs are considered as a class, which could be recommended to a user. Finally, seeking to determine explicitly the users' interests, the authors employed statistical methods to find the DVs features that are important to an individual user.

Semeraro et al. [36] described an intelligent Web-based digital library, named CDL, which incorporates Machine Learning techniques both for document analysis and classification, as well as for user modeling. Users can access CDL in several ways, even through a dial-up connection to Internet, and interact with it via either a form-based, a tree-based, or a topic-map interface. The topic map provides a global view of the semantic content of the documents by showing the document topics. The topics have been defined incorporating standard thesaurus building techniques and represented by vectors. The navigation in the map or in the tree interfaces results into the automatic query composition. Regarding user modeling, CDL incorporates the supervised learning algorithm C4.5 as a module of the "Application Server" which is embedded in the Learning Server component. C4.5 takes as input the data stored in the log files, and classifies the users interacting with CDL, inducing a decision tree as well as a set of rules. Each entry of the interaction log files is labeled indicating three main registered user categories: Novice, Expert and Teacher. Furthermore, each class is associated with one of the mentioned interfaces. In this manner the CDL architecture uses Machine Learning techniques for managing user models and providing a weak form of user interface adaptivity.

3.2   Intelligent Agents and Multi-agent Systems

Fragoudis and Likothanassis [16] provided a complete comparative study of the user modeling approaches of the most well-known information discovery intelligent agents, such as Lira, Letizia, Amalthea, Arachnid, Webmate, Webace, Syskill & Webert, Webwatcher, Siteseer, Law and Fab. They stated that Intelligent agents help people in two different ways: They can provide assistance while browsing or they may autonomously discover documents of interest, based on the results of a query to some search engine. The main conclusion of this work is that "none of the referred solutions seems to outperform the others and in any case the result is the same: Intelligent systems that help people on their battle against information overload".

The paper by Moukas [24] described "Amalthaea", a multi-agent user modeling and information discovery system. Amalthaea is implemented by creating an "ecosystem" of two kinds of cooperating agents: the Information Filtering Agents which are responsible for the acquisition and maintenance of the user profiles and the Information Discovery Agents which monitor and adapt user profiles to the various information sources. Both documents and user preferences are represented using the Vector Space Model. The results of the users' queries on existing search engines are used to define the interestingness of the documents. The user receives only the most "interesting" documents and rates them in a scale from 1 to 7, providing the ecosystem with relevance feedback. Amalthaea assigns to each user model a population of Information Filtering and Information Discovery agents. The user profiles are updated dynamically by the Information Filtering Agents, which, evolve by three operators: cloning, crossover and mutation. The agents' survival, offspring generation, or diminishment depends on the values of two measures: the *individual* and *overall fitness*. Agents with low individual fitness are purged and new ones are created, while the evolution rate is determined by the overall fitness of the ecosystem.

3.3   Student Modeling

Chiu and Webb [13] dealt with two issues confronted during the student behavior prediction process. First, what mechanisms could be employed in order to increase the predictions without degrading prediction accuracy and second, for contexts in which accuracy is of primary importance, how the prediction accuracy could be further improved. The paper improved previous work of the authors known as the Dual model. This approach utilizes temporal data in order to improve the prediction rate of a student modeling system. Specifically, Dual model creates a temporal model, namely *fresh model* - built using data from the most recent observations - in addition to a conventional model, which is referred to as an *extended model* - inferred from data of all historical observations. When a Dual-model system predicts a student's future actions, both models will be consulted. In this paper the authors, aiming to further increase the prediction rate, propose an alternative Dual-model strategy that consults the two models in parallel. Moreover they present and evaluate three new variants of Dual-model, which improve its prediction accuracy.

3.4   Web Mining

Spiliopoulou et al. [38] described WUM (Web Utilisation Miner), an algorithm which keeps track of all traversals of the paths through the pages of a site and aggregates them in a graph. The authors specify MINT, a mining language, which forms SQL-like queries to extract useful information from the "aggregated" graph. Specifically, MINT provides "interesting" navigation patterns (paths). Finally, the authors define the concept of "interestingness" according to the structure of a MINT-query.

The paper by Paliouras et al. [28] proposed a methodology for constructing user communities (i.e., groups of people with common interests) from Web logs and they applied it on the logs of the ACAI'99 Web site. The methodology deals with three major issues: The fisrt issue is that of data engineering, which includes selecting the right representation for the training data and reducing the dimensionality of the problem. Regarding this issue, the authors propose the representation of access sessions as transitions between pages, or as bags of pages. The second issue concerns the selection of the clustering method. The authors construct user groups using the conceptual clustering algorithm COBWEB. The last issue, in which they pay substantial attention, is the characterization of the community models, i.e., the construction of meaningful communities. For this purpose, they introduce *frequency increase*, a metric to decide which are the representative features for each community of visitors. One of the results of this paper is that representing access sessions by means of transitions between pages produces interesting navigation patterns for the community models. Finally the authors conclude that Web usage analysis is much more insightful than the approach of examining simple usage statistics of a Web site and that the employment of machine learning and user modelling techniques are very promising tools for this analysis.

4   Discussion

After the paper presentations an interesting discussion took place, debating the following issues:

1. The impact of ML in the development of adaptive interfaces and UM software.
2. What kinds of ML techniques are needed in UM.
3. Whether it is worth-while using "heavy" ML algorithms in the development of on-line interactive systems such as tutoring systems, or personilized Web-based applications.

The conclusions of this discussion could be summarized as follows:

1. ML offers a suite of powerful techniques either for user model acquisition or for user community induction.
2. ML techniques support complex decision making tasks and improve the prediction quality of a UM software.
3. UM should focus on the utilization of rapid and on-line learning techniques. This means that accurate and descriptive user models should be generated from small sets of training cases and that the models should be updated each time a user interaction occurs or at least before the next session.

References

1. Albrecht, D.W., Zukerman, I. and A.E. Nicholson: 1998. Bayesian Models for Keyhole Plan Recognition in an Adventure Game. User Modelling and User-Adapted Interaction 8, 5 - 47.
2. Balabanovic, M. and Y. Shoham: 1997. Content-Based, Collaborative Recommendation. Communications of the ACM 4 (3), 66-72.
3. Basu, C., Hirsh, H., and W. Cohen: 1998. Recommendation as Classification: Using Social and Content-Based Information in Recommendation. Fifteenth National Conference in Artificial Intelligence, Madison, Wisconsin, MW.
4. Bauer, M.: 1999. From Interaction Data to Plan Libraries: A Clustering Approach. International Joint Conference on Artificial Intelligence, Stockholm, Sweden, 962-967.

5. Benaki, E., Karkaletsis, V. and C. D.Spyropoulos: 1997. Integrating User Modelling Into Information Extraction: The UMIE Prototype. Sixth International Conference on User Modelling, 55-57.
6. Billsus, D. and M. Pazzani: 1999. A Hybrid User Model for News Story Classsification Seventh International Conference on User Modelling, Banff, Canada, 99-108.
7. Bloedorn, E., Mani, I. and T. R. MacMillan: 1996. Machine Learning of User Profiles: Representational Issues. Thirteen National Conference on Artificial Intelligence, Portland, Oregon, 433-438.
8. Brajnik, G. and C. Tasso: 1994. A Shell for Developing Non-monotonic User Modelling Systems. International Journal of Human-Computer Studies 40, 31-62.
9. Brajnik, G., Guida, G. and C. Tasso: 1987. User Modelling in Intelligent Information Retrieval. Information Processing and Management 23, 305-320.
10. Brusilovsky, P., and E. Schwarz: 1997. User as Student: Towards an Adaptive Interface for Advanced Web Applications. Sixth International Conference on User Modelling, 177-188.
11. Chin, D.N.: 1989. KNOME: modelling what the user knows. In: A. Kobsa and W. Wahlster (eds.): User models in dialog systems. Berlin: Springer-Verlag, 74-107.
12. Chiu, B.C., and G. Webb.:1998. Using Decision Trees for Agent Modeling: Improving Prediction Performance. User Modelling and User-Adapted Interaction 8, 131-152.
13. Chiu, B.C., and G. Webb: "Dual-model: An Architecture for Utilizing Temporal Information in Student Modeling". In [41].
14. Crabtree, I.B. and S.J. Soltysiak: 1998. Identifying and tracking changing interests. International Journal on Digital Libraries 2, 38-53.
15. Esposito, F., Malerba, D., Semeraro, G., Fanizzi, N. and S. Ferilli: 1998. Adding Machine Learning and Knowledge Intensive Techniques to a Digital Library Service. International Journal on Digital Libraries 2, 3-19.
16. Fragoudis, D. and S. Likothanassis: "User Modelling in Information Discovery: An Overview". In [41].
17. Giangrandi P. and C. Tasso:.1997. Managing Temporal Knowledge in Student Modelling. Sixth International Conference on User Modelling, 415-426.
18. Joachims, T., Freitag, D. and T. Mitchell: 1997. WebWatcher: A tour guide for the World Wide Web. Fifteenth International Joint Conference in Artificial Intelligence, Nagoya, Aichi, Japan.
19. Kay, J.: 1995. The um Toolkit for Cooperative User Modelling. User Modelling and User Adapted Interaction 4, 149-196.
20. Langley, P.: 1999. User Modelling in Adaptive Interfaces. Seventh International Conference on User Modelling, Banff, Canada, 357-370.
21. Langley, P.: "User Modeling in Adaptive Interfaces". In [41].
22. Maes, P.: 1994. Agents that Reduce Work and Information Overload. Communications of the ACM 37(7), 31-40.
23. Moukas, A.: 1997. Amalthaea: Information Discovery and Filtering using a Multiagent Evolving Ecosystem. Applied Artificial Intelligence: An International Journal 11(5), 437-457.
24. Moukas, A.: "User Modeling in a MultiAgent Evolving System". In [41].
25. Mueller, M.: 1999. Inducing Conceptual User Models. ABIS-99, 7. GI Workshop on Adaptivity and User Modelling in Interactive Software Systems.
26. Orwant, J.: 1995. Heterogeneous Learning in the Doppelgänger User Modeling System. User Modelling and User-Adapted Interaction 4, 107-130.

27. Paliouras, G., Karkaletsis, V., Papatheodorou, C., and C. D. Spyropoulos: 1999. Exploiting Learning Techniques for the Acquisition of User Stereotypes and Communities. Seventh International Conference on User Modelling, Banff, Canada, 169-178.

28. Paliouras, G., Papatheodorou, C., Karkaletsis, V., Tzitziras, P. and C.D. Spyropoulos: "Learning Communities of the ACAI'99 Web-site Visitors". In [41].

29. Pazzani, M. and D. Billsus: 1997. Learning and Revising User Profiles: The Identification of Interesting Web Sites. Machine Learning 27, 313-331.

30. Perkowitz, M. and O. Etzioni: 1998. Adaptive Web Sites: Automatically synthesizing Web pages. Fifteen National Conference in Artificial Intelligence, Wisconsin, MW.

31. Perkowitz M., and O. Etzioni: 1999. Adaptive Web Sites: Conceptual Cluster Mining. Sixteenth International Joint Conference in Artificial Intelligence, Stockholm, Sweden, 264-269.

32. Raskutti, B. and A. Beitz: 1996. Acquiring User Preferences for Information Filtering in Interactive Multi-Media Services. Pacific Rim International Conference on Artificial Intelligence, 47-58.

33. Resnick, P. and H.R. Varian: 1997. Recommender Systems. Communications of the ACM 4(3), 56-58.

34. Rich, E.: 1983. Users are Individuals: Individualizing User Models. International Journal of Man-Machine Studies 18, 199-214.

35. Schwab, I. and W. Pohl: "Learning User Profiles from Positive Examples". In [41].

36. Semeraro, G., Costabile, M.F., Esposito, F., Fanizzi, N. and S. Ferilli: "Machine Learning Techniques for Adaptive User Interfaces in a Corporate Digital Library Service". In [41].

37. Sison, R., Numao, M. and M. Shimura: 1998. Discovering Error Classes from Discrepancies in Novice Behaviors via Multistrategy Conceptual Clustering. User Modelling and User-Adapted Interaction 8, 103-129.

38. Spiliopoulou, M., Faulstich, L. and K. Winkler: "A Data Miner Analyzingthe Navigational Behaviour of Web Users". In [41].

39. Suryadi D. and P.J. Gmytrasiewicz: 1999. Learning Models of Other Agents Using Influence Diagrams. Seventh International Conference on User Modelling, Banff, Canada, 223-232.

40. Weber, G.: 1999. Adaptive Learning Systems in the World Wide Web. Seventh International Conference on User Modelling, Banff, Canada, 371-377.

41. Proceedings of the Workshop on Machine Learning in User Modeling, Advanced Course on Artificial Intelligence (ACAI '99), Chania, Greece, 1999
(http://www.iit.demokritos.gr/skel/eetn/acai99/Workshops.htm).

Data Mining in Economics, Finance, and Marketing

Hans C. Jessen[1] and Georgios Paliouras[2]

[1]Initiative Consulting, London SW1V 1PX, UK
hans.jessen@initiativemedia.com
[2]Inst. of Informatics and Telecommunications, NCSR "Demokritos", 15310 Athens, Greece
paliourg@iit.demokritos.gr

1   Introduction

Data Mining has become a buzzword in industry in recent years. It is something that everyone is talking about but few seem to understand. There are two reasons for this lack of understanding: First is the fact that Data Mining researchers have very diverse backgrounds such as machine learning, psychology and statistics. This means that the research is often based on different methodologies and communication links e.g. notation is often unique to a particular research area which hampers the exchange of ideas and the dissemination to the wider public. The second reason for the lack of understanding is that the main ideas behind Data Mining are often completely opposite to mainstream statistics and as many companies interested in Data Mining already employ statisticians, such a change of view can create opposition.

There are many definitions of Data Mining, the one we favour can be summarised as follows:[1]

> *"Data Mining is concerned with secondary data analysis of large data bases where the aim is to identify unsuspected relationships of interest or value."*

Classical statistics is mostly based on hypothesis testing. The researcher makes assumptions about the structure of the data and then uses statistical tests to either prove or disprove these assumptions. The result of such an exercise is that a lot of careful consideration goes into building a model and that the researcher should have a good understanding of the data involved. The drawback is, of course, that the quality of a model becomes dependent on the quality of the researcher, his ability to formulate interesting hypotheses and his experience in handling a given date source.

Data Mining does not have hypotheses testing at its heart and this is its main difference from classical statistics. Instead, Data Mining aims to find interesting relationships within the data that are of value to the researcher. The most appealing aspect of Data Mining is that it removes the need for the researcher to be an expert in model building and therefore reduces the cost of the analysis. It also offers the possibility that the tools might come up with ideas that the researcher would not have thought of. Although this sounds excellent for applied researchers there are unfortunately also some drawbacks. Here are a couple that are of particular interest:

Are the identified relationships of interest? Most Data Mining is used on medium or large-scale databases. With a large enough number of observations, it is all too

---

[1] This note draws on ideas from Prof. David J. Hand's RSS (Royal Statistical Society) presentation: "Data Mining: puff or potential".

G. Paliouras, V. Karkaletsis, and C.D. Spyropoulos (Eds.): ACAI '99, LNAI 2049, pp. 295-299, 2001.
© Springer-Verlag Berlin Heidelberg 2001

easy to identify spurious or obvious patterns. Spurious patterns are caused by pure chance and do not relate to the general structure of the data, whereas obvious patterns are relationships in the data caused by data collection procedures or inherent in a particular type of data e.g. the colder it is, the fewer ice creams are sold. Many examples have been presented where Data Mining techniques have come up with solutions that are trivial for an expert in the field.

Selection bias. Much work has been done on selection bias in statistics but Data Mining research has largely ignored this issue. One way to think about selection bias is "how did the people on which I have data happen to be in the data set in the first place?" One often sees forecasts, say from decision trees, being applied to the whole population without recognising that the data from which the tree was derived was non-random.

Few people in industry doubt that Data Mining is here to stay and that it offers significant improvements over classical analysis when used on large databases. The challenge for the Data Mining research community is to incorporate knowledge from other fields, like econometrics and statistics, in order not to make obvious mistakes or to re-invent the wheel. The Workshop on "Data Mining in Economics, Finance and Marketing", which took place during the Advanced Course on Artificial Intelligence (ACAI '99) aimed to address this challenge, by bringing together people from different disciplines who share a common interest for developing and using data mining techniques. This chapter presents an overview of the papers presented in the workshop [15] and some of the general conclusions that were drawn.

2   Overview of the Workshop Papers

Data mining or Knowledge Discovery in Databases (KDD) is an exploratory and iterative process that can be decomposed into a number of stages. The paper by Feelders and Daniels [4] describes the different activities in the data mining process and discusses some pitfalls and guidelines to circumvent them. Despite the predominant attention for analysis, data selection and pre-processing is usually the most time-consuming activity, and has a substantial influence on the ultimate success of the process. The involvement of a subject area expert, data mining expert as well as a data expert is critical to the success of data mining projects. Despite the attractive suggestion of "fully automatic" data analysis, knowledge of the processes behind the data remains indispensible in avoiding the many pitfalls of data mining. Although company databases are usually quite large, proper formulation of the data mining problem combined with sampling techniques often allows reduction to manageable sized data sets. In the majority of applications the data were originally not collected with the intention of data mining, but merely to support daily business processes. This may give rise to low quality data, as well as biases in the data that reduce the applicability of discovered patterns.

Dikaiakos [3] presented the architecture of a Financial Information Gathering Infrastructure (FIGI). FIGI helps investors collect, filter, combine and integrate portfolio-related information, provided through various Internet services, like World-Wide Web sites and Web-databases. FIGI is being developed with Java-based Mobile Agent technology by Mitsubishi Electric Information Technology Center [5]. The employment of Java and Mobile Agents provides a framework for unifying the various financial information services currently available on Internet and for sustaining continuous information provision to mobile users.

The vast improvement of hardware and software technology in the last years has made it possible for companies to store large amounts of data in a reliable and inexpensive way. Although this may appear to be very positive at first, it has led in very many cases to large collections of data, where it has become impossible for humans to maintain the right understanding of the data they hold. The paper by Karamanlidou et al. [6] concentrates on data related to stock markets and especially on the stock market in Athens. It presents the system Stock Miner, which intends to deal with problems related to large volumes of data in financial areas. Stock Miner combines technical analysis, which is used by stockbrokers, and Knowledge Discovery in Databases, which is a new field concerned with analyzing data and discovering useful information.

The approach introduced by Piasta [11] for analysing business databases is based on the idea of rule induction. The ProbRough system [10] for inducing rough classifiers was inspired by the methodology of the rough set theory. The search strategy of ProbRough, through the set of partitions of the attribute space, is guided by the global cost criterion. Because of the specific shape of partition elements, the resultant rough classifiers may be presented as sets of simple and transparent decision rules, easily understood by humans. The domains of rules are disjoint and fill up the whole attribute space. ProbRough accepts databases with noisy and inconsistent information delivered by attributes of any mixed qualitative and quantitative type. Moreover, it enables the use of background knowledge in the form of prior probabilities of decisions and different costs of misclassification. The ProbRough system is capable of inducing decision rules from databases with practically unlimited number of objects and attributes. The paper presents the behavior of the ProbRough system on several real-life business databases. Two real-world marketing databases [8], [14] are being used to illustrate the way of discovering the decision rules for identifying customers who are likely to accept or reject an offer. Furthermore, the US Census Bureau database is being analysed and applications of ProbRough in credit evaluation and financial ratio analysis are being illustrated.

The exploration of huge quantities of stored data and the extraction of useful knowledge, which is formally referred to as data mining, is now believed to be a critical factor in the decision that a company or any other interested individual may take. Recently, Evolutionary Algorithms (EAs) have been applied with very good results to various types of data mining problems. EAs are stochastic search techniques that explore combinatorial search spaces, using simulated evolution. The primary objective of an EA is to either find something – whether this is known or not – or accomplish a goal, or more generally solve a problem. The paper by Adamidis and Koukoulakis [1] presents initial results of data mining from TV program databases using EAs. It compares the performance of different operators and different operator parameters of EAs. The EA mining system is used to extract rules from a database that contains TV broadcast data. The database has historical data, i.e., broadcasted schedules. Therefore, the interested individual, that is the owner of the station, given the rules, can be informed about possible relations between attributes and plan future schedules accordingly. Initial results show that EAs can discover previously unknown knowledge in the TV database that we used.

Direct mail is a typical example for the use of response modelling. In order to decide which people will receive the mailing, potential customers are divided into two groups or classes (buyers and non-buyers) and a response model is created. The main aim of the paper by Coenen et al. [2] is the improvement of response modelling. For this purpose, a combined approach of rule-induction and case-based reasoning is being proposed. The initial classification of buyers and non-buyers is done by means of the C5 algorithm, the more recent version of C4.5 [12]. In order to improve the ranking of the classified cases, a new method, called rule-predicted typicality, is being introduced. The combination of these two approaches is tested on synergy by elaborating a direct mail example.

Corporate bankruptcy prediction is a usual problem in financing and management. Several approaches have been proposed for the solution of this problem. These can be classified into two categories: conventional classification (e.g. discriminant analysis and multicriteria analysis) and data mining methods (e.g. neural networks, genetic algorithms, decision trees). In the paper by Thomaidis et al. [13] a new approach is proposed based on Machine Learning and Fuzzy Logic. This new approach uses a fuzzy system, in order to classify firms into efficient and inefficient ones. The system uses the *Fuzzy- ROSA* (*Rule Oriented Statistical Analysis*) [7] methodology, which is found in *Winrosa©* [9] and is a combination of the *Standard-ROSA* methodology and Fuzzy Logic. It is shown that the proposed method produces better results than the conventional ones. Furthermore, it produces rules with fewer statements in their premise, which are more 'general', and thus have greater prediction capability.

3   Conclusions

The workshop papers clearly showed how Data Mining can be applied to many different economic and/or financial prediction problems. What is perhaps the most interesting observation is just how quickly this research area has become popular in the otherwise conservative world of business. Statistical analysis has been available to businesses for years but somehow Data Mining has captured the interest of businesses in a way that classical statistical analysis never did. Cynics may believe that this is due to better marketing of Data Mining with labels such as "artificial Intelligence, Neural Networks, Decision rules" instead of the usual statistical labels like "nonlinear regression, discriminant analysis". This may be partly true but without a real financial benefit to businesses, Data Mining would not have gained so widespread popularity.

Although the future looks very rosy for Data Mining both as a research area and as a tool to increase profitability for businesses, there are still teething problems that need to be dealt with more rigorously. For example, several of the papers drew attention to data issues. Without a thorough understanding of how data is collected and pre-processed, it is unlikely that Data Mining can offer unbiased results. Understanding your data is not a glamorous undertaking and many businesses tend to ignore this and go straight to doing the analysis. Perhaps there is a need for some caveats to the usual selling of Data Mining as do-it-all-without-thinking techniques. Another example raised at the workshop was the need to keep the output of the Data

Mining analysis easily understandable. Most business leaders will be uncomfortable with things they do not at least have some understanding of and "black boxes" will never be acceptable.

The papers contained many examples of innovative technical developments. One of the most attractive things about this research area is the diversity of approaches to data analysis. In fact, Data Mining probably incorporates a greater variety of different techniques than any branch of numerical analysis. It is highly likely that this coming together of ideas and innovations from so many sources will continue to inspire developments in the Data Mining area and that businesses will be increasingly interested in what Data Mining can offer them.

References

1. Adamidis, P, and Koukoulakis, K. Evolutionary Data Mining applied to TV Databases: A First Approach. In [15].
2. Coenen, F., Swinnen, G., Vanhoof, K. and Wets, G. The Improvement of Response Modelling: Combining Rule-Induction and Case-Based Reasoning. In [15].
3. Dikaiakos, M. FIGI: Using Mobile Agent Technology to Collect Financial Information on Internet. In [15].
4. Feelders, A. and Daniels, H. Discovery in practice. In [15].
5. Horizon Systems Laboratory. *Mobile Agent Computing. A white paper.* Mitsubishi Electric ITA., January 1998.
6. Karamanlidou, M. Tuffier, O. and Vlahavas, I. Stock Miner: A System for Knowledge Discovery in Financial Data. In [15].
7. Krone, A. and Kiendl, H. Rule-based decision analysis with Fuzzy-ROSA method, *Proceedings of EFDAN'96*, Dortmund (Germany), 1996, 109-114.
8. Kowalczyk, W., Piasta, Z. Rough-set inspired approach to knowledge discovery in business databases. In: X. Wu, R. Kotagiri, K. R. Korb, *Research and Development in Knowledge Discovery and Data Mining,* Proceedings of the Second Pacific-Asia Conference on Knowledge Discovery and Data Mining, PAKDD-98, Melburne, 15-17 April, Springer-Verlag, Berlin, Heidelberg, New York, 1998, 186-197.
9. MIT GmbH. *WINROSA: Handbook*, Aachen, Germany, 1997(b).
10. Piasta, Z., Lenarcik, A. Learning rough classifiers from large databases with missing values. In: L. Polkowski, A. Skowron, (eds), *Rough Sets in Knowledge Discovery*, Physica Verlag, 1998, 483-499.
11. Piasta, Z. Analyzing business databases with the ProbRough rule induction system. In [15].
12. Quinlan, J.R., *C4.5: Programs for Machine Learning*, Morgan Kaufmann, 1993.
13. Nikolaos Thomaidis, George Dounias, Costas D. Zopounidis: A fuzzy rule based learning method for corporate bankruptcy prediction. In [15].
14. Van den Poel, D., Piasta, Z. Purchase prediction in database marketing with the ProbRough system. In: L. Polkowski, A. Skowron, (eds), *Rough Sets and Current Trends in Computing*, Physica Verlag, 1998, 593-600.
15. Proceedings of the Workshop on Data Mining in Economics, Finance and Marketing, Advanced Course on Artificial Intelligence (ACAI '99), Chania, Greece, 1999 (http://www.iit.demokritos.gr/skel/eetn/acai99/Workshops.htm).

Machine Learning in Medical Applications

George D. Magoulas[1] and Andriana Prentza[2]

[1] Department of Information Systems and Computing, Brunel University,
Uxbridge UB8 3PH, UK
George.Magoulas@brunel.ac.uk
[2] Department of Electrical and Computer Engineering, National Technical University of
Athens, GR-15773 Athens, Greece
aprentza@biomed.ntua.gr

1   Introduction

Machine Learning (ML) provides methods, techniques, and tools that can help solving diagnostic and prognostic problems in a variety of medical domains. ML is being used for the analysis of the importance of clinical parameters and their combinations for prognosis, e.g. prediction of disease progression, extraction of medical knowledge for outcome research, therapy planning and support, and for the overall patient management. ML is also being used for data analysis, such as detection of regularities in the data by appropriately dealing with imperfect data, interpretation of continuous data used in the Intensive Care Unit, and intelligent alarming resulting in effective and efficient monitoring. It is argued that the successful implementation of ML methods can help the integration of computer-based systems in the healthcare environment providing opportunities to facilitate and enhance the work of medical experts and ultimately to improve the efficiency and quality of medical care. Below, we summarize some major ML applications in medicine.

Medical diagnostic reasoning is a very important application area of intelligent systems [18], [35], [36]. In this framework, expert systems and model-based schemes provide mechanisms for the generation of hypotheses from patient data. For example, rules are extracted from the knowledge of experts to construct expert systems. Unfortunately, in many cases, experts may not know, or may not be able to formulate, what knowledge they actually use in solving their problems. Symbolic learning techniques (e.g. inductive learning by examples) are used to add learning, and knowledge management capabilities to expert systems [5]: given a set of clinical cases that act as examples, learning in intelligent systems can be achieved using ML methods that are able to produce a systematic description of those clinical features that uniquely characterize the clinical conditions. Thus, knowledge can be expressed in the form of simple rules, or often as a decision tree. A classic example of this type of system is KARDIO, which was developed to interpret ECGs [7].

This approach can be extended to handle cases where there is no previous experience in the interpretation and understanding of medical data. For example, Hau and Coiera [11] describe an intelligent system, which takes real-time patient data

G. Paliouras, V. Karkaletsis, and C.D. Spyropoulos (Eds.): ACAI '99, LNAI 2049, pp. 300-307, 2001.
© Springer-Verlag Berlin Heidelberg 2001

obtained during cardiac bypass surgery and creates models of normal and abnormal cardiac physiology to detect changes in patient's condition. Additionally, in a research setting, these models can serve as initial hypotheses that can drive further experimentation.

Learning from patient data one encounters several difficulties, since datasets are characterized by incompleteness (missing parameter values), incorrectness (systematic or random noise in the data), sparseness (few and/or non-representable patient records available), and inexactness (inappropriate selection of parameters for the given task). ML provides tools for dealing with these characteristics of medical datasets [20]. Subsymbolic learning methods, especially neural networks are able to handle these datasets and are mostly used for their pattern matching abilities and their human like characteristics (generalization, robustness to noise), in order to improve medical decision making [1], [21], [22], [26], [31].

Another field of application is biomedical signal processing [9], [17], [24], [30]. Since our understanding of biological systems is not complete, there are essential features and information hidden in the physiological signals that are not readily apparent. Also, the effects between the different subsystems are not distinguishable. Biological signals are characterized by substantial variability, caused either by spontaneous internal mechanisms or by external stimuli. Associations between the different parameters may be too complex to be solved with conventional techniques. ML methods use these sets of data, which can be produced easier, and can help to model the nonlinear relationships that exist between these data, and extract parameters and features which can improve medical care.

Computer-based medical image interpretation systems comprise a major application area providing significant assistance in medical diagnosis [10], [12], [13], [27]. In most cases, the development of these systems is considered as an attempt to emulate the doctor's expertise in the identification of malignant regions in minimally invasive imaging procedures (e.g., computed tomography, ultrasonography, endoscopy, confocal microscopy, computed radiography or magnetic resonance imaging). The objective is to increase the expert's ability to identify malignant regions while decreasing the need for intervention, and maintaining the ability for accurate diagnosis. Furthermore, it may be possible to examine a larger area, studying living tissue *in vivo*, possibly at a distance [8], and, thus, minimize the shortcomings of biopsies, such as discomfort for the patient, delay in diagnosis, and limited number of tissue samples. The need for more effective methods of early detection, such as those that computer assisted medical diagnosis systems aim to provide is obvious. The potential of ML in this area is significantly high since it provides us with computational methods for accumulating, changing and updating knowledge in intelligent medical image interpretation systems, and, in particular, learning mechanisms that will help us to induce knowledge from examples or data. Especially in minimally invasive imaging procedures that apply new imaging principles, such as fluorescence imaging or laser scanning microscopy, ML methods can be useful since algorithmic solutions are not available, there is lack of formal models, or the knowledge about the application domain is poorly defined due to lack of previous experience and/or medical expertise in the interpretation of the acquired images.

In general, it seems that as the healthcare environment is becoming more and more reliant on computer technology, the use of ML methods can provide useful aids to assist the physician in many cases, eliminate issues associated with human fatigue and habituation, provide rapid identification of abnormalities and enable diagnosis in real time.

Next, we will summarize successful applications of ML methods that were presented at the *Workshop on Machine Learning in Medical Applications* held on July 15th, 1999, and hosted by the ECCAI Advanced Course on Artificial Intelligence for 1999 (ACAI '99) at Chania, Island of Crete, in Greece. The goals of the workshop were to foster fundamental and applied research in the application of ML methods to medical problem solving and medical research, provide a forum for reporting advances in the area, determine whether ML methods are able to support the research and development on intelligent systems for medical applications, and identify those areas where increased research is likely to yield advances.

The workshop comprised eleven refereed papers [38] and one invited, which looked at the theories and approaches that underpin the use of ML methods in medicine. A number of recommendations for a research agenda were produced, including both technical and human-centered issues. In the next section, a brief description of these contributions is presented and the chapter concludes with a general discussion on the development and use of ML methods in a medical context.

3   Overview of the Workshop Papers

The invited talk by Schurr [34] focused on endoscopic techniques and the role of ML methods in this context. The speaker referred to current limitations of endoscopic techniques, which are related to the restrictions of access to the human body, associated to endoscopy. In this regard, the technical limitations include: restrictions of manual capabilities to manipulate human organs through a small access, limitations in visualizing tissues and restrictions in getting diagnostic information about tissues. To alleviate these problems, international technology developments focus on the creation of new manipulation techniques involving robotics and intelligent sensor devices for more precise endoscopic interventions. It is acknowledged that this new generation of sensor devices contributes to the development and spread of intelligent systems in medicine by providing ML methods with data for further processing. Current applications include suturing in cardiac surgery, and other clinical fields. It was mentioned that particular focus is put by several research groups on the development of new endoscopic visualizing and diagnostic tools. In this context, the potentials of new imaging principles, such as fluorescence imaging or laser scanning microscopy, and ML methods are very high. The clinical idea behind these developments is early detection of malignant lesions in stages were local endoscopic therapy is possible. Technical developments in this field are very promising, however, clinical results are still pending and ongoing research will have to clarify the real potential of these technologies for clinical use.

The paper by Moustakis and Charissis [23] surveyed the role of ML in medical decision making and provided an extensive literature review on various ML applications in medicine that could be useful to practitioners interested in applying ML methods to improve the efficiency and quality of medical decision making systems. In this work the point of getting away from the accuracy measures as sole evaluation criteria of learning algorithms was stressed. The issue of comprehensibility, i.e. how well the medical expert can understand and, thus, use the results from a system that applies ML methods, is very important and should be carefully considered in the evaluation.

The paper by Alexopoulos et al. [2] focused on the application of inductive ML methods in medical diagnosis of stroke. The proposed approach was based on the See5 algorithm, which is an updated version of the C4.5 algorithm. In the experiments reported, this approach exhibited the capability to learn from examples and handle missing information by constructing a decision tree, which could be transformed to IF/THEN rules. Special attention was given to the determination of the complexity and comprehensibility of the acquired decision rules by consulting medical experts.

In the paper by Zelič et al. [37], the Magnus Assistant decision tree learner and the Bayesian classifier were used for the diagnosis and prognosis of first cerebral paroxysm. Despite the fact that best predictions were obtained using the naive Bayesian classifier, the most interesting results from a medical point of view were obtained using the Magnus Assistant decision tree learner. Data and attributes that were considered by expert neurologists as obvious and meaningless turned out to be very important for automatic diagnosis and prognosis. In this case, ML methods provided a different estimation of some clinical attributes and motivated clinicians to generate new hypotheses and ultimately to improve their standard diagnostic and prognostic processes.

An interactive system for the ascertainment of visual perception disorders was presented by Ruseckaite [33]. The system performed data analysis and extracted interesting dependencies between visual perception disorder and damage of the brain by applying a modified version of the ML algorithm Charade. Preliminary results indicated the effectiveness of the proposed approach in rehabilitating persons with certain brain anomalies.

The paper by Bourlas et al. [6] extended previous work of the authors on medical expert systems for ECG diagnosis by incorporating ML methods to continuously improve the knowledge base of a medical expert system. According to the reported results, the new system exhibits continual learning capabilities using an extended version of the ID3 algorithm to extract, from time to time, a set to diagnosis rules based on a training set of ECGs. The extracted rules are merged into the older ones and the duplicates are removed. In order to optimize the performance of the system, a knowledge management subsystem provides monitoring of the performance of the final rules, in terms of their diagnostic accuracy, and modifies the knowledge base.

The work presented in Neves et al. [25] demonstrated the need for Health Care Unit's medical imaging models and introduced the concept of a generic and deductive/inductive model of operation, which supports scheduling, forecasting, and accounting. Following this approach, several agents concurred in generating hypotheses, each one of them having a different role in evaluating parts of the data, and neural networks were used to discover associations in the dataset.

Asteroth and Möller [4] investigated the use of neural network-based approximation of structural information to the identification of individualized models of the human cardiovascular system. This approach allowed them to achieve robust real-time identification.

The problem of identifying the structure of a population of patients with brain disorder was investigated by Pranckeviciene [29]. A single layer neural network evaluated the similarity among patients' electroencephalograms (EEGs). Experiments indicated that this approach successfully revealed similarities in the electrical activity of the brain of different patients.

In the paper by Jankowski [14] the use of incremental neural networks was suggested for approximation and classification tasks. The proposed model was based on neurons with a new form of rotated bi-radial transfer functions and was dynamically generated to match the complexity of the training data. In simulation experiments, the model exhibited superior generalization performance in the classification of medical data when compared with other popular methods.

The paper by Karkanis et al. [15] proposed the use of textural descriptors for the discrimination of cancer regions in endoscopic images. Second order gray level statistics were used for texture description and a multi-layer feedforward neural network was employed for classifying regions of interest. In preliminary experiments, this simple scheme was able to detect abnormalities in colonoscopic images with high accuracy.

The paper by Karkanis et al. [16] outlined a new approach to texture classification applied to lung endoscopic images. Feature selection was based on the texture spectrum of the image and a clustering method was used to distinguish the features with the most discriminative ability.

4   Discussion

Research in ML methods for medical applications to-date remains centered on technological issues and is mostly application driven. However, in order to answer fundamental questions and acquire useful insight in the performance and behavior of ML methods in a medical context, it is important to enhance our understanding of ML algorithms, as well as to provide mathematical justifications for their properties. Furthermore, we have to cope with a number of difficulties which concern the process of learning knowledge in practice, such as visualization of the learned knowledge, extraction of understandable rules from neural networks and identification of noise and outliers in the data. Other issues that arise in ML applications in medicine, like the control of overfitting and the scaling properties of the ML methods, so that they can apply to problems with large datasets, and high-dimensional input (feature) and output (classes-categories) spaces need also further investigation.

A common concern for ML applications in a medical context is the need for comprehensibility of the learning outcome, relevance of rules, criteria for identifying applications and assessing their feasibility, integration with the patient records, as well as the description of the appropriate level and role of intelligent systems in healthcare. These issues are very complex, as technical, organizational and social issues become intertwined. Previous research and experience suggest that the successful implementation of information systems (e.g., [3], [28]), and decision support systems in particular (e.g., [19], [32]), in the area of healthcare relies on the successful integration of the technology with the organizational and social context within which it is applied. Medical information is vital for the diagnosis and treatment of patients and therefore the ethical issues presented during its life cycle are critical. Understanding these issues becomes imperative as such technologies become pervasive. Some of these issues are system-centered, i.e., related to the inherent problems of the ML research. However, it is humans, not systems, who can act as moral agents. This means that it is humans that can identify and deal with ethical issues. Therefore, it is important to study the emerging challenges and ethical issues from a human-centered perspective by considering the motivations and ethical dilemmas of researchers, developers and medical users of ML methods in medical applications.

References

1. Akay, Y.M., Akay, M., Welkowitz, W., and Kostis, J.B. "Noninvasive detection of coronary artery disease using wavelet-based fuzzy neural networks". *IEEE Engineering in Medicine and Biology,* 761-764, 1994.
2. Alexopoulos, E., Dounias, G.D. and Vemmos, K. "Medical diagnosis of stroke using inductive machine learning". In [38].
3. Anderson, J.G. "Clearing the way for physician's use of clinical information systems". *Communications of the ACM,* 40, 8, 83-90, 1997.
4. Asteroth, A. and Möller, K. "Identification of individualized models of the human cardiovascular system". In [38].
5. Bourlas, Ph., Sgouros, N., Papakonstantinou, G., and Tsanakas, P. "Towards a knowledge acquisition and management system for ECG diagnosis". In *Proceedings of 13th International Congress Medical Informatics Europe-MIE96*, Copenhagen, 1996.
6. Bourlas, Ph., Giakoumakis, E. and Papakonstantinou, G. "A knowledge acquisition and management system for ECG diagnosis". In [38].
7. Bratko, I., Mozetic, I., and Lavrač, N. *KARDIO: A study in deep and qualitative knowledge for expert systems*, Cambridge, Massachusetts: MIT Press, 1989.
8. Delaney, P.M, Papworth, G.D, and King, R.G. "Fibre optic confocal imaging (FOCI) for in vivo subsurface microscopy of the colon". In *Methods in disease: Investigating the Gastrointestinal Tract,* Preedy, V.R. and Watson, R.R. (eds.), Greenwich Medical Media, London, 1998.

9.   Gindi, G.R., Darken, C.J., O' Brien, K.M., Sterz, M.L., and Deckelbaum, L.I. "Neural network and conventional classifiers for fluorescence-guided laser angioplasty". *IEEE Transactions on Biomedical Engineering*, 38, 3, 246-252, 1991.

10. Hanka, R., Harte, T.P., Dixon, A.K., Lomas, D.J., and Britton, P.D. "Neural networks in the interpretation of contrast-enhanced magnetic resonance images of the breast". In *Proceedings of Healthcare Computing,* Harrogate, UK, 275-283, 1996.

11. Hau, D., and Coiera, E. "Learning qualitative models of dynamic systems". *Machine Learning*, 26, 177-211, 1997.

12. Ifeachor, E.C., and Rosen, K. G. (eds.) *Proceedings of the International Conference on Neural Networks and Expert Systems in Medicine and Healthcare*, Plymouth, UK, 1994.

13. Innocent, P.R., Barnes, M., and John, R. "Application of the fuzzy ART/MAP and MinMax/MAP neural network models to radiographic image classification". *Artificial Intelligence in Medicine*, 11, 241-263, 1997.

14. Jankowski, N. "Approximation and classification in medicine with IncNet neural networks". In [38].

15. Karkanis, S., Magoulas, G.D., Grigoriadou, M. and Schurr, M. "Detecting abnormalities in colonoscopic images by textural description and neural networks". In [38].

16. Karkanis, S., Galoussi, K. and Maroulis, D. "Classification of endoscopic images based on texture spectrum". In [38].

17. Kennedy, L.R., Harrison, R.F., Burton, A.M., Fraser, H.S., Hamer, W.G., MacArthur, D., McAllum, R., and Steedman, D.J. "An artificial neural network system for diagnosis of acute myocardial infarction (AMI) in the accident and emergency department: evaluation and comparison with serum myoglobin measurements". *Computer Methods and Programs in Biomedicine*, 52, 93-103, 1997.

18. Kralj, K. and Kuka, M. "Using machine learning to analyze attributes in the diagnosis of coronary artery disease". In *Proceedings of Intelligent Data Analysis in Medicine and Pharmacology-IDAMAP98,* Brighton, UK, 1998.

19. Lane, V.P., Lane, D., and Littlejohns, P. "Neural networks for decision making related to asthma diagnosis and other respiratory disorders". In *Proceedings of Healthcare Computing,* Harrogate, UK, 85-93, 1996.

20. Lavrač, N. "Data mining in medicine: Selected techniques and applications". In *Proceedings of Intelligent Data Analysis in Medicine and Pharmacology-IDAMAP98,* Brighton, UK, 1998.

21. Lim, C.P., Harrison, R.F., and Kennedy, R.L. "Application of autonomous neural network systems to medical pattern classification tasks". *Artificial Intelligence in Medicine,* 11, 215-239, 1997.

22. Micheli-Tzanakou, E., Yi, C., Kostis, W.J., Shindler, D.M., and Kostis, J.B. "Myocardial infarction: Diagnosis and vital status prediction using neural networks". *IEEE Computers in Cardiology,* 229-232, 1993.

23. Moustakis, V. and Charissis, G. "Machine learning and medical decision making". In [38].

24. Nekovei, R. and Sun, Y. "Back-propagation network and its configuration for blood vessel detection in angiograms". *IEEE Transactions on Neural Networks,* 6, 1, 64-72, 1995.

25. Neves, J., Alves, V., Nelas, L., Romeu, A. and Basto, S. "An information system that supports knowledge discovery and data mining in medical imaging". In [38].

26. Pattichis, C., Schizas, C., and Middleton, L. "Neural network models in EMG diagnosis". *IEEE Transactions on Biomedical Engineering*, 42, 5, 486-496, 1995.

27. Phee, S.J., Ng, W.S., Chen, I.M., Seow-Choen, F., and Davies, B.L. "Automation of colonoscopy part II: visual-control aspects". *IEEE Engineering in Medicine and Biology*, May/June, 81-88, 1998.

28. Pouloudi, A. "Information technology for collaborative advantage in health care revisited". *Information and Management*, 35, 6, 345-357, 1999.
29. Pranckeviciene, E. "Finding similarities between an activity of the different EEGs by means of a single layer perceptron". In [38].
30. Prentza, A. and Wesseling, K.H. "Catheter-manometer system damped blood pressures detected by neural nets". *Medical and Biological Engineering and Computing*, 33, 589-595, 1995.
31. Reategui, E.B., Campbell, J.A., and Leao, B.F. "Combining a neural network with case-based reasoning in a diagnostic system". *Artificial Intelligence in Medicine*, 9, 5-27, 1996.
32. Ridderikhoff, J. and van Herk, B. "Who is afraid of the system? Doctors' attitude towards diagnostic systems". *International Journal of Medical Informatics* 53, 91-100, 1999.
33. Ruseckaite, R. "Computer interactive system for ascertainment of visual perception disorders". In [38].
34. Schurr, M. "The Role of Machine Learning Methods in Endoscopic Techniques". In [38].
35. Strausberg, J. and Person, M. "A process model of diagnostic reasoning in medicine". *International Journal of Medical Informatics*, 54, 9-23, 1999.
36. Zupan, B., Halter, J.A., and Bohanec, M. "Qualitative model approach to computer assisted reasoning in physiology". In *Proceedings of Intelligent Data Analysis in Medicine and Pharmacology-IDAMAP98*, Brighton, UK, 1998.
37. Zelič, I., Lavrač, N., Najdenov, P. and Rener-Primec, Z. "Impact of machine learning to the diagnosis and prognosis of first cerebral paroxysm". In [38].
38. Proceedings of the Workshop on Machine Learning in Medical Applications, Advanced Course on Artificial Intelligence (ACAI '99), Chania, Greece, 1999
(http://www.iit.demokritos.gr/skel/eetn/acai99/Workshops.htm).

Machine Learning Applications to Power Systems

Nikolaos Hatziargyriou

Department of Electrical & Computer Engineering, National Technical University of
Athens, 9 Iroon Polytechniou, 15773 Athens
nh@power.ece.ntua.gr

1   Introduction

The recent developments in the power system area, i.e. the on-going liberalization of
the energy markets, the pressing demands for power system efficiency and power
quality, the increase of dispersed, renewable generation and the growing number of
interconnections and power exchanges among utilities, dictate the need for
improvements in the power system planning, operation and control. At the same time,
the power equipment industry faces new challenges in nowadays ever-increasing
competition. Artificial Intelligence techniques together with traditional analytical
techniques can significantly contribute in the solution of the related problems. Indeed,
during the last 15 years, pattern recognition, expert systems, artificial neural
networks, fuzzy systems, evolutionary programming, and other artificial intelligence
methods have been proposed in an impressive number of publications in the power
system community.

Among the various power system functions, security remains a source of major
concern. Power system deregulation and the increasing need to operate systems closer
to their operating limits imply the use of more systematic approaches to security in
order to maintain reliability at an acceptable level. Security assessment has proved
therefore one of the most versatile ML applications leading to a large number of
publications and an advanced application stage. Research started with Pattern
recognition in the late sixties T.E. Dy Liacco [5], and seventies , C.K. Pang et al [13],
etc. New methods have been developed next, able to handle the complexity and nonlinearity of power system security problems, like ANNs and machine learning
methods [6], [3]. Since the mid-eighties significant interest is expressed by various
electric Utilities that has contributed significantly to formalize the application
methodology and to develop software tools. L. Wehenkel [21] provides an excellent
overview of these developments.

Forecasting is another very popular application of ML techniques, developed since
the early seventies. A number of ANNs have been proposed, mainly in the areas of
short-term load forecasting, e.g. Papalexopoulos et al. [14], and various real-life
applications have been presented. The increasing wind power penetration mainly in
isolated power systems poses the need for short-term wind power forecasting for
efficient operation scheduling. Fuzzy models, genetic approaches and neural networks
have proven to outperform traditional approaches [11].

Power system operation optimization is another versatile field for ML applications.
The problems of Unit Commitment and Economic Dispatch, traditionally tackled as
non-linear, constrained optimization problems, have lent themselves recently to
genetic algorithm approaches, e.g. Sheble [17]. Other applications of ML techniques

G. Paliouras, V. Karkaletsis, and C.D. Spyropoulos (Eds.): ACAI '99, LNAI 2049, pp. 308-317, 2001.
© Springer-Verlag Berlin Heidelberg 2001

concern the areas of monitoring, ranging from monitoring of individual devices and power plants to sophisticated system monitoring. For example, ML applications to transformer monitoring and power plant monitoring based on real time measurements of high accuracy can detect critical situations and predict failures. Modeling of the physical behavior of the system is yet another area open to ML applications, e.g. load modeling. ML techniques have also been used to accelerate traditional analytical techniques, as Finite Element methods, to calculate electromagnetic inference problems.

The papers presented in this Workshop broadly correspond to the above areas of ML applications. These papers are classified in two groups, the first deals with ML applications at power system level, while the second focuses mainly on applications at power system component level. In the first group the problems of Dynamic Security Assessment and Control, Economic Dispatch, Power Flows and Restoration are tackled. The second describes applications in Transformer Manufacturing, in Wind Power Forecasting, in prediction of electromagnetic fields due to Inductive Inference and in aiding the application of the Finite Element method to solve electromagnetic field problems. It should be noted however, that this list is only indicative of the large potential of ML applications in the Power system area. The interested reader can find an impressive number of related publications in the Proceedings of various Conferences, particularly ISAP (Intelligent System Applications to Power Systems), PSCC (Power System Computation Conference) etc., in CIGRE publications and in journals, such as the IEEE (Transactions of Power Systems), IEE (Proc. Generation, Transmission and Distribution), EPES (Electric Power and Energy Systems), EIS (Engineering Intelligent Systems), etc. Admittedly however, today only a few large Utilities in North America and Europe actually use ML applications for planning, operation and control of their power systems. In Europe, at least one of them (EdF) is presently using the ML methodology for dynamic security assessment in real field studies. Field tests on load forecasting by ANNs have been reported by Electric Companies like Pacific Gas & Electric Co., ABB Systems Control, Tractebel S.A., Siemens A.G., Puget Sound Power & Light, EPRI, EdF, etc. [6]. A number of ML functions tailored to island systems with increased wind power penetration have been developed within the European project CARE [1] and applied to Load and Wind Power Forecasting, Unit Commitment, Economic Dispatch and On-line Dynamic Security Assessment. The CARE system has been integrated in the Control Center of Crete and provides operating advice to the system operators.

2   Description of Workshop Papers

This section presents an overview of the papers presented during the workshop on "Machine Learning Applications to Power Systems" organized as part of the Advanced Course on Artificial Intelligence (ACAI '99) [22].

2.1   Machine Learning Applications at the Power System Level

The paper by Sobajic et al. [18] describes an intelligent neural controller for optimal regulation and maximal stabilization of a power system. This is achieved by adding an additional neural network-supplied control signal into the excitation system voltage summing function. Simulations on a 6-bus-4-generator system show that neural network controllers are trained to provide better voltage regulation than conventional controllers and previously unstable systems can be stabilized by a properly trained neural network controller. This is quite a remarkable finding. It is also shown that optimal recovery after a major disturbance is achieved by training neural network controllers to provide optimal regulation for non-catastrophic faults and also to provide stabilization for some catastrophic faults.

In the paper, optimal control of nonlinear systems using the open-loop dynamic optimization algorithm, as well as the neural network state-feedback approach trained by the backpropagation-through-time algorithm are reviewed. Comparing the adaptation equations of the two, it can be seen that backpropagation-through-time and dynamic optimization are related in the sense that a neural network can be trained to give results that are very similar to those that dynamic optimization would give. In other words, neural networks can give dynamically optimal solutions.

This is fortuitous, as dynamic optimization is not a practical algorithm for on-line applications. Runs could take a few hours, depending on the complexity of the plant and the computer speed. Even the fastest, most advanced computers still would not make dynamic optimization practical. On the other hand, neural networks can be trained off-line, when time is not crucial. After adequate training, the weights of the neural network can be loaded and used on-line. Response speeds would be in a matter of milliseconds. However, dynamic optimization serves as a good benchmark for determining the goodness and optimality of a trained neural network. Isolated cases could run with dynamic optimization, and the solution can be compared with the neural network solution as a test.

The paper by Vasconcelos et al. [20] presents the capabilities provided by Kernel Regression Trees - a hybrid non-parametric regression technique - to on-line dynamic security assessment and monitoring of isolated power systems with high penetration of wind power. In the applied technique, to avoid overfitting a pruning algorithm is used to extract the security structure. This approach, is demonstrated on the electrical power system of Crete Island, and proves very suitable to extract simple, interpretable, and reliable security structures. A description of the security problem and the data set generation procedure are included. Comparative results regarding performances of Regression Trees and Decision Trees are presented and discussed.

The security evaluation structures provided by the Kernel Regression Trees approach have been integrated into CARE [17], the advanced control system that aims to achieve optimal utilization of renewable energy sources, in a wide variety of medium and large size isolated systems. The security evaluation structures obtained provide a classification on dynamic security. Moreover, the degree of security is provided, expressed as the expected minimum value of system frequency and maximal rate of frequency change for a selected disturbance. For the creation of the data set, a large number of initial operating points (OPs) were obtained by varying randomly the load for each load busbar, the wind power for each wind park and the wind margin. For each of the produced OPs a number of possible disturbances has been simulated.

From the results obtained with the various approaches the following conclusions are derived:

1. The Kernel Regression Tree approach is able to provide security classification results and emulation of the numerical security index f_{min} in a coherent way and with good accuracy. Besides, KRTs provide simple interpretable security rules that can be adopted by operators in the control rooms to help them in operating the system.
1. Decision Trees (DT) provide classification structures of comparable performance but with a simpler structure, which makes easier any interpretation of the phenomena and of the influence of the relevant parameters. KRTs however have the advantage of producing simultaneously a classification structure and giving the degree of robustness of the system.

The paper by Matos et al. [12] tackles the same problem as the previous paper with a different technique. It reports on the application of fuzzy reasoning to the fast assessment of the dynamic security of isolated power systems with high wind power penetration. The inference method is a Takagi-Sugeno type system with a small number of rules, optimized for each specific learning set by a standard method included in the MATLAB Fuzzy Logic Toolbox. The methodology is demonstrated in a contingency study in the network of Crete that showed interesting results in the test set. The paper discusses some implementation issues and possible future developments of the approach, now in a preliminary phase.

Two approaches have been used regarding the classification problem: direct classification of the operating state, or inference of the value of some index or important variable, then used for classification. Some of the techniques can work with either philosophy. In the present case, frequency is considered as the most important variable, and both f_{min} and df/dt_{max} values constitute usual security indices that lead straightforward to decision rules based on thresholds to their values. In this paper, both approaches are used and results are compared.

Most of the paper is devoted to the analysis of the example and results. Results of the application of fuzzy inference systems to dynamic security assessment are very promising, even when a general purpose package is used to design the system. However, more extensive tests are certainly needed, with different learning sets and contingency situations, in order to draw more definite conclusions. Future development of this work includes the use of different types of fuzzy inference systems (first-order Takagi-Sugeno, different logical operators, etc.), new training algorithms and new training philosophies, namely for the direct classification procedures, with minimization of the classification error instead of the RMSE.

A Genetic Algorithm (GA) solution to the Economic Dispatch (ED) problem is presented in the paper by Saramourtsis et al. [15]. Economic dispatch analysis schedules the outputs of the online generating units so as to meet the system load at minimum cost. Improvements in scheduling the unit outputs can lead to significant cost savings. Traditional dispatch algorithms (i.e. lambda iteration) are based on the concept of equal incremental cost: the total production cost of a set of generators is minimized when all the units operate at the same incremental cost. When considering transmission losses, the unit incremental costs are modified to account for incremental transmission losses. Traditional algorithms however, require that the unit cost curves ($/h vs MW) be convex functions. Hence, they cannot handle non-monotonically increasing incremental cost curves.

Solution to the economic dispatch problem with non-convex unit cost functions can be achieved using dynamic programming (DP). Unlike the traditional solution, the DP solution imposes no restrictions on the generating unit characteristics. However, it suffers from the dimensionality problem: as the number of generators to be dispatched increases and higher solution accuracy is needed, the storage requirements and the execution time increases dramatically.

The GA solution proposed in this paper is integrated in CARE and applied to Crete with very satisfactory results. A binary genetic algorithm was implemented in order to achieve the operating cost minimization. The algorithm's aim is to maximize the GA objective function (which is the inverse of the operating cost) while satisfying the constraint relations that are set by the generators' operating limits, as well as by the power demand. GA solutions do not impose any convexity restrictions on the generators' cost functions making them ideal for use with generator units non-convex cost functions. Test cases with different numbers of online generators showed that the proposed GA gives comparable results with the well-known $\bullet$-iteration method that was used as benchmark. In addition the encoding strategy, the penalty policy for constraints violation and the importance of special operators that were designed specifically for the economic dispatch problem are analyzed.

The paper by Gavoyiannis et al. [8] addresses the problem of computing the probability density functions (pdfs) of power flows as approximated by a weighted sum of a finite number of Gaussian kernels. The parameters and weights of these kernels are iteratively estimated from the actual power flow input samples using the EM (Expectation-Maximization) algorithm implemented by a suitable Neural Network. In this way, probabilistic load flows can be calculated avoiding assumptions about the input data regarding their pdfs and correlation among them. The proposed method, still at its infancy, presents interesting prospects for planning applications.

2.2   Machine Learning Applications at the Power System Component Level

The paper by Kalles et al. [10] proposes a novel approach to intelligent monitoring and predictive maintenance of power plants based on reinforcement learning. This is a new computational approach to automating goal-directed learning and decision-making emphasizing on learning from direct interaction with its environment without relying on exemplary supervision or complete models of its environment.

Proper maintenance of power plant equipment is essential to high system availability. The complexity of modern power plant equipment is such, that few plant maintenance personnel are truly experts in diagnosing faults and even fewer are capable of predicting them. An effective approach to equipment maintenance is *predictive maintenance*, and has been used to monitor the health of rotating equipment by recording the vibrations and temperatures of their bearings. These measurements, or *signatures*, are taken periodically, analysed using well-known DSP techniques and compared with desired signatures or with earlier signatures to observe how they evolve. When significant deviations occur, these are flagged so that appropriate action can be taken. The decision on whether or not the equipment requires maintenance is taken by human experts though expert systems are commercially available to this end. Maintenance is carried out only when necessary and not at regular intervals as in *preventive maintenance*, thereby reducing maintenance costs and the possibility of major breakdown significantly.

Essential to predictive maintenance is any platform capable of data acquisition from suitable sensors, which supply a continuous flow of data on the condition of the plant in addition to a real-time decision mechanism to predict impending faults so that immediate remedial action can be taken. Both *qualitative* as well as *quantitative* information from the plant can be fused in the inference mechanism to decide on the condition of the plant equipment and *what* maintenance is required and most importantly, *when*. The diagnostic problem starts with the observation of some deviation in the behavior of the plant equipment as compared to that desired or expected. When a malfunction is observed, maintenance personnel hypothesize on its causes, based on their knowledge and experience. Attempting to accept or reject some of these hypotheses leads to further tests or uses specific or *deep* knowledge of the specific piece of malfunctioning equipment. This knowledge usually concerns the structural and behavioral characteristics of the equipment. *Qualitative reasoning* has attracted much attention in the past. Rule-based diagnostic systems with deterministic or fuzzy reasoning have been proved capable of reaching conclusions using only *shallow* knowledge about the plant. Artificial Neural Networks, by their very nature, allow for learning by viewing this problem as a pattern classification activity. Their mapping ability can be exploited to perform associations between input patterns derived from plant sensors and patterns representing fault conditions. Input patterns are represented by vectors of measurements while the output data from the system are vectors of the fault space representing the condition of the health of power plant equipment.

The paper by Damousis et al. [4] presents a genetic fuzzy model that utilizes special features, for the prediction of the wind speed variations in various time windows in the future. The model utilizes a set of meteorological stations that encircle the wind turbine clusters at a radius of 15km or more. The system has been applied using data collected over a period of 2 years at locations in the Crete Island and Northern Greece. A user intervention to assist the training process is not needed while there is also no need for parameter initialization, like in other methods, contributing to the model's robustness.

Studies have also been made for spatial correlation of wind turbulence regarding short distances (700 m to 15 km) and short time scales (wind changes per 4, 10, 30 min and also 1-minute deviations from 30-min averaged value). Correlation coefficients are concluded to be related to the wind direction, terrain roughness and height above the ground.

The paper induces a genetic fuzzy system that uses local and spatial relations of the wind speed so as to improve the efficiency of forecasting, ranging from minutes to several hours ahead. Since the efficiency of a genetic algorithm based solution depends greatly on the coding scheme, the proposed GA for the training of the fuzzy system uses an effective coding scheme as well as special operators, tailored to the problem. The model is flexible and self-sufficient so as to easily learn and adapt in data of any special case without any guidance or constraint by the user.

The paper by Georgilakis et al. [9] uses machine learning to predict iron losses in the transformer manufacturing process. Prediction of iron losses is an important task in the transformer manufacturing industry, since iron losses constitute one of the main parameters of transformer quality. Furthermore, accurate prediction of transformer iron losses protects the manufacturer from paying loss penalties. In order to avoid this risk, and in view of the fact that iron losses cannot be accurately predicted in the current practice, one possible method is to design the transformer at a lower magnetic induction, resulting in an increase of the transformer cost since more magnetic material is required. Satisfactory prediction of iron losses, however, can be achieved only if various parameters involved in the process, both qualitative and quantitative, are taken into consideration. Instead, in the current practice, only the loss curve is used, i.e., the influence of the rated magnetic induction on iron losses for each specific magnetic material. This is dictated by the fact that there is no analytical relationship expressing the effect of the other parameters on transformer iron losses.

The origin of this paper is the effective use of measurements taken at the first stages of transformer construction, in order to minimize iron losses of transformer. These measurements are collected and stored in databases. Each database corresponds to different conditions (environment), i.e. to a certain supplier, grade and thickness of magnetic material. When a satisfactory number of measurements has been collected, machine learning is applied in order to learn the information included in the databases. More specifically, decision trees are used to select the most relevant attributes among a large set of candidate ones and to produce "if-then-else" decision rules. These rules are applicable at the early stages of core production, and allow possible corrective actions during the manufacturing process.

Moreover, neural networks are used to predict iron losses at the early stages of transformer manufacturing. Each neural network model is suited to a different environment. Selection of the most appropriate network (or equivalently environment) is based on the satisfaction of customers' requirements and several technical and economical criteria. The attributes selected by the decision trees are used as inputs to the neural networks. The intelligent iron loss model (i.e., the model of iron losses obtained through the neural network) is applied on-line in order to optimally combine the individual cores and reduce the iron losses of assembled transformers.

Finally, based on the good performance of the neural network structure, a new grouping algorithm has been proposed. This algorithm selects, among the various possible combinations of grouping cores, the one providing the minimal deviation of predicting iron losses from the guaranteed to the customer losses. Application of the proposed method to transformer manufacturing industry has verified the accurate prediction of iron losses in all the examined environments. Moreover, reduction of the transformer losses is achieved.

Triantafyllidis [19] presented a method for prediciting mesh density with the use of Artificial Neural Networks (ANN). The Finite Element Method (FEM) has been widely used to solve electromagnetic field problems, mainly due to its ability to handle cases of geometrical complexity. One of the main disadvantages of the method is the need for an experienced user to provide a quality mesh, i.e. a mesh with which the method will converge to an accurate solution quickly. One way around this problem is the adaptive use, i.e. starting with an initial coarse mesh the problem is solved, then the solution error is estimated for each element and finally the elements with error that exceeds a given threshold are split into smaller elements, thus refining the initial mesh. This technique will provide very accurate results, but is very time and memory consuming.

The use of Artificial Neural Networks (ANNs) has been proposed for predicting the mesh density of specific electromagnetic problems [2]. For this purpose a prototype mesh is generated for a magnetic device, which includes all features expected to be found in future devices to be meshed. The device is sampled at specific sample points and a set of geometric features is associated to the mesh density at the neighborhood of the given sample point. The data gathered constitute the training database for the ANN. Although these mesh density prediction methods work well for the magnetic devices that they were designed for, they fail in cases of faulted overhead power transmission line systems (TLS), carrying a zero-sequence current. The paper presents an ANN trained to reproduce the mesh density vector of open-boundary faulted power transmission line problems under the presence of small features, such as conductors. In order to produce the data for the training database of the ANN a technique for recursively subdividing the solving area is proposed. A Delaunay-based mesh generator is used to produce the final mesh. Several test cases show that this method significantly reduces solving time.

The paper by Satsios et al. [16] presents a novel application of *genetically evolved* Fuzzy Logic Systems (FLSs), to transmission line electromagnetic field modeling. A sophisticated artificial intelligence system (AIS), consisting of a sequence of FLSs which evolve until the optimum FLS is achieved, has been developed by the combination of FLS and GA techniques. The artificial intelligence system (AIS) proposed uses a rule base adaptation mechanism. Instead of using fixed-length chromosomes, new rules are added when necessary to form a variable-length FLS-chromosome.

The AIS presented consists of a population of fuzzy logic systems (FLSs) evolving with time. The evolution of the FLSs is accomplished by using a rule base adaptation mechanism combined with a genetic algorithm (GA). The number and parameters of fuzzy rules of each FLS are changed, until an optimum is achieved. To implement this, a vector of variable length is defined for every FLS, containing its parameters. This vector corresponds to an FLS-chromosome that will be processed by the GA. After some generations, the population of the FLS-chromosomes converges to the optimum FLS. The developed AIS is used to predict the electromagnetic field induced by an overhead transmission line. This field depends on multiple variables, such as the position of the phase conductors, the currents flowing through all conducting materials, the earth resistivity and other operational parameters. The AIS was trained using data resulting from finite element method calculations, for different configuration cases of the above electromagnetic field problem. The performance of the optimum FLS, derived after the training, is tested for new configuration cases, differing significantly from the cases used for training. It is shown that the proposed method may be very effective in predicting electromagnetic fields.

The architecture of each FLS of the AIS has been designed to solve the inductive interaction problem between a faulted overhead transmission line and a nearby-buried pipeline. This problem is of growing practical interest, due to restrictions currently imposed on public utilities in the use of right-of-ways resulting in overhead transmission lines, pipelines, railroads, telecommunication lines etc. to be laid in narrow corridors for several kilometers.

Fountas and Hatziargyriou [7] proposed the use of *Petri Nets* **for planning power system restoration.** Experience from the development of system restoration plans based on knowledge bases has indicated the effective role of these systems to the overall restoration process. Recognizing the maturing capabilities of the expert systems, it is believed that the suitable integration with existing facilities will enable many elements of restoration planning to be carried out in an on-line environment. This environment shall provide powerful on-line assistance to operators of the type they most need, at the time they most need it. The result will be a significant reduction in the time required for major restoration incidents, and significant reduction in the losses that are incurred.

In this paper *Petri Nets* are used to plan power system restoration. Petri Nets constitute a reasoning tool that has been used in modeling discrete event dynamic systems, mainly in the areas of computers, communication protocols and factory automation. This model-based approach is based on *Petri Net formulation* of the power system procedures. Illustrative examples are provided, showing the applicability of Petri nets in power system restoration (PSR) following a total or partial blackout. Common features regarding power system behavior are highlighted, and the equivalent models are explained.

By implementing the state-space analysis techniques, all important net properties can be analytically explained and verified. Through the analysis of the 1989 Hellenic power system blackstart, the dynamic behaviour of the modelled power system was evaluated and the suggested sequence of generic restoration tasks proved to be meaningful and well-defined. The cumulative required restoration time was estimated, assigning practical time delays to transition firings.

3   Conclusions

In the Workshop a wide variety of ML techniques for solving timely problems in the areas of Generation, Transmission and Distribution of modern Electric Energy Systems have been proposed. In particular, applications of Artificial Neural Networks, Kernel Regression and Decision Trees, Fuzzy Systems and Genetic Algorithms have been proposed or applied to security assessment, control, economic dispatch, power flows calculations, forecasting, restoration, plant monitoring, transformer manufacturing, faulted transmission line problems, and inductive inference problems. In all cases, the application of ML techniques has proven their efficiency to tackle difficult power system operation, planning and manufacturing issues. These applications, by no means exhaustive, are indicative of a booming activity in Power System applied research, as shown by the impressive number of related publications in the literature. In conclusion, ML techniques coupled with mature analytical techniques promise to provide significant support to power systems in the new era.

References

1. "CARE: Advanced Control Advice for power systems with large scale integration of Renewable Energy sources", contract JOR3-CT96-0119, Proceedings of CARE Workshop, Heraklion 16-17 July 1999 and Final Project Report, September 1999.
2. Chedid and Najar, "Automatic Finite-Element Mesh Generation Using Artificial Neural Networks - Part I: Prediction of Mesh Density," IEEE Trans. on Magnetics, pp. 5173-5178, Vol. 32, n. 5, Sep. 1996.

3. IGRE TF38-06-06, "Artificial Neural Networks for Power Systems: A Literature Survey", Engineering Intelligent Systems, Vol. 1, No. 3, pp. 133-158, Dec. 1993.
4. I.G. Damousis, P.D. Dokopoulos: A Genetic Fuzzy Model for Wind Speed Prediction and Power Generation in Wind Parks. In [22].
5. T.E. Dy Liacco, "Control of power systems via the multi-level concept", PhD Thesis, Case Western Reserve University, 1968.
6. M. El-Sharkawi, D. Niebur (editors). "Artificial Neural Networks with Applications to Power Systems", IEEE PES, 96 TP 112-0.
7. N. Fountas, N. Hatziargyriou: Artificial Intelligence Approaches to the Problem of Power System Restoration. In [22].
8. A.E. Gavoyiannis, N. Vlassis, N.D. Hatziargyriou: Probabilistic Neural Networks for Power Flow Analysis. In [22].
9. P. Georgilakis, N. Hatziargyriou: Machine Learning Applications in the Transformer Manufacturing Industry. In [22].
10. D. Kalles, A. Stathaki, R.E. King: Intelligent Monitoring and Maintenance of Power Plants. In [22].
11. G. Kariniotakis, G.S. Stavrakakis, E.F. Nogaret, "Wind Power Forecasting using advanced neural network models", IEEE Trans. on Energy Conversion, 96 SM 552-0 EC, pp. 762-767, Vol. 11, No. 4, Dec. 1996.
12. M. Matos, J.A. Pecas Lopes, M.H. Vasconcelos: Dynamic Security Assessment by Fuzzy Inference. In [22].
13. C.K. Pang, F.S. Prabhakara, A.H. El-Abiad, A.J. Koivo, Security evaluation in power systems using pattern recognition, IEEE Trans. on PAS 93, no. 3, 1974.
14. A.D. Papalexopoulos, S. hao, T-M. Peng, "An Implementation of a Neural Network based Load Forecasting Model for the EMS", IEEE Trans. on Power Syst., pp. 1956-1962, Vol. 9, Nr. 4, Nov. 1994.
15. A. Saramourtsis, J. Damousis, A. Bakirtzis, P. Dokopoulos: Genetic Algorithm Solution to the Economic Dispatch Problem - Application to the Electrical Power Grid of Crete Island. In [22].
16. K.J. Satsios, I.G. Damousis, D.P. Lambridis, P.S. Dokopoulos: An Innovative Genetic Fuzzy System for the Prediction of an Inductive Interference Problem. In [22].
17. G.B. Sheble, K. Brittig, "Refined Genetic Algorithm – Economic Dispatch Example", 94 WM 199-0, pp. 117-124, IEEE Trans. on Power Systems, Vol. 10, No. 1, Febr. 1995.
18. D.J. Sobajic, R. Shen, B. Widrow: Supplementary Neural Controls for Improved Transient Behavior of Power Systems. In [22].
19. D. Triantafyllidis: Mesh Density Prediction for Open Boundary Faulted Power Transmission Line Problems Using Artificial Neural Networks. In [22].
20. M.H. Vasconcelos, J.A. Pecas Lopes: Pruning Kernel Regression Trees for Security Assessment of the Crete Network. In [22].
21. L. Wehenkel, "Automatic Learning Techniques in Power Systems", Kluwer Academic Publ., 1998.
22. Proceedings of the Workshop on Machine Learning Applications to Power Systems, Advanced Course on Artificial Intelligence (ACAI '99), Chania, Greece, 1999 (http://www.iit.demokritos.gr/skel/eetn/acai99/Workshops.htm).

Intelligent Techniques for Spatio-Temporal Data Analysis in Environmental Applications

Nikolaos Vassilas[1], Elias Kalapanidas[2], Nikolaos Avouris[2], and Stavros Perantonis[3]

[1]Dept. of Computer Science, T.E.I. of Athens, 12210 Egaleo, Attica, Greece
nvas@teiath.gr
[2]Electrical and Computer Engineering Dept, University of Patras, 265 00 Rio-Patras, Greece
{ekalap,N.Avouris}@ee.upatras.gr
[3]Inst. of Informatics and Telecommunications, NCSR "Demokritos", 15310 Athens, Greece
sper@iit.demokritos.gr

1 Introduction

Environmental applications share common features that make them distinct from typical applications of other areas of applied computer science. This fact has lead during the last years to the development of *Environmental Informatics*, a novel specialty of Applied Informatics, which studies specific problems related with the application of computer science techniques in environmental problems. In environmental applications often many different, non homogeneous information sources can be found, such as text data e.g. environmental legislation or research projects results, measurement data from monitoring networks, structural data on chemical substances, satellite data etc. In particular, environmental data is often geographically coded, i.e. information is attached to a particular point or region in space. Secondly, some of the data objects are multidimensional and have to be represented by means of complex geometric objects (polygons or curves).

The processing of measurement data and related statistical analysis methods as well as handling of vague, uncertain and incomplete knowledge is a major concern in Environmental Informatics. In addition easy user access on heterogeneous distributed environmental data bases has to be supported. And finally, environmental data must be presented and evaluated in a subject-overlapping way. As a requirement, this information has to be often deducted from different subject specific primary data bases beforehand and then combined in an appropriate way [1]. As described in [7], Environmental Informatics need to play a mediating role since, on one hand, it is called to analyse real-world problems in the environmental sector field, while on the other hand, brings the problem solving potential of Information Technology to this application field.

Machine Learning techniques are particularly relevant to Environmental Informatics. Artificial Intelligence, Neural Networks, Fuzzy Logic, Genetic Algorithms, Decision Trees and Expert Systems together with powerful techniques from Statistics, Signal and Image Processing, Computer Vision and Pattern Recognition are recently applied to homogeneous or inhomogeneous multisource spatio-temporal and/or structural data in order to extract useful information and produce solutions to a variety of difficult problems related to the environment.

G. Paliouras, V. Karkaletsis, and C.D. Spyropoulos (Eds.): ACAI '99, LNAI 2049, pp. 318-324, 2001.
© Springer-Verlag Berlin Heidelberg 2001

There has been an ongoing discussion on the role of computer science in the environmental field. Concerns have been expressed that computer science can miss some of the issues that surround an environmental problem, and that the solution provided may be structured, but also incomplete or inflexible. One of the main goals of the workshop on "Intelligent Techniques for Spatio-Temporal Data Analysis in Environmental Applications" [13], which was organised during the Advanced Course on Artificial Intelligence (ACAI '99), was to show that Environmental Informatics can benefit a lot by modern research in computer science in dealing with the various real world environmental problems.

2   Short Description of Workshop Papers

Tsatsoulis et al. [10] use a Dempster-Shafer rule base to integrate data from multiple sources in order to classify sea ice. Their system, named ARKTOS, fuses SAR imagery, digital grid climatology and classified SSM/I images of polar regions in order to classify sea ice into four categories (old ice, first-year ice, fast ice and open water). ARKTOS is currently installed at the U.S. National Ice Center and at the Canadian Ice Services and is integrated in the operations flow of these organizations.

After some basic preprocessing of the SAR image that includes a mask to separate land from sea ice, ARKTOS segments the image into non-intersected regions (areas of neighboring pixels) using the Watershed algorithm, whereby regions are characterized by low image intensity gradient and region boundaries correspond to pixels of high gradient. Next, a set of 17 features (numerical descriptors) is extracted for each identified region such as the following: *area, average intensity, perimeter, outer perimeter, centroid, orientation, roundness* and *irregularity*. These features are then used to generate symbolic facts (as suggested by the experts) which together with facts from digital climatology (historically compiled data and the last ice chart) and SSM/I passive microwave data are used in the Dempster-Shafer rule-based system for classification.

The rule-base was developed by interviewing sea ice experts using the *protocol, blind test* and *reference* knowledge acquisition methods. Uncertainty in the classification rules was expressed by the experts through a degree of belief and the Dempster-Shafer theory was then used to combine the uncertainty values of the classification rules. Finally, all rules are subject to change by the system users.

Benediktsson and Arnason [2] provide a logarithmic consensus rule for combining multi-temporal and multi-type earth-observation data sources. Application of this rule is used for land cover classification and for detecting and mapping of land cover changes.

In particular, the classification decisions produced by using each of the different data sets are combined through a statistical consensus rule in order to make the final decision. By assuming that the data sets correspond to experts the authors combine the individual decisions using a logarithmic opinion pool with the following advantages: a) it is externally Bayesian (unlike a linear consensus rule), and b) it obeys the data independence property (i.e., it treats data sources independently). Various methods are suggested to assign weights to the various sources (experts). For example, in the absence of any knowledge regarding the reliability of the experts the combination weights should be equal, otherwise they should reflect the individual reliabilities. If self-rating of the sources is possible then the weights should be proportional to the corresponding scores. Finally, scoring rules can be used to comparatively assess the performance of each expert.

Experimental classification results in fifteen land-cover categories using multispectral SPOT, Landsat-TM, panchromatic SPOT and Landsat MSS satellite data on a 30 km by 30 km test site from southwest Iceland were obtained using the maximum likelihood statistical classifier. The results based on logarithmic consensus rules with various weight combinations show improvement in terms of test accuracies when compared to the single source classifications.

Vassilas et al. [12] present an automatic lineament detection method based on a weighted Hough transform. Geophysical grid data (airborne magnetic and electromagnetic measurments) are used for this purpose. Where the application of the original Hough transform fails to delineate the existent geological lineaments due to the arc-like shape of the surrounding objects, the use of a continuous function of the shape descriptors greatly improves the overall results. In the process, Self-Organizing Maps and a scheme for fast indexed classification are used.

More specifically, lineament extraction is performed using the following processing stages: a) unsupervised classification of the spatial data using a self-organizing map (SOM) with simultaneous production of an array of pointers to the SOM prototypes (the *index table*), b) binarization of the classification result by using one of four thresholding options, c) identification of connected regions in the binary image using image processing techniques, d) evaluation of shape descriptors for each connected region, and e) extraction of lineaments using a modified (weighted) Hough Transform.

The shape descriptors evaluated for each region are the following: a) the area, b) the angle of the principal axis relative to the x-axis, and c) the elongation. Each region is then represented by its geometrical center and the original Hough Transform is modified by introducing a voting kernel to reduce interference effects and avoid spurious accumulator array maxima. The voting kernel is a continuous function of the shape descriptors and is constructed by taking into account the following considerations: a) elongated regions should be weighted mostly in the direction of the principal axis, i.e., the closer the line (with respect to angle) to the principal axis the higher its accumulator array value should be, b) the influence of a region in the accumulator array cells should increase with the elongation parameter, c) nearly circular regions should be allowed to vote equally for all directions while very elongated ones should vote only for the direction of the principal axis, d) suppression of the contribution from regions with large areas and small elongation since such lines would be spurious, e) suppression of regions with very small areas as they introduce random noise, and f) regions of small elongation whose area is comparable to a characteristic intermediate area scale may be part of a chain of regions contributing to a disrupted linear structure and should be taken into account.

Experimental results using airborne magnetic and electromagnetic data from the Vammala area in Finland showed a significant speedup in automatic classification as well as meaningful lineament structures by using the modified Hough Transform. On the contrary, direct application of the original Hough Transform on the binarized classification result or its coresponding edge image failed to reveal lineaments mainly due to interference from unwanted pixels.

Tsoumakas and Vlahavas [11] present ISLE, an intelligent system for land evaluation supporting GIS capabilities and expert analysis through a sophisticated user interface. Presented with a digital map of an area and its geographical database, the system displays this map, evaluates the land units selected by the user and finally visualises the results colouring properly the analysed land units.

The features supported by ISLE are the following: a) capability of displaying the digital map of the land, b) automation of the land evaluation process for the displayed map (or part of it) based on an expert system in accordance with the FAO-SYS system for land evaluation, c) visualization of the evaluation result by map coloring, and d) provisions of spatial analysis tools and other GIS functions. In addition, ISLE is designed in such a way as to integrate the functionality of a geographical information system with an expert system for land evaluation and consists of the following main parts: a) the *front end* that provides the interface to the expert system, encapsulates the mapping object and provides the user interface, b) the *digital map* and the *geographical database* of the area under evaluation, and c) the *expert system* which is responsible for the evaluation process.

The knowledge base consists of production and deductive rules and the information flow between the fron end and the expert system is implemented with Prolog predicates. An example of land evaluation using ISLE is provided for an area of the Kilkis prefecture in northern Greece.

Demyanov et al. [4] study the efficiency of modeling the problem of land surface contamination utilizing Radial Basis Functions Neural Networks (RBFNNs). Parallel to the main model, another one based on the residual error of the former is constructed for handling the prediction uncertainty problem. A methodology exploiting the variography of the prediction and of the error residuals is proposed for decision support.

RBFNNs are supervised nonparametric methods and known to possess the property of universal approximation. It is for this reason that they are used for spatial estimations in two case studies dealing with: a) radioactive soil contamination with caesium 137 originated after the Chernobyl Nuclear Power Plant accident, and b) nickel contamination of the Geneva Lake. In both cases the training and test sets consist of contamination levels as a function of the 2-D coordinates.

To incorporate error estimates and confidence intervals placed on the neural network estimates, the so called *predictive error bars* (PEB) approach has been implemented. During training, the network weights are optimized with a two-stage procedure: a) the first stage determines the weights for the typical regression problem, i.e., find the weights that best approximate the target values (known contamination levels) of the training set, and b) the second stage keeps the weights of the hidden layer fixed, presents the same inputs as before and determines the weights of another set of output nodes (connected to the same hidden nodes) so as to best approximate the variance (conditional error values computed at the first stage using the training samples).

Finally, geostatistical methods are applied throughout the decision-oriented mapping, that is from the beginning of the analysis (exploratory data analysis, declustering, data splitting, spatial continuity description – variography) until the interpretation of the results. The results on the above data sets are presented in the form of *thick* contour isolines for both the function estimation and the variance predictions. Such kind of visualization combines regression mapping with spatial uncertainty given by confidence intervals around the estimated isolines.

Gilardi et al. [5] investigate the use of several kernel functions for a Support Vector Machine (SVM) applied on a water contamination problem. Comparison with probabilistic mapping is made, using a non-parametric geostatistical model.

SVMs constitute a recently developed statistical theory that can be used as a universal constructive learning procedure for classification and regression problems. The strength of this method is that it attempts to simultaneously minimize the empirical risk of the error (estimation of the error on the training data) and the structural risk (model complexity). The SVM paradigm was used on the following two data sets: a) chemical analysis of Lake Leman sediments, and b) chemical analysis of Lake Leman water at various depths.

Data classification was performed with respect to Cadmium concentration by considering two thresholds on the concentration levels. For the design of the SVM classifier three basic kernel types were examined, i.e., polynomial, hyperbolic tangent and radial basis function kernels. Next, the specific parameters of each kernel were selected, the support vector coefficients were calculated according to the training data and, finally, the efficiency of those coefficients and the kernels' parameters were estimated using the test data set. The data were also processed using geostatistical methods for comparison. Both classification approaches gave smooth output results.

Kalapanidas and Avouris [8] compare three methods from the machine learning area on local air pollution data. A Case-Based Reasoning (CBR) prototype along with a MLP neural net and a CART-like decision tree are competing at predicting the point maximum measurement of the day for nitrogen dioxide.

The case-based reasoning algorithm uses past knowledge to solve new problems; the basic idea behind CBR is the use of a systematically recorded repository of past cases of the problem to be solved. All metrics (modification heuristics, similarity metrics) have been replaced by the Knowledge Base. NEMO consists of three main modules. Two of them are assigned with the retrieval and the filtering of the similar cases, while the third one adapts the solutions proposed by the remaining similar cases to form the proposed solution for the new problem.

Through the use of the remaining two techniques, some knowledge about each attribute's importance in the data is required. Results are presented in quantitative way through confusion tables, test set error, rms error and mean absolute distance calculations. Also qualitative presentation of the results is done through efficiency charts and rules visualisation.

The three algorithms compete with each other and obtain very close results. Overall they constitute an efficent decision support ensemble that can function as a predictive working system in an air quality operational centre.

Grosser and Conruyt [6] concentrate on a knowledge description methodology for identification of coral specimens. The authors indicate the problem of complex knowledge representation and the need for updates of the knowledge base, from expert users. For these tasks a modified C4.5 decision tree is implemented.

A working definition for the purposes of biology adopted in this paper views knowledge as consisting of the following three kinds: a) *domain knowledge* that refers to what is observable, b) *instantiated knowledge* that refers to the description of observed instances, and c) *derived knowledge* that is discovered from domain and instantiated knowledge and can be compared with produced hypotheses. An *iterative knowledge base system* (IKBS) is then used to extract knowledge from domain and instantiated knowledge through a three step cyclical process: a) *knowledge acquisition* (domain knowledge, observed facts or cases), b) *knowledge processing* using *decision trees* and *case-based reasoning*, and c) knowledge validation and refinement.

The descriptive model built during the acquisition phase is organized in a structured tree scheme. The nodes of the tree represent objects defined by a list of attributes with their respective values. Case bases are created by the users through automatically generated questionnaires by the program. Next, inductive learning algorithms such as the C4.5 decision tree algorithm are used for classification (tree-based knowledge processing). IKBS extends some functionality of the C4.5 algorithm for dealing with: a) structured objects, b) taxonomic attribute-values, and c) multi-valued attributes.

Finally, the reliability of the IKBS system was tested on coral identification with different users. The update of the descriptive model through the validation and refinement phase significantly improved the accuracy of identification.

Da Rocha et al. [3] propose a Bayesian Network topology for detecting and for identifying changes in images. A Bayesian Network for Environmental Monitoring (BNEM) model has been designed for multitemporal information fusion, knowledge representation and uncertainty handling. An application of this topology is shown concerning the change of land use between two images of the same area at different time instants.

Bayesian networks constitute a probabilistic knowledge representation framework that incorporate: a) uncertainty representation based on probability theory, b) possibility to model causal and temporal influence, and c) evidential reasoning capabilities. It is for these reasons that have been used for the design of BNEM for remote sensing postclassification comparison and change analysis. Besides remote sensing spatio-temporal data, other GIS contextual data that describe soil properties, vegetation, hydrology, climate, biomass and economic activities can also be incorporated in BNEM and provide valuable evidences for environmental analysis.

The applicability of the BNEM model is shown in the evaluation of wood cover changes using two Lansat TM images taken at 1984 and 1991 from the Port Renfrew, Canada, region. The vegetation status (classification categories) detected was one of the following: a) *mature*, b) *in regeneration*, and c) *ausent*.

Toivonen et al. [9] present a Bayesian Network for the reconstruction of environmental conditions in the past (paleoecological reconstruction), by determining the relation between environmental variables and fossil data. Two such models are shown, and an experimental comparison of them with other methods is made.

The aim of the paper is to obtain good estimates of the environmental variable in the past (such as the temperature) based on fossil assemblages of abundances. The requirements for the reconstruction results are twofold: a) to obtain information about the reliability of the estimates of environmental variables, and b) to be able to extrapolate from the training samples as it cannot be assumed that all historical variance is covered by the modern training data.

Quantitative reconstruction based on two Bayesian networks is compared favorably to regression trees, nearest neighbor learning methods and other Machine Learning techniques such as rule induction, naive Bayes classifiers and neural networks, by examining the ecological plausibility of the response function used in the reconstruction.

3   Conclusions

The papers included in the workshop covered a wide range of environmental problems, such as sea ice monitoring, land surface classification and geological evaluation, soil and water contamination control, air pollution assessment, bio-life monitoring, to name a few. They also targeted on the following major tasks: feature classification, prediction, modeling and function approximation / interpolation by making use of a variety of techniques from the Machine Learning community. Decision Trees, Neural Networks, Bayesian Modeling, Support Vector Machines, Case-Based Reasoning, Self-Organized Maps, and several hybrid techniques, exhibited their potential in solving complex real-life problems. Of course, special attention was paid to the use of pre- and post-processing spatial and/or temporal analysis, due to the fact that most of the problems are of such multi-dimensional nature.

References

1. N. Avouris, B. Page, Environmental Informatics, Introduction, Kluwer Academic Publishers, pp. ix, 1995.
2. J.A. Benediktsson, K. Arnason, Fusion and Classification of Multitype Data. In [13].
3. J. Carlos Ferreira da Rocha, D. L. Borges, C.A.A. Kaestner, Bayesian Networks for Change Analysis in Environmental Monitoring. In [13].
4. V. Demyanov, N. Gilardi, M. Kanevski, M. Maignan, V. Polishchuk, Decision-Oriented Environmental Mapping with Radial Basis Function Neural Networks. In [13].
5. N. Gilardi, M. Kanevski, M. Maignan, E. Mayoraz, Environmental and Pollution Data Classification with support vector machines and Geostatistics. In [13].
6. D. Grosser, N. Conruyt, Tree-based classification approach for dealing with complex knowledge in natural sciences. In [13].
7. L.M. Hilty, B. Page, F.J. Radermacher, W.-F. Riekert, Environmental Informatics as a New Discipline of Applied Computer Science, in Environmental Informatics (N. Avouris, B. Page editors), Kluwer Academic Publishers, 1995.
8. E. Kalapanidas, N. Avouris, Machine Learning Techniques for Air Quality Prediction. In [13].
9. H. Toivonen, K. Vasko, H. Mannila, A. Korhola, H. Olander, Bayesian modeling in paleoenvironmental reconstruction. In [13].
10. C. Tsatsoulis, Leen-Kiat Soh, Cheryl Bertoia, Kim Partington, Intelligent Fusion of Multisource Data for Sea Ice Classification. In [13].
11. G.Tsoumakas and I.Vlahavas, ISLE: An Intelligent System for Land Evaluation. In [13].
12. N. Vassilas, S. Perantonis, E. Charou, K. Seretis and Th. Tsenoglou Automatic Lineament Detection from Geophysical Grid Data Using Efficient Clustering and Weighted Hough Transform Algorithms. In [13].
13. Proceedings of the Workshop on Intelligent Techniques for Spatio-Temporal Data Analysis in Environmental Applications, Advanced Course on Artificial Intelligence (ACAI '99), Chania, Greece, 1999
    http://www.iit.demokritos.gr/skel/eetn/acai99/Workshops.htm).

Author Index

Lecture Notes in Artificial Intelligence (LNAI)

Lecture Notes in Computer Science

GPSR Compliance

The European Union's (EU) General Product Safety Regulation (GPSR) is a set of rules that requires consumer products to be safe and our obligations to ensure this.

If you have any concerns about our products, you can contact us on

ProductSafety@springernature.com

In case Publisher is established outside the EU, the EU authorized representative is:

Springer Nature Customer Service Center GmbH
Europaplatz 3
69115 Heidelberg, Germany

www.ingramcontent.com/pod-product-compliance
Ingram Content Group UK Ltd.
Pitfield, Milton Keynes, MK11 3LW, UK
UKHW021828160226
468080UK00003B/16